MOON

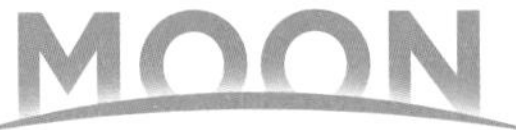

CAPE COD
MARTHA'S VINEYARD & NANTUCKET

RAY BARTLETT

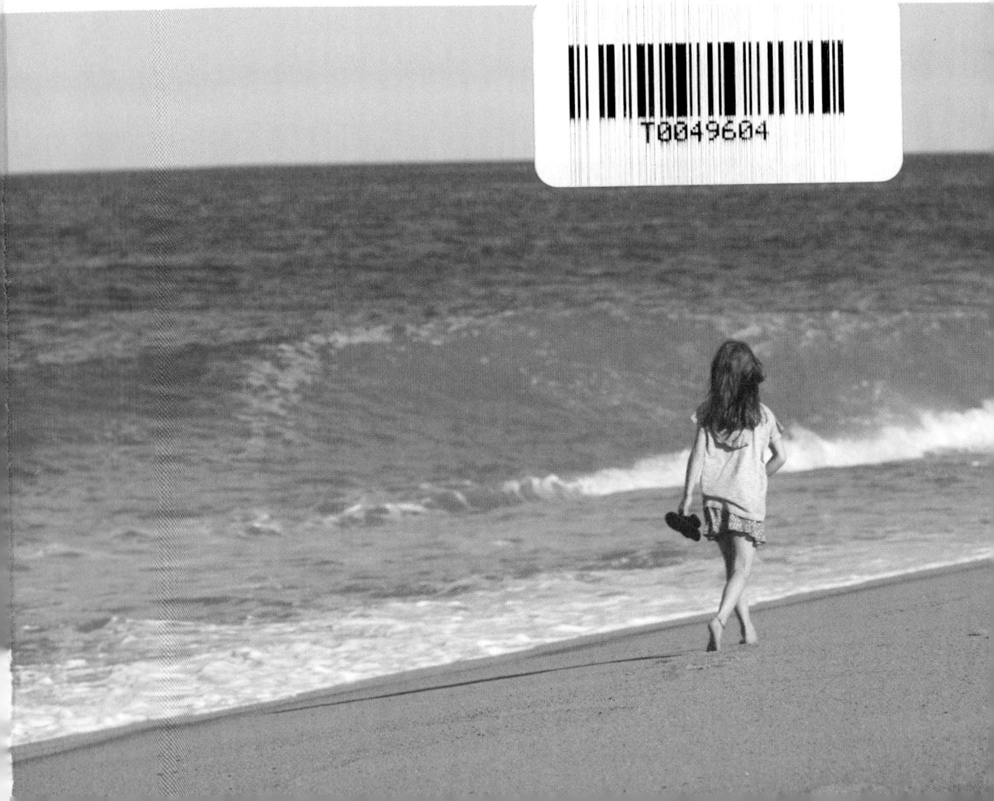

Contents

Although every effort was made to make sure the information in this book was accurate when going to press, research was impacted by the COVID-19 pandemic and things may have changed since the time of writing. Be sure to confirm specific details, like opening hours, closures, and travel guidelines and restrictions, when making your travel plans. For more detailed information, *see p. 265.*

CAPE COD, MARTHA'S VINEYARD & NANTUCKET

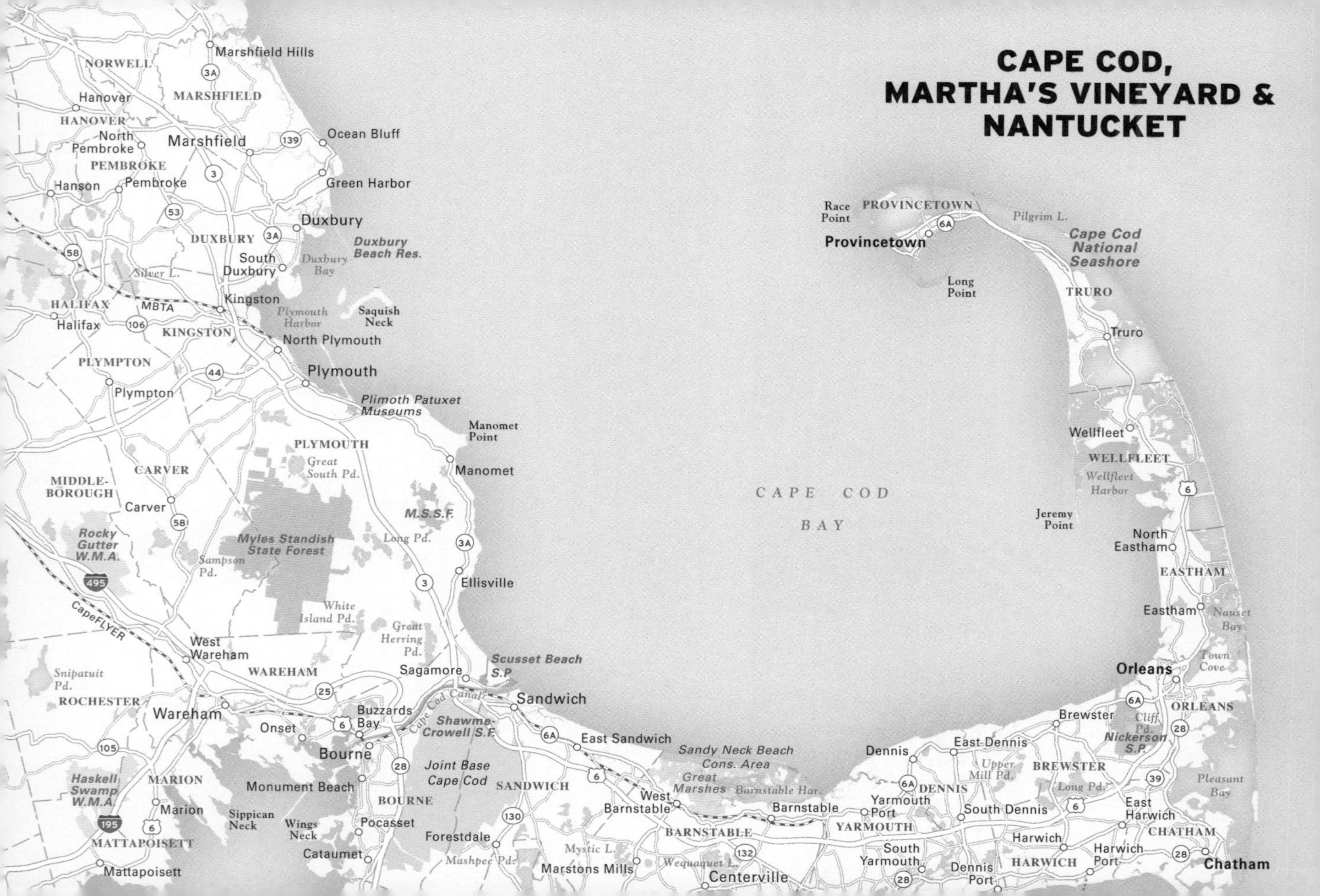

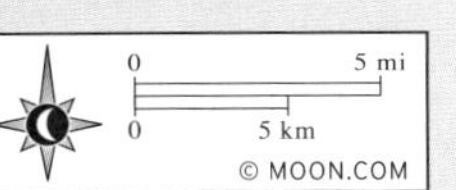
0
5 mi
0
5 km
© MOON.COM
Mattapoisett Neck
BUZZARDS BAY
West Island
North Falmouth
West Falmouth
F.A. Crane W.M.A.
MASHPEE
Johns Pd.
151
Mashpee N.W.R.
FALMOUTH
28
East Falmouth
Teaticket
Waquoit Bay
Falmouth
Falmouth Heights
Woods Hole
Nobska Point
Cotuit
Cotuit Bay
Osterville
Popponesset Bay
Popponesset
New Seabury
South Cape Beach S.P.
Hyannis
Centerville Harbor
Hyannis Harbor
Great Island
Monomoy N.W.R.
Monomoy Island
Naushon Island
Nonamesset Island
GOSNOLD
Pasque Island
Vineyard Sound
West Chop
East Chop
TISBURY
Vineyard Haven
Oak Bluffs
OAK BLUFFS
WEST TISBURY
North Tisbury
West Tisbury
Manuel F. Correllus State Forest
Edgartown
EDGARTOWN
Martha's Vineyard
Edgartown Great Pd.
Chappaquiddick Island
Katama Bay
Cape Poge
Wepua Point
CHILMARK
Tisbury Great Pd.
Aquinnah
AQUINNAH
Chilmark
Squibnocket Point
Nomans Land N.W.R.
NANTUCKET SOUND
ATLANTIC OCEAN
Muskeget Island
Tuckernuck Island
Medaket Harbor
Madaket
NANTUCKET
Coatue Point
Nantucket Harbor
Nantucket
Nantucket
Great Point
Middle Moors
Siasconset

DISCOVER

Cape Cod, Martha's Vineyard & Nantucket

Cape Cod takes its name from its wealth of marine resources, and that's what still makes this area so special today. People come here to enjoy the seafood, the beaches, and the lazy summer days. This is true of all three of the area's land masses, both the Cape and its neighboring islands. Each, however, retains a distinct character that makes it unique. A Cape getaway will be very different from a trip to the Vineyard or Nantucket. Get to all three, and you'll have three vacations wrapped into one.

Cape Cod is where you will find fresh bait shops and fine-art galleries side by side. Think summer-league baseball, live music on town bandstands, double features at the drive-in, and miniature golf with a quirky maritime theme. Here you'll eat ice cream for lunch and fried clams for dinner (yum!). There are also beaches, of course—hundreds of miles of them: slack-water estuaries, freshwater ponds, rock-strewn coves, long sandy strands lapped by the rhythmic ebb and flow of the bay, and surf-scoured barrier beaches that occasionally bare the bones of old ships.

Martha's Vineyard ("the Vineyard"), the larger, more populous, and more readily accessible of the two offshore islands, has become best known for its

Clockwise from top left: Pilgrim Monument in Provincetown; The Lobster Pot in Provincetown; kayak on a wild beach in Chatham; Eastham Windmill; lily pads on the surface of a kettle pond; Cape Cod beach at sunset.

big-name celebrities and yacht owners. While it's hardly inexpensive, it doesn't thumb its nose at budget travelers either. Its small, easily strollable towns brim with one-of-a-kind shops and galleries, interesting architecture, and good food.

Nantucket is a pretty little pearl, with rose-draped cottages hugging narrow lanes and low shrubby moors ringed by wide sandy beaches. This port town swathes itself in a mantle of history; arriving ferry passengers will feel like they've opened a doorway to the 19th century. Distance and affluence have kept some of the diversity of its neighbors firmly at bay, but it warmly welcomes day-trippers of all stripes.

You may assume that the small size of this region will make it possible to pack everything you want to see and do into a single trip, but it's best to take it slow. Allow yourself time to get lost in slow pleasures and seaside charm, to explore not only what's within these pages but also what's between the lines and beyond the margins. Save some discoveries for your next visit to the Cape. You'll be back.

Clockwise from top left: Truro's Highland Light; seeing whales from the *Whale Watcher*; pail and shovel on a beach; monarch butterflies from Mexico.

6 TOP EXPERIENCES

1 **Hit the beach:** Whether you pick a windswept, wave-scrubbed Atlantic shore or a tidal flat on the Bay side teeming with critters, you'll find yourself lost in wonder at the beauty of beaches here (page 25).

2 **Bike and hike:** Winding through white pine forests or tucked right next to the sea, the Cape's many bike paths and hiking trails offer a wealth of ways to experience the wildlife-rich landscape (page 28).

3 **Explore Provincetown:** Part fishing town, part LGBTQ+ mecca, part nature preserve, part fine-dining destination and art hotspot, you really can't say you've seen the Cape until you've stopped in P-town (page 98).

4 **Feast on fresh seafood:** From rich lobster bisque to an old-fashioned clam bake, the Cape and Islands offer New England comfort food from the sea, fresher here than anywhere else (page 22).

5 See whales: Just offshore from Provincetown's breakwater is a prime feeding area for whales, so sightings are virtually a sure bet on whale-watching excursions (pages 57 and 102).

6 Catch a wave: Find year-round surfing and a range of breaks. In the colder months you may have the waves all to yourself (page 84).

Planning Your Trip

Where to Go

This trio of destinations is visited in mix and match, any order you please. Some travelers want to get to all three, busing or driving from Boston or Providence and using the ferries to the islands after (or before) cruising the Cape. Others use the Cape only as a springboard to get to one or both of the islands, still others skip the islands and stay on the "mainland" only. There's no "right" way to come here, just the way that works best for you.

Cape Cod

No doubt about it, the big draws of Cape Cod are those seasonal verities of **sun, sand, and surf,** followed closely by **golf greens and shopping.** There are points of interest indoors too—around every bend in the road is a historic landmark, a local historical museum, or a uniquely themed attraction inviting exploration. **Art galleries** and artisans' studios abound. Antique stores are equally ubiquitous. And given the vital importance of safe navigation to the regional economy, it should come as no surprise to learn that a number of **19th-century lighthouses** still stand as beacons over the Cape. At the tip of the Cape, funky Provincetown offers a mix of fisherfolk, artists, and natural beauty, as well as being a proud gay and lesbian travel destination.

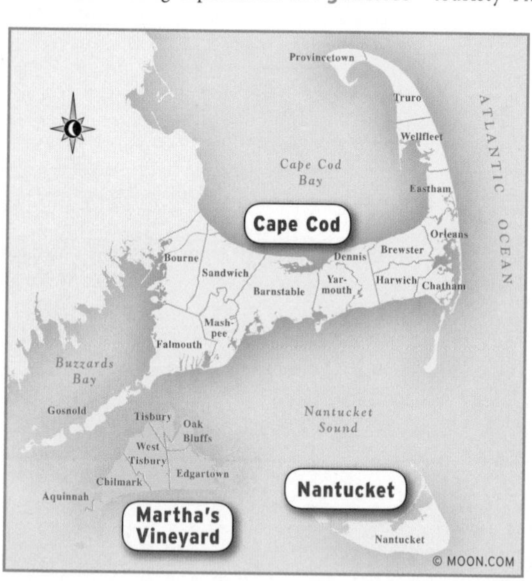

Martha's Vineyard

The island of Martha's Vineyard features **endless beach roads** and **peaceful saltwater ponds,** often lit by the stunning golden light that has drawn artists to the island for centuries.

Residents divide the island into down-island (east) and up-island (west). The former is home to the island's three main population centers: touristy **Vineyard Haven,** chic **Edgartown,** and charming **Oak Bluffs.** Up-island is more rural, with the cow pastures of **West Tisbury** and **Chilmark** sharing space with the scenic fishing village of **Menemsha** and the cliffs of **Aquinnah.**

Nantucket

Life doesn't get more idyllic (or more preppy) than in the **cobblestoned main streets, saltbox homes, and creaking docks** of this community, renowned for its past life as the whaling capital of the world. It was that status—enjoyed from about 1800 to 1840—that brought great wealth to the community, which is to this day studded with

lavender blooming in summer

the immense captains' homes of yore. That wealth is still readily apparent today in the form of new mansions, sometimes complete with a helipad or two in the backyard, and boutique shopping throughout central Nantucket town.

When to Go

Beach lovers and sun worshippers heed the call of Cape Cod's **summertime** offerings; the sandy beaches, warm-weather festivals, and sea-centric and conservation land-based activities available here are all an outdoor enthusiast needs to get hooked on the area in high season. But for those who'd rather see the area than muddle through the crowds it attracts, in **late September to early October** the hordes thin out and give way to those who want more one-on-one time with the towns, the beaches, and the land.

Deeper into the cold **winter season,** December-March, things get even calmer. Stores tend to reduce hours drastically, restaurants go dark for weeks at a time, and only die-hard visitors keep the inns and housing rental market busy. Starting as early as April, things begin to perk up again, but the season doesn't really get rolling until early June, when **beach weather** once again turns dependable.

Before You Go

Unlike the rest of Cape Cod, the islands by definition have limited space and are thus almost always fully booked in high season. Heed warnings to book accommodations and make restaurant reservations well in advance. For the former, it's best to secure arrangements several weeks ahead of time, and several months in advance for holiday and festival periods.

Transportation

Only major town centers of **Cape Cod** are easily accessible by **bus.** From Boston's South Station terminal, Plymouth and Brockton buses depart daily year-round for Hyannis and the Outer Cape from Orleans to Provincetown, while Peter Pan buses run from Logan Airport and South Station to Bourne, Falmouth, and Woods Hole on the Upper Cape. Peter Pan also runs from both upstate New York and Manhattan to Hyannis via Providence. In summer there are **ferries** between Boston and Provincetown. Local **public buses** serve all 15 towns of the Cape, although service is often only to the town center, not to outlying areas like beaches or hiking trails.

Getting to and from the **islands** relies on **ferry** schedules that vary according to season. On **Martha's Vineyard,** unless you are going to be spending a lot of time up-island, a car is by no means essential and can be a nuisance on the narrow, crowded roadways. The Martha's Vineyard Regional Transit Authority runs **buses** among all of the island's towns. On **Nantucket,** the Nantucket Regional Transit Authority does continuous loops from Straight Wharf in Nantucket Town to Madaket, Surfside, Siasconset, and the airport. By far the best way to avoid the frustration of summertime traffic on either island is to avoid contributing to it by renting a **bicycle.**

What to Pack

Packing for a visit to Cape Cod and the islands depends on what time of year you go. In **spring and fall,** when temperatures can be unpredictable, sweaters and a medium-weight jacket are key to rolling with the weather's changes. In **winter,** a heavy winter coat, umbrella, and snow boots are essential. And in **summer,** when most visitors swarm to the area, a rain jacket is still recommended, as are a few sweaters to throw on when nights get chilly. Beach lovers should be sure to bring along the usual surf-side gear (bathing suits, flip-flops, beach bags, sunscreen, a good book, and the like), although beach towels are provided at many hotels and inns. Meanwhile, in **all seasons,** comfortable shoes make walking the area's meandering town sidewalks a lot more pleasant.

The Best of the Cape

Diving into the unique attractions the coast and its islands have to offer is easy with just a little basic planning; many of the region's gems are found together in accessible clusters. It's not exactly easy to get around the Cape and islands using public transportation. A car allows you the freedom to take leisurely drives and explore the many sights along the way at your own pace.

Day 1

Begin your journey in **Sandwich** and head east along Route 6A toward **Brewster** (50 minutes), stopping at **Heritage Museums and Gardens** in Sandwich (10 minutes), **Sandy Neck** (15 minutes), or **Millway Beach** in Barnstable (20 minutes), the **Edward Gorey House** in Yarmouthport (30 minutes), and at whatever **antiques shops** or **art galleries** strike your fancy. Watch the sun set over **Cape Cod Bay** from the **Bass Hole Boardwalk** (35 minutes) in Yarmouthport, or from one of the town's lovely bay-side beaches. Stay in **Brewster,** near the east end of the Old King's Highway, where a number of historic sea captain's mansions have been converted into B&Bs, any one of which will make a good base for these first three nights.

Day 2

Spend a few hours cycling the **Cape Cod Rail Trail.** The route is most varied to the south, with ponds, cranberry bogs, and deeply wooded stretches. This being Massachusetts, there's even a nifty little bike rotary where the main rail trail intersects with the Old Colony spur to **Chatham.** In the afternoon, visit Brewster's **Cape Cod Museum of Natural History.**

Day 3

Head north to the **Cape Cod National Seashore** in Eastham (20 minutes) and Wellfleet (25 minutes). Spend time at **Coast Guard Beach**

Heritage Museums and Gardens

Best Places to Stay

Whether you want time alone, with the family, or with a special someone, you deserve the perfect getaway, and it's worth a little splurge. Check out this list of top spots to stay; not all offer in-ground pools and 24-hour room service, but it's location, location, location that makes these spots special:

- **Gull Cottage B&B (Wellfleet):** This is a quiet boathouse studio on the grounds of a property that's nearly 300 years old, nestled between two of the town's most beautiful kettle ponds. The rustic studio apartment has a microwave, a fridge, and even a stove for those chilly nights—but it's what's outside the room that makes this spot so special.
- **Land's End Inn (Provincetown):** Atop one of the highest hills in town, this lovely and eclectic inn has fantastic views of the harbor, the boats, the tides, and the sunset. Sit out on the deck and watch the world go by.
- **Chatham Bars Inn (Chatham):** Opulent enough to be worthy of a Gatsby, with spectacular beachfront access and a multi-level swimming pool, the Chatham Bars Inn is about as upscale as the Cape gets.
- **The White Elephant (Nantucket):** If price is not a problem, go out of your way to grab one of the White Elephant's lofts for a night or two. These enormous rooms have a full kitchen, a dining table that could seat a football team, and giant flat-screen TVs. But it's the details that make the stay special: a Vitamix blender for mixing up a morning smoothie, a variety of pillows, and heated floors in the bathrooms. One of these lofts even comes with a BMW SUV.

Play a game of oversize chess at the Winnetu Oceanside Resort.

- **Winnetu Oceanside Resort (Martha's Vineyard):** Here, being family-friendly is taken seriously, and it's a win for parents and children alike. Big boxes of toys and games are in various places around the resort. A variety of kid-size life jackets are at the pool. The restaurant has a mini day care, so when kids are done eating they can play with toys, color, or get their hair braided while their parents enjoy some time alone.

(20 minutes), favorite of the state's corps of wetsuited surfers, beneath the red-flashing beacon of **Nauset Light.** Continue to **Wellfleet Bay Wildlife Sanctuary** (10 minutes), occupying the extensive salt marshes and wooded shore on the calm western side of the Outer Cape. Explore the galleries and shops of **Wellfleet** (10 minutes), perhaps the Cape's least touristy town. If you've never experienced a drive-in movie, you'll have your chance tonight after sundown at the **Wellfleet Drive-In Theatre** (15 minutes).

Day 4

Bid adieu to your Brewster B&B hosts and proceed to **Provincetown** (50 minutes), the Cape's answer to Key West. Spend today visiting the galleries and shops of **Commercial Street.** While strolling around, don't miss stepping into the public library for excellent aerial views from the **Pilgrim Monument.** In the afternoon, go on a **dune tour.** You owe it to yourself to go whale-watching, so if you won't be here for Day 5, do this now.

Day 5

P-town redux: Go **whale-watching** in the morning, and then rent a bike and spend the afternoon riding the National Seashore's **Province Lands** trails (5 minutes from MacMillan Wharf). Time your ride so that you end up at **Herring Cove Beach** for the best show in town: sunset.

Day 6

Pack up the car and head south to Chatham (60 minutes) to the **Monomoy National Wildlife Refuge.** Take a wildlife-watching cruise with **Monomoy Island Excursions,** or make a full day trip of it with a naturalist-guided **walking tour,** including a visit to the historic lighthouse at its tip.

Day 7

Take the morning ferry from Harwich Port to **Nantucket.** Spend the day strolling the town and visiting the **Whaling Museum.** Walk to tiny **Brant Point Light** in the late afternoon and watch the sailboats and ferries. If it's open, go star-gazing at the **Loines Observatory.**

Day 8

Still on Nantucket, wake up in the downtown vicinity and take the shuttle to quiet **'Sconset** for a beach walk or lunch at **The Summer House.** Alternatively, rent a bike and ride to Wauwinet for a tour at **Coskata-Coatue Wildlife Refuge** with the Trustees of Reservations (reserve this as far in advance as you possibly can).

Day 9

Take the ferry back to Harwich Port and drive to Falmouth (45 minutes), making a quick stop in **Hyannis** (20 minutes) to check out the **John F. Kennedy Hyannis Museum** or wares in the funky stores on **Main Street.**

iconic Nauset Light

Fresh Catch

Cape Cod's reputation as a treasure trove of ultrafresh delicious sea creatures is well earned. Start the feast by tucking into raw oysters (some of the best in the world are served on menus around Cape Cod, hailing from the town of Wellfleet). Local clams too are a favorite (medium-size, hard-shell bivalves known as quahogs) and show up in restaurants stuffed, in fried clam cakes (called fritters), or in the area's cream-based clam chowder.

Entrées dig even deeper into the sea: you'll find delicacies like lobster, crab, shrimp, mussels, and clams on offer. Fish like cod, striper, salmon, mackerel, and bluefish are also readily available here, and you'll find them cooked every which way—fried, boiled, sautéed, marinated, braised with wild mushrooms, or filled with bacon and stuffing, then baked.

Here's a list of some of the best places for seafood throughout Cape Cod and the islands.

CAPE COD

- **Brewster Fish House (Brewster):** Fancy, pricey seafood done to perfection.
- **Sir Cricket's Fish & Chips (Orleans):** Fried platters are the ticket here.
- **Mac's Shack (Wellfleet):** The usual fried platters plus unique and healthy options, like sushi-grade tuna wraps in sesame vinaigrette.
- **The Wicked Oyster (Wellfleet):** Oysters aren't the only thing on the menu, but they sure are good.
- **The Lobster Pot (Provincetown):** Portuguese and Cape-style casual spot with great chowder and fish entrées.
- **The Mews Restaurant & Cafe (Provincetown):** A contemporary American seafood favorite for both locals and tourists.
- **John's Foot Long (Provincetown):** You can't get better fried scallop platters, and they're (almost) affordable, even in summer.

MARTHA'S VINEYARD

- **Sandy's Fish & Chips (Vineyard Haven):** Fresh fish and great clams.

fresh lobster roll

- **The Sweet Life Café (Oak Bluffs):** With quirky hits like strawberry gazpacho, this is a locavore paradise: island-caught seafood, locally grown vegetables, and in-season ingredients are all on the menu.
- **Alchemy (Edgartown):** Delicious seafood and burgers.
- **Larsen's Fish Market (Menemsha):** Great raw bar, clam cakes, and stuffed quahogs.

NANTUCKET

- **Bar Yoshi:** Enjoy fresh sushi rolls with a full bar presented by an impressive Tokyo-born and trained chef.
- **Òran Mór:** Haute cuisine at its island best.
- **Straight Wharf Restaurant:** Go for the lobster roll at lunch or the poached lobster at dinner.
- **The SeaGrille:** Year-round standby for great seafood.

From Falmouth, secure passage on one of the ferries to **Martha's Vineyard,** landing in either **Oak Bluffs** or **Vineyard Haven.** Spend the day in either town, ducking through the souvenir shops and art galleries and walking the downtown harbors of each.

Day 10

Take the island shuttle or rent a bike and cycle to **Gay Head Cliffs** and **Menemsha,** where the island really opens up and the crowds give way to incredible views and authentic island living. If you've still got energy left after the bike ride, hike the stunningly beautiful **Menemsha Hills.**

Day 11

Switch gears and spend the day in **Edgartown,** taking in the historic **captains' houses** and pristine waterfront homes. When you've had enough ogling, rent a bike and bring it across on the ferry to **Chappaquiddick** island, home to the serene **Mytoi** Japanese-style gardens.

Day 12

Make your return to **Falmouth** by boat, then be sure to visit **Woods Hole Oceanographic Institute** to advance your depth of knowledge of local sealife (10 minutes' walk from the ferry terminal). Then, further that education at the **Woods Hole Science Aquarium.**

the beautiful gardens of Mytoi

painted cliffs at Gay Head

A Weekend in Nantucket

Friday

Start the day in the center of **Nantucket town,** where quaint cobblestone streets and generations-old shops sit next to upscale boutiques. After strolling around, settle in at a table for lunch at **Straight Wharf Restaurant** for fresh seafood overlooking the water. Along the way back to the hotel, check out the many art galleries, souvenir shops, and craft stores.

Saturday

Pack a beach bag, rent a bike, and ask for a map to **Madaket Beach.** The well-paved, beautiful bike paths along the way are lined with beach plums and wind past neighborhoods exhibiting the island's traditional saltbox houses. Along the way, stop and pick up first-rate sandwiches and cookies at **Something Natural.** Bring the lunches with you to enjoy during your day on the shore.

Sunday

Make it a day filled with local history. Begin after breakfast at **African Meeting House,** an 1827 site once used as a meeting place and schoolhouse for the island's African American residents. After lunch, make your way to Nantucket's **Whaling Museum** and spend the remainder of the day taking in giant whale skeletons and more whaling lore than you can shake a harpoon at.

the Nantucket Whaling Museum

The Cape and Islands' Best Beaches

No matter where you are on the Cape, you're never more than 10 minutes from a beach, and they're all lovely. Here are the top picks among the many wonderful options.

- **Nauset Light Beach:** Lighthouses and Cape Cod go together like ice cream and apple pie, and this one in Eastham is as picture-perfect as any, with its beautiful red-and-white tower and the light itself, still in operation today.
- **Race Point Beach:** Include a little pink from a nice sunset or some blue ocean in the background, and you'll have a memory of the sand dunes at the Cape Cod National Seashore that you'll cherish for years.
- **Sandy Neck Beach:** This Cape beach is as scenic as it gets, with wood fences, wave-rounded stones, silky white sand, and terns that wheel through the sky. There's a snack bar and restrooms in summer, as well as 4WD camping (permit required).
- **The Knob:** Not technically a beach per se, the Knob is a great spot for beachcombing, with rocks, shells, sea critters, and wading. You can hike up to the top for a bird's-eye view or just grab a towel and park somewhere on the sand and watch the boats go by.
- **Gray's Beach:** Another top Cape beach, this picture-perfect beach is inside a bay estuary, with a boardwalk and ever changing scenery with the tide. At low tide you can walk out across azure puddles and beautiful sand flats. At high tide it's perfect for swimming and kayaking.
- **Madaket Beach:** Located in Nantucket, this unmissable beach is powdery white sand, surf (strong currents at times), and lovely photogenic dunes.
- **Gay Head:** The beach beneath these painted cliffs in Martha's Vineyard are pretty enough to warrant their own trip. Swim in the warm waters of Nantucket Sound or sunbathe beneath artfully eroded cliffs that will have you setting your camera into panoramic mode.
- **Craigville Beach:** This stretch of white south-facing sand has almost no current and looks out at the scintillating waters of Nantucket Sound. It's one of the spots with a "beach scene" and thus is a great choice for college students looking to make friends or party. There are facilities, some restaurants in summer, and parking, though not nearly enough of it. Arrive early to make sure you get a spot.
- **Old Silver Beach:** This Falmouth beach is on the Buzzards Bay side and as such gets great views of ships and other vessels headed for the Cape Cod Canal. The water is warmer than the Atlantic and Cape Cod Bay sides, and currents are family friendly, usually without waves or undertow.
- **Coast Guard Beach:** Consistently ranked as one of America's top beaches, Coast Guard really has it all. The evocative ranger station overlooks a marsh estuary and miles of unbroken white Cape shores. Seals and great whites are here, as are surfers and sunbathers. The "elbow" location means it's accessible to nearly any Cape visitor—which means parking can be tricky; most visitors will need to use the free shuttle.

Be prepared to share the sand in summer.

Martha's Vineyard Getaway

Day 1

Arrive in Vineyard Haven and charter a windjammer with **Black Dog Tall Ships** for a day on the water. Afterward, take a shuttle to Oak Bluffs and stroll the winding lanes of colorful cottages in **Oak Bluffs Campground.** In the evening, take a 10-minute drive into downtown Edgartown and visit **Edgartown Lighthouse** (Edgartown Harbor), built in 1828.

Day 2

Pack a picnic lunch and spend the morning experiencing a serene reservation area with a trip to **Mytoi.** The pine-forest Japanese-style enclave has rare and exotic plants and trees and a quiet 0.25-mile trail. Follow that bit of natural splendor with a bit more: The nearby **Cape Poge Wildlife Refuge** includes 14 miles of walking trails and beachfront. Take a break from hiking to have lunch at one of the picnic tables. After the return hike, grab the ferry back and settle into **The Newes from America** for a pint and some solidly restoring pub fare. Then get back on the road leading out of Edgartown.

Day 3

Up-island, check out **Grey Barn Farm,** where, among other things, you can have milk that, if it were any fresher, would still be in the cow. Take a free tour of the picturesque property, peruse the boutique's shelves filled with homemade gourmet foodstuffs and bottles of wine, and make sure to bring some back for you and your friends. Spend what's left of the day exploring the art galleries and cafés in nearby **West Tisbury.**

Day 4

You'll see the island's most magnificent corners on foot, but see more of them equally up-close and personal by bike. In Edgartown, rent bikes

feeding the goats at Grey Barn Farm

at Wheel Happy and turn your handlebars toward the Massachusetts Audubon Society's Felix Neck Wildlife Sanctuary. Bike riding will get you there, but is not allowed while within the wildlife sanctuary: Park your bike and explore on foot the sanctuary's six miles of trails and remote beaches surrounded by woodlands, meadows, pond, and marshes.

Day 5

The paragon of Martha's Vineyard beauty glows with every evening's sunset: Aquinnah's Gay Head Cliffs, a National Natural Landmark. Spend some time perusing the stable of shops and eating some lunch, then spend the rest of the time gawking at the striated red and amber walls of the bluffs—and catch a glimpse of the Elizabeth Islands across Vineyard Sound.

Water Fun for Everyone

Whether it's fishing, boating, surfing, swimming, sea kayaking, sunbathing, or something else, Cape Cod has something for water lovers of all kinds. Check the list below for top tips on your favorite water activities.

Fishing

Reel Deal Fishing Charters offers full-day or half-day fishing charters you can plan your vacation around. Catch striped bass, blues, bluefin tuna, and a variety of groundfish from one of their two vessels in Pamet Harbor in Truro.

Kayaking and Canoeing

Nauset Marsh and the Cape Cod National Seashore offer spectacular chances for great marsh vistas. Few experiences are more quintessentially Cape Cod than gliding silently along a brackish creek, watching as great blue herons and ducks appear through morning mist. It's an experience that's as ethereal and enlightening as it was when the Nauset people rode these same waters in their hand-carved canoes.

Bridge Creek, part of Barnstable Great Marsh, is one of the nicest spots for canoeing and kayaking in the Mid- and Upper Cape. It's for advanced-level paddlers, but offers an almost Everglades-like feel at times as one slips around blind corners, surprising herons, ducks, and shorebirds.

Surfing

While Coast Guard Beach in Eastham is one of the most popular, the entire Outer Cape, from the elbow of Chatham to the wrist of P-town, is one huge 40-mile-long beach break. The same shifting sandbars that claimed so many ships in these waters make for great waves when conditions are right. The best times of year are spring and fall, when the ground swell is longer due to storms in the Atlantic and there are fewer tourists competing for the waves.

Swimming

Not many kettle ponds match Gull Pond in Wellfleet for freshwater Cape Cod bliss. This pond, the fragile head of the Herring River, is a great spot for a dip anytime from early June to mid-September.

Saltwater wave lovers will want to head to Coast Guard Beach or any of the other Outer Cape spots, whereas families with little ones will prefer the more placid Cape Cod Bay areas of Sandy Neck and Millway Beach, which feature gentle currents and small (if any) waves.

Boating

Quissett Harbor is one of the nicest spots for a sail, and, if winds favor it, you can go all the way out into Buzzards Bay or down to Woods Hole and still be back before sunset.

Cape Cod Bay, via Millway Beach, is the premier spot for boating. The gentle protective arm of the Cape proper keeps currents to a minimum, and it's not uncommon to see dolphins, sharks, turtles, or even whales as you take in the scenery.

Biking and Hiking

cyclists on the Cape Cod Rail Trail

Few places offer such a wealth of options for hiking and biking as the Cape. Mile upon mile of unused railway track have been converted to bike paths, and each town has numerous conservation lands that are crisscrossed with trails. Many are multiuse areas too: In addition to avid cyclists on mountain bikes, you'll find people out walking their dogs, families with young kids going birdwatching, joggers, runners, and more. Best of all, parking in many of these diverse areas is actually free, or at least far less expensive than at the beaches.

Martha's Vineyard and Nantucket are so easy to bike around that it's hardly worth mentioning, but there are a number of lovely walking routes.

- **Cape Cod Canal Bike Path:** Spanning both sides of the Cape Cod Canal, this paved and well-maintained biking and walking path offers great views of the Cape's three bridges, plus waterbirds, fishing, and the boats going by on the canal.
- **Shining Sea Path:** You can start in Woods Hole and bike all the way to Falmouth center and beyond on this paved trail that goes right by some stunning beaches, as well as through woods and marshes.
- **West Barnstable Conservation Area:** This unpaved area, also known as the Trail of Tears, is a network of wooded trails that crisscross a large, roughly triangular area bordered by the road, the airport, and a set of power lines. It's great for mountain bikers, as the rugged up-and-down terrain offers challenging rides.
- **Cape Cod Rail Trail:** One of the first paved trails, the Cape Cod Rail Trail is nearly flat and takes you past lovely cranberry bogs, kettle ponds, pine forests, and quaint Cape villages.
- **Cape Cod National Seashore:** Not exactly an official bike trail, this route can connect the Rail Trail with Provincetown, though there are large sections that must be shared with cars.
- **Province Lands:** A gorgeous and well-maintained network of trails lets you explore the rugged, salt-stunted worlds of the P-town dunes. You'll see blueberry and huckleberry bushes, beech forests, pine and scrub oak thickets, sand dunes, beaches, and a host of birds and wildlife as you go.
- **Lily Pond Park (Nantucket):** Tucked behind homes and with the lovely steeple of the First Congregational Church presiding in the background, this partial boardwalk, partial grass, and partial mud meander is a lovely spot for families to take kids or for couples to hold hands. It's also one of the few nature walks where one could bring a wheelchair, at least for parts of it. The wooden walkway allows access over the muddiest parts, and it connects several areas of grass and lawn.
- **Cedar Tree Neck (Martha's Vineyard):** Along Martha's Vineyard's northwest shoreline, this conservation land is stunning—leading from a wooded parking lot down to unhurried, rock-strewn coastal beaches and then back to cliff-side bluffs. It's well worth seeking out if you've got a car and a morning or afternoon free to explore (not accessible to wheelchairs).

Cape Cod

Ah, Cape Cod: "A man may stand there and put all America behind him," wrote Henry David Thoreau, longingly summing up his several 19th-century visits.

Jutting 40 miles into the Atlantic, this relatively young "flexed arm" of sandy soil and pitch pine forest, appreciated by Thoreau for its desolation, has become one of the nation's preeminent seaside resorts; its 15 towns and hundred-odd beaches draw millions of summer residents and visitors each year.

Cape Codders have always lived off the sea in some form or other. For centuries, the Cape brought in much of the area's fish and shellfish; now, its livelihood depends on people coming to whale-watch, swim, surf, or sunbathe.

Highlights

Look for ★ to find recommended sights, activities, dining, and lodging.

★ **Heritage Museums and Gardens:** Two centuries of Americana live on at this palatial garden estate (page 37).

★ **Sandwich Glassblowers:** Artisans first brought the art of glassblowing to this town centuries ago, and the tradition is still going strong (page 39).

★ **Woods Hole Oceanographic Institute:** Deep-sea explorers reveal the mysteries of the real final frontier (page 48).

★ **Old King's Highway:** Winding through one quaint village after another, this route runs through the Cape Cod of yesteryear (page 56).

★ **Monomoy National Wildlife Refuge:** This sandy spit off the end of the Cape's "elbow" is home to a colony of gray seals and hundreds of migratory bird species (page 77).

★ **Cape Cod National Seashore:** Stroll miles of sandy beaches and marvel at the vast, seemingly endless ocean (page 81).

★ **Highland Light:** Towering 123 feet over the dunes, this is the Cape's most impressive working lighthouse, and the only one regularly open to the public (page 95).

★ **Provincetown's Commercial Street:** Drag queens, local characters, and wide-eyed tourists all add up to a people-watcher's paradise (page 100).

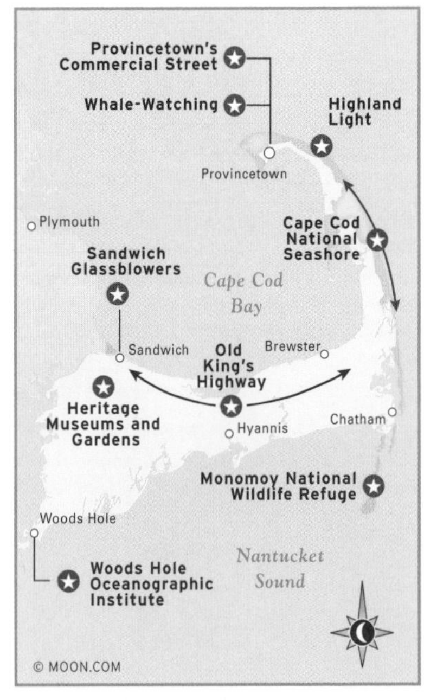

★ **Whale-Watching:** Seeing the leviathans in their natural habitat on one of P-town's trusty vessels is anything but a fluke (page 102).

You'll notice as you meander "up" and "down" (note, not "west" or "east") the Cape that some parts are prettier than others. In fact, each town has its own unique character. Stately Sandwich, with its ancient houses and history; the Yarmouth south-side beaches, mini golf, and nightclubs, all catering to the college here-to-party crowd; the artsy and quaint stretch of Old King's Highway in Dennis and Brewster, with its clapboard houses and trellises full of Cape roses; the melting pot of Provincetown, with its eclectic mix of gays, lesbians, fishermen, and tourists—each part of this quirky peninsula has a different vibe.

Of course, the biggest attraction for most visitors is the quantity and variety of Cape Cod's beaches. Seeing as the peninsula is pretty much a giant sandbar plopped here by glaciers during the last ice age, it makes perfect sense that on the Cape, all roads don't lead to Rome—instead, they lead to a beach, bay, estuary, inlet, boardwalk, or salt marsh. Add a freshwater pond for every day of the year (yes, there are 365 named ponds on the Cape), and you've got a haven for just about any kind of water-related activity you might imagine. Hover over the canal on a Friday afternoon and you'll see miles of on-Cape traffic, most vehicles crammed with surfboards or sea kayaks, beach chairs, and umbrellas.

With all those visitors, you might think you'd have a hard time finding anywhere with any privacy, but you'd be surprised. Over 40 miles of unbroken outer Cape beach means all you have to do is walk 5-10 minutes from a parking area and you'll essentially have a spot all your own. Add a little overcast weather (or better, come in the off-season) and you might find the beach almost as lonesome and desolate as Thoreau found it when he walked here over a century ago.

Another benefit of off-season visits is skipping the hefty parking fees—$15 or even $25 May-mid-September. Around 4:30pm, many beaches stop collecting the fee, so the budget-minded can save a bundle if they come after prime suntanning hours.

Visitors who never leave the car will still find a lot to marvel at. Morning mist rising over water lilies in a kettle pond might be pulled straight from a Monet canvas. Antiques, curios, and art give bargain-hunters plenty to find as they tootle along Route 6A (the Old King's Highway). Even the jumble of wacky mini-golf stops and restaurants on Route 28 can offer a chuckle or two. But the real magic starts when you get out of the car.

Ditch the wheels for a while and discover that at any time of year the Cape's local conservation lands and privately managed sanctuaries offer world-class vacationing that—for many New Englanders—is only a day trip from home. Kayaking along a salt marsh estuary among blossoming white beach plum, sitting beside a kettle pond listening to a kingfisher's call, spotting red-winged blackbirds among the cattail reeds of an eelgrass estuary, or encountering bright lady's slippers *(Cypripedium acaule)* scattered amid the moist coolness of a maturing stand of oaks—all are available here. One or two such experiences, and you too may find yourself repeating the phrase that has come so easily to generations of visitors: See you next year, back down on the Cape.

ORIENTATION

First-timers are often rightly confused by highway directions here. Signs are often equally frustrating, as a particular route "south" may actually travel due north for miles.

The operative principle on the Cape is "up" and "down." **Up Cape** means westward—toward the Upper Cape and that big hummock known as **off-Cape** to locals and as North America to everyone else. **Down Cape** means eastward—toward the Outer Cape and eventually Provincetown. What's tricky is that

Previous: Falmouth; Wellfleet; maple trees in the fall.

Cape Cod

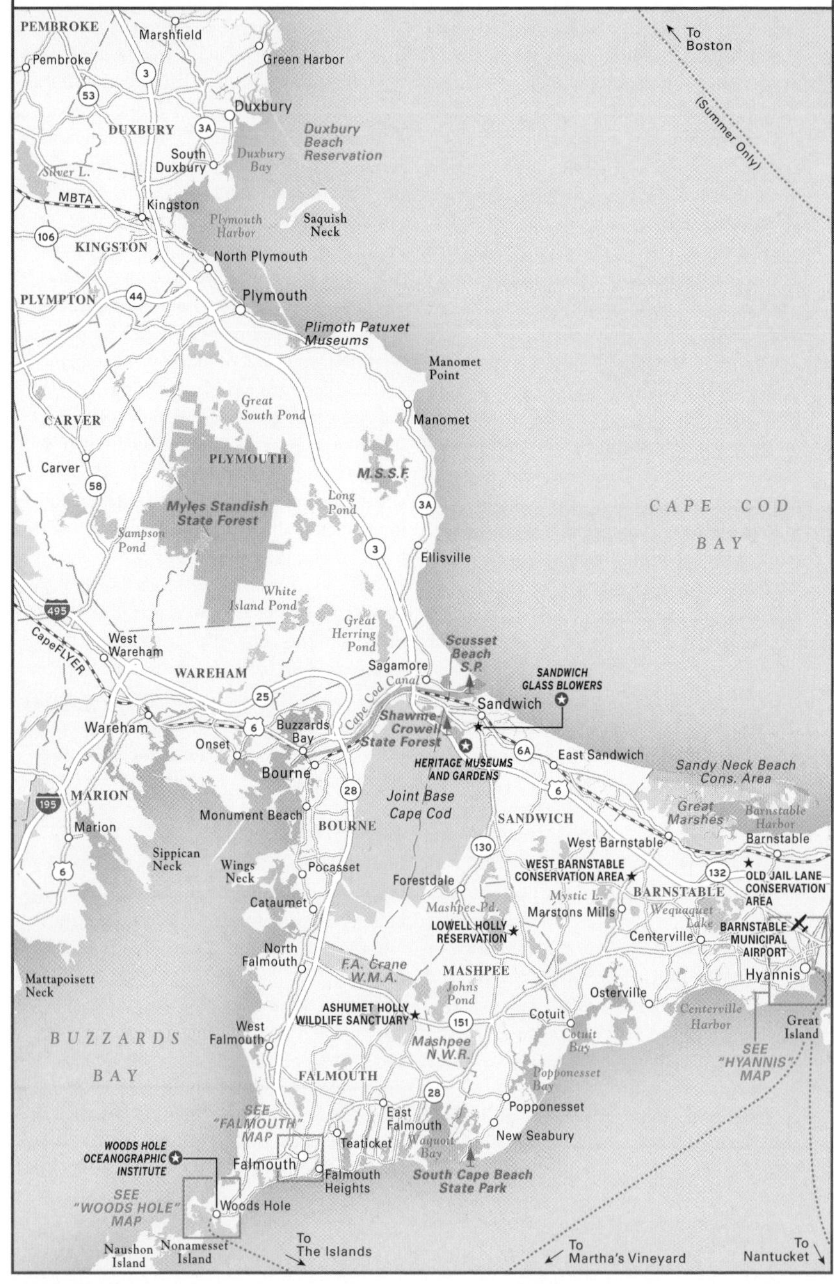
PEMBROKE
Marshfield
Pembroke
Green Harbor
Duxbury
DUXBURY
Duxbury Beach Reservation
South Duxbury
Duxbury Bay
Silver L.
MBTA
Kingston
Plymouth Harbor
Saquish Neck
KINGSTON
North Plymouth
PLYMPTON
Plymouth
Plimoth Patuxet Museums
Manomet Point
Great South Pond
CARVER
Manomet
PLYMOUTH
Carver
M.S.S.F.
Myles Standish State Forest
Long Pond
Sampson Pond
Ellisville
CAPE COD BAY
White Island Pond
Great Herring Pond
West Wareham
CapeFLYER
Scusset Beach S.P.
WAREHAM
Sagamore
Cape Cod Canal
SANDWICH GLASS BLOWERS
Sandwich
Shawme-Crowell State Forest
Wareham
Buzzards Bay
Onset
HERITAGE MUSEUMS AND GARDENS
East Sandwich
Sandy Neck Beach Cons. Area
Bourne
MARION
Joint Base Cape Cod
Monument Beach
BOURNE
SANDWICH
Great Marshes
Barnstable Harbor
Marion
West Barnstable
Barnstable
Sippican Neck
Wings Neck
Pocasset
WEST BARNSTABLE CONSERVATION AREA
OLD JAIL LANE CONSERVATION AREA
Forestdale
BARNSTABLE
Mystic L.
Cataumet
Mashpee Pd.
Marstons Mills
Wequaquet Lake
LOWELL HOLLY RESERVATION
BARNSTABLE MUNICIPAL AIRPORT
Centerville
North Falmouth
F.A. Crane W.M.A.
MASHPEE
Hyannis
Mattapoisett Neck
Johns Pond
Osterville
ASHUMET HOLLY WILDLIFE SANCTUARY
Cotuit
Centerville Harbor
Great Island
West Falmouth
BUZZARDS BAY
Mashpee N.W.R.
Cotuit Bay
SEE "HYANNIS" MAP
Popponesset Bay
FALMOUTH
Popponesset
East Falmouth
SEE "FALMOUTH" MAP
Teaticket
New Seabury
Waquoit Bay
WOODS HOLE OCEANOGRAPHIC INSTITUTE
Falmouth
Falmouth Heights
South Cape Beach State Park
SEE "WOODS HOLE" MAP
Woods Hole
Naushon Island
Nonamesset Island
To The Islands
To Martha's Vineyard
To Nantucket
To Boston
(Summer Only)

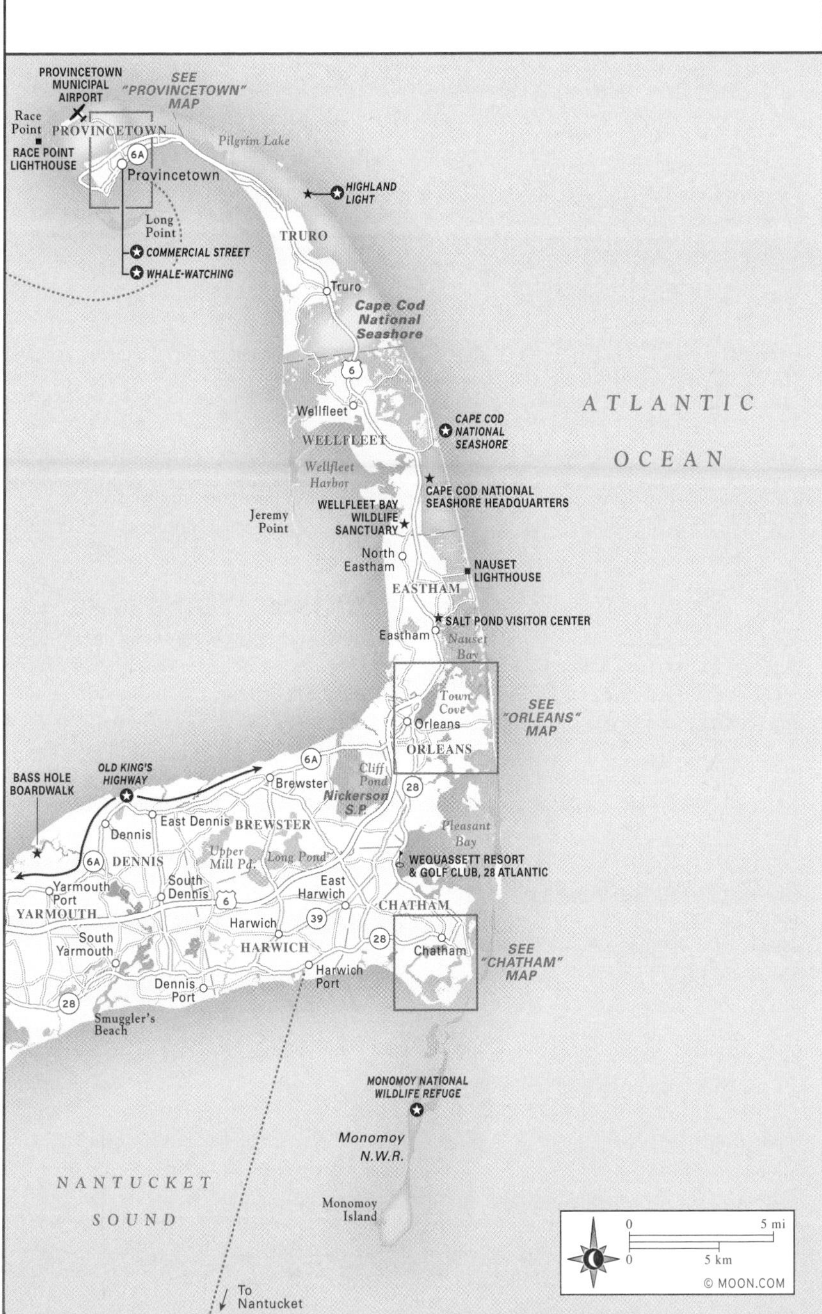
PROVINCETOWN MUNICIPAL AIRPORT
SEE "PROVINCETOWN" MAP
Race Point
PROVINCETOWN
Pilgrim Lake
RACE POINT LIGHTHOUSE
6A
Provincetown
HIGHLAND LIGHT
Long Point
TRURO
COMMERCIAL STREET
WHALE-WATCHING
Truro
Cape Cod National Seashore
6
ATLANTIC OCEAN
Wellfleet
CAPE COD NATIONAL SEASHORE
WELLFLEET
Wellfleet Harbor
CAPE COD NATIONAL SEASHORE HEADQUARTERS
WELLFLEET BAY WILDLIFE SANCTUARY
Jeremy Point
North Eastham
NAUSET LIGHTHOUSE
EASTHAM
SALT POND VISITOR CENTER
Eastham
Nauset Bay
Town Cove
SEE "ORLEANS" MAP
Orleans
ORLEANS
OLD KING'S HIGHWAY
BASS HOLE BOARDWALK
Cliff Pond
Brewster
28
Nickerson S.P.
East Dennis
BREWSTER
Pleasant Bay
Dennis
Upper Mill Pd.
Long Pond
WEQUASSETT RESORT & GOLF CLUB, 28 ATLANTIC
DENNIS
Yarmouth Port
South Dennis
East Harwich
YARMOUTH
CHATHAM
Harwich
39
South Yarmouth
HARWICH
Chatham
SEE "CHATHAM" MAP
Harwich Port
Dennis Port
Smuggler's Beach
MONOMOY NATIONAL WILDLIFE REFUGE
Monomoy N.W.R.
NANTUCKET SOUND
Monomoy Island
0 5 mi
0 5 km
© MOON.COM
To Nantucket

Where to Stay on Cape Cod

There's a lot of Cape Cod that overlaps, and towns may seem similar, but knowing right where to go to get the most from your stay here can make a real difference—especially if you're not keen to fight traffic to get where you want to go. The following is a list of top spots based on activity or interest that can help you plunk down and never want to leave.

- **If you want beaches:** Go to Orleans.
- **If you want bicycling:** Go to Falmouth.
- **If you want bird-watching:** Go to Wellfleet.
- **If you hate traffic:** Go to Provincetown.
- **If you want dancing and bars:** Go to Hyannis.
- **If you like fine dining:** Go to Brewster.
- **If you want to get away from it all:** Go to Truro.

depending on where you are, "down" can either mean to head east, or, if you're already at the "elbow" of Chatham-Orleans, north. If you're in Wellfleet, "up Cape" will mean to travel south to the elbow and then west. Make sense?

Further important distinctions are made between the three sides of the Cape's bent arm: **Bayside** refers to the entire rim of Cape Cod Bay, from the canal at Sandwich down to MacMillan Pier in Provincetown. The first half comprises historic and picturesque Cape villages, as venerable as Thanksgiving, along what was once the Old King's Highway (now Rte. 6A). The **south shore** faces Nantucket Sound, between Buzzards Bay and the Cape's **elbow** at Chatham. Blatantly commercial Route 28, as casual as a beer belly over the barbecue and as gaudy as the Fourth of July, is the main artery of this side. And the **backside** denotes that segment that braves the open Atlantic from the Chatham elbow to the "fist" of Provincetown; most of this area is preserved for posterity as part of Cape Cod National Seashore.

It's also worth remembering that towns on the Cape are all subdivided into distinct villages, whose names can also be confusing. But eventually, if you keep coming back, it will make perfect sense that South Dennis would be north of West Dennis or that West Chatham would be east of South Chatham.

PLANNING YOUR TIME

Cape Cod isn't large, but it's long, meaning that many people opt for a "base" town and then take day trips or overnights to other parts of the Cape or the islands, but another option to consider is staying a night up Cape and a night down Cape in order to see most of what there is to see. With a car, you can get from the bridges to P-town in about 2 hours, so it's better to overnight here at least one night than try to do "all the Cape" as a day trip. By far the biggest frustration visitors have coming to or leaving the Cape is the traffic, which is to some degree unavoidable because the public transportation options, especially to the more scenic out-of-the-way spots, are poor, if they exist at all. Backpackers may find that Martha's Vineyard and Nantucket, while more expensive, are a lot more walking-friendly. Improvements over the years have made it easier to get around, but if you're coming from Asia, Europe, or any of the larger American cities with subways and bus systems, you'll find non-car navigation around the Cape a challenge.

You can skip the bridge traffic by flying directly, and depending on the time of year the cost may not be jaw-droppingly exorbitant. Barnstable Municipal Airport, in Hyannis, is the largest and most used. Provincetown Municipal Airport is a convenient option if you're coming from Boston. Both are served by Cape Air, as well as other airlines.

It's possible to reach almost every town on the Cape with the **Cape Cod Regional Transit Authority** (CCRTA, www.capecodrta.org) and its collection of year-round bus lines and summer trolleys, in combination with the all-season **Plymouth & Brockton** (508/746-0378, www.p-b.com) and **Peter Pan** (888/751-8800, www.peterpanbus.com) buses.

Depending on the timing of your visit, you may also want to consider arriving into Provincetown by ferry from Boston.

Locals know to never, ever leave the Cape on a Sunday afternoon, and never return to it on a Friday, when vacationers from New England and beyond pile onto the arteries leading south to the Cape, and **traffic** can back up for miles at bridges. The worst weekends are the two that bookend the Fourth of July and Labor Day. **High season** typically runs from Memorial Day weekend in late May through Labor Day weekend in early September. Most people come expecting, even enjoying, the crowds. It's a great time to meet new friends, have that "crazy" summer, or make good money waiting tables, doing housekeeping, or tending bar.

The key to enjoying a peak-season July or August stay is to plan as far ahead as possible, particularly with lodging, as the massive demand for hotel rooms brings up prices. People arriving on the spur of the moment expecting to pull into a cheap motel may find themselves nearly back in New York or Connecticut before they find a place that doesn't have a "No Vacancy" sign. With a little time spent calling ahead or making reservations online, you can ensure that your days or weeks here are frustration-free.

Vacationers with more leeway in their schedules may prefer the spring and fall **shoulder seasons,** which are quite popular but not quite as packed. These are the months when prices are a tad lower—the 30-percent-off signs can start appearing in front of T-shirt and beachwear shops as early as the last weekend of August, and many lodgings offer Sunday-Thursday discounts. Many repeat visitors regard fall, in particular, as the Cape's best season because the water and weather remain warm but the crowds dissipate.

The exact lengths of the shoulder seasons greatly depend on the weather and location. The spring shoulder begins at Easter and ends in late May. The fall shoulder is more elastic, running from Labor Day through October across most of the Cape, and from Columbus Day to early November in selected pockets that have romantic B&Bs, such as Provincetown and areas along the Old King's Highway.

By Thanksgiving in most places, and by New Year's everywhere, the **off-season** has arrived and remains until the daffodils bloom in April. Businesses close up or start keeping malleable hours. How strictly they keep to the posted signs depends on where you are. Hyannis and Falmouth remain fairly open year-round. Orleans and the Route 28 section of Harwich and Yarmouth are spotty, and from the "elbow" to P-town become ghost towns. This suits many locals and even some visitors just fine. As the leaves turn red and golden or as the snowfall starts to blanket the dunes in cottony white, you'll discover great scenic beauty and meet the year-round residents who turn out for nightlife, gallery events, and to support the local restaurants that stay open throughout the winter.

The Upper Cape

One of the great attractions of the Cape is the diversity of its towns. Behind the uniform weathered-gray shingles and simple little saltbox houses, clam shacks and soft-serve ice cream machines, pitch pine and scrub oak forests, are differences in history and demographics that keep each town unique and surprising. The four Upper Cape towns—Sandwich, Mashpee, Woods Hole, and Falmouth—which by turns either embrace or ignore tourism, are highly commercialized or nearly rural and can feel either country-clubbish or working-class. With about one-third fewer lodgings than any of the other parts of the Cape, it's an area often bypassed by visitors bound for the motel-lined shore of the Mid-Cape, the carnival of Provincetown, or the Woods Hole ferry. The people who do stop here can start enjoying a Cape vacation while other travelers are still braving traffic on U.S. 6.

The Upper Cape also benefits from having a nearly forgotten side to it: the Buzzards Bay shore. Although only a few of the beaches here are open to outsiders who come by car (one, Monument Beach, even has free parking), simply driving or cycling the route closest to the bay is as good an introduction as you can get to the sedative charms of the Cape landscape. Although it led the region in catering to summer tourists in the late 1800s, with fancy beachfront hotels along the then-new railroad to Woods Hole, the area has since slid gently into a lower gear. Despite some new developments that have cut swaths in the scenic value, there is still a lot to enjoy on a quiet Upper Cape trip. Modest homes tucked behind trees, marsh-edged inlets, undeveloped woods, and salt-blasted signs for boatyards all offer great snapshots. Birding is good at almost any time of year. And for those on the fence about whether to push farther down Cape (east, toward P-town) it's comforting to cut a full 1.5 hours off the drive.

SANDWICH

Sandwich, settled by a group of 60 families from north of Boston in 1637, was the first town to be established on the Cape and could easily pass for the most historic even today. Buildings that retain the look and feel of "olde Cape Cod," some lovely museums and scenery, and a number of excellent dining and lodging choices make it a perfect vacation in itself, or a great overnight before heading farther down Cape.

Cape Cod Canal

Few things are more iconic of arrival on the Cape than the **Bourne** and **Sagamore Bridges,** whose silver girders and rounded arches are the only two entry points, save for those who plan to swim. The Cape used to be fully connected to the mainland, separated from the rest of the state only by a valley with two opposite-flowing rivers, the Manomet and the Scusset. The Pilgrims recognized as early as the 1670s that a canal between them would be a good idea. It wasn't until 1909, however, that construction began in earnest, and the first vessels passed through the completed eight-mile canal in July 1914. The federal government bought the canal in 1928, nearly doubled its width, and built the two huge highway bridges that now provide the Cape's principal link to the rest of the nation. More recently, bike trails have been made on both sides of this waterway, offering locals and visitors alike a wonderful way to access fishing holes, snapshot vistas, or just an easy, pretty way to get some exercise.

Operation and maintenance of the canal is overseen by the U.S. Army Corps of Engineers, which also runs the **Cape Cod Canal Visitors Center** (60 Ed Moffitt Dr., Sandwich, 508/833-9678, www.nae.usace.army.mil, 10am-5pm May-late Oct., free) at the eastern end of the canal. Drop by to learn about the canal's history and wildlife, view traffic video and radar monitors, and shop for Cape-related books at the small gift shop. For a more extensive selection of regional titles, head up Route 6A to the excellent **Titcomb's Book Shop** (432 Rte. 6A, 508/888-2331, www.titcombsbookshop.com, 9am-6pm Mon.-Sat., 11am-5pm Sun. year-round), a little ways past the Father's Kitchen & Taphouse in East Sandwich.

The 6.5-mile **Cape Cod Canal Bike Path**—comprising service roads on the banks of both sides of the canal—is paved for use by skaters, joggers, and cyclists. It's a family-type trail, so be prepared to slow down for toddlers on training wheels and people fishing with tackle. Expect great views of the canal's ship traffic. If it's windy, try veering off onto Shore Road in Bourne (parallel with the west end of the Cape-side path) and bicycling a short distance west to the beaches at Gray Gables, facing the canal, or Phinney's Harbor, on the causeway to Mashnee Island. Parking is limited to residents at the former and is nonexistent at the latter, so cycling is about the only way to experience either beach in summer.

The best lot to access the mainland side of the Canal Path is tucked almost underneath the Sagamore Bridge. Follow the aptly named Canal Road past Friendly's to its terminus. An alternate entry is midway down that road, beside speedy U.S. 6 westbound, at the only canal-side stoplight. On the Cape side, parking is available at the east (Sandwich) end beside the big boxy electricity-generating station off Route 6A (turn on Tupper Road and follow signs with the U.S. Army Corps of Engineers logo), and at the west (Bourne) end off Shore Road, by the railroad lift bridge that resembles the two towers of London's Tower Bridge.

Historic Sandwich Village

The village of Sandwich—with its restored 1640 gristmill grinding cornmeal for visitors, its classically inspired Town Hall and meetinghouse, its Christopher Wren church on a hill, and its carefully crafted imitation stagecoach inn—almost epitomizes what people think of when they imagine an old Cape Cod town. The density of historic buildings, museums, shops, antiques stores, and scenery make it easy to stop for lunch and not leave by nightfall. Even better, unlike many spots on the Cape, Sandwich village is something you can walk through. Highlights are listed here, but don't be afraid to parallel-park that car of yours and discover some cool spots on foot.

SANDWICH GLASS MUSEUM

One of the early visitors who came to Sandwich for the hunting, Deming Jarves recognized in the woods a potential source of fuel for a glass factory's furnaces. (Daniel Webster, for one, complained that the subsequently diminished forests were no longer adequate for "good sport.") For much of the 19th century, Jarves's Boston & Sandwich Glass Company dominated the nation's nascent glassmaking industry, turning an expensive import item into a domestic commodity well within the means of most Americans.

At the **Sandwich Glass Museum** (129 Main St., 508/888-0251, www.sandwichglassmuseum.org, 9:30am-4pm Wed.-Sun. Feb.-Mar., 9:30am-5pm daily Apr.-Dec., closed Jan., adults $12, ages 6-14 $2, under age 6 free), in the single-story clapboard building on Main Street opposite Town Hall and First Church, gallery after gallery of samples illustrates the evolution of this early mass-produced glassware. While the factory's artisans were capable of remarkable work, it helps to have a collector's interest in the cut saucers, plates, lamp chimneys, and other household items displayed in such great numbers.

★ HERITAGE MUSEUMS AND GARDENS

About 0.75 miles south of Town Hall is Sandwich's king of collecting, the **Heritage Museums and Gardens** (67 Grove St., 508/888-3300, www.heritagemuseumsandgardens.org, 10am-5pm daily late Apr.-mid-Oct., adults $20, ages 3-12 $10, under age 3 free). Here is Americana by the acre, a diverse assemblage encompassing

1

2
SANDWICH
GLASS
MUSEUM
of the
SANDWICH
HISTORICAL
SOCIETY
SHOP
MUSEUM STORE
ANYTIME
GLASSBLOWING
DAILY

antique autos, military miniatures, Currier & Ives prints, landscape paintings, trade signs, and carved cigar-store figures, just to name a few of the items. A working 1912 carousel is among the larger specimens in the collection, although even the gallery buildings themselves are architectural showpieces and the grounds are a horticultural collection of show gardens. The famous hybrid rhododendrons alone draw busloads of gawkers when in bloom (the first half of June). Added highlights include changing art exhibits and a summer concert series; call or check the website for details.

★ SANDWICH GLASSBLOWERS

Many people visit the Sandwich Glass Museum without ever knowing that the glassblowing tradition continues on the Cape to this day. Only a few minutes' drive south will take you to **McDermott Studios** (272 Cotuit Rd., 508/477-0705, www.mcdermottglass.com, 10am-5pm Tue.-Sun.), where David McDermott and Yukimi Matsumoto create amazing glass art at a studio behind their home. Locally famous for a number of charity projects they've partnered with and for some stunning works of art, David and Yukimi are happy to show guests the studio and give them a tour of their gallery as well.

Drive east along Route 6A and you'll find the studio of **Michael Magyar** (470 Rte. 6A, 508/888-6681, www.capecodglass.net, 10am-4pm daily), a Japanese-inspired glassblower who has found fame in a popular "sea glass" motif. And right near the canal (though technically in Sagamore), in the shadows of the Sagamore Bridge, is **Pairpoint Glass** (851 Rte. 6A, 774/338-4004, www.pairpoint.com, 10am-5pm Mon.-Sat., 11am-4pm Sun.), one of the oldest continually operating glassworks in the United States. It's a common stop for bus tours, and the studio has a large window where you can look down at the artisans without suffering the heat of the kilns.

1: a replica of the *Pinta* getting tugged through the Cape Cod Canal 2: the Sandwich Glass Museum

Beaches

SCUSSET BEACH

The only Sandwich beach on the mainland side, Scusset Beach is often mistakenly thought not to be part of the Cape, and thus it is one of the area's gems. The Sandwich power plant looms prominently from the other side of the canal—so this isn't quite a beach in the middle of nowhere—but the clean quartz-based sand, the scenic beauty of Cape Cod Bay, glimpses of the boats going through Cape Cod Canal, and the relatively few crowds are all reasons to come here. Follow the large signs to Scusset Beach as you go off-Cape over the Sagamore Bridge. Day parking is $14 for residents, $40 for out-of-state visitors.

Shopping

THE WEATHER STORE

Weather buffs or the just plain curious may want to stop in for a peek at **The Weather Store** (146 Main St., 508/888-1200, www.theweatherstore.com, by chance or appt. only), which demonstrates as much single-minded dedication as any of the town museums to its fascinating inventory of weathervanes, whirligigs, tide clocks, sundials, rain gauges, lightning detectors, anemometers, thermometers, barometers, and the like, both new and antique.

Food

A good bet for any meal of the day is the homestyle **Marshland Restaurant** (109 Rte. 6A, 508/888-9824, www.marshlandrestaurant.com, 7am-8pm daily, $10-24), a combination bakery-eatery at the Shell gas station 1.5 miles east of the Bourne-Sandwich line. (Their T-shirt logo: "Eat here and get gas!") Lobster bisque, fish-and-chips, spaghetti and meatballs, steak tips, chicken parmesan, and homemade desserts are examples of the rib-sticking fare. (If you visit in autumn, try the Pilgrim pie, with apples, cranberries, and walnuts.) Prices are low enough to produce lines of patient diners on summer weekends: Two people can eat breakfast for under $20, and other meals are just as friendly to the wallet.

Repeatedly in the Cape's top 10 breakfast and lunch lists is the delightful **Cafe Chew** (4 Merchants Square, 508/888-7717, www.cafechew.com, 8am-3pm daily, $8-12), everything a great coffee shop should be and then some. It has fantastic homemade breads, breakfasts, and a variety of unique sandwiches. Try the French if you don't know where to start: a ciabatta roll with egg and spinach topped with warm gooey brie cheese. Cafe Chew also offers a cornucopia of delightful baked goods, from flaky croissants and breads to tasty brownies, cookies, and "cobbler bars" that are a Chew specialty. On Sunday morning the place is packed, even in the off-season, which tells you people from up and down the Cape are lining up to come here.

Captain Scott's Seafood Restaurant (71 Tupper Rd., 508/888-1675, www.captainscotts.com, 11:30am-8:30pm Sun.-Thurs., 11:30am-9pm Fri.-Sat., $12-27) is a mainstay for locals looking for casual ambiance, cheap eats, and friendly service. It's nothing fancy, but that's exactly how people like it.

Off the Grid (91 Rte 6A, 508/241-8684, http://offthegridcapecod.com, noon-7pm Thurs.-Sun., $8-20) is a food truck that offers great burgers, wings, and some of the Cape's best pulled pork. It's "sandwiched" (get it?) between the Old King's Highway (Rte 6A) and Tupper Road, and is accessible from either direction.

Accommodations

Outside the four hostels in Hyannis, Eastham, Truro, and Provincetown, some of the most affordable rooms on the Cape are found at the **Spring Garden Inn** (578 Rte. 6A, 508/888-0710, mid-Apr.-Nov., $79-159 d), a small motel near milepost 7 on Route 6A in East Sandwich. The 11 pine-paneled nonsmoking guest rooms facing a bird-filled marsh are only a 0.5-mile walk from a bay-side beach (there's also a shallow in-ground pool). Rates include complimentary bagels and fresh-baked goods in the morning. Each room has a flat-screen TV and a coffeemaker.

You'll find a half-dozen other small motels and cottages, none exactly inexpensive, along Route 6A west and east of the Spring Garden Inn. For not too much more, you could also try one of the handful of bed-and-breakfast places in the center of Sandwich's historic village—especially if you don't need the motel-standard second double bed for your kids, or such "unromantic" amenities as in-room TVs and phones. Most of the B&Bs are found within a short stroll of the scenic gristmill on Shawme Pond.

A perfect example is the very Victorian **Isaiah Jones Homestead** (165 Main St., 508/888-9115 or 800/526-1625, www.isaiahjones.com, $199-329 d). Behind the wicker porch furniture are seven guest rooms decorated in authentic late-19th-century style—floral chintz fabric here, a full canopy bed there, and everywhere fresh flowers and candles. As a concession to modern romance, a couple of guest rooms have gas-fueled fireplaces and whirlpool baths. Rates include full breakfast (with a strata if you're lucky) and afternoon refreshments.

Nearby, the **Dan'l Webster Inn & Spa** (149 Main St., 508/888-3622 or 800/444-3566, www.danlwebsterinn.com, $148-335) is an old standby...literally: It's one of the oldest inns in Sandwich, touting its hospitality for over 300 years. The furnishings reflect its historic past, with canopy and four-poster beds, a lobby that feels like you've stepped back in time, and cheery, helpful staff.

On Route 6A, **The Sandy Neck Motel** (669 Rte. 6A, 508/362-3992, www.sandyneck.com, $89-135) is casual but well maintained, offering guest rooms with a fridge, a microwave, and coffee. There is an outdoor common barbecue area, but the real reason to stay is the proximity it offers guests to Sandy Neck beach and the villages of Sandwich and West Barnstable. Rooms for 2-4 people with full kitchens ($150-199) are also available.

Camping

Sandwich has two state campgrounds, both of which may be booked in advance

(877/422-6762, www.reserveamerica.com, $4.50 nonrefundable reservation fee). If you need a place to hook up your RV, try **Scusset Beach State Reservation,** on the mainland side of the canal on Cape Cod Bay due east of the Rte. 3/U.S. 6 intersection. At the foot of the Sagamore Bridge, follow the signs. Five tent sites (mid-Apr.-mid-Oct., $70, state residents $22) are tucked in among the scrub oaks and small pines at the back of the campground. The other sites are available year-round to self-contained vehicles ($20). There is also a $2 Scusset Beach Trust Fund fee.

A more scenic option is **Shawme-Crowell State Forest** (42 Main St., off Rte. 130, 508/888-0351). No RV hookups are available, but the campground has a disposal station, full restrooms with hot showers and modern conveniences, and even a store selling firewood and minor supplies. The 285 sites ($55, state residents $17), generously spread throughout the pine woods, are available mid-April-mid-October during the week and year-round on weekends (barring blizzards). A few dozen spaces are also open to RVs through the winter. They even have small/large **yurts** ($120/140, state residents $45/60). Although overnighters are granted free day use of Scusset Beach, saving $2, this property's distance from the Cape Cod Rail Trail and the National Seashore ensures that it never fills as quickly as Nickerson State Park in the lower Cape.

Getting There and Around

Sandwich is just under 60 miles (60 minutes) southeast of Boston and 61 miles (67 minutes) from Providence. It is nestled at the "shoulder" of the Cape on its north side. The Sagamore Bridge runs over the Cape Cod Canal in Sandwich. The town has easy access to Cape Cod Bay and to the Sagamore bus stop, served by **Plymouth & Brockton Street Railway Co.** (1 Canal Rd., 508/746-0378, www.p-b.com) just across the bridge. The town is a good spot to stop if you're planning a long weekend here from Boston or western Massachusetts, as going to Orleans is another hour (more with traffic) and Provincetown is at least another hour and forty-five minutes (also longer if there's traffic). Both destinations make it a bit too far for a day trip.

While the village is dense and can easily be walked, getting from your hotel or B&B to the beaches, shopping, or restaurants could be difficult without a car, since the village center is miles away from some of these spots. If you've got a bike, it can be doable if you plan to stay only in Sandwich. Going to Bourne or Barnstable will require careful planning or some extended use of your legs.

BOURNE

This area had one of the only Native American settlements to have survived to the end of the colonial era, a place called Comassekumkanet, until its residents, members of the Herring Pond band of the Wampanoag people, succumbed to the preaching of missionaries. Although the resulting "praying Indian" reservation was eventually absorbed by Sandwich, the band is memorialized on the north side of the canal by the namesake Herring Pond Recreation Area, a small turnout with parking and picnic tables off U.S. 6 in Bournedale. The site is popular in spring, when thousands of alewives (in the herring family) return to the pond to spawn; come in mid-late April to watch the run at its peak.

Aptucxet Trading Post

Wall Street may be the seat of the country's capital markets today, but to see the "Birthplace of Free Enterprise in America," pay a visit to the **Aptucxet Trading Post Museum** (24 Aptucxet Rd., 508/759-8167, www.bournehistoricalsociety.org, 10am-4pm Fri.-Sat. late May-Oct., adults $6, seniors $5, children $4, family $12) beside the canal bike path in Bourne. Here, off Shore Road west of the Bourne Bridge, is a replica of the seasonal 1627 trading post where Pilgrims, Native Americans, and Dutch from New Amsterdam bargained and bartered to change wampum into furs and vice versa. There's also a saltworks, a windmill, and the minuscule private depot that President Grover Cleveland had built when he escaped malarial Washington DC to visit his "summer White House," the home he bought and named Gray Gables, at the mouth of what was then the Manomet River.

Food

If you're looking for a fix of Cambodian or Vietnamese food (as opposed to Thai, which has become quite popular on the Cape), make a beeline down Route 28 to **Stir Crazy** (570 MacArthur Blvd., 508/564-6464, https://stircrazycapecod.com, 3pm-8:30pm daily, $15-25), in the Bourne village of Pocasset. Look for the big Onset Computer Corp. sign on Route 28's southbound lanes, and shortly after you'll see this tiny eatery. It has a nice menu of tasty stir-fried meals and other Cambodian-inspired dishes. Beef Lock Lack (Cambodian *lok lak,* sirloin tips on a bed of watercress) and *nhem shross* (vegetables and shrimp in rice shells) are good choices. Vegetarians can have most of the menu items prepared without meat; just ask.

A number of restaurants near the Cape Cod Canal have good water views, but if you're looking for a meal to match the panorama, you've got to go to the **Chart Room** (1 Shipyard Lane, 508/563-5350, www.chartroomcataumet.com, 11:30am-10pm Thurs.-Sun. May-Oct, $18-25), overlooking Red Brook Harbor from the Kingman Marine boatyard in the Bourne village of Cataumet. The place serves traditional surf and turf, from broiled swordfish and baked stuffed lobster to steaks and lamb chops, but prepares them to a higher standard than most Cape waterfront places, which seem to believe you pay for the view rather than the food. Entrées are in the $20-and-up range, but sandwiches, served all day, are quite a bit cheaper. Reservations are nearly essential; ask for a porch table if you want the best seat for a Buzzards Bay sunset.

On the mainland side, **Mezza Luna** (253 Main St., 508/759-4667, www.mezzalunarestaurant.com, 11am-9pm Sun., 11am-10pm Mon.-Sat., $17-35) has been family-owned and operated since the 1930s. It has good old American-style Italian food, lots of choice on the menu, and wheelbarrow-size portions. Staff is helpful, and it's kid-friendly. **Leo's Breakfast Restaurant** (249 Main St., 508/759-7557, 6am-1pm Tue.-Sun., daily late-May-early-Sept., $7-15) is a greasy spoon without the grease; it's clean, bright, casual, and cheap, and offers a lovely alternative to mega-chains.

On the Cape side, in Cataumet, hunt for the **Daily Brew** (1730 Rte. 28A, 508/564-4755, www.thedailybrewcoffeehouse.com, 7am-2pm daily, $7-16), with lovely lattes and other espresso-based caffeine, plus uniquely named sandwiches, great smoothies, and a very tasty cheddar cheese and chive scone. Plan for a wait on the weekends; it gets busy here.

Accommodations

Bourne's accommodations are generally of the roadside-motel style, as few high-end types stop here rather than in Falmouth or Sandwich. There's a convenient though characterless **Quality Inn** (100 Trowbridge Rd., 508/759-0800 or 800/528-1234, www.qualityinn.com, $100-240 d), at the foot of the Cape side of the Bourne Bridge. A number of other options line the U.S. 6 section across the canal.

Getting There and Around

Bourne, about 60 miles (60 minutes) from Boston, is on the Cape's southern Buzzards Bay side, and is served by several Peter Pan buses (www.peterpanbus.com) that connect it to Boston and Providence and destinations beyond. They drop off right at the Tedeschi convenience store (105 Trowbridge Rd., 508/759-9295) at the Bourne rotary, so it's not particularly easy to get from there to other parts of the Cape or Falmouth.

Taxis or ride sharing services are probably the best bet for short trips: try **Town Taxi** (508/775-5555, www.towntaxicapecod.com).

If you'll be doing a lot of travel around the Cape, you may want to take the bus to Hyannis first from off-Cape locations, then rent a car and zip back to your Bourne destination.

FALMOUTH

Connections to Nantucket and Martha's Vineyard made Falmouth a conduit for both island-bound Sunday day-trippers and resident "summer folk" as early as 1836—the dawn of offshore tourism. But it wasn't until the railroad came down the Buzzards Bay coast to Falmouth's port-side village of Woods Hole in 1872 that the town started to capture a piece of the tourism pie for itself. Today, Falmouth is a prime destination in its own right, offering lovely waterside and water-sports activities as well as shopping and great restaurants. It's a quirky place to spend time, as parts of the town feel almost blue-collar and other spots very country-club. Boat lovers will have plenty to feast their eyes on just looking at the harbors, which are filled with a mix of old wooden sailboats and sleek fishing diesels. Sea kayakers and even snorkelers enjoy exploring the marshlands, rocks, and estuaries. And bass and bluefish are often caught right from shore.

If you want to read more about the town's history, drop by **Eight Cousins** (189 Main St., 508/548-5548, www.eightcousins.com, 10am-6pm Mon.-Sat. Jun.-Aug., 10am-5pm Mon.-Sat. Sept.-May, 11am-4pm Sun.), the award-winning downtown bookstore that, in addition to specializing in children's books, carries adult fiction and nonfiction (they stock the full Book Sense list of independent-bookstore best-sellers) and devotes several shelves up front to titles about Falmouth.

Waquoit Bay

If you study the Upper Cape shoreline on a map, you'll notice how the sea, rising after the end of the last ice age, has pushed up the water table and flooded the valleys carved by glacial meltwater through the coastal sandplain along Falmouth's southeastern coast. The largest of these fingerlike valleys breached by Vineyard Sound is now largely protected within the state-owned **Waquoit Bay National Estuarine Research Reserve** (Rte. 28, 508/457-0495, www.waquoitbayreserve.org), whose visitors center (10am-4pm daily Jul.-Aug.) is down the road from Edwards Boatyard. A vast open-air laboratory of ponds, salt marsh, barrier beaches, and a large wooded island, the reserve is used in part to study the effects of non-point-source pollution. That means the collected runoff from a wide area of petroleum-stained pavement, overfertilized yards, and leaky septic systems—which add up to a major environmental hazard, as serious as any pipeline spill or untreated factory discharge. The effects are ominous: algal blooms, fish kills, and declining eelgrass beds, for a start (eelgrass is a vital nursery habitat for shrimp, crabs, and over a dozen fish species, including such commercial varieties as flounder, pollack, and hake). Waquoit Bay is hardly alone in these problems—from sea to shining sea, the nation's wetlands and the fisheries they support are seriously threatened—but it's one of the few subjected to careful study. On the outreach side, the reserve sponsors a number of seasonal interpretive programs to inform visitors of the bay's special qualities and raise awareness about watersheds. You can also explore on your own—some five miles of trails run through the place, including boardwalks in the marshes.

Beaches

Thanks to shallow underwater topography and the nature of offshore currents, Falmouth is blessed with the warmest average water temperatures of any town on the Cape—it's often a full 10 degrees warmer here than on the Outer Cape spots like Coast Guard Beach. Eight of the town's dozen or so beaches are public, with parking available ($15-20 daily) in season. Visitors can also purchase stickers for a week or longer at the Surf Drive bathhouse and at the town hall. Beaches are free by other means of access (foot, bike, taxi).

By far the most popular of the public beaches is **Old Silver Beach,** off Quaker Road in North Falmouth. This wide, curving half-mile or so along the edge of Buzzards Bay

Falmouth

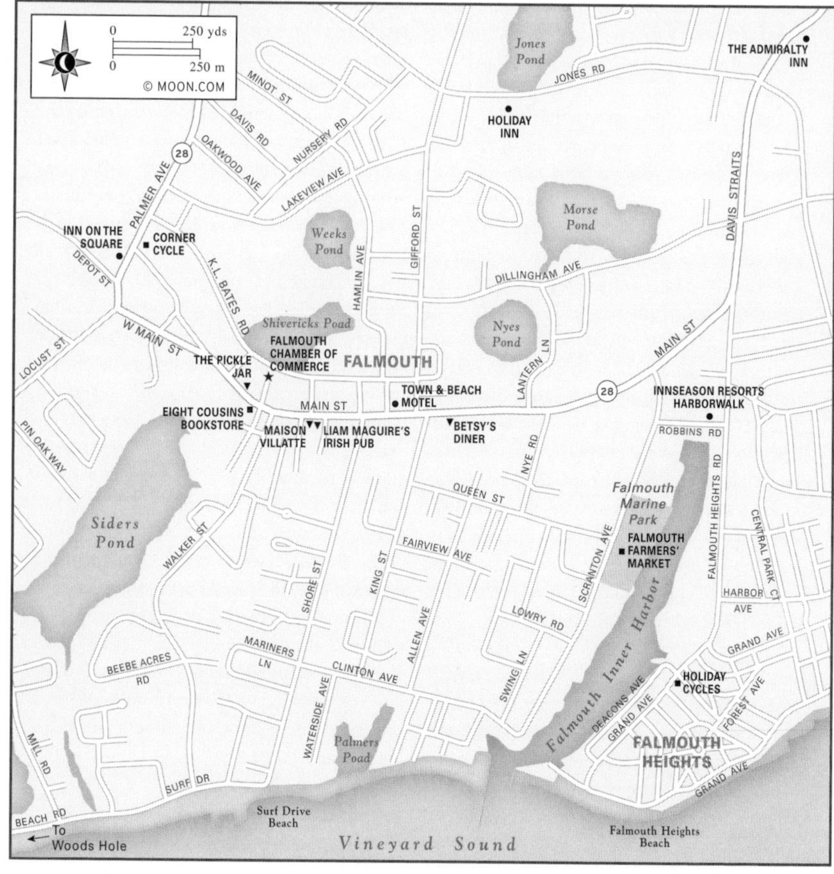

has a front-row seat for the setting sun, and the stone breakwaters that bracket it make for interesting exploration anytime. Come early or late, or be prepared to find the parking area filled to overflowing.

Two other public parts of the shore face the more wind-whipped waters of Vineyard Sound: centrally located **Surf Drive Beach** (from downtown, follow Walker St. to its end), and **Menauhant Beach** (end of Central Ave., East Falmouth). Water is still warmer here than Cape Cod Bay, and the views of ferries and sailboats is quintessential Cape Cod. The last public beach is **Grew's Pond** (Goodwill Park, between Rte. 28 and Gifford St.), a little over one mile north of downtown, a freshwater beach with entirely different scenery: turtles, frogs, reeds, and lily pads.

Sports and Recreation

Biking opportunities in the Falmouth area include the scenic 10.7-mile **Shining Sea Path,** a paved rail trail extending from North Falmouth to Woods Hole. It runs by some stunning beaches and passes through woods and marshes.

Several shops in Falmouth rent bicycles, including downtown **Corner Cycle** (115 Palmer

Ave., 508/540-4195, www.cornercycle.com, 9am-6pm daily mid-May-mid-Oct., hours vary off-season, $24 2-8 hour day, $33 overnight), 0.25 miles north of the Shining Sea Path on Route 28, and the seasonal **Holiday Cycles** (465 Grand Ave., 508/540-3549, 9am-6pm daily mid-May-mid-Oct. $25 full-day, $20 half-day), located among the inns and motels along Falmouth Heights.

Food

Falmouth has good dining options, no matter what meal you're hungry for. **Liam Maguire's Irish Pub** (273 Main St., 508/548-0285, www.liammaguire.com, 11:30am-1am Wed.-Sat., 10:30am-1am Sun. year-round, dinner from $12) isn't your run-of-the-mill Irish pub. It's got the Irish favorites, sure, but that's where the similarity ends. Liam Maguire himself owns and runs the place, and he does his own live music. The food isn't fancy, but it's flavorful, varied, and well-priced. It's even far more family-friendly than popular chains. Come here and enjoy a night out or a drink with friends knowing that your dollars are supporting a great local spot and not a mega-franchise.

Maison Villatte (267 Main St., 774/255-1855, 7am-5pm Tues.-Sun.) is a tasty French bakery offering a delectable variety of pastries, desserts, and breads to suit even the most Francophile of customers. The croissants are flaky and moist, the tarts aren't cloying, and the olive bread disappears faster than they can put it on the shelves; grab a loaf if you can.

The Pickle Jar (170 Main St., 508/540-6760, 7am-3pm Thurs.-Mon., $10-16) is a delightful spot for a bite, sandwich, soup, or sweet. Table seating is both rustic and elegant, and a counter area with retro bar stools lines part of one room. All items are handmade on the premises and yes, they actually have pickles too—in lovely large glass jugs or as garnishes. Crispy Tofu Salad is a perennial favorite. Their "Sammies" are good too, as is the pulled pork. They can be quite busy at peak times in the summer.

Betsy's Diner (457 Main St., 508/540-0060, 7am-2pm daily, $7-13) is a good place to begin the day—breakfast is served all day long, and many lunch entrées are under $10. It's a classic stainless-steel 1950s Mountain View diner, in perfect shape inside and out. The omelets are tasty and the coffee refills are free. In true diner fashion, there are half a dozen varieties of pie, but alas, they taste of canned filling, and the crusts are made tough by microwaving. Stick to the puddings instead.

Here on Falmouth's Main Street, you may just pop into an ice cream shop and discover that the small cone runs a hefty $5 and change, $6 with a tip. People line up almost out the door, but it's a mystery why when places like the Polar Cave (in Mashpee) offer cones twice as good for half the price.

Another fine choice for folks who care about good food is the **Chapoquoit Grill** (410 W. Falmouth Hwy./Rte. 28A, 508/540-7794, www.chapoquoitgrillwestfalmouth.com, 5pm-9pm Tue.-Sat., $10-26), in the village of West Falmouth, near the eponymous beach on the Buzzards Bay shore. Creative and attractive menu choices include a variety of brick oven pizzas, Korean BBQ salmon, and tornelli with chicken and broccoli, good artisanal house breads for dipping up sauces, and fine freshly made desserts. The casual, warm-toned surroundings mean that there's almost always a line out the door. Wear comfortable shoes, get a libation from the bar, and settle in. Once you finally get to lift your fork, you'll find that good things do indeed come to those who wait.

Accommodations

Falmouth proper has ample accommodations, but they're in strong enough demand to fill in summer. For the absolute lowest prices in high season, about your only option—outside of the cabins for rent at Sippewissett Campground—is one of the small motels found between downtown and the Inner Harbor, like the **Town & Beach Motel** (382 Main St., 508/548-1380, www.townandbeachmotel.com, $75-95 d).

A much better value is found on the shore of finger-shaped Green Pond in East Falmouth at **Green Harbor Waterfront Lodging** (134 Acapesket Rd., 508/548-4747 or 800/548-5556, www.gogreenharbor.com, mid-Apr.-Nov., $162-264 d), about 0.3 miles south of Route 28. It's well maintained, and the staff is very friendly. All units overlook the water, and conservation land across the water preserves the scenic view. Guest rooms come with two beds and have at least a microwave and fridge, if not a complete kitchenette. Most pets are welcome, but confirm when booking. Two outdoor pools (one for kids), volleyball, shuffleboard, croquet, badminton, and free use of rowboats and paddleboats ensure there's nary a dull moment. With charcoal grills and laundry facilities as well, you might never need to budge from the premises once you put away your groceries. Since resident flocks of Canada geese occupy the shallow waters of the pond, swimmers will want to use those free boats to venture farther from shore, or head two miles down to Acapesket Beach, the barrier beach beside the pond's outlet to the sea. Expect a 3-5-day minimum stay requirement in high season, depending on the unit, and full-week minimums during selected summer holidays and special events. Inquire about the three-bedroom cottage if your clan needs lots of elbow room.

Another good bet much closer to town—and without the minimum stay requirement—is **The Admiralty Inn** (51 Teaticket Hwy., 508/548-4240, www.theadmiraltyinn.com, $100-295), on Route 28 opposite the Stop & Shop plaza at the east end of town. Guest rooms, most with two queens, a fridge, and all the standard chain motel amenities (color cable TV, ironing board, blow-dryer, coffee, and microwave), run from large to larger, with some "townhouse suites" ($145-305) on two levels connected by (cool!) spiral stairs. Both indoor and outdoor swimming pools are onsite. Up to two kids stay free. There's a nightclub in the main building over the entrance, so if thumping music isn't your idea of a lullaby, be sure to ask for a guest room away from the front.

Several familiar national chains or their near-equivalents are found on or near Route 28 as it bends through the center of town, including, from north to southeast, **Holiday Inn** (291 Jones Rd., 508/540-2000 or 800/465-4329, www.ihg.com); **Inn on the Square** (40 N. Main St., 508/457-0606, www.innonthesquare.com); and **InnSeason**

Falmouth's Main Street

Resorts HarborWalk (26 Robbins Rd., 508/548-4300 or 800/228-2968, www.innseason.com), off East Main Street a few hundred feet from the *Island Queen* ferry to Martha's Vineyard. All are open year-round and meet or exceed the $200 mark mid-June-Labor Day—although rates may vary up to $80 higher from weekdays to weekends.

Camping

The much-loved camping spot in the Falmouth-Woods Hole area has changed ownership and become a luxury location, with Airstream trailers, tents, and funky cottages that have high-end appliances, high-thread-count sheets, sleek furniture and amenities, and thus it's either the best of both worlds or taking the camping out of camping, depending on your viewpoint. **AutoCamp** (836 Palmer Ave., 508/548-2542, https://autocamp.com, mid-May-mid-Oct., $249-419), is in a well-wooded semirural residential area 1.5 miles northwest of downtown Falmouth. It's technically still camping, but a budget- and backpacker-friendly lodging option it is not.

There are 10 primitive public campsites on 300-acre Washburn Island in the **Waquoit Bay National Estuarine Research Reserve** (Rte. 28, 508/457-0495, www.waquoitbayreserve.org, mid-May-mid-Sept., $8), but you'll need a boat to reach them; depending on where you put in your boat, it's at least a 20-minute paddle. All freshwater has to be packed in, and no campfires of any sort are permitted; the risk of fires getting out of control on the windblown island is just too high. Reservations (877/422-6762 or 877/422-6762, www.reserveamerica.com, $9.25 non-refundable reservation fee) are required. Unfortunately, canoe and kayak rentals aren't available nearby, but these may be rented from **Sea Sports** (1441 Iyannough Rd., Hyannis, 508/790-1217, www.capecodseasports.com, 10am-5pm Mon.-Wed. & Fri.-Sat., 11am-4pm Sun., 10am-6pm Thurs., $75 per day), which includes a car-topping kit in the rental price.

Getting There and Around

Falmouth is bordered by Bourne, Sandwich, and Mashpee on the north, northeast, and east, respectively (and by Martha's Vineyard, if you count a bit of water in between!). Coming from Bourne, Route 28 or Route 28A take 10 or 15 minutes, depending on the traffic. Sandwich shares a border, but there is no access. The other access is from Route 28 on the Mashpee side, or from Route 151, which is less than 10 miles but subject to unpredictable traffic.

Falmouth center is served by **Cape Cod Regional Transit Authority buses** (CCRTA, 800/352-7155, www.capecodrta.org), but getting to the off-route locations requires rental bikes, walking, ride-share, or a car. People not wanting to take a car to the islands have to park it at the shuttle lots and use the Steamship Authority shuttle to get to the docks in Woods Hole. Parking in Woods Hole can be quite beastly at times, so pad your visit with plenty of time for circling around, or use the abundant free daytime parking in Falmouth at the Falmouth Plaza (Rte. 28, east of downtown, park on the Starbucks side) and from there take the CCRTA's **Sealine** (5:30am-9pm Mon.-Sat.) to Woods Hole. Another option is to bike to Woods Hole via the **Shining Sea Path,** a paved rail trail running through the intersection of Woods Hole Road and Mill Street (south of Main St.) in Falmouth center and ending at the Steamship dock. The northern end of the bike path is in North Falmouth.

WOODS HOLE

Woods Hole has the distinction of being Massachusetts's only seaside college town (okay, not really a town, it's officially a part of the town of Falmouth, but it does feel like its own separate world). This isn't just any college either—the tiny village at the Cape's "other tip," ensconced by the town of Falmouth, is home to the Woods Hole Oceanographic Institution (WHOI, pronounced "hooey"), a private, largely federally funded research

Woods Hole

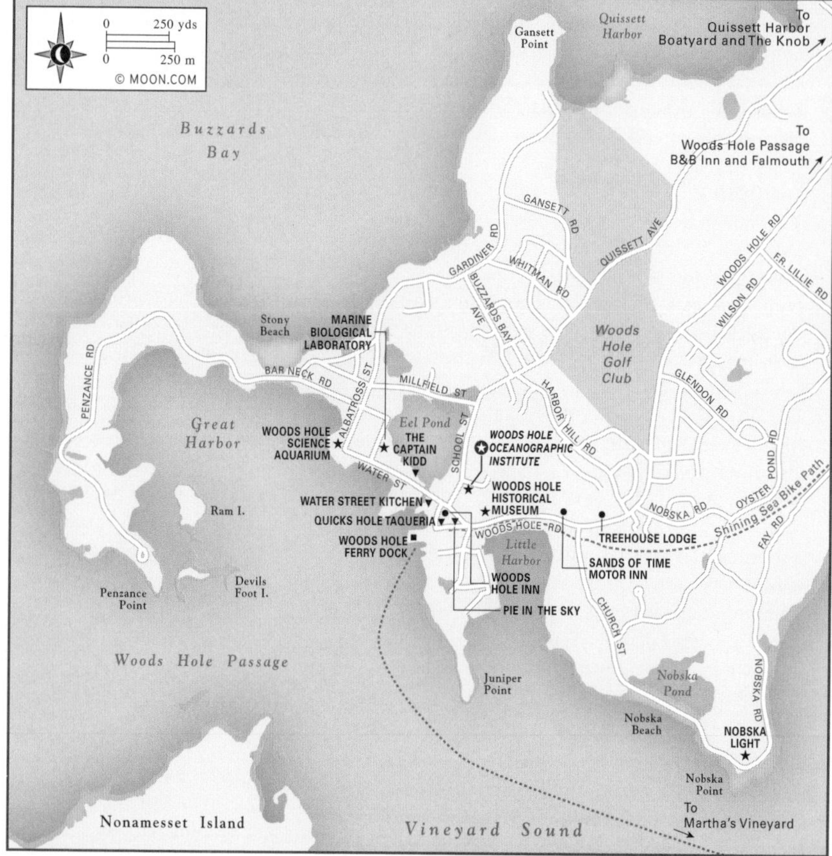

center known most widely for the work of its pioneering little deep-sea submersible, *Alvin*, and other high-profile marine research vessels. The U.S. Geological Survey (USGS), the National Marine Fisheries Service (NMFS), the Marine Biological Laboratory (MBL), the undergraduate Sea Education Association (SEA), and Woods Hole Research Center, an environmental think tank, are also based here in whole or in part, making Woods Hole the 800-pound gorilla in the world of marine science and education. Though the presence of the Martha's Vineyard ferry gives the village all the trappings of the Cape's other tourist towns in summer—overflowing parking lots, scores of cyclists, strolling shoppers, eateries crowded with out-of-towners—during the off-season, the community of some 1,500 scientists and students reveals its true nature: It's essentially one big academic campus.

★ Woods Hole Oceanographic Institute

The work of Woods Hole's scientific community isn't concealed entirely behind closed lab doors or beneath distant oceans. The **WHOI Ocean Science Discovery Center** (15 School St., 508/289-2663, www.whoi.

edu, 11am-4pm Mon.-Sat. late-May-Sept., 10am-4:30pm Mon.-Fri. Oct.-Dec., closed Jan.-mid-Apr., suggested donation $3-5), in a chapel-like clapboard building a block north of Water Street, has two floors of displays and videos on coastal ecology and discoveries made through WHOI-sponsored research, from understanding the lives of jellyfish in local Atlantic waters to strange life-forms around the ocean floor's hydrothermal vents. The center also showcases the tools of the oceanographer's trade, including a full-size mock-up of the remarkable titanium sphere *Alvin,* a 30-some-year-old pioneer of deep-sea exploration, discoverer of the *Titanic,* and doorway to the world up to 14,700 feet under the sea. A small gift shop sells selected books, magazines, and souveniers. As a complement to these exhibits, the WHOI Visitor Center & Store, downtown on 86 Water Street, sponsors guided 75-minute walks around the campus in July and August, giving an overview of the institution's history while taking in its dockside ship operations and even, if you're lucky, a laboratory or two. The walks commence at the Visitor Center (508/289-2252, information@whoi.edu). Reservations required, as space on the tours is limited.

Marine Biological Laboratory

The village center is shared by shops, restaurants, and the buildings of the **Marine Biological Laboratory** (7 MBL St., 508/289-7623, www.mbl.edu), a private nonprofit that hosts marine-related undergraduate and graduate programs for students of two East Coast universities as well as the sponsored research of hundreds of scientists from around the world. Free tours (1pm and 2pm Mon.-Fri. late June-Aug.) start at the **Pierce Exhibit Center** (100 Water St.); look for the half-hulled ship model poking out of the facade. Reservations are required. The visitors center also offers exhibits and features live animals during its hours of operation (generally 10am-3pm or 4:30pm, depending on the time of year). The center is open Monday, Wednesday, and Friday-Saturday in May-June; Monday-Saturday in July-August; Monday, Wednesday, and Friday in September-October; and by appointment only November-April.

Woods Hole Science Aquarium

At the end of Water Street stands the NOAA **Woods Hole Science Aquarium** (166 Water St., 508/495-2001, www.fisheries.noaa.gov, 11am-4pm daily, free). You've seen their names on menu cards at sushi bars, but here's where you can see what cod, haddock, yellowtail flounder, salmon, octopus, and other denizens of local waters really look like. The creatures in this exhibit of the village's oldest science institution (NOAA's forerunner established a collecting station in Woods Hole in 1871) are all the subjects of the facility's research into fish biology and fisheries resource management—so they may change to reflect what's turning up on twice-weekly sampling trips. There's usually at least one scene-stealing harbor seal in the outdoor pool by the entrance too. Which creature is featured depends on who's been rescued from shore stranding and is being fattened up or allowed to regain flipper strength before being released again into the wild. Seal feedings are at 11am and 4pm daily.

Woods Hole Historical Museum

A fine overview of the community at the end of the 19th century is offered by the **Woods Hole Historical Museum** (579 Woods Hole Rd., 508/548-7270, www.woodsholemuseum.org, 10am-4pm Tues.-Sat. mid-June-mid-Oct., free); among the exhibits providing a local angle on maritime history in the main house is a scale model of the village circa 1895, complete with an operating Z-scale railroad. The adjacent barn houses the museum's ship models and small wooden boat collection, which is highly recommended for learning the difference between a catboat, knockabout, dory, and dinghy—useful knowledge in this region, where many kids still learn to sail not long after they learn to walk. The museum publishes an attractive quarterly journal, *Spritsail,* and has produced a number of award-winning books, from collections of historic photos to a cookbook, all of which are available on the premises. You may also join museum volunteers on a free walking tour (4pm Tues. July-Aug.) around the historic village center.

Sports and Recreation

Picture-perfect **Quissett Harbor** remains one of the most sought-after spots to sail on the Cape, but it's primarily locals (often those who've waited for years) who can moor their vessels here. Travelers can enjoy the scenic beauty or put in for day jaunts, and the secluded, wind-protected water is a superb place for sea kayaking. The **Quissett Harbor Boatyard** (508/548-0506, www.quissettharborboatyard.com) assists boaters with slips and information.

Dedicated cyclists may want to try the scenic route along Buzzards Bay, following Sippewisset Road from West Falmouth to Woods Hole. Along the way are wood-shingled houses nestled in trees like elfin cottages, glimpses of the bay through backyards, and **The Knob** (Cornelia L. Carey Bird Sanctuary), a curious bluff at the very end of Quissett Harbor Road, notable for breathtaking views out at the end of its causeway. Rent a bike for this route at **Art's Bike Shop** (91 County Rd., 508/563-7379, www.artsbikeshop.com, 8am-5pm Mon.-Sat., 11am-4pm Sun. May-Sept.), on the corner of Old Main Street in North Falmouth, slightly west of Route 28A.

Another scenic option for bicyclists is the **Shining Sea Path,** a paved rail trail extending from North Falmouth to Woods Hole, which passes by beaches that look out on Nantucket Sound before heading into pretty woodlands.

Food

In Woods Hole, around the corner from the Steamship Authority ferry, is **Water Street Kitchen** (56 Water St., 508/540-5656, 5pm-10pm Wed.-Sat., $20-34). This spot embraces local ingredient options for its ever-changing menu that includes fresh seafood, meats, and seasonal delicacies. There's even a kimchi pancake if you're looking for something different. Though the mains are mostly not vegetarian, there are plenty of side dishes that are veggie-friendly, and excellent desserts too.

Other good options abound. Just across the street is year-round **The Captain Kidd** (77 Water St., 508/548-8563, www.thecaptainkidd.com, 11:30am-10pm daily, $23-30), half casual dining, half turn-of-the-20th-century sailors bar on the edge of Eel Pond. **Quicks Hole Taqueria** (29 Railroad Ave., 508/495-0048, noon-9pm daily May-Sept., $11-27) is across from the ferry and has near-legendary clam chowder, which is odd for a place that advertises itself as a "Baja California" taco joint. The tacos are tasty and include a lobster option (what could be more Cape Cod?), and the wide variety of other seafood options and burgers means everyone will find something to love.

Pie in the Sky (10 Water St., 508/540-5475, www.woodshole.com/pie, 6am-6pm daily, $5-8.50) is not just the spot to go for pies: There are lovely baked goods, fair-trade coffee, a host of teas, and the usual tattooed baristas one expects from a fine caffeine purveyor.

Accommodations

The only year-round accommodations within Woods Hole are smack-dab in the village center at **The Woods Hole Inn** (28 Water St., 508/495-0248, www.woodsholeinn.com, $219-387 June-Aug., rates lower Oct.-May), a stone's throw from just about everything. It's a sweet little family-run place with just a handful of sunny guest rooms, most featuring a double bed and a small private bath, and a pleasantly modern decor in keeping with the year of its

1: The Knob, a bluff in Woods Hole **2:** Woods Hole's iconic Captain Kidd restaurant **3:** the scientific research vessel *Neil Armstrong* at dock in Woods Hole

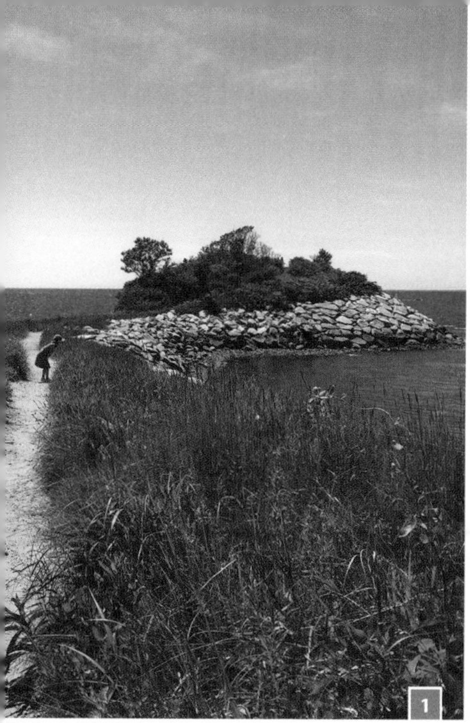

1

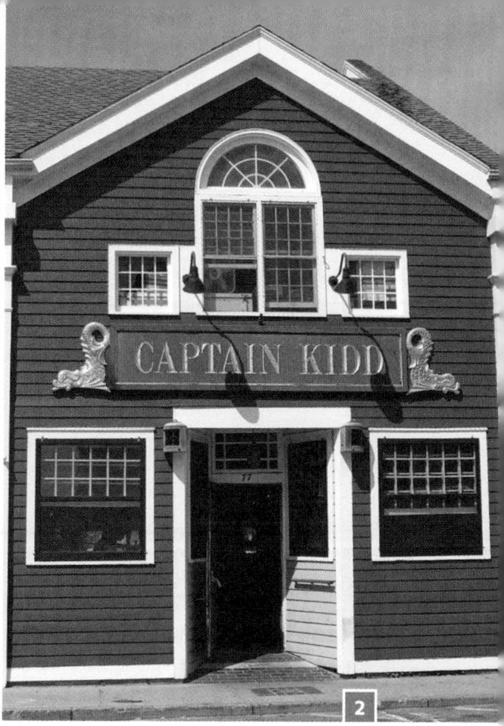

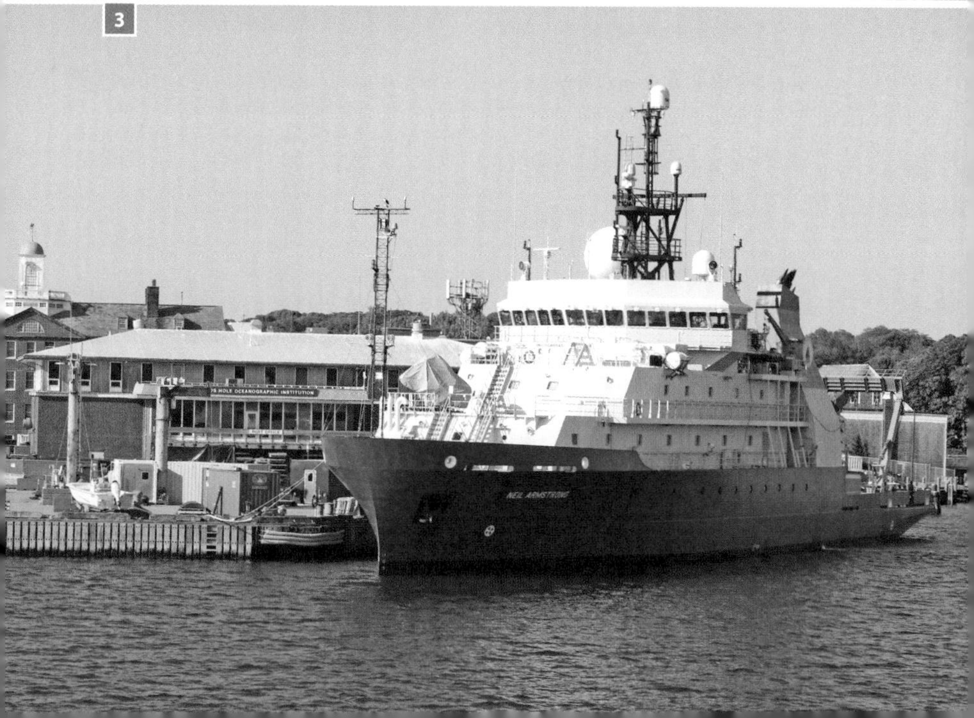

2

3

renovation (2002) rather than the age of the building (1890). Rates include morning beverages and baked goods in the lobby, and guests have easy dining at the street-level restaurant, under the same ownership.

A pair of small seasonal motels flanks Woods Hole Road as it enters the village from Falmouth: the **Treehouse Lodge** (527 Woods Hole Rd., 508/548-1986, www.mytreehouselodge.com, $149-319 d) and the **Sands of Time Motor Inn** (549 Woods Hole Rd., 508/548-6300 or 800/841-0114, www.sandsoftime.com, $114-289 d). Both are open mid-April through October or early November. The former has some newly renovated rooms with a mini fridge, coffeemaker, and sitting area.

About three miles away from the heart of the village—conveniently close to the start of the Shining Sea Path just south of Falmouth center, and right on the route of the summer WHOOSH trolley to Woods Hole—is the year-round **Woods Hole Passage B&B Inn** (186 Woods Hole Rd., 508/548-9575 or 800/790-8976, www.woodsholepassage.com, $183-219). This century-old carriage house and attached barn, formerly belonging to an adjacent private estate, have been fully renovated for B&B use, so the guest rooms, all with queen beds and modern private baths, are furnished in a tasteful contemporary country style. A huge yard and acres of conservation land surround the property. Full breakfast is included, and bikes are available for guests. Innkeeper Deb Pruitt can point you to a variety of pleasant walks in the vicinity, including a pair of residents-only beaches; she also has good taste in restaurants.

Getting There and Around

Woods Hole is a five-mile (15-minute) drive from Falmouth center along Woods Hole Road. If congestion is a problem, opt for Quissett Road instead. The terminus of the **CCRTA's Sealine** (800/352-7155, www.capecodrta.org) is at the ferry terminal. **Peter Pan** buses (888/751-8800, www.peterpanbus.com) also stop here.

The heavy volume of summer traffic to the Steamship Authority ferry, along with the dearth of even paid parking around Woods Hole, can make a peak-season visit frustrating for drivers. One solution is to take advantage of the acres of free daytime parking back in Falmouth at the Falmouth Plaza (Rte. 28, east of downtown, park on the Starbucks side) and from there hop aboard the **Sealine** (5:30am-9pm Mon.-Sat.), the regular Hyannis-Falmouth and Woods Hole bus. WHOOSH trolleys between Falmouth center and Woods Hole are a service of the CCRTA, meaning that all-day CCRTA passes are valid (otherwise standard adult fare is $2).

A second option is to bike to Woods Hole via the **Shining Sea Path,** a paved rail trail running through the intersection of Woods Hole Road and Mill Street (south of Main St.) in the heart of Falmouth and ending right at the Steamship dock. The northern end of the bike path is in North Falmouth.

MASHPEE

Of the several Cape towns with Native American names, this is the only one that still has many residents who take personal pride in that fact. Mashpee (*massa* and *pe*, meaning "great" and "water," an eastern Algonquian variant of *Mississippi*) is one of two towns in Massachusetts with a significant Native American population; like the other, Aquinnah on Martha's Vineyard, the tribal affiliation is Wampanoag. It remained largely rural until relatively late in the 20th century, when a burst of development created a town within a town—New Seabury, a resort community along Popponesset Beach on the south shore—and giant shopping malls at the junction of Routes 28 and 151. Mashpee has been engaged in a residential and commercial building boom ever since; between 1980 and 2000, its population growth made Mashpee the fastest-growing town in Massachusetts.

Recognizing the threat of unbridled development on the town's character, a coalition of private and public entities has fostered an ambitious plan for land preservation, leading to the creation of a new national wildlife refuge covering parts of both Mashpee and next-door Falmouth. Mashpee has thus become one of the best places on the Cape to see firsthand such globally rare habitats as pine barrens, cedar swamps, and salt marsh. So, although there are no museums, next to no accommodations, and relatively few restaurants, you'll want to pay Mashpee a visit if you have any interest in exploring the outdoors.

Mashpee National Wildlife Refuge

Closed for a government assessment at the time of writing, the **Mashpee National Wildlife Refuge** (Mashpee NWR, Great Neck Rd., 978/443-4661, www.fws.gov/refuge/mashpee) hopes to ultimately protect some 5,800 acres of critical watershed for several rivers feeding the deep bays along the south shore. For now the refuge is divided into sections on the north and south sides of Route 151. The north section includes upland oak forest around the deep headwater ponds of the Childs, Quashnet, and Mashpee Rivers. There are miles of walking trails and backwoods roads suitable for mountain biking, plus a popular **swimming beach** at Johns Pond, one of the deeper (65-foot) kettle-hole ponds on the Cape. The south section encompasses the riparian corridors of those three rivers and many smaller brooks, along with hundreds of acres of hot dry scrub oak and pitch pine belonging to the South Mashpee Pine Barrens. Abutting the eastern side of the refuge is the **Mashpee River Reservation** (Quinaquisset Ave. and Meetinghouse Rd., 508/636-4693, www.thetrustees.org), a property of the Trustees of Reservations that protects the lower reaches of what experts consider to be one of the state's finest streams for anadromous brook trout, or "salters" (hatched in freshwater, but reaching maturity at sea). An interpretive trail guide covering both the woodlands and the pine barrens, available from the Waquoit Bay National Estuarine Research Reserve visitors center (Rte. 28, Falmouth), is highly recommended for its detailed descriptions and clear illustration of trailhead access. The visitors center also carries the *Mashpee NWR Trail and Recreation Guide,* which gives precise locations of all the refuge's put-in points for canoes, kayaks, or sailboards as well as parking areas for trailheads. Both guides are free.

If, after exploring the refuge on foot or bike, you need to cool off with a swim, head for the **South Cape Beach State Park** (508/457-0495, www.mass.gov) on Vineyard Sound. It's located near the end of Great Oak Road—not at the very end, that's the town beach for residents only—and parking is $40 (state residents $15) in July-August.

Ashumet Holly Wildlife Sanctuary

Mashpee and Falmouth sport separate preserves bearing the mark of "the Holly Man"—Wilfrid Wheeler, the State Secretary of Agriculture who gained fame during the first half of the 20th century as one of the world's leading propagators of holly trees. His personal collection, donated after his death to the Massachusetts Audubon Society, is now the **Ashumet Holly Wildlife Sanctuary** (Ashumet Rd. and Currier Rd., 508/362-7475, www.massaudubon.org, dawn-dusk daily, free), off Route 151 on the Falmouth-Mashpee line. The 65 varieties of holly from around the world now occupying the few dozen pond-side acres were all planted by Wheeler, along with a number of other exotics such as Japanese umbrella pine, a Manchurian dawn redwood, and a late-flowering *Franklinia,* the garden offspring of a Georgian native now extinct in the wild. In addition to summer natural history programs on the property, the sanctuary sponsors naturalist-guided trips to the Elizabeth Islands, including occasional outings to some islands not served by the usual public ferries or tours. Ashumet is free to Massachusetts Audubon members.

Lowell Holly Reservation

Wheeler's other bit of handiwork is the **Lowell Holly Reservation** (508/636-4693, www.

Nothing Frigid about Polar Cave Ice Cream

Polar Cave Ice Cream in Mashpee

On Route 28 in Mashpee, you'll find the one-of-a-kind **Polar Cave Ice Cream** (22 Rte. 28, Mashpee, 508/477-5553, http://polarcave.com, 2pm-8:30pm Thurs.-Tue., longer in summer, shorter hours May-June and Sept.-mid-Oct., Sat.-Sun. mid-Oct.-late Dec., closed Jan.-Apr.), where some of the friendliest ice cream on Cape Cod is served. The place is a testament to bears of all kinds (the owner's daughter even wears a Boston Bruins jersey as her "uniform"), but among other things, you'll find brain-teaser puzzles to play with while you wait, a cooler filled with Jarritos brand soda (a non-corn syrup, real-sugar brand from Mexico), and the "world's smallest" ice cream cone (just $0.50; it really is small). It's well worth seeking out if you're in the mid-Cape area. The flavors offered are nearly uncountable, including all the usual ones and a number of unique specialties, plus one or two seasonal favorites, like blueberry in spring, peach in summer, or apple pie and pumpkin in fall.

thetrustees.org, dawn-dusk daily, free) on Conaumet Neck, jutting out between a pair of joined ponds on the Mashpee-Sandwich town line. Unlike Ashumet, this 135-acre peninsula already had a large stand of native American holly, for which Cape Cod marks the northern edge of its natural range; Wheeler supplemented the indigenous population with new trees selected for their fruitfulness. But what's unique about this property of the Trustees of Reservations is that it's the Cape Cod equivalent of an old-growth forest, untouched by brushfires, chainsaws, or plows since at least the Revolutionary War. As such, it's one of the few places on the Cape whose mix of trees suggests how the region's landscape might have appeared to its early inhabitants. But the place is not wholly untouched; its previous owner introduced a number of flowering shrubs to provide a showy floral display each spring. Open year-round, the reservation is found on South Sandwich Road off Route 130, adjacent to Sandwich's Ryder Conservation Lands; turn at the cursive-script white sign for Carpe Diem (the private residence shares the Trustees driveway), then follow signs. Free parking is available at South Sandwich Road year-round, and there is also a lot that opens late-May-early-Sept. that's much closer to the swimming beach on the Ryder side of Wakeby Pond.

Food

Bleu (10 Market St., 508/539-7907, www.bleurestaurant.com, 11:30am-3pm and 4pm-9pm daily, $23-36) is a sophisticated French bistro set smack in the middle of Mashpee Common. A decidedly uncommon spot to dine, Bleu has a great wine selection, excellent French-inspired dishes, lovely duck, and a dessert menu you'll want to save room for. There is a prix-fixe menu (5pm-8pm Sun.-Thurs., $35). Though classy, this restaurant does not require you to dress up: Cape casual is fine.

Naukabout Beer (13 Lake Ave., 508/419-6273, www.naukabout.com, noon-8pm Wed.-Thurs., 11am-9pm Fri.-Sat., 11am-7pm Sun., $4) brews a number of fresh lagers and ales in its clean wood-and-steel brewery off Route 130. Small food items are served, and they invite local food trucks to set up outside in the parking lot. Stop by and quench your thirst after a day at the beach.

Bangkok Cuisine (681 Falmouth Rd., 508/539-9991, www.bangkokcapecod.com, 11am-10pm Mon.-Fri., 11:30am-10pm Sat., 4pm-9:30pm Sun., $12-20) is this area's only Thai option. Part of a friendly chain, it's a clean, quiet spot with lots of Asian art on the walls and ceramics decorating the booth dividers. It serves all the classic dishes plus a few that aren't on most menus, like *pad voonsen* or *mee siam*.

Accommodations

Santuit Inn (6 Rte. 28, 508/428-6433, www.thesantuitinn.com, $99-155) is an 18-unit boutique motel with modern decor and a central location that's good for day trips to Woods Hole and the Vineyard, or, in the other direction, Hyannis and the beaches of the southern Cape. Cottages go $199-339.

Getting There and Around

Mashpee is a central town, and as such, is about 10 miles (20 minutes) east of Falmouth center, 10 miles (25 minutes) west of West Barnstable's exit 68 (old exit 6), and 13 miles (30 minutes) west of Hyannis's bus terminal near Main Street. Numerous back routes offer alternate options if there's congestion.

The Mashpee area has **CCRTA bus service** that runs between Hyannis and Woods Hole, via Mashpee Common, but that's the only real option for public transportation. The CCRTA's door-to-door **DART** (800/352-7155, www.capecodrta.org), taxi companies, or online ride share apps are the only other choices.

Mid-Cape

If you're imagining the Cape as an arm that someone's flexing to show muscle, the Mid-Cape is the bicep—the middle—and both the most populous and the most developed part of the peninsula. You'll see a marked difference between the tree- and B&B-lined historic districts to the north along the Old King's Highway (Rte. 6A) and the motels and mini-golf spots that flank the south shore. On a rainy summer afternoon (or any non-beach day), the traffic can be beastly, but don't think this means the area should be avoided. There's lots to see, do, eat, drink, and enjoy here. Mountain-biking trails, beachcombing hikes, a number of international-cuisine restaurants, affordable motels, and stores with the widest selection of whatever you're looking for are all (*ahem,* if there's no traffic) a few minutes' drive away. It's also the prime gateway for ferry service to Nantucket. Even the miniature golf, saltwater taffy shops, and beach gear and novelty shops along Route 28 can be a sensory delight, expressions of local color unlikely to be franchised across the country. Some of the signs, stores, or attractions have been around long enough to be institutions or antiques in their own right.

To keep your cool in the inevitable traffic

tie-up, be sure to pad any plans with some extra time. It may help to know that the Cape version of "fashionably late" gives you 15-30 extra minutes to arrive, so if you're meeting friends and not trying to make it to a movie, you'll be fine if you arrive a little late. And best of all, you can always say there was traffic even though you actually stopped off for an extra ice cream cone along the way.

BARNSTABLE

Barnstable Town (not to be confused with Barnstable County, which encompasses the entire Cape) is the biggest town around, cutting across the entire Cape from the northern bay side to the south and Nantucket Sound. The metropolis—er, village—of nearby Hyannis is more hip and happening, while its stately, refined sister Barnstable is on its northern shore. Barnstable is the Cape's commercial hub, the largest shopping area, and a spot for excellent dining as well. The town has great beaches, among other things, and scenic vistas nearly everywhere you go.

Sights

SCUDDER LANE TOWN LANDING

Few visitors know about this spot, and be advised—there is only parking for a handful of vehicles, and local beach permits are required. However, this spot is lovely for a whole host of beach-scavenging activities, and particularly fun for families, because there are many tidal pools in the peat bogs that offer great peeks at marine fauna such as green crabs, spider crabs, a host of minnows, and all varieties of mollusks. There are several differing environments as well: The mud and sand flats have entirely different animals than the eelgrass shallows, which are different again from the spartina grass peat bogs. Have the kids collect things from the wrack line (the detritus left by the high tide) and take it back to color or sketch from at home on a rainy day.

★ OLD KING'S HIGHWAY

Drive Cape Cod long enough and you'll see that it's very different from town to town, and even village to village; it's hard to believe this is all the same basic sandbar. The Mid-Cape portion of Old King's Highway (now Rte. 6A) is one of the best Sunday drives you'll have here, passing through village center after village center that seem cut from a postcard of the 1800s: West Barnstable, Barnstable Village, Cummaquid, Yarmouthport, Dennis, East Dennis, and Brewster. Shingle-sided saltbox or steep-roofed Cape houses, white clapboard churches, and fancy Federal or Greek Revival shipmasters' mansions abound—as do antiques shops, B&Bs, art galleries, pottery studios, and—surprise—more antiques shops. Despite the scenic quality of the road, it's actually a road, so plan on pulling over in a safe spot if you want to take a picture. Prepare to be beeped at or see unmentionable gestures from drivers behind you if you're backing up traffic for miles.

You'll notice that each town has a historical house or museum vying for your attention along Route 6A, most of which suggest donations rather than charge admission. The volunteers who generally staff these places are often the very reason to stop and pay a visit; their knowledge can breathe life into a museum you might easily have overlooked. The best places within the various towns are noted in this section.

Beaches

SANDY NECK

On Cape Cod Bay by the Sandwich-Barnstable town line is the largest salt marsh ecosystem north of Chesapeake Bay, along with its accompanying six-mile beachfront of creeping barrier dunes. Although access to **Sandy Neck** (495 Sandy Neck Rd., 508/362-8300) isn't cheap (nonresident parking $20 late May-early Sept.), a visit pays many dividends, offering hours of potential walking along the shore, with its wrack line of tide-borne curiosities and its busy population of shorebirds. 4WD driving and camping is also possible (with permits). You might find coyote tracks in the arid swale between the parallel formation of protective dunes—whose accreting sands, augmented by eroded material from the western rim of Cape Cod Bay, are slowly closing off Barnstable Harbor—or the sight of tree and barn swallows swooping through the Great Marsh behind the dunes, snapping insects out of the air (plenty of leftovers remain, however, so bring repellent). Early-summer visitors may also see the carefully monitored nests of the endangered piping plovers and least terns, two tentative but regular visitors to the Cape's shores.

A Cape Cod resident launched the Kindness Rocks Project at Sandy Neck in 2015, leaving inspirational messages on rocks for others to find. The kindness movement has since become a global phenomenon.

To reach Sandy Neck from Route 6A, turn north on Sandy Neck Road in East Sandwich, next to the Sandy Neck Motel, and proceed to the ranger station and parking lot at the end.

MILLWAY BEACH

Another nice beach option is the much smaller mainland-side Millway Beach, just a stone's throw from Barnstable Village. Turn north at the village stoplight, past the Unitarian Church on your right, and follow the road past the marina to the end. You'll see some lovely marsh views and scenic boats (this is where you embark for whale-watching cruises if you're not going from Provincetown). The beach is at the end of the road. Parking is limited to residents, but it's a lovely spot and gives nice views of the mouth of Barnstable Harbor and Barnstable Great Marsh where it opens out into Cape Cod Bay. **Millway Marina** (253 Millway, 508/362-4904, www.millwaymarina.com, 8:30am-4:30pm Mon.-Fri., by appointment Sat.-Sun.) can assist with boat rentals and slip information.

Follow the channel out here and within minutes you'll be in **Cape Cod Bay,** the large water body contained within the "arm" of the peninsula. In addition to excellent fishing and sailing opportunities, in season Cape Cod Bay offers one of the only places in the world where endangered right whales can be seen. Several species of endangered sea turtles also make the bay their home.

CRAIGVILLE BEACH

No question, many of the Cape beaches are pretty chilly if you're planning to swim. The Outer Cape offers spectacular scenery, but dip a toe in and you'll feel Atlantic currents coming right from the Gulf of Maine. If you find that even Cape Cod Bay is a bit too "refreshing" for comfort (read: numbingly cold), then **Craigville Beach** (997 Craigville Beach Rd., 508/790-9888) or other Nantucket Sound-facing beaches will suit you. You will either love it or wonder why anyone comes here, but if you come, expect to share the sand with a lot of other people. That can be part of the fun, of course. If you're here to meet up, hang out, and socialize, this is the beach to seek out. It's a particularly hot scene throughout the summer for the 20-something sun-worshippers, the families with 2.3 kids, honeymooners who aren't looking for solitude, and just about anyone else. The currents aren't as strong as the Outer Cape shores, but be cautious at all times when swimming.

Sports and Recreation

TOP EXPERIENCE

WHALE-WATCHING

The only whale-watching excursions available between Plymouth and Provincetown are the **Hyannis Whale Watcher Cruises** (Barnstable Harbor, 800/287-0374, www.whales.net, daily May-Oct., adults $65, seniors $55, ages 4-12 $45, under age 4 $3), off Route 6A in Barnstable Village. The company's speedy boat departs the Millway Marine boatyard for Stellwagen Bank off the tip of Cape Cod in search of Stellwagen's most frequently sighted species: the finback, blue, sei, humpback, and North Atlantic right whales, all of which are endangered (as is the minke whale; both are seasonal visitors). Excursions are scheduled according to ocean tides and can change from day to day. Reservations for the four-hour outings are advised.

1

2

HIKING AND BIKING

Inland of Barnstable Harbor are several municipal conservation properties encompassing portions of the glacially formed moraine underlying U.S. 6. The hilly upland woods are choice spots for hiking on days too cool for the beach. You can also leave the crowds behind and find out how dry and hot a pitch pine forest can get in summer. The largest is the 1,100-acre **West Barnstable Conservation Area** (also known as the Trail of Tears), bounded by U.S. 6, Route 149, a small airport, and the town of Sandwich; look for parking off Route 149 south of U.S. 6's exit 65 (old exit 5), on Popple Bottom Road nearly opposite the Olde Barnstable Fairgrounds golf course. ("Popple" is an old colloquialism for poplar trees.) Two smaller parcels sandwich the Mid-Cape Highway from beside Phinney's Lane, slightly east of exit 68 and due south of the one stoplight on Route 6A in Barnstable: **Old Jail Lane Conservation Area,** with parking beside the eponymous access road on the north side of U.S. 6, and **Hathaway's Pond,** a popular freshwater swimming beach on U.S. 6's south side (parking $10 in summer). All three welcome hikers as well as mountain bikers and feature the kind of terrain that justifies having hiking boots or a mountain bike. The nearest bike rental shop is **Bike Zone** (323 Barnstable Rd., 508/775-3299, www.bikezonecapecod.com, 9am-5pm daily, $25-45, e-bike $60 daily), located across the street from Staples, near the Hyannis Airport.

Excellent computer-generated and GPS-tested trail maps and guides to these and six other town conservation properties are available for download from the website of the **Barnstable Conservation Commission** (200 Main St., Hyannis, 508/862-4093, http://town.barnstable.ma.us).

BRIDGE CREEK

This lovely place to paddle is ideal for serious canoeists and kayakers who have two cars. The put-in is right near where the train tracks cross over Route 6A on their way into West Barnstable. This is a live track, so be particularly wary if walking on it, and don't hesitate to jump to either side if a train comes. Bridge Creek runs under Route 6A, and the tracks and goes all the way out to Barnstable Great Marsh and the tidal estuaries of Barnstable Harbor. Several sandbars offer great birding and, in season, excellent chances to see horseshoe crabs. Time this one carefully, putting in just after the high tide starts to recede. Park your second vehicle at Scudder Lane Town Landing's ramp. Once you reach the flat waters of the harbor, with Sandy Neck on your left, make for the mainland, and Scudder Lane will be just around the first promontory. The trip will take most paddlers most of an afternoon, 4-6 hours, with a few stops for birding or lunch along the way.

Entertainment and Events

Even in summer the Cape can be pretty sleepy, and in winter it can be downright dull, but the **Barnstable Comedy Club** (508/362-6333, www.barnstablecomedyclub.com, 7:30pm, 2:30pm matinees on Sun), in Barnstable village, can tickle your funny bone with seasonal plays, shows, skits, and other such merriment.

Food

The town of Barnstable, including Hyannis, has more variety in dining options than anywhere else on the Cape. If you're hungry and you've got to have that plate of (fill in the blank: Thai, Italian, Indian, Mexican, Brazilian, and so on) food, then you'll want to look for it in Barnstable and Hyannis. Great seafood goes without saying. Find fancier places along Main Street in Hyannis or along Route 6A. The Cape Cod Mall has the usual cheap chain eats, and other usual-suspect chains are here as well.

For traditional New England seafood with a lovely view, try **Mattakeese Wharf** (273 Mill Way Rd., Barnstable, 508/362-4511, www.mattakeese.com, 11:30am-8:30pm daily May-mid-Oct., $22-38), on Barnstable

---

1: Sandy Neck Beach **2:** Biking is a popular Cape Cod activity.

Take Me Out to the Ballgame

the Cotuit Kettleers' home field

One of the purest pleasures of summertime on the Cape is not on the beach by the rolling surf but on the baseball diamonds of the **Cape Cod Baseball League** (www.capecodbaseball.org), an NCAA-sanctioned amateur league that has been around since 1885. In any given year, nearly one-sixth of all the current ball players in the majors have swung a bat for one of the Cape's 10 teams, and one-third of all collegiate baseball players who graduate to Major League Baseball are Cape League alumni. These stats give the league an outsize reputation as a font of that most holy of baseball grails, professional-level play without big-league attitudes or the warped influence of big-league money. Games are, in fact, free—a hat is passed for donations. On nearly every evening from mid-June to early August there are up to five different games from which to choose.

The league's two divisions extend between Wareham—the first off-Cape town on the shore of

Harbor; turn at Route 6A's traffic light east of Barnstable Village. The preparations aren't overly fancy, but neither are the prices, and for seaside views this spot is an excellent value. Whether the sun is sinking in the west or the harbor is blanketed in atmospheric fog, it's a great spot to sup, and well worth coming from out of town for.

American diner-style fare may be abundant in these parts, but not all vendors of the stuff are equal. If you want to rub elbows over breakfast with residents rather than day-trippers, head up-Cape to Marstons Mills, one of the rural Barnstable villages about eight miles west of downtown Hyannis. There you'll find the **Fig Tree Cafe** (149 Cotuit Rd./Rte. 149, 508/428-9814, www.figtreecafecapecod.com, 7:30am-2pm Wed.-Mon., $11-16), on Route 149 next to the Mobil station. Though under new ownership, it's still an extremely popular place known for its solid country breakfasts, healthy vegetarian omelet choices, weekend specials, and great service.

Accommodations

Most of the small inns and B&Bs in this area are readily visible to passing motorists along Route 6A between Route 132 in Barnstable and Union Street on the east side of neighboring Yarmouthport. No two are alike, although the prevailing theme is colonial rather than Victorian. If you want a comfortable inn within a block of a beach, head to the south shore on the other side of Route 28, but expect

Buzzards Bay—in the west to Orleans in the east, playing on community and high school fields lovingly tended by a small army of dedicated volunteers. Since most of the games regularly attract 10 times as many fans as can sit in the average venue's few sets of bleachers, most attendees bring blankets or folding chairs to set out on the grass overlooking the outfields. Such casual seating arrangements and breezy outdoor settings wrap games in the distinctive easygoing ambience of a friendly community picnic.

Here's a list of the league's home fields:

- **Bourne Braves:** Upper Cape Tech Field (Rte. 6A, Bourne, just east of the Bourne Bridge rotary)
- **Brewster Whitecaps:** Stoney Brook School Field (384 Underpass Rd., Brewster, off Rte. 137)
- **Chatham Anglers:** Veterans Field (Depot Station, Chatham, north side of Rte. 28, just west of town center)
- **Cotuit Kettleers:** Lowell Park (Lowell St., Cotuit, 1.2 miles south of Rte. 28 on Main St., then left)
- **Falmouth Commodores:** Elmer "Guv" Fuller Field (Main St., Falmouth, 0.6 miles south of Jones Rd.)
- **Harwich Mariners:** Whitehouse Field (Oak St., Harwich, next to Harwich High School; take Queen Anne Rd. east from Rte. 124, then turn right on Oak for 0.8 miles)
- **Hyannis Harbor Hawks:** McKeon Field (at the end of High School Rd., Hyannis)
- **Orleans Firebirds:** Eldredge Park (Rte. 28 and Eldredge Parkway, Orleans)
- **Wareham Gatemen:** Clem Spillane Field (55 Viking Dr., off U.S. 6, Wareham, behind the town hall parking lot)
- **Yarmouth-Dennis Red Sox:** Red Wilson Field (Dennis-Yarmouth High School, 180 Station Ave., South Yarmouth, 1.4 miles west of Union St.)

to pay at least half again as much as you would here.

A good example of what you'll find in this area is **The High Pointe Inn** (70 High St., 508/362-4441 or 888/362-4441, www.thehighpointeinn.com, year-round, $165-325 d May-Oct.), a large, homey spot near West Barnstable village center. Light-filled guest rooms have a more contemporary feel than many antiques-laden B&Bs, but it's still quaint, quiet, and unhurried. Some rooms have a view of Sandy Neck's barrier beach, and full breakfast is included.

Getting There and Around

Barnstable is the largest Cape town and borders Sandwich, Mashpee, and Yarmouth. From Sandwich center, it's a 10-mile (15-minute) drive east on U.S. 6 or Route 6A. From Mashpee, it's about 10 miles (20 minutes) to the northeast on Route 28. Yarmouth is accessed by a number of roads, the main ones being Route 6A, U.S. 6, and Route 28.

The town of Barnstable comprises of several villages. To reach Barnstable village (in the historic district), use U.S. 6 to exit 68, then drive north to Route 6A. Follow Route 6A east for three miles and you'll arrive at the village. To reach the more commercial "center" of Barnstable, such as the Cape Cod Mall or Hyannis's Main Street, take exit 68 and go south on Route 132, first hitting the mall, then the airport.

Barnstable is one area fairly well served

by public transportation. You can take the **CCRTA bus** from the Hyannis bus station to the Cape Cod Mall and then to various villages of Barnstable, Mashpee, Falmouth, and all the way to Woods Hole. **Ferry service** takes you to Nantucket and the Vineyard. And the **P&B bus line** connects Hyannis to Boston, Providence, and other major transportation hubs.

For trips northward, however, such as spots on Route 6A, you'll find it's hard to get around without a car. The **DART bus** (800/352-7155, www.capecodrta.org) offers call-in-advance pickup and drop-off, but if you're unsure of your schedule, there's really no good option to get around. Several car rental agencies operate out of Hyannis airport, so this may be a good time to spring for a rental car.

HYANNIS

One of the Cape's early resort areas, Hyannis, the largest village in Barnstable town, and the neighboring villages of Hyannisport and Osterville have been known since the 1920s for their oceanfront estates. Today, Hyannis is the most urban of Cape towns, despite having a population of only 16,000, as a major commercial center attracting Mid-Cape visitors and residents to shopping plazas along busy Route 132. Come summer it's an absolute boomtown, filled with families spending summer at Grandma's, renting kitchenette-equipped efficiencies by the week, or joining streams of island-bound passengers making their way down to the ferry.

In addition to having the most passenger rail, bus, boat, and airline connections to the off-Cape world, Hyannis boasts the region's highest concentration of guest rooms, with over 40 motels, hotels, and inns around town. It's also a hub for Cape nightlife.

Kennedy Sights

Fans of the Kennedy clan—and anyone else wanting to trip lightly down the path of nostalgia—should be sure to check out the JFK photos and videos on display at the **John F. Kennedy Hyannis Museum** (397 Main St., 508/790-3077, www.jfkhyannismuseum.org, 11am-5pm Thurs.-Sat. Apr. 29-May 28, 11am-5pm Mon.-Fri. May 30-Sept. 3, adults $13, seniors $11, ages 6-17 $7, free under age 6), on the ground floor of bunting-draped Old Town Hall, covering the years he spent vacationing at the local family spread from the 1930s until his assassination in 1963. There's also a **JFK Memorial** on Ocean Street past the ferry staging area, overlooking the sheltered Veteran's Park Beach next to the yacht club (fee for beach parking in summer). The famous **Kennedy Compound**—whose nucleus is the much-expanded 1902 cottage that Joe and Rose Kennedy and their nine kids used for a summer home—is located in the well-heeled residential neighborhood of Hyannisport, south of downtown. But given the frequent traffic restrictions, voyeurs are better off taking one of the several cruises that parade past the compound's waterfront, out by the harbor breakwater. At the Ocean Street docks, look for the boat with the grinning Cheshire Cat-like puss on the sail. The 12:15pm and 2:15pm excursions sail closest to the Kennedy Compound.

Cape Cod Potato Chip Factory Tour

It once was that potato chips meant bland, dull, and uninspiring. Then along came the **Cape Cod Potato Chip Factory** (100 Breed's Hill Rd., 800/438-1880, www.capecodchips.com, self-guided tours 9am-5pm Mon.-Fri., free), and everything changed. Soon crisp, snappy indie chips were popping up everywhere, almost as fast as microbreweries. The tour is great fun for parents and kids alike, who get to marvel as potatoes are sliced, fried, and shaken along a conveyor belt to their final destination: the bag (or your mouth). As with beer tours, you get freebie tastings at the end of the line.

The Dinner Train

Taking the **Cape Cod Central Railroad** (252 Main St., 888/797-7245, www.capetrain.com, adults $30-140, children $25-50) through the

Hyannis

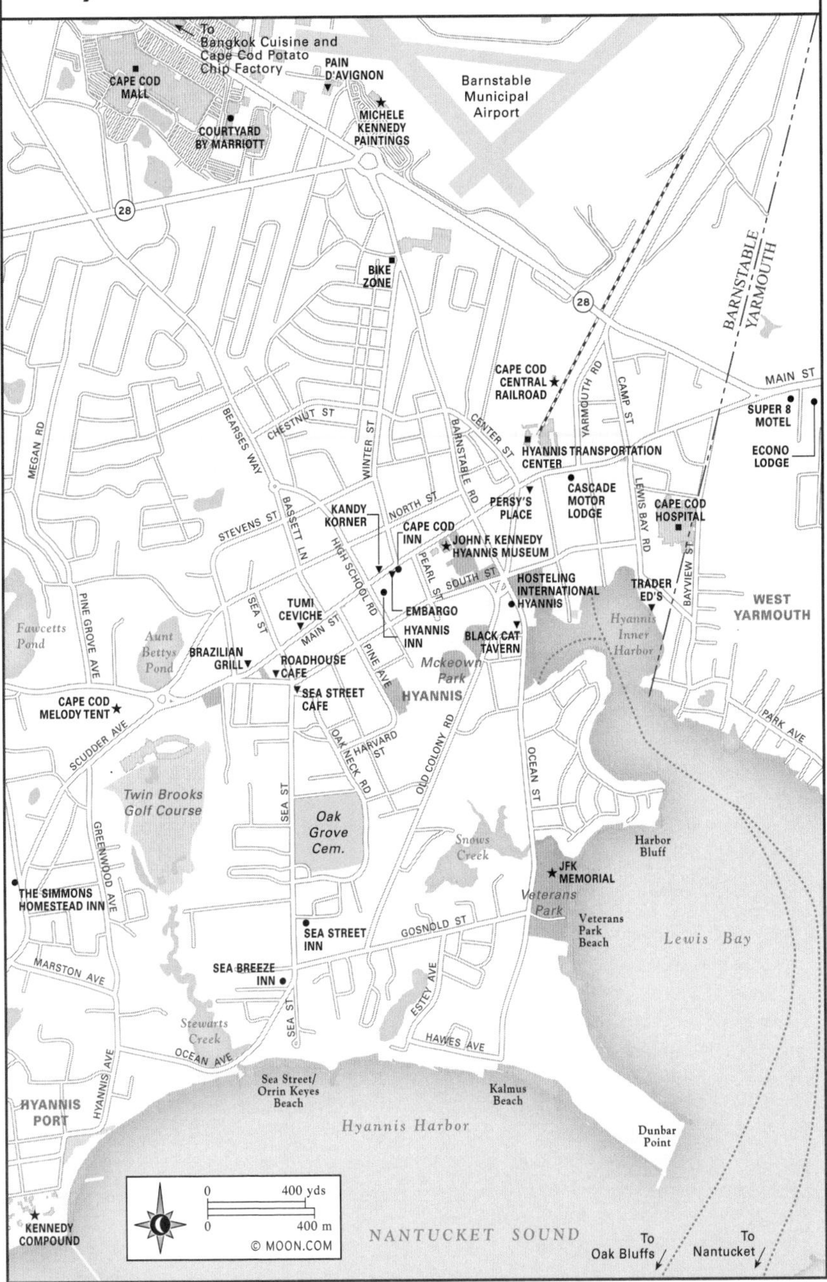
To Bangkok Cuisine and Cape Cod Potato Chip Factory
CAPE COD MALL
COURTYARD BY MARRIOTT
PAIN D'AVIGNON
MICHELE KENNEDY PAINTINGS
Barnstable Municipal Airport
28
BIKE ZONE
BARNSTABLE
YARMOUTH
CAPE COD CENTRAL RAILROAD
MAIN ST
SUPER 8 MOTEL
ECONO LODGE
HYANNIS TRANSPORTATION CENTER
CASCADE MOTOR LODGE
CAPE COD HOSPITAL
PERSY'S PLACE
KANDY KORNER
CAPE COD INN
JOHN F. KENNEDY HYANNIS MUSEUM
HOSTELING INTERNATIONAL HYANNIS
TRADER ED'S
WEST YARMOUTH
EMBARGO
HYANNIS INN
TUMI CEVICHE
BLACK CAT TAVERN
BRAZILIAN GRILL
ROADHOUSE CAFE
SEA STREET CAFE
HYANNIS
Mckeown Park
Hyannis Inner Harbor
Fawcetts Pond
Aunt Bettys Pond
CAPE COD MELODY TENT
MEGAN RD
PINE GROVE AVE
BEARSES WAY
CHESTNUT ST
WINTER ST
BARNSTABLE RD
CENTER ST
YARMOUTH RD
CAMP ST
LEWIS BAY RD
BAYVIEW ST
STEVENS ST
NORTH ST
BASSETT LN
HIGH SCHOOL RD
PEARL ST
SOUTH ST
SEA ST
MAIN ST
PINE AVE
SCUDDER AVE
OAK NECK RD
HARVARD ST
OLD COLONY RD
OCEAN ST
PARK AVE
Twin Brooks Golf Course
Oak Grove Cem.
Snows Creek
Harbor Bluff
JFK MEMORIAL
Veterans Park
Veterans Park Beach
Lewis Bay
GREENWOOD AVE
THE SIMMONS HOMESTEAD INN
SEA STREET INN
GOSNOLD ST
MARSTON AVE
SEA BREEZE INN
ESTEY AVE
Stewarts Creek
HAWES AVE
OCEAN AVE
HYANNIS AVE
HYANNIS PORT
Sea Street/ Orrin Keyes Beach
Kalmus Beach
Hyannis Harbor
Dunbar Point
0
400 yds
400 m
© MOON.COM
KENNEDY COMPOUND
NANTUCKET SOUND
To Oak Bluffs
To Nantucket

varied topography of the Upper Cape is a relaxing alternative to stewing in traffic, and the railroad right-of-way is pleasantly free of the commercial clutter that increasingly mars sightseeing by car. Dome cars (adults $150) and first-class cars (adults $120) offer additional snazz. Round-trips from Hyannis include stops in historic Sandwich and at the Cape Cod Canal; some trips include dinner or guided marsh walks. Regular scenic trips are offered Tuesday-Thursday and Saturday-Sunday June-October. Dinner trains featuring deluxe five-course meals are available at additional cost (12 and older only, $90-150) and begin on Saturdays in April, expand to Thursdays and Saturdays June-August, and then return to Saturday operation through the end of October. A three-course Yankee Clipper Brunch Train (adults $60) runs at 11am. Trains depart from the downtown railroad station next to the Hyannis Transportation Center bus terminal.

Entertainment and Events

Hyannis serves as a hub for Cape nightlife, with bars, cafés, and nightclubs drawing the legion of young workers who flock to the region to earn next year's college money. While the party abates after summer ends, this is still just about the only Cape town where you can schmooze over some brews with the under-35 single set off-season.

emBargo (453 Main St., 508/771-9700, www.embargorestaurant.com, 4:30pm-midnight, entrees $7-15) is a tapas-and-more spot with a great martini selection and live music in the summer, and one of the few spots that have almost a nightclub feel. It's chic and upscale and as the dinner crowd leaves the bar fills up with 20-and-30-somethings looking to meet and mingle. Wednesday is karaoke night.

For a libation poolside, head to **Trader Ed's** (25 Arlington St., 508/790-8686, https://traderedsrestaurant.com, 11:30am-1am daily late-May-early-Sept., 11:30am-1am Thurs.-Sat. early-Sept.-late-May, entrees $13-26) in the Hyannis marina, where you can party, eat, drink, or even swim around their large outdoor pool. There's live entertainment in the summer most nights, and great views of the water.

Throughout the summer, you can catch up with America's ageless pop, rock, and country-western stars at the **Cape Cod Melody Tent** (21 W. Main St., 508/775-5630, www.melodytent.org, from $10). This in-the-round venue is certainly more intimate than any Vegas stage; no seat is more than 50 feet from the stage. Ticket prices depend on the act but are usually quite reasonable.

If you're in town around the Fourth of July, catch the **Cape Cod Symphony** (508/362-1111, www.capesymphony.org) on the Town Green, where they perform their annual free summer concert on the Saturday of the Fourth of July holiday weekend. The Boston Pops Esplanade Orchestra also puts in an annual appearance on the Town Green on the first or second Sunday evening in August; tickets for this special **Pops by the Sea** concert are sold in advance through the **Arts Foundation of Cape Cod** (508/362-0066, www.artsfoundation.org).

Shopping

There are so many places to shop here that it's hardly worth pointing things out—you only have to have your eyes open to find some place for postcards, Cape Cod T-shirts, key chains, or other souvenirs. If you aren't looking for something that's Cape Cod branded, head to the Cape Cod Mall on Route 132 or to Main Street in Hyannis. Bargain shoppers beware: The Cape in season isn't an ideal spot to get things cheap; the best prices will be at the end of the season when stores are trying to clear out the unsold summer items. But it's easy to wait too long and discover that the stores already have the "See You Next Year" sign in the window. The best time for a good deal is between Labor Day and Columbus Day

1: the Whydah Pirate Museum in Yarmouth **2:** the *Cape Flyer* **3:** Pain D'Avignon in Hyannis **4:** the Cape Cod dinner train, offering a great meal on wheels

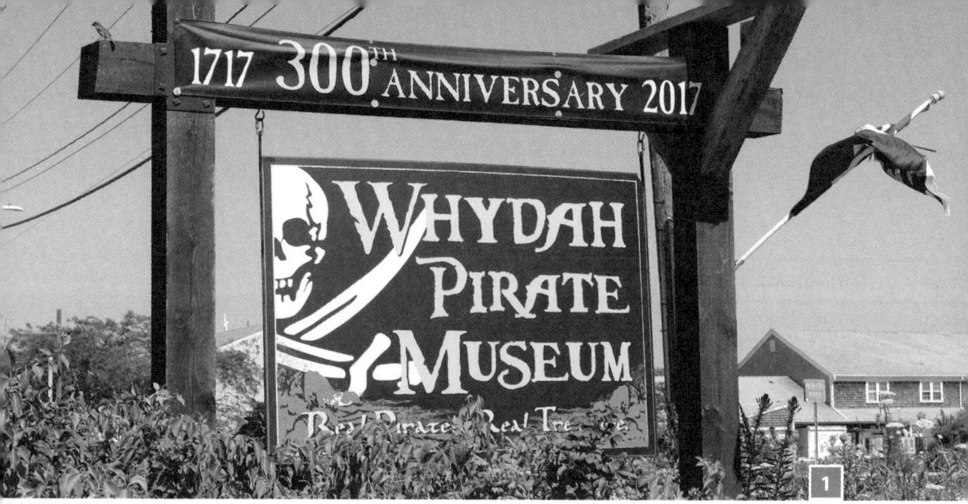

1717 300TH ANNIVERSARY 2017
WHYDAH PIRATE MUSEUM
1

2

CAFÉ
PAIN D'AVIGNON
BAKERY
3

4
2006
2006

weekend, when there's a hint of autumn in the air but the beaches aren't totally empty.

There's a myriad of shopping opportunities on the Cape, and none so numerous as in Hyannis. But the choice is made simpler by detailing where to start out. Depending on your needs, you'll either head to the **Cape Cod Mall** (769 Iyannough Rd., 508/771-0200, 10am-9pm Mon.-Sat., 11am-6pm Sun.), a Simons-owned branch where all your favorite brand names await, plus some quirkier indie-type stores, where you'll find a great selection of CDs, jokes, games, and gimmicks—if you're heading to a Halloween party or need a costume of any kind, stop by the Cape Cod Mall.

The other main shopping mecca in Hyannis is **Main Street,** where block after block of souvenir-type clothes, trinkets, key chains, and so on mixed in with ice cream parlors, restaurants, and a whole lot of passersby. If you need that Cape-branded logo sweatshirt or a T-shirt to give a girlfriend back home, a meander down Main Street will surely satisfy.

Tucked nicely into a gallery inside the Hyannis Airport, **Michele Kennedy Paintings** (480 Barnstable Rd., 508/737-5346, www.michelekennedy.com, 10am-5pm daily) is a great place to go for fine art as well as portraits and caricatures, often depicting the rich and famous. A self-proclaimed voyeur, Kennedy hones in immediately on the "essence" of a scene and manages to capture all aspects with humor, playfulness, love, and passion. Kennedy also does commissions. There's no better way to kill time in the airport than stopping by for a look.

Food

Persy's Place (247 Main St., 508/790-8200, http://persysplace.com, 7am-3pm Tue.-Sun. year-round, $8-16) is part of a small regional chain of eateries known for their prodigious breakfast menus. A head-spinning number of pancake options, locally traditional cornmeal johnnycakes, at least four daily quiches, chipped beef on toast, finnan haddie (smoked haddock) for homesick Scots, omelets with or without seafood, and even catfish or trout—not to mention all manner of baked goods—guarantees there's no excuse for leaving hungry.

Celebrate something truly special with dinner at **Pain D'Avignon** (15 Hinckley Rd., 508/788-8588, http://paindavignon.com, 7am-5pm Mon., Tues. & Sun., 7am-7pm Wed.-Sat., $18-40), one of the Cape's finest French dining spots, and also an excellent bakery. During the day it's a casual bistro with simple sit-down or take-out fare, but in the evening the white tablecloths come out along with candles, and if you squint, you might think you're in Paris rather than Cape Cod. The food is excellent—this is one of the few places where you can find French specialties like foie gras and truffles. Bring someone special and prepare to enjoy. Don't be afraid to take a loaf of bread or two home with you as well. Baked that day, it's so fresh it will keep for days even in the humid summer's heat. The Red Bar is open later most nights.

At the **Black Cat Tavern** (165 Ocean St., 508/778-1233, www.blackcattavern.com, 11:30am-9:30pm daily Mar.-Dec., $13-35), across the street from the Hy-Line ferry landing, red-meat eaters seeking relief from the relentless barrage of fried seafood can also put an end to their "we're not in Kansas City anymore, Toto" lament with a thick slab of prime rib beneath the crew-racing paraphernalia decorations. Of course, seafood lovers won't go unrewarded. You can also belly up to the bar and have a simple burger or bowl of chowder while jawing with the friendly barkeep over a decent microbrew.

Excellent Thai food in an elegant setting is at **Bangkok Cuisine** (20 Independence Dr., 508/771-1388, 11am-10pm Mon.-Sat., 4pm-9:30pm Sun., $12-23), tucked into a small strip mall. It offers popular Thai dishes as well as some specials that change weekly and is a good place for groups since it's usually not necessary to have reservations.

Cape Cod doesn't have the vast variety of dining options that exists in Boston, but the widest variety of choices is in Hyannis.

Traditional *rodizio* is on the menu at **Brazilian Grill** (680 Main St., 508/771-0109, www.braziliangrill-capecod.com, 11:30am-9:30pm daily, $35-40 all-inclusive), where waiters carve skewer after skewer of beef, pork, and sausage at your table.

Not far away is **Tumi Ceviche** (592 Main St., 508/534-9289, www.tumiceviche.com, 11:30am-10pm daily June-Aug., 11:30am-10pm Thurs.-Sun. Sept-May, $21-30), a Peruvian-Italian fusion spot that offers fresh ceviche and a lovely prix fix menu in the off-season. Choose from their nine different ceviches plus raviolis, pasta, and other Italian delicacies. A truly special spot, it's tucked away off Main Street and reached via a small alley.

Nearby, the **Sea Street Cafe** (50 Sea St., 508/534-9129, www.seastcafe.com, 7am-2:30pm daily, $9-18) is an excellent breakfast and lunch spot, with diner ambiance but way better food. It's popular enough that you should plan on a bit of a wait in the peak of summer—it's worth it.

If you've got a sweet tooth, you can indulge it at **Kandy Korner** (474 Main St., 508/771-5313, www.kandykorner.com, 10am-6pm daily, $3-10), a Hyannis Main Street mainstay for handmade saltwater taffy (you can watch), chocolates, hard candy, and souvenirs.

Accommodations

Hyannis, on the other side of Barnstable, is first and foremost a motel town. The half-dozen establishments sharing the waterfront district can legitimately claim to be within walking distance of the beach, but the other 30 or so are more likely to offer views of asphalt than water. Most of the national chains found on the Cape are here in Hyannis as well, generally along mall-lined Route 132.

Affordable and within walking distance of Main Street restaurants, shops, and all forms of local transportation, including bike rentals on the premises, is the very modest **Cascade Motor Lodge** (201 Main St., 508/775-9717, cascade@meganet.net, year-round, $120-160 d June-Aug., $82-102 d Sept.-May), opposite the train station.

A handful of no-frills B&Bs and guesthouses are found a little under one mile south of the downtown business district, within the residential neighborhood a few hundred yards from Sea Street Beach. **Sea Street Inn** (328 Sea St., 508/360-6389, www.seastreetinn.com, $100-340, includes shuttle to bus or train) is a prime example: very simple guest rooms with plain white bedcovers, floral wallpaper, no TVs or phones, window air-conditioning units, and common rooms that may evoke memories of Grandma's house. Families are welcome, although no cribs are available, and continental breakfast is included. An efficiency is available, although it's usually booked six months in advance.

If you're looking for something that really embodies the "location, location, location" mantra, **Hyannis Inn** (473 Main St., 508/364-3468, www.hyannisinn.com, year-round, $310-550 Jun.-Aug., $107-270 Sept.-May) is hard to top, despite the fact that you're paying premium for the convenience. There's a pool, a bar, and a cafe right there, and you're on Hyannis' Main Street, steps away from the dining and nightlife, and only a few blocks away from the bus, train, and ferry terminals. Rooms are fine overall, though it feels more well-kept motel than artsy or unique. Staff are friendly and helpful, but it's not a spot to expect them to remember your name.

Not far away, on Ocean Street, the **Sea Breeze Inn** (270 Ocean Ave., 508/771-7213, www.seabreezeinn.com, year-round, $98-225 d June-early Sept., $80-125 off-season) provides simple accommodations with a simple amenities—small TVs, radios, phones, canopy beds, all private baths, lots of frilly fabrics and doilies, and not much of a personal touch.

A cozier option is found in Hyannisport at **The Simmons Homestead Inn** (288 Scudder Ave., 800/637-1649, www.simmonshomesteadinn.com, year-round, $150-230 mid-June-mid-Sept., less in winter), an 1820 sea captain's mansion converted into a rambling country inn. Bill, the innkeeper, doesn't stand for formality, so the decor won't intimidate you with matchless antiques and accessories placed just so. Comfort is paramount, from the evening wine to the morning's full breakfast. Free bicycles are available, and you can practice your pool-hustling moves in the billiard room when the weather is inclement. A couple of guest rooms have fireplaces—needless to say, they're the first to be booked in the off-season. Perhaps best of all, the owner prides himself on his vast collection of single-malt scotches: over 1,600 of them.

Iyannough Road (eye-ANN-oh), also known as Route 132 at one end and Route 28 at the other, is a veritable hotel highway entering Hyannis. Among the major chains or their nearly identical imitators are these, listed in driving order from U.S. 6's exit 68, via Route 132 and Route 28 to Main Street:

The **Best Western** (1470 Iyannough Rd./Rte. 132, opposite Hyannis Chamber of Commerce, 508/771-4804 or 877/424-6423, www.bestwestern.com, $119-269 d) is pet-friendly and offers an included continental breakfast, an indoor swimming pool, and a sauna. **Courtyard by Marriott** (707 Iyannough Rd./Rte. 132, at the south end of Cape Cod Mall, 508/775-6600 or 800/321-2211, www.marriott.com, $146-454 d) has a breakfast café and an indoor swimming pool.

From the Yarmouth side of the town line to the west end of Main Street, there's the **Super 8 Motel** (41 E. Main St./Rte. 28, 800/454-3213, www.super8.com, $69-379 d), which has an outdoor swimming pool. **Econo Lodge** (59 East Main St./Rte. 28, 508/771-0699 or 877/424-6423, www.econolodge.com, $109-209 d May-Sept., $77 d off-season) is pet-friendly and has an indoor swimming pool. The **Cape Cod Inn** (447 Main St., 508/775-3000, www.capecodinnhyannis.com, May-late Oct., $74-220 d) has a restaurant and an indoor swimming pool.

Hosteling International in Hyannis (111 Ocean St., 508/775-7990 or 877/683-7990, www.hiusa.org, 8am-10am and 3pm-10pm late May-early Oct., dorm $29-39, rooms $79-175) is in a private house that was donated to create the Hyannis hostel. It's airy and close to everything Hyannis has to offer, including the bus station and both ferry terminals. Best of all, it's genuinely affordable, though you'll want to reserve far in advance to ensure a bed in the prime summer months. Note that check-in is 3pm-10pm, but guests have 24-hour access.

Getting There and Around

AIR

Cape Air (508/771-6944 or 800/227-3247, www.capeair.com) has a fleet of nine-passenger Cessnas that flies year-round from Boston's Logan Airport to **Barnstable Municipal Airport** (HYA) in Hyannis.

The airport is about four miles (20 minutes) south from Barnstable's Main Street, Route 6A. Main Street, Hyannis, is only a five-minute drive east.

CAR

Barnstable is a large town comprising ten villages. To reach the more commercial "center" of Barnstable, such as the Cape Cod Mall or Hyannis's Main Street, take exit 68 and go south on Route 132, first hitting the mall, then the airport. Hyannis Main Street runs the entire length of North Street, Hyannis. Barnstable village and Hyannis village are about 4.5 miles apart, via one of several routes, such as Route 132 or Phinney's Lane. The drive from Boston to Hyannis is about 70 miles (70 minutes), using Routes 93, 3, 6, and finally 132 (Iyannough Rd.).

BUS

Peter Pan (no phone, www.peterpanbus.com) provides service from New York City via Providence, Fall River, and New Bedford to Hyannis. To reach Hyannis from Boston's Logan Airport or Boston's South Station, however, you must take one of the dozen daily buses of the **Plymouth & Brockton Street Railway** (P&B, 508/746-0378, www.p-b.com). The Hyannis Transportation Center, where all buses arrive, is about a 15-minute walk from either the Hy-Line or Steamship ferry docks. A free Steamship Authority shuttle van swings by the transportation center as it makes its rounds between satellite parking lots and the South Street ferry terminal, but frankly, walking is often just as quick.

The Hyannis Transportation Center serves as an endpoint for all three year-round **Cape Cod Regional Transit Authority** (CCRTA, 800/352-7155, www.capecodrta.org) bus routes: the **Sealine,** running west to Falmouth and Woods Hole; the **Villager,** heading north to Barnstable Harbor via the Route 132 malls; and the easterly **H2O Line,** connecting Hyannis to Orleans via Route 28 through Yarmouth, Dennisport, Harwich Port, and Chatham. All routes operate daily late June-early September, and then mostly Monday-Saturday the remainder of the year.

RAIL

The ***Cape Flyer*** (215 Iyannough Rd., 508/775-8504, http://capeflyer.com, 2 hours 20 minutes, $22 one-way, $40 round-trip) train operates weekend-only service between the Hyannis terminal and Boston. On Friday evening, the train leaves Boston at 3:55pm and the return train departs Hyannis at 7:40pm. On Saturday and Sunday, the train leaves Boston at 7:40am and the return train departs Hyannis at 6:10pm. Bikes and pets are welcome, and there is free Wi-Fi on board.

FERRY

As the year-round Mid-Cape gateway to the island of Nantucket, Hyannis Harbor bustles with the horn-blasting boats of **Hy-Line Cruises** (508/778-2600, www.hylinecruises.com) and the **Steamship Authority** (508/477-8600, www.steamshipauthority.com). If you'll be taking the bus to Hyannis, intending to connect straight to an outbound ferry, you can save yourself a wait in line by purchasing your ferry ticket when you pay your bus fare. Drivers will notice that all directional signage avoids mentioning either company's name. If you want the Hy-Line, follow signs to the Ocean Street docks; for Steamship Authority, follow signs to South Street. If you have time to kill, next to no luggage (or can drop someone off to watch it), and don't mind walking a fair piece, the cheapest in-town parking is east of the Steamship dock. Don't let the authoritative red flag-waving guys with the too-cool shades dupe you into turning into the super-expensive lots immediately opposite the Hy-Line passenger drop, as you can save several bucks a day (and be just as close to the ferry) by simply taking the next left.

Connecting bus service to both ferry docks is provided via the Villager route of the **Cape Cod Regional Transit Authority** (CCRTA, 800/352-7155, www.capecodrta.org, adults $2, seniors $1), which runs every 20 minutes throughout the day. A third satellite parking facility is located off Route 28/132 closer to the edge of downtown; count on signage at exit 68 to direct you to the nearest empty lot.

Both ferry companies offer a choice between fast and expensive or slow and cheap ferries to Nantucket, while Hy-Line adds a seasonal vessel to Martha's Vineyard.

BOAT

You'll want to call ahead to reserve a slip at the **Hyannis Marina** (508/790-4000, www.hyannismarina.com). There, on the inner harbor across from all the island ferries, you'll find all the repair, rigging, pump-out, hookup, shower, and laundry facilities you could want. Trolley service to Main Street is available aboard the CCRTA bus.

YARMOUTH

Primarily a pass-through conduit for people heading to then prosperous and upscale Wellfleet along the Old King's Highway and eventually the railroad, Yarmouth has always been an inn and tavern spot, and much of that flavor remains even to this day. Many of the buildings, if not untouched, retain a look and feel of yesteryear thanks to strict historic building codes that recognize that clapboard siding and gabled houses are part of what give the Cape it's character. Although most of the action takes place in nearby Hyannis, there are some nice restaurants, quirky spots, and charming B&Bs here.

Sights

EDWARD GOREY HOUSE

Illustrator and author Edward Gorey lived beside the Old King's Highway in Yarmouthport for 14 years until his death in 2000; now his life and art are the subject of an appropriately idiosyncratic museum. Located in a traditionally gray-shingled Cape house near the town common, the **Edward Gorey House** (8 Strawberry Lane, 508/362-3909, www.edwardgoreyhouse.org, 11am-4pm Thurs.-Sat., noon-4pm Sun. mid-Apr.-June, 11am-4pm Wed.-Sat., noon-4pm Sun. July-Sept., 11am-4pm Fri.-Sat., noon-4pm Sun. Oct.-Dec., closed Jan.-Mar., adults $8, students and seniors $5, ages 6-12 $2, under age 6 free) has both a permanent biographical exhibit—from his first baby shoes to his last sneakers, and significant steps in between—and twice-yearly displays of original art, first editions of his books, and other treasures drawn from Gorey's prolific career. The museum also sells those of his books that remain in print. One of Gorey's most memorable works, *The Doubtful Guest,* is reproduced in topiary form in the backyard.

Whydah Pirate Museum

Thanks to Johnny Depp and a certain string of Hollywood blockbusters, pirates have once again become cool. Fans of those films will love the **Whydah Pirate Museum** (674 Rte. 28, 508/534-9571, www.discoverpirates.com, 10am-5pm Tues.-Sun., adults $15, seniors 65 and older $13, youths 5 to 15 $11, under age 5 free). This museum details the history and wreck of the pirate ship *Whydah* and its subsequent discovery in 1984 off the shoals of the Outer Cape—the only pirate shipwreck ever authenticated. The museum does a great job tracing the history of the ship from its origins as a slave vessel to its command under "Black Sam" Bellamy in the early 1700s, using many original artifacts from the wreck to illustrate the tale.

Beaches

BASS HOLE BOARDWALK

This stretch of road has the added distinction of passing by one of the more interesting places to obtain a panoramic view of the Cape. A water-level vantage point at the long Bass Hole boardwalk looks out over Yarmouth's bay-side tidal marsh. This favorite sunset-viewing spot among Mid-Cape residents is two miles north of Route 6A at the end of Center Street. Beside it is **Gray's Beach,** so small as to be free of charge even in high season.

the Bass Hole Boardwalk

SMUGGLER'S BEACH

This beach, one of many on Yarmouth's south shore, offers warm waters and calm seas, and it can be packed in the peak summer months of July-August. Come here for a Miami Beach feel: lots going on, plenty of people out to meet other sunbathers, and lots of nighttime activities as well.

Golf

Blue Rock Golf Course (48 Todd Rd., South Yarmouth, 508/398-9295, http://bluerockgolfcourse.com, May-Sept., $24-60) is a popular par-3 course for fans of all levels and abilities and a nice spot for travelers in the mid-Cape area to get a bit of time on the green.

Food

For a snack, step into **Hallet's** (139 Main St., Yarmouthport, 508/362-3362, www.hallets.com, 11am-5pm Tues.-Sun.), an 1889 pharmacy turned ice cream parlor. The apothecary cabinet along the wall is a real beauty, with Latin names inscribed on the brass drawer pulls, and the malted frappes are darn good too. Hours may vary according to the season and the owner's whim.

A few doors from Hallet's is the Japanese restaurant **Inaho** (157 Main St./Rte. 6A, 508/362-5522, www.inaho-sushi.com, 5pm-9pm Tue.-Sat. year-round, $22-37), occupying the ground floor of a historic house. Perhaps no restaurant on the Cape shows off the fresh bounty of the local waters like this small establishment, whose sushi, tempura, and whole-fish dishes are served in the welcoming atmosphere of a private home. The flourless chocolate cake is one of the best desserts in the region—light and not too sweet.

A minute's drive farther down Route 6A brings you to **Happy Fish Bakery** (173 Main St., 774/994-8272, 9am-3pm Thurs.-Sun., $4), perhaps the only place on Cape Cod to stay open longer in the off-season than during the peak of summer. Why? Because it "takes longer to bake things in the summer," that's why. This airy bread shop boasts absolutely to-die-for sticky buns, so sticky that they will give you a plastic glove to use if you plan on eating them in the car. (Hint: Get the glove.) But the buns may disappear before you've even made it to your car.

Almost across the street from Happy Fish is the **Optimist Café** (134 Main St., 508/362-1024, 8am-3pm daily late-May-early-Oct., $8-17), with its can't-miss-it whale sculpture and bright gingerbread-style building. It serves gourmet breakfasts and lunches and even a British-style high tea. There's a full bar too for those who want their optimism served shaken or stirred.

Di Parma (175 Rte. 28, 508/771-7776, http://diparmarestaurant.com, 4pm-10pm daily, bar 3pm-midnight daily year-round, late-night menu 10pm-midnight daily summer, $15-28) is a family-owned establishment on Route 28 that has offered casual but tasty Italian "pastabilities" since long before the similar Italian chains arrived on Cape Cod. In addition to all-you-can-eat soups and salads and a variety of excellent main courses, there's a late-night menu.

Captain Parker's Pub (668 Rte. 28, 508/771-4266, www.captainparkers.com, 11:30am-9pm daily year-round, $13-33) has won the Cape's clam chowder contest multiple times and is renowned for being open 363 days a year, come rain, shine, hurricanes, snowstorms—you name it. The only holidays are Christmas Day and Thanksgiving. Some of the tables have a lovely view of the marsh and river. They have somewhat irregular hours and typically close when guests leave.

Accommodations

In the center of Yarmouthport, you can't miss the ★ **Liberty Hill Inn** (77 Main St., 508/362-3976, www.libertyhillinn.com, year-round, $209-349 d June-mid-Oct.), a distinctive 1825 Greek Revival estate atop a low hill behind the broad sloping lawn at the corner of Willow Street and Route 6A. Originally built by a prominent local shipwright, it's the epitome of a classic New England inn—stately white clapboard, black shutters, a wrap-around porch with wooden rocking chairs on the outside, and hardwood floors, high ceilings, and a tasteful collection of period furnishings on the inside. The bright sunlit guest rooms are furnished for comfort, with thoughtful attention to real traveling needs (you'll never have to leave your luggage all over the floor) and every modern amenity you would expect of a top-rated inn. Just as importantly, the innkeepers' hospitality is second to none, which explains why so many returning guests wouldn't dream of staying anywhere else. And if you pick where you stay based on the breakfast served, look no farther: outstanding multicourse repasts and fresh-baked afternoon cookies will ensure your stay here is a memorable one.

The Inn at Cape Cod (4 Summer St., 508/375-0590 or 800/850-7301, www.innatcapecod.com, $259-319) is a delightful, spacious, well-located inn right on Route 6A in Yarmouthport center. The guest rooms are gorgeous, as is the graceful spiral stairway to reach them. If the weather is nice, you'll eat breakfast outside surrounded by flowers and hummingbirds. It's perfectly located for anyone planning a Route 6A antiquing expedition. Most visits require a 2 or 3 night stay.

The Escape Inn (1237 Rte. 28, 508/694-7153, www.theescapeinn.com, $95-159) is on the south side, a Route 28 option that is a clean, bright, charmingly decorated motel. The open common area means that it's easy to meet other travelers; the only downside is that some of the guest rooms are quite near the noisiness of Route 28.

It is hard to get closer to the water than **The Ocean Club at Smuggler's Beach** (329 South Shore Drive, 508/398-6955, www.oceanclubsmugglersbeach.com, from $149), a hotel that presides over the packed summer beach. What it lacks in flair it makes up for by being in a great location, whether you're wanting to beach bathe or explore up and down Cape. If you happen to be here when the weather's crummy (and on the Cape, it often is!), have no fear—a glassed-in heated pool means you will not be without swimming opportunities.

Getting There and Around

Yarmouth is another town that, like Barnstable, runs the entire width of the Cape from north to south. It is 3 miles (7 minutes) from Barnstable village's center and 4.5 miles (15 minutes) from Hyannis Main Street. Getting to Yarmouth is easy—the Hyannis bus terminal is within walking distance of the town line. From there, however, you'll have to keep on walking (and walking, and walking) if you want to get to Route 6A (the north side). The CCRTA **DART door-to-door shuttle** (800/352-7155, www.capecodrta.org) is an option, as is the **CCRTA bus service** south to Orleans, but it's infrequent and doesn't allow for easy beach or sightseeing access. If you're planning on spending any serious traveling time in Yarmouth, you'll want to rent a car or depend on ride-share services.

The Lower Cape to the Elbow

The Lower Cape, if we continue the "Cape is a flexed arm" analogy, starts in the middle of the bicep-tricep region and moves to the elbow, including the towns of Dennis and Harwich (bordering Yarmouth), then Brewster and Chatham. While it has a few nice parks, it's not as well-known for the nature as for the other things that make Cape Cod so fun: ponds to swim in or paddle around, great food at a variety of seafood restaurants (fitting budgets from pricey to costs-and-arm-and-a-leg), more of that lovely white sand that people crave, and (depending on the time of year) the chance to spot endangered right whales from the shore.

Whether you choose a pond or an ocean beach, a fried fish platter or a towering soft-serve cone, a beachfront cottage or a boutique B&B, you'll find a lot to love here.

DENNIS

Dennis, another town edging both Cape Cod Bay and Nantucket Sound, lives and breathes by summer tourism. Most of the houses are either summer homes or nine-month rentals, and the entire south side (along Rte. 28) is geared toward the one-week or two-week beachgoing crowd. Accommodations range from basic motels all the way up to the fairly fancy; restaurants likewise cater to crowds who want something cheap and fried and those who want to luxuriate over a lovely meal.

Scargo Tower

Farther east in Dennis is Scargo Tower, a simple stone observation tower built high atop the hill overlooking its namesake lake; turn south at the village green on Old Bass River Road, then take the next left on Scargo Hill Road and watch for the sign.

Beaches

Aside from those in Sandy Neck, the nicest beaches in this Cape Cod Bay facing part of the Cape are in Dennis: **Mayflower Beach** (at the end of Beach St.), with a picturesque view of the bay and far fewer rocks than Sandy Neck; adjacent **Chapin Memorial Beach** (turn left on Taunton Ave., near the end of Beach St.) meanderers a nice (sometimes secluded) stretch of sands that end at a point that looks toward Gray's Beach and its boardwalk; and **Corporation Beach** (at the end of Corporation Rd.), which is a fun beach due to Nobscusset Point, a promontory that offers fun exploration and sea critter discoveries. Mayflower Beach and Corporation Beach have concession stands in July-August; Mayflower has seasonal restrooms.

Entertainment

O'Shea's Olde Inne (348 Main St./Rte. 28, 508/398-8887, www.osheasoldeinne.com) has live music in the summer season and a classic watering-hole ambiance.

Food

The **Marshside Restaurant** (28 Bridge St., 508/385-4010, www.themarshside.com, 11:30am-close daily, $13-25) is aptly named: It has a great view of the marsh from three different picture windows. Families with small children will enjoy the plethora of toys to play with, and the staff seem to take it upon themselves to entertain. While they don't take reservations, the wait is usually compensated for by the nice views.

Scargo Cafe (799 Main St., 508/385-8200, www.scargocafe.com, 11am-9pm daily, $16-32) is a delightful gem on Route 6A, offering a host of natural foods with some organic and vegan options in a tavern-like atmosphere. It's a good place to go with groups, as there's space enough to pull tables together and feel like you've got the place all to yourselves, even if you don't.

Good Friends Café (83 School St.,

508/760-2727, http://goodfriendscafe.com, 7am-noon Mon.-Fri., 7am-1pm Sat.-Sun. $7-10) has excellent breakfasts known for being hearty, satisfying, and at near-diner prices. The apple-walnut french toast and eggs benedict are popular.

Accommodations

The comfy **Inn at Swan River** (829 Main St., 508/394-5415, www.innatswanriver.com, from $235) is an elegant option for Dennis-bound travelers, with a beautiful garden, lovely trees, nice Cape-style architecture with gabled roofs and shingles, and easy proximity to the beaches. At the opposite end of the quaintness scale are the large LED tvs. Kids or couples sick of sleeping in the same bed might enjoy their bunk bed-equipped rooms. Some rooms include kitchenets as well.

Getting There and Around

Dennis (like Barnstable and neighbor Yarmouth) spans the width of the Cape, with beaches on the Bay and Nantucket Sound sides. Dennis center, on Route 6A, is about 9.5 miles (15-20 minutes) northeast of Hyannis. It's far enough away that you'll need to have a car or other four-wheeled form of transportation to get here if you arrive by bus or train. There is service from the **Cape Cod Regional Transit Authority** (CCRTA, www.capecodrta.org) to stops along Route 28 and the south side. For north-side destinations, you'll need to call a cab or ride-share.

HARWICH

Harwich, on the Cape's south side, has a bit of a rural, off-Cape feel, with some farms and fields mixed in with the Route 28 kitsch. Wooded conservation lands mix with suburban homes and quaint backyards, without the grandeur and nose-in-the-air of Chatham. If you're looking for peace and quiet that's not too far from Hyannis or the Cape Cod National Seashore, it's a nice spot to be.

Sights

Cranberry Bog Tours (1601 Factory Rd., 508/432-0790, www.cranberrybogtours.com, by appointment only year-round, $15) gives you a look at what goes on behind the scenes at the Cape's most ubiquitous agricultural crop. Depending on the season, Andrea and Leo Cakounes will show you the machinery used in their bogs, introduce you to the animals in the farm, even drive you around in a special cart so you can see them up close. Since the cranberry bogs you see as you drive around the Cape are private property and walking on them will harm the berries, this is a great chance to see what you may not be able to see on your own. Kids will enjoy the farm animals as well.

Cape Cod Lavender Farm (Weston Woods Rd., 508/432-8397, www.capecodlavenderfarm.com, 10am-4pm daily, Mar.-Dec.) is a lovely spot to stroll amongst lovely lavender fields and surrounding conservation land. Bees buzz merrily in the blossoms and the quiet, peaceful paths make you feel a bit like you're on a movie set. There's a shop with lavender-based gifts and souvenirs, and free parking.

Entertainment

Harwich Junior Theatre (105 Division St., 508/432-2002, https://capecodtheatrecompany.org) is more than just an acting opportunity for kids. For over 70 years, the HJT has been offering acting classes and great theatrical performances for kids of all ages. Shows are often sold out and include everything from modern works *(The Giver)* to timeless classics like *The Secret Garden* and *The Wizard of Oz*. Check the website for their current performance schedule, or swing by and audition sometime!

Food

Bucas Tuscan Roadhouse (4 Depot Dr., 508/432-6900, www.bucastuscanroadhouse.com, 5pm-close daily, $25-54) is a very popular high-end Italian restaurant—so popular, in fact, that you will likely need reservations even midweek in summer. Portions are large enough to make an Italian grandmother nod in approval; the potato gnocchi is tasty, and the seafood is excellent as well. The red-checked tablecloths seem pulled out of a family album from Naples or Rome. Assuming you're in the mood for something on the pricey side, Bucas won't disappoint.

Accommodations

The **Harwich Inn & Tavern** (77 Route 28, 774/237-0848, www.harwichinn.com, $450, 2-night minimum stay required) has both rooms and meals on tap here, giving you a chance to kick back and not venture out unless you want to. The building is beautiful, with wrap around porches, varnished wood stairways, fireplaces, and Victorian charm. Rooms are smallish, but adequate and clean.

Getting There and Around

Harwich is on the south side of the Lower Cape, bordered by Dennis on the west, Brewster on the north, and Chatham to the east. Harwich center is about 13 miles (30 minutes) drive from Hyannis center on Route 28, though U.S. 6 can be a valid alternate. The town is served by the **Peter Pan bus** (www.peterpan.com) which stops at the Fontaine Outpatient Center, and by the CCRTA's **H2O** line (www.capecodrta.org), stopping along Route 28 between Hyannis and Orleans.

BREWSTER

Brewster is another town rich in history and old, Cape-style houses with clapboards and widow's walks. On both the Old King's highway and the railway that once reached Wellfleet, the town has always catered to tourists and travelers and still does, with the Cape's best camping, fine dining, and interesting things to see and do.

Cape Cod Museum of Natural History

The Cape Cod Museum of Natural History (869 Main St./Rte. 6A, 508/896-3867, www.ccmnh.org, 10am-4pm daily June-Sept., erratic off-season hours, closed Jan., adults $15, seniors $10, ages 3-12 $6, under age 3 free) has two floors of salt and fresh aquariums showcasing aquatic flora and fauna of the local waters, plus a pair of interpretive trails behind the museum offering views of a salt marsh, a cranberry bog, and a beech grove.

Numerous items cater specifically to kids, from the glass-enclosed live beehive to the big rocking horse-like whale vertebrae; adults, meanwhile, should check out the museum's nature trips, scheduled throughout summer-fall. Day trips and rustic overnights to Monomoy Island's National Wildlife Refuge and guided full-day or half-day canoe trips are among the various options; all require preregistration.

Golf

The Jack Nicklaus-designed course at **Ocean Edge Resort** (2907 Main St., 508/896-9000, www.oceanedge.com, 7:30am-7pm daily, $62-140) is the crème de la crème for Cape golfing, though it comes at a price. Peak summer fees for this par-4 course are three or more times what other courses cost. Like much of the Cape, shoulder season golfing here gets much more affordable. Expect challenging holes, lots of variation on the green, and a few swear words to be uttered as you play.

Biking and Hiking

Nickerson State Park (508/896-3491, sunrise-sunset, $8/30 resident/non-resident parking May-Nov.) is a prime campground (listed below), easily the Cape's best and most popular, but it's a mecca for those seeking outdoor activities as well. Its meandering bike paths connect kettle ponds and woodlands, and link to the popular Cape Cod Rail Trail as well. Boating and swimming are possible, and the ancient white pines and scrub oaks make for beautiful, relaxing walks if you're in need of a bit of "forest bathing."

Food

Reservations would be essential for **Brewster Fish House** (2208 Main St./Rte. 6A, Brewster, 508/896-7867, www.brewsterfishhousecapecod.com, noon-3:30pm and 4:30pm-close Wed.-Sun. year-round, $21-37)—if they took them. But since they don't, your only hope is to show up early (at least 5:30pm) to get one of the 30-some tables at this unassuming Brewster establishment. Once you snag a seat, however, you can sit back and relax with some of the best seafood on the Cape. The restaurant eschews the same old fried fish and lobster combos that typify so much of Cape cuisine to offer the freshest fish in simple preparations that bring out, rather than obscure, the flavors. If the bluefish are jumping, don't hesitate.

For those really looking for something special, **Chillingsworth** (2449 Main St., 508/896-3640, www.chillingsworth.com, 5pm-9pm Tues.-Sun. mid-May-Thanksgiving weekend, entrees $22-42) offers fine French cuisine and has remained visible in the Cape's restaurant scene for decades. There is both a casual bistro side and a fancier fine dining option. Come here expecting to be treated well, and if you're at all a fan of dessert soufflés, you're well advised to order one (note: it must be preordered when you sit down).

Accommodations

Brewster by the Sea (716 Main St., 508/896-3910, www.brewsterbythesea.com, $245-390) offers gorgeously decorated adult-only guest rooms and is surrounded by a large flower and vegetable garden. Keep in mind there's a two- or three-night minimum stay, depending on the season. The gourmet breakfasts are not to be missed and include popovers filled with fruit and veggies from Brewster's own garden, among other delicacies. Yum!

Camping

The largest campground in this area is in Brewster's **Nickerson State Park** (508/896-3491, www.mass.gov, reservations 877/422-6762, www.reserveamerica.com, $4.50 transaction fee, mid-Apr.-mid-Oct., $22/70 resident/non-resident), west of Orleans on Route 6A. The 420 sites are broken up into many small cul-de-sac clusters throughout the park's dense pine- and oak-covered hills, whose stones and sand are well carpeted with a comfortable mat of pine needles. Although a number of sites are rather too close to their neighbors, most are adequate—you won't feel as if you're sleeping under the flags, signs, and laundry lines that some of the more settled-in residents use to stake out their perimeters, and a few choice spots—number 32 in area 7, for one—are quite secluded indeed. Although no hookups exist, a disposal station is available,

Nickerson State Park offers the area's largest campground.

along with full restrooms, showers, a camp store, and bike rentals (next door) for use on the park's many paved trails or the Cape Cod Rail Trail, which crosses Route 6A beneath Nickerson's front entrance. If you don't have a tent, inquire about renting one of Nickerson's yurts ($45).

Getting There and Around

Brewster, on the Cape Cod Bay side, is about eight miles (15 minutes) from Dennis' historic center along Route 6A. The CCRTA's **Flex** line (www.capecodrta.org) makes several stops here between Harwich and Provincetown.

The Outer Cape

Most of the human settlement of the Outer Cape, right up to this century, has come from its proximity to excellent fishing grounds. The name Cape Cod, of course, reflects this. Here, Native Americans spent summers fishing and gathering shellfish, 15th- and 16th-century European fishing vessels put ashore to dry fish and engage in minor trade, and post-*Mayflower* colonists built a fishing industry from these exposed shores. But what the sea giveth, it can also taketh away—like a video on fast-forward, the effects of wind, tide, and erosion are probably more visible on the Outer Cape than anywhere else along the Massachusetts coast, not only from year to year but sometimes from day to day. The barrier beaches and cliffs that bear the brunt of this process include the region's crown jewel of natural wonders: the 44,000-acre Cape Cod National Seashore, extending the length and sometimes the breadth of the Outer Cape. Small museums and historic sights pepper the area as well. Most of the museums are best characterized as houses of memory—idiosyncratic collections of commonplace objects now rendered rare or unusual by the passage of time.

CHATHAM

Situated at Cape Cod's "elbow," Chatham presides over the hazardous waters whose "dangerous shoulds and roring breakers" sent the *Mayflower* scurrying for the protection of Provincetown harbor, according to her chronicler William Bradford. Now that the Cape's economy has shifted from harvesting cod to attracting tourists, this old sea captains' town of about 7,000 year-round residents has become one of the Cape's best gifts to visitors who appreciate the aesthetics of "olde Cape Cod": you'll find clapboard mansions, boutiques, art galleries, summer concerts in the old bandstand, and historic lighthouses. While it's one of the Cape's most fashionable addresses, Chatham is even coveted by the sea itself; unfortunately for oceanfront homeowners, negotiating with Poseidon is an extremely one-sided deal. Since the protective outer barrier beach was breached in a 1987 winter storm, the town's coastline has been more dramatically altered than perhaps anywhere else on the Cape. See the results for yourself at the vast South Beach, in front of the Coast Guard station and lighthouse on Shore Road, which was once separated from town by the harbor.

★ Monomoy National Wildlife Refuge

Monomoy Island, which is actually two separate islands, used to be a peninsula connected to town, as South Beach is now, with bus service down to the lighthouse station at its tip. A 1958 storm breached the sandy strand, and today, the only residents of this 2,700-acre national wildlife refuge are birds, a winter colony of harbor seals, and several hundred gray seals, year-round residents since 1991. These seals seem to have liked what they saw; they not only came to stay but told a lot of their friends—most of whom seem to be Canadian bachelors from Nova Scotia's Sable Island,

Chatham

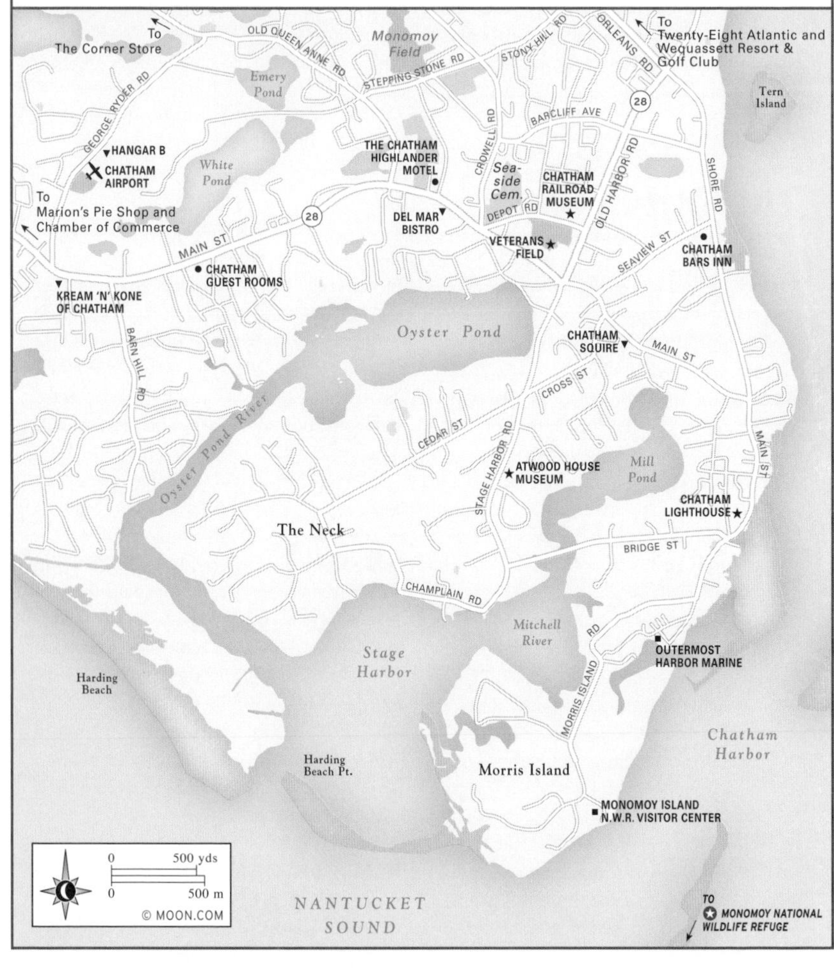

home to 90 percent of North America's gray seals. With the seals have come seal predators: Great White sharks. Needless to say, Monomoy is great bird-watching territory—two-thirds of all avian species recorded in Massachusetts have been sighted here—and good for strolls on the beach without stepping over thousands of sunbathers.

The refuge's **headquarters and visitors center** (508/945-0594, www.fws.gov/refuge/Monomoy, 9am-5pm daily late May-Labor Day, 10am-2pm Mon.-Fri. off-season, staff permitting) are located on Morris Island, south of Chatham Lighthouse and Coast Guard Station; follow Morris Island Road until you see the refuge entrance sign. The one-room center offers displays about the natural forces that influence the refuge, interpretive brochures for the short trail looping along the shoreline marsh behind the building, and information sheets on some of the significant wildlife protected here. You can also pick up an annotated bird-watcher's list of nearly 300 species sighted on Monomoy.

Managed by the U.S. Fish and Wildlife Service, the islands are open to the public as long as you observe certain guidelines with respect to their ecology and inhabitants. Simple but informative wildlife-watching cruises around the refuge are offered by **Monomoy Island Excursions** (508/430-7772, www.monomoysealcruise.com, $40/person), departing from Saquatucket Harbor in Harwich Port. The ticket office on Main Street (Rte. 28) is shared with the Nantucket Island Ferry. For transit to the beaches of South Monomoy, Keith Lincoln's **Monomoy Island Ferry** (774/722-1336, www.monomoyislandferry.com, $450/1-6 people) offers chartered seal, shark, or whale watching trips.

Located about 0.5 miles south of the Chatham Lighthouse, **Outermost Harbor Marine** (83 Seagull Rd., 508/945-2030, www.outermostharbor.com, $15) also operates seal tours ($30-35, 1 hour), staying closer to Chatham harbor.

A final note: Between early June and the last full moon in August, Monomoy island is overrun by greenhead horseflies, whose voracious appetites are not to be underestimated. Take all the usual precautions—covering every inch of exposed skin with clothing and bug repellent, for example—but recognize that no matter what you do, you're likely to meet that one cloud of greenheads who lap up DEET as if it were soda pop.

Food

If you aren't staying in a B&B and need solid food, search out **hangar B** (240 George Ryder Rd., 508/593-3655, https://hangarbchatham.com, 8am-2pm, 5pm-8pm Wed.-Sun. $12-20). If it's lunchtime or later, consider a visit to that king of the fried clam, **Kream 'N' Kone of Chatham** (1653 Main St., West Chatham, 508/945-3308, www.kreamnkonechatham.com, 11am-8pm Wed.-Mon. Apr.-Oct., market prices), up the road. A signature Cape dish, fried clams are one of many choices to come out of the fryers of this fast-food joint across from the supermarket.

For a sweet finish, head farther west to **Marion's Pie Shop** (2022 Main St., 508/432-9439, www.marionspieshopofchatham.com, 8am-5pm Mon.-Sat., 8am-4pm Sun.) in South Chatham. Fruit pies, pecan pies, and lemon meringue pies are among the offerings, all for takeout only, from family size down to mini two-person portions. If you have a kitchen at your disposal, Marion's also has heat-and-serve quiches, casseroles, and savory meat pies. To say the lemon meringue is Massachusetts's best is awfully faint praise given the lack of competition, so let's be more specific: The crust is perfectly crisp and flaky; the filling has a nice custardy texture, not too sweet; and the meringue is lofty enough to reach from your chin to your nose.

One of the Cape's finest restaurants is located on the grounds of the Wequassett Resort & Golf Club: the impeccable **Twenty-Eight Atlantic** (2173 Route 28, 508/430-3000, https://wequassett.com, 7am-11am and 5:30pm-10pm, dinner entrees $34-75, tasting menu $150). Elegant dining at its Cape Cod best here, with beautiful water views through the floor-to-ceiling windows, dark wood finishes, spotless white tablecloths, candlelight, and impeccable service as well. Entrees are as delicious to look at as they are to taste.

The menu at ★ **The Chatham Squire** (487 Main St., 508/945-0945, http://thesquire.com, 11am-1am Mon.-Sat., 12noon-1am Sun., $15-37) isn't as fancy as some other local restaurants, but its village tavern atmosphere enhances any meal. Selections include center-cut sirloins, linguine with clams, shrimp scampi, and chicken *piccata.* The Squire has a fine raw bar for oysters and other shellfish, and it makes an earnest effort at offering attractive vegetarian selections.

Slightly upscale and with an excellent drink menu is **Del Mar Bistro** (907 Main St., 508/945-9988, www.delmarbistro.com, 5pm-9pm Tue.-Sat., $17-40). Located right on Main Street, this spot offers a variety of unique entrées and wood-fired pizzas as well as signature cocktails and desserts.

The Corner Store (1403 Old Queen Anne's Rd., 508/432-1077, www.freshfastfun.com, 6:30am-6:30pm Wed.-Sun., $5-11) has specialty paninis, sandwiches, wraps, burritos, soups, and pastries in a building that's been a corner store for generations.

Accommodations

Quaintness enhances the price of lodgings everywhere on the Cape, and Chatham is no exception. The dozen small inns and B&Bs within a reasonable stroll of downtown almost all charge well over $150 for a double room in summer, although before mid-June or after Labor Day rates on some of the larger properties dip under $100. For example, **The Chatham Highlander Motel** (946 Main St., 508/945-9038 or 877/945-9038, www.chathamhighlander.com, Apr.-early Dec.), a family-friendly motel on Route 28 west of the rotary, has double rooms for $109-169 in the pre- and postseason shoulder months. Even during the height of summer, double rooms are $199-259 (kids under 18 stay free but require a $10 cot). There are two heated pools, the children's beach at Oyster Pond is nearby, it's an easy 0.5 miles up the sidewalk to Main Street, and there are breakfast cafés within walking distance. Two efficiency units are also available for stays of five nights or more.

Chatham Guest Rooms (1409 Main St., 508/945-1660, www.chathamguestrooms.com, $155-215, $115-175 off-season) is a cute, quaint, remodeled 1700s-era house with private entrances to all guest rooms. No breakfasts are served, but one of the guest rooms has a full kitchen, and the others have fridges and coffeemakers.

On the other end of the budget range is the understated yet stately **Wequassett Resort & Golf Club** (2173 Route 28, 508/432-5400, https://wequassett.com, $475-3000), one of the nicest hotels in the region. If you're honeymooning, been saving for a splurge, or just have that kind of money to throw around, you'll feel pampered and beautifully taken care of here. The resort sits on the edge of a lovely bay and a thin peninsula, giving rooms incredible water views; despite its caliber, there's a pleasant, comfortable feel, as if you're in your own Cape cottage for the week and not at a fancy resort. Flag down a friendly golf cart driver to get from one spot to another, or walk along the brick-lined meandering paths. Tennis, beaches, and a host of water-related activities are steps away. You can even take dance lessons! It's Cape Cod-style luxury at its best.

If you're looking for a motel style spot with a good location, check the **Chatham Tides Beach Motel** (394 Pleasant St., 508/432-0379, www.chathamtides.com, from $183). The rooms are typical of a clean, well-kept motel, but the reason to come is to enjoy the chance to open the door and walk fifty feet to the white sand. Minimum stays may be required in peak season.

Another premier resort, ★ **Chatham Bars Inn** (297 Shore Rd., Chatham, 508/945-0096 or 800/527-4884, www.chathambarsinn.com, $470-989 d) is also a spot to soak in luxury. With a full-service spa, a restaurant serving food that's nothing short of impeccable, and a breezy spot on gorgeous Pleasant Bay, it's easy to see why.

The **Chatham Chamber of Commerce** (508/945-5199 or 800/715-5567, www.chathaminfo.com) can give you the skinny on what else is available—and usually even has an idea about who has last-minute availability; visit its high-season **information booth** (533 Main St.) next to Chatham Town Hall or its **visitors center** (2377 Main St., 10am-5pm Mon.-Sat. July-Aug., 10am-2pm Mon.-Sat. May-June and Sept.-Dec., closed Jan.-May).

Getting There and Around

Chatham is at the "elbow" of Cape Cod, about 20 miles (45 minutes) east of Hyannis Main Street on Route 28. U.S. 6 to the Orleans Rotary is an alternate. It is about 37 miles (60 minutes) due south of Provincetown. The CCRTA's **H2O** line (www.capecodrta.org)

stops in Chatham on its way from Harwich to Orleans.

ORLEANS

Thinking of Cape Cod as an arm, Orleans is the upper part of the elbow. It's lucky to have both ocean and bay-side beaches, a fair variety of restaurants (one of the area's only large supermarkets), and plenty of inns and hotels. Needless to say, the proximity to great swimming, sunbathing, and other beach activities makes the "elbow" one of the hottest places to be in the summer season.

Lacking sufficiently deep harbors to attract the shipbuilding and other maritime industry adopted by many other Cape towns, this area remained invested in agriculture well into the early 1900s, managing to carve out a unique niche for travelers on the Old King's Highway and later those who came on the railway line. Today, Orleans provisions and outfits the entire outer Cape with its shopping centers and offers this area's best year-round options for dining and entertainment.

Nauset Marsh

The salt marsh estuaries protected by the Nauset barrier beach are a world often unseen by Cape visitors and well worth seeking out for anyone with an interest in the outdoors. The vast majority of this large salt marsh is actually in neighboring Eastham, but seasonal boat access is available from Town Cove in Orleans courtesy of guided two-hour **pontoon-boat trips** ($49) sponsored by the **Massachusetts Audubon Society** (508/349-2615). Preregistration and advance payment are required.

You can experience the marsh even more closely with a four-hour guided kayak tour from **Goose Hummock** (Rte. 6A, Orleans, 508/255-0455 or 508/255-2620, www.goosehummockshops.com, $85/person for 2 hours) on Town Cove, Cape outdoor outfitters for over half a century. If you're a paddler bringing your own gear, the good folks at Goose Hummock can also give pointers on where to go and what to avoid.

★ Cape Cod National Seashore

Few Cape attractions rival the wonders of Cape Cod National Seashore, a 43,500-acre park that is unique in being relatively populated. It extends the entire "forearm" of the Cape, from P-town and the Province Lands in the north all the way to Monomoy Island and Chatham in the south. While rampant development has made it clear where the park boundaries are, you'll find shingle cottages and the occasional mansion tucked here and there throughout this fragile network of dunes, beaches, swamps, and pines. Thank heaven for the foresight of those who worked to set this vast area aside, as the preservation has created a haven of green space on the Cape. **Doane Rock,** the largest of the Cape's glacial erratics (boulders), can be found on the way to Coast Guard Beach, in Eastham.

Begin your visit to the Cape Cod National Seashore at the **Salt Pond Visitors Center** (508/255-3421, www.nps.gov/caco, 9am-4:30pm daily year-round, longer hours in summer), conveniently located beside U.S. 6, about three miles north of the big Orleans rotary. The center itself has been closed for structural reasons, but there are outdoor info centers with staff to help answer questions. They offer handy publications that will orient you to what's available in the park, from historic lighthouses and abandoned cranberry bogs to beautiful beaches and rigorous bike trails.

Inform yourself with a briefing on the park's natural history from the museum exhibits, pick up a field guide from the small shop, and inquire about the tempting lineup of ranger-guided activities: Playing amateur naturalist by wading around in muddy salt marshes, learning to surf-cast, canoeing one of the park's kettle ponds, listening to campfire storytelling, and taking part in after-dark wildlife searches are among the many activities offered daily and weekly in high season. Reservations are occasionally required, and fees may be charged, especially where equipment is provided; call in advance for details.

Orleans

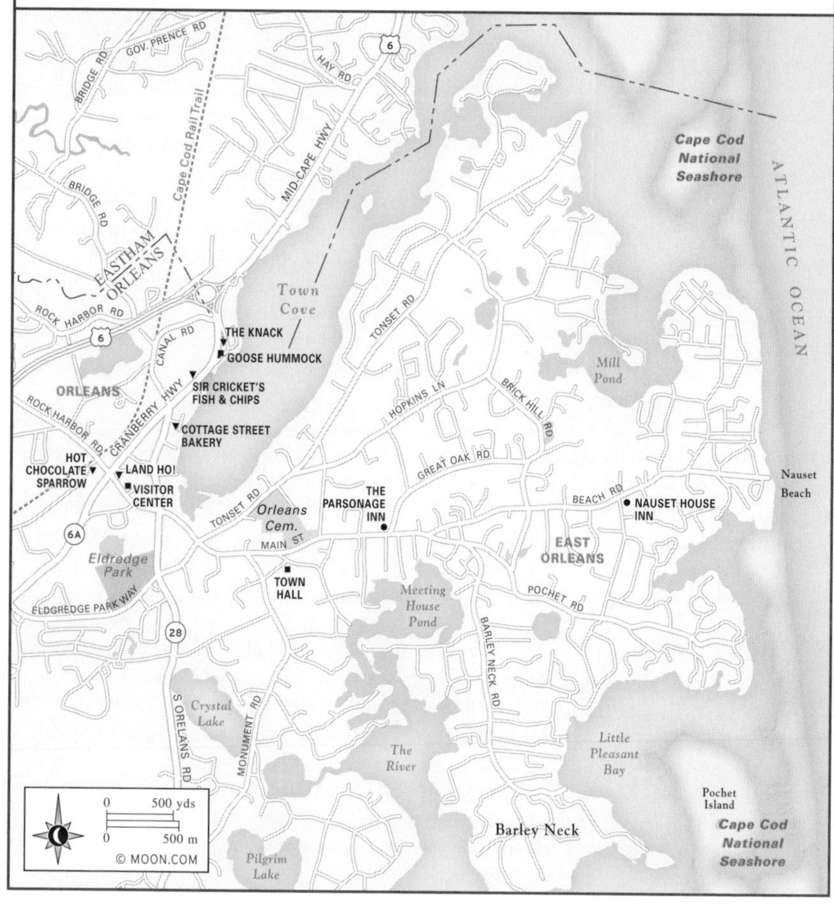

One of the attractions northbound drivers will pass prior to reaching the visitors center is the 1867 **Captain Edward Penniman House** (daily in season), on Fort Hill Road off U.S. 6. In sharp contrast to the plain Cape houses that were the prevailing standard of his time, this whaling captain's fancy Second Empire-style mansion and its ornamental carpentry illustrates how lucrative a seaman's career could be in the days when the nation's lamps were lit with whale oil. And yes, that front gate is indeed a pair of whale jawbones.

Bird-watchers and anyone curious about what remains of the indigenous Nauset people that once lived here should walk the short trail around panoramic Fort Hill just beyond the mansion, overlooking Nauset Marsh.

Beaches

Orleans has one beach on its ocean side and one on its bay side, and both are available to visitors for a parking fee ($25 per day, $100 for a weeklong sticker, $250 for the season); the beaches are free to cyclists and walkers. Bay-side **Skaket Beach** is warmer and relatively waveless, by far the calmer of the two.

Nauset Beach, on the other hand, is considered one of the best on the Cape—mile after mile of sandy shore with nothing beyond those waves until you hit the Iberian peninsula on the other side of the Atlantic. In summer, it often appears as if every day-tripper on the Cape has ended up here, but determined walkers can generally find some space way down the beach.

Food

When it comes to batter-dipped seafood, Orleans has one of the Cape's best purveyors. Try the perfectly fried sweet scallops at **Sir Cricket's Fish & Chips** (38 Rte. 6A, 508/255-4453, www.nausetfishandlobsterpool.com, 11am-8pm daily year-round, $13-25), for example, a hole-in-the-wall south of the rotary and next to the Nauset Lobster Pool.

If your heart pauses at the thought of another day's dining on fried anything, repair to the tiny ★ **Cottage Street Bakery** (5 Cottage St., 508/255-2821, www.cottagestreetbakery.com, 7am-3pm Thurs.-Mon.), just off downtown Route 28 a block south of its junction with Route 6A. Enjoy breakfast items such as French toast or the bakery's own granola with fruit, or lunch on sandwiches, soups made from scratch, quiches, and vegetable pies. The owner knows not to ruin her fine handiwork in the microwave—she warms the savory pastries in an oven, preserving the tender crusts. If you're on any sort of sugarless diet, stay away—she bakes up a fragrant storm of meringues, tarts, cookies, cakes, fruit danish, pies (generally sold whole), and luscious buttery croissants (try the almond crème with rum and frangipani). The deceivingly named (and very delicious) Dirtbomb muffin is another favorite. Luckily for off-season visitors, this place has a strong local following, so its delights can be savored year-round.

Another Orleans eatery that doesn't live and die by the tourist trade is **Land Ho!** (38 Rte. 6A, 508/255-5165, www.land-ho.com, 11:30am-10pm daily year-round, sandwiches $9-13, market prices for seafood), a genuinely local joint smack-dab in the center of Orleans at the corner of Main Street. Affectionately nicknamed "The Ho," it has charbroiled burgers, deli sandwiches, beer-boiled knockwurst, fried and broiled seafood, and an excellent kale soup among the casual menu items available, all at prices aimed at attracting neighbors more than gouging visitors.

For dessert, step over to **The Hot Chocolate Sparrow** (5 Old Colony Way, 508/240-2230, www.hotchocolatesparrow.com, 6:30am-8pm daily), a block and a half away next to the Cape Cod Rail Trail. Fudges, nut barks, truffles, caramels, toffee crunch, cream-filled and solid chocolates, cranberry cordials, chocolate-dipped dried fruits and ginger, chocolate-covered espresso beans—you get the picture. The place is half bakery and half café, so your companion who pretends not to like sweets can have a complete meal while you experimentally reevaluate whether you prefer milk or dark chocolate. Just be warned: The heady aromas of cocoa butter, coffee beans, and baked goods are impossible to resist, so don't think you'll get away with "just looking."

Right at the Orleans rotary, using as much local farm produce as possible to craft higher-quality burgers is **The Knack** (5 Rte. 6A, 774/316-4595, www.theknackcapecod.com, 11am-8pm daily Apr.-Sept., $6-19), which offers burgers with distinction and a charitable attitude (10 percent of all dessert sales go to charity). Fish tacos are popular, but their classic burgers are what bring people back for more. Owned by local guys with a dream for great local food, it's worth stopping for.

Accommodations

Places to stay in Orleans are about evenly split—half are on Route 28 south from downtown toward Chatham, and half are in East Orleans near the popular Nauset Beach. One that is sure to please is **The Parsonage Inn** (202 Main St. E., Orleans, 774/722-7403, www.parsonageinn.com, year-round, $269-299 d June-Oct., much less in winter) in Orleans, opposite Nauset Farm, 1.5 miles from Nauset

TOP EXPERIENCE

Surfing the Cape

The author heads out to catch some swell at Coast Guard Beach.

Cape Cod may not have pipeline or reef breaks, nor does it have perfect swell every day like some Pacific spots, but when the waves are good, they're really, really good—especially for **beginners,** who can enjoy friendly, even forgiving beach breaks, assuming they're willing to paddle out through the impact zone.

The Atlantic facing beaches all have good swell at times, with **Marconi Beach** being the sole high-tide surf spot. Other popular beaches are **Coast Guard Beach, Nauset Light Beach, White Crest Beach,** and even the south-facing Nantucket and Martha's Vineyard beaches when the swell and wind are right.

Note that these Cape beaches are very similar, all on the same stretch of Atlantic-swept "forearm" that makes up the Outer Cape. What makes one beach better for surfing than the others is individual conditions—the serious will drive to each spot and check out the swell before opting to park and head out. For online conditions at Coast Guard, check out www.morebeach.com; they have an up-to-the-minute cam.

Surfing on the Cape—despite winters that dip below freezing—is a **year-round** activity. Summers require only the thinnest of wetsuits, a 3/2 or even just a rash guard. Spring and fall (which many consider to be the ideal time to surf) require a 3/4 and possibly a hood. For true winter die-hards, you'll want a 6/5 with all the trimmings, seams taped and sealed. And remember that the hardest part isn't being in the water, but changing into and out of the suit in subzero temps. The waves may be great, but you also might want to bring some Thera-Flu.

As with surfing anywhere, there's a small risk of shark interaction, as Great Whites frequent the area looking to munch on the plentiful seals. The only other safety issue you may run into is the human one: In summer these waves get crowded, often with beginners who don't know the Surfer's Creed or which side of the board to stand on. Be alert for people cutting in, and (if possible) try not to curse too loudly . . . these are family waves, after all.

Rent boards, grab cold-water wax, or take lessons at **Sacred Surf School** (4900 Rte. 6, 508/514-1555, www.sacredsurfschool.com, group lessons $100/2 hours). **Nauset Surf Shop** (2 Rte. 6A, 508/255-4742, https://nausetsurfshop.com,10am-5pm, closed Tues. Oct.-May) does not do lessons but has a wide variety of gear, boards, wetsuits, and accessories, as well as daily or weekly board rentals.

Beach. Friendly, casual comfort is the rule at this 1770 Cape-style house and its rambling additions, amid country antiques and atmosphere. Rates include full breakfast.

In addition to B&B homes found through reservations services—some of which still fall below $90 for a double with a shared bath in high season—a number of highly regarded B&B inns are also found in this area. Also high on the hospitality index is the **Nauset House Inn** (143 Beach Rd., Orleans, 508/255-2195, www.nausethouseinn.com, mid-Apr.-Oct., $95-225), a mile farther east toward the beach. With a plant-filled conservatory, painted furniture, whimsical trompe l'oeil, and extensive quilts, this place has an insidious fun streak running through it—the kind that gives rise to dangerous thoughts about quitting your job and moving to the Cape to putter around enjoying yourself, entertaining friends, and sharing your life with tourists. If you catch yourself thinking what a delight it would be to run an inn like this, you'd better pack up and leave right away—don't even think of staying around for that big breakfast smorgasbord. Off-season rates run $130-195 double with a private bath, $85-110 double with a shared bath—an excellent value for budget travelers.

Getting There and Around

Orleans is a hub of sorts. At the very least, it's where the two main highways, U.S. 6 (the Mid-Cape Highway) and Route 6A (Old King's Highway) merge into one at the Orleans Rotary. If you're heading anywhere down Cape (Eastham to Provincetown) you'll need to pass through Orleans.

Orleans is about 10 miles (20 minutes) from Chatham center and 5 miles (10 minutes) from Brewster. Coming from Provincetown, the closest town north is Eastham, which is about 3 miles (5 minutes) away. The town lies at the elbow of Cape Cod and is the location of the landmark Orleans Rotary, where U.S. 6 comes into the circle from the west and then leaves 270 degrees later heading due north all the way to Provincetown. Route 6A and Route 28 both empty out here. One of the reasons traffic is so heavy here is that between the Orleans Rotary and Provincetown there's only one main road. If any tie-ups happen, it affects the entire stretch in both directions.

The **Peter Pan bus** (www.peterpan.com) stops here four times daily in summer and twice daily in winter at the CVS on Route 6A. The hourly **Flex** and **H2O** lines (www.capecodrta.org) stop the Orleans Stop & Shop (24 Rte. 6A).

EASTHAM

In truth, Eastham isn't known for its spectacular attractions. It's a quiet part of the lower Cape with scrub pine and some quaint off-the-beaten-trail roads that are actually quiet enough to walk, jog, or dog-walk on. It's a great location for its proximity to the town of Orleans, the beaches north and south, and day trips to Provincetown or even Hyannis if the whim hits. The **Eastham Windmill** is the oldest mill on Cape Cod, dating back as far as the late 1600s. It's a picturesque reminder of days long gone, when villagers came to grind their corn and wheat using the power of the wind.

Beaches

Unlike many Cape towns, Eastham permits visitors to use all nine of its freshwater and saltwater beaches, provided you purchase a week ($100), two week ($150), or seasonal pass ($250). Taxpaying residents pay only $25. The town also permits day use ($25 per car) at four of its beaches (First Encounter, Campground, Cooks Brook, and Wiley Park). Its bay-side shore, while boring for anyone hoping to do some bodysurfing, can be lovely, especially as the sun gets low over the water and the crowds head home for dinner.

First Encounter Beach, named for the initial meeting of the Pilgrims and the locals back in 1620, has the most parking, along with restrooms, but others that are not as well sign-posted on U.S. 6 are equally deserving, with similar views of Cape Cod Bay.

Turn onto Massasoit Road in North Eastham to access **Campground Landing Beach, Cooks Brook Beach,** and **Sunken Meadow Beach** (only Cooks Brook has restrooms). If you're cycling the Rail Trail, consider detouring to **Kingsbury Beach** or **Thumpertown Beach,** where you can turn the lack of public parking to your advantage: "bikes only" means far fewer people.

From the cliff-top parking lot at **Nauset Light Beach,** located one mile north of the National Seashore's Salt Pond Visitors Center, you can often watch surfers among the breakers, looking like board-riding seals in their full-body wetsuits. Eastham is one of the only places in Massachusetts that attracts serious surfers. This is due to fierce erosion off Eastham's backshore beaches, where loss of a dozen feet a year is not uncommon. Most erosion goes to build up offshore sandbars, some of which become visible at low tide. It's these sandbars that prove so appealing to surfers.

Turn around, though, and you'll have a great view of **Nauset Light,** which looks amazing in early morning or late afternoon light. Both the lighthouse and the beach are managed by the National Park Service. Nauset Light Beach has a lifeguard during summer months and charges $20 for parking in season.

The National Park Service also manages nearby **Coast Guard Beach** on the Atlantic, 1.5 miles east of Salt Pond Visitors Center on Nauset and Doane Roads. Coast Guard is lovely, with a white-and-red ranger station, an estuary behind, and good surf swell much of the season. Note, however, that this beach has very limited parking; during high season, cars must use the satellite lot on Doane Road and take the shuttle bus or walk the remaining 0.5 miles.

Food

The Hole in One Donut Shop (4295 U.S. 6, 508/255-9446, http://theholecapecod.com, 6am-2pm daily summer, 6am-noon daily off-season) is a local chain with another location in Orleans. It's a favorite with locals and has great freshly made doughnuts and pastries.

Royal Thai Cuisine (4550 U.S. 6, 508/240-3888, www.royalthaieastham.com, noon-9pm daily, $13-22) is one of those hole-in-the-wall spots that's easy to miss. With small windows and a primarily brick wall that faces the street, people often zip by thinking this spot has closed. Yet there's decent Thai food here, and it's one of the few spots in the area to offer it, including all the big-time favorites *(pad thai)* and some quirkier specials that change season to season. **Red Barn Pizza and More** (4180 U.S. 6, 508/255-4500, www.theredbarnpizza.com, 11am-9pm daily, pizzas $8-25) is one of many joints along the U.S. 6 strip, but what sets it apart is the obvious giant red barn and the not-so-obvious excellent ice cream. Pasta and pizza round out the dining experience.

Accommodations

Eastham's lodgings are concentrated along U.S. 6, with a dozen others scattered close by. For out-of-town seclusion with beautiful views out over Nauset Marsh to the ocean, nothing beats **Fort Hill Bed & Breakfast** (75 Fort Hill Rd., Eastham, 508/240-2870, www.forthillbedandbreakfast.com, year-round, $365 d May-Oct., $325 d Nov.-Apr., lower without breakfast and at off-season times). This attractive 1868 Greek Revival farmhouse, built by the brother-in-law of Captain Penniman (whose own home across the street now belongs to the National Seashore), has been converted into an all-suites property with charm and amenities to match its unique location; one three-room suite even has a piano. They offer a cottage ($400 d spring, $450 d summer; rates much higher holiday weeks in summer) for rent as well.

There's a year-round **Sheraton Four Points Hotel** (508/255-5000 or 800/325-3535, www.fourpointseasthamcapecod.com, $285-360 d June-early Sept.) on U.S. 6 in Eastham about one mile north of the Salt Pond Visitors Center—the "best available" rack rates off-season start at a very reasonable $156 for a double, though the rates vary daily based on a host of factors.

Getting There and Around

Eastham is about 22 miles (30 minutes) south of Provincetown, 3 miles (5 minutes) from Orleans. Wellfleet, its northern neighbor, is 8 miles (11 minutes) away.

Like much of the Outer Cape, Eastham is most convenient if you have a car, though it is served four times daily in summer and twice daily in winter by the **Peter Pan bus** (www.peterpan.com), which stops at the Eastham Town Hall and at the Village Green.

Flex bus service (www.capecodrta.org), from the Cape Cod Regional Transit Authority, runs along U.S. 6 with up to

1: Eastham's windmill **2:** Nauset Light Beach on a sunny summer day **3:** the Captain Edward Penniman House in Eastham

1
2
3
Penniman House

0.75-mile deviations for prescheduled pick-ups, with official stops at the Salt Pond Visitors Center and several other locations. Disembark at Nauset Regional High School and you will be within walking distance of Nauset Light Beach.

WELLFLEET

Wellfleet, once the home port for one of the largest cod fleets in 19th-century New England and a top oyster producer for over 40 years, is now more an enclave for retirees, writers, and psychiatrists than fishmongers. Most visitors, anchored by the more extensive accommodations in neighboring Provincetown or Orleans, know only of Wellfleet's ocean beaches, if they know the town at all, but those who do make the short detour from the highway to the bay will find a pleasantly becalmed community of small art galleries, a working pier, and almost no T-shirt shops.

Instead of competing with the motel rooms and retail capacity of its neighbors, Wellfleet prefers to be an oasis for the long-term rental crowd, with restaurants and shops sprinkled among old houses and town offices on narrow winding streets.

While Wellfleet had some early ups and downs in fishing, shipbuilding, and coastal trading, its lasting fame has come from its oysters. The foot-long specimens gathered by Native Americans—so plentiful that Champlain named the harbor after them when he charted Wellfleet waters in 1606—were gone before the American Revolution, but imported stock kept Wellfleet synonymous with oysters well into the Victorian era (which seems appropriate for a town whose namesake is an English village known for its bivalves). Virtual monopoly over New England's supply of this alleged aphrodisiac was attained in the middle decades of the 1800s, abetted by the newly arrived railroad, fast schooners, and fussy tycoons who could afford to be particular about their Wellfleets on the half-shell. The oysters' popularity was such that by 1870 as many as 40 vessels were engaged in ferrying Virginia seed to the Outer Cape for proper upbringing. Chesapeake's partisans may choose to focus on this Southern pedigree, but chefs and gastronomes claim Wellfleet's water imparts agreeable and incomparable flavor to its shellfish. A deadly parasite known as the oyster drill devastated the industry in the early 1900s, but renewed interest in aquaculture may restore the Wellfleet *Crassostrea virginica* to its lost throne.

Songs of praise for the oyster aside, the town was no slouch in the fishing industry back in the days when cod and mackerel outnumbered tourists. A few working boats still exist, along with plenty of good clam-digging mudflats (required permits are sold at the Town Pier), but these days Wellfleet is better known for its cluster of art galleries and pottery studios than for what it catches from the sea. Fortunately, despite shifting demographics, the town retains some of the look and feel of a place in which mending nets is more important than peddling knickknacks—a true anachronism on the Cape.

The town center is within earshot of the First Congregational Church: Listen carefully whenever its bells chime, and perhaps you'll figure out how to use "ship's time." According to *Ripley's Believe It or Not,* this is the only town clock in the world that uses this two-, four-, six-, and eight-bell system for marking the hours.

Uncle Tim's Bridge, a Wellfleet landmark named for a shop owner from the 1800s, was restored from disrepair in 2008. It crosses scenic **Duck Creek,** connecting Commercial Street with Cannon Hill. It's a popular stop for birders, hikers, and photographers.

Great Island

Thanks to the continual reshaping of the Outer Cape, this former island has developed a link to the hilly shore west of Wellfleet's village center, and as a result has become one of the more exceptional hiking spots in the National Seashore. Since walking the length of the island can easily take a full afternoon, visitors generally enjoy great solitude even on the most frenzied summer holiday weekends. It's a good place for bird-watching and an excellent spot to play amateur naturalist, like Thoreau did. The farthest part of the trail, out to Jeremy Point, gets submerged at high tide; know when this occurs, or be prepared to do some wading or swimming if it's a moon tide. Since summer's prevailing southwesterly winds can be brisk and unabated, extended wading isn't as pleasant as you might think, so plan ahead and be careful—it's easy to misjudge how quickly the tide can rise. The National Seashore visitors centers can help plan an outing, or you can join Park Service rangers for their free guided tours in season; call the Salt Pond Visitors Center (508/255-3421) or visit www.nps.gov/caco for a schedule.

Marconi Station

In 1903, President Theodore Roosevelt sent greetings to King Edward VII of England via the magic of Guglielmo Marconi's wireless telegraph—a historic event made possible by an enormous set of radio masts erected two years earlier at this Wellfleet cliff. The antennae are long gone—coastal erosion has undermined the site, although a couple of the concrete anchor posts remain at the cliff's edge—but a small pavilion managed by the National Seashore holds a model, along with interpretive signs recalling the facility and explaining the scientific achievement it represented. Here also is the trailhead for the National Seashore's Atlantic White Cedar Swamp Trail, an easy 45-minute ramble through an ecosystem more typical of the wetlands along the southern New England coast than the Cape's well-drained, sandier glacial moraine. Along with the towering native pines, the rot-resistant white cedars were aggressively harvested by European settlers as building material. Imagine the specimens along this trail replaced by mammoth trees five feet wide, and you'll appreciate what the colonists and Native Americans saw when they came here.

Numerous ships have been wrecked on the shoals off this stretch of shore, but none as famous as the *Whydah*, a pirate ship that sank here in 1717. "Black Sam" Bellamy and over 100 of his crew washed up dead, but no treasure was recovered until 1985, when salvager Barry Clifford located the first of the ship's artifacts. You can see some of the millions of dollars' worth of recovered coinage and hardware in South Yarmouth at the Expedition Whydah museum.

Wellfleet Bay Wildlife Sanctuary

Wellfleet Bay Wildlife Sanctuary

Salt marsh, ponds, and moors, home to numerous species of terrestrial and marine animals, are part of the landscape found within the Massachusetts Audubon Society's **Wellfleet Bay Wildlife Sanctuary** (291 State Hwy./U.S. 6, at West Rd., 508/349-2615, www.massaudubon.org, 8:30am-5pm daily late May-mid-Oct., 8:30am-5pm Tues.-Sun. mid-Oct.-late May, trails 7:30am-dusk daily year-round, adults $5, seniors and ages 2-12 $3), whose entrance and parking are located off U.S. 6 just north of the Eastham-Wellfleet town line. Turtles, horseshoe crabs, migratory and nesting birds, bats, and owls are among the denizens of the sanctuary's 1,000 acres, which include what was once part of President Grover Cleveland's favorite duck-hunting habitat. Brush up on your wetland ecology at the visitors center, or join one of the **guided walks** or **bird-watching programs** scheduled during the busiest months of the year (prepaid reservations required). More active events are also sponsored, such as snorkeling around the bay in search of crabs and snails, twilight canoeing, and various off-site excursions to places like the Pleasant Bay estuary south of Orleans. All require advance registration; costs run about $20 or more, depending on the program, with a discount for members.

Beaches

Between the third weekend in June and Labor Day, most of Wellfleet's 10 saltwater beaches require a beach sticker ($30 daily, $65 for 3 days, $100 per week, $325 for the season), available to visitors with proof of Wellfleet lodging from the booth at the end of Commercial Street in the Town Pier parking lot. Exceptions include three of the five long backside beaches—**Marconi, White Crest,** and **Cahoon Hollow** (parking $15 in season)—and the still free **Mayo Beach** along Kendrick Avenue near the Town Pier. Due to the increased chance of collisions with swimmers, those with personal watercraft such as windsurfers, kite-boarders, and surfers are asked to stay outside the areas that are lifeguarded or otherwise prohibited. The first three beaches, all on the same stretch of Atlantic-facing coastline, are nearly identical except for ever-shifting sandbars and cliffscapes. Marconi currently offers the only high-tide surf break; however, this is subject to change.

Permit or not, parking is never guaranteed—and yes, you will get ticketed if you ignore the "No Parking" signs. If this seems harsh, remember that much of Wellfleet is a National Park or private property. You wouldn't want someone parking on your front lawn or backyard at home, so be respectful of people who live here and have to contend with this kind of thing daily—they're not even on vacation. Since parking restrictions don't have to be posted in rural areas, confirm where it's safe to park when buying your beach sticker.

Sports and Recreation

Gull Pond, one of the prime Wellfleet kettle ponds, offers clear sand and good visibility, and is large enough to support (stocked) trout and a variety of other freshwater fish like pickerel and bass. Swimming is lovely, and a variety of boats (windsurfers, Sunfish, and paddleboats) can be rented from **Jack's Boat Rental** (U.S. 6 and Cahoon Hollow Rd., 508/349-9808, www.jacksboatrental.com, 9am-4pm daily June-Sept., kayaks $55 per day, SUPs $65 per day, Sunfish $270 for 3 days).

Festivals

One of Wellfleet's biggest yearly events is the **Wellfleet OysterFest** (508/349-3499, http://wellfleetspat.org, weekend after Columbus Day), held in mid-October and dedicated to promoting sustainable shellfishing. This two-day extravaganza draws so many people that it clogs the roads all over Cape Cod—expect live music, refreshments and alcohol, nonprofits with displays and info, costumes and characters, and (of course!) oysters. There's even a "Shuckoff" competition to see who can shuck

The Last Drive-In Show

the Wellfleet Drive-In Theatre

Drive-in movies have become an endangered species across the country, but even more so in New England, where spiraling real-estate values have sped the demise of many once-memorable drive-ins. Luckily for Cape visitors, one fine local example not only still survives but thrives: the **Wellfleet Drive-In Theatre** (51 U.S. 6, South Wellfleet, 508/349-7176, www.wellfleetcinemas.com, adults $15, seniors and ages 4-11 $12, under age 4 free), right beside the highway at the Eastham-Wellfleet town line.

Built in 1957, the Wellfleet shows first-run double features nightly almost year-round, rain or shine. Come summer, you can spend your entire day here: Play mini golf on the 18-hole course; dine on burgers, fish-and-chips, and ice cream at the **Dairy Bar & Grill** (508/349-0278); and browse the giant **flea market** (508/349-0541, 8am-3pm Wed.-Thurs., Sat.-Sun., and holidays) that takes over the parking lot during the day. Finally, after the sun has fully set, park in front of the giant screen, tune your car radio to the FM stereo sound system (door-mounted mono speakers are still available on request too), and enjoy the show.

Be sure to come early—not only to avoid hunting for a spot in the dark, but also to see the preshow animated countdown, a piece of retro 1950s Americana almost worth the price of admission by itself.

the fastest. Tickets often sell out, so get yours in advance if you want to join the fun.

Entertainment

Wellfleet Harbor Actors Theater (WHAT, box office 508/349-9428, www.what.org) brings wonderful and award-winning theater to people who would otherwise have to go to Boston. Guild actors, great plays, and many televised dramas (such as *Downton Abbey*) are all performed right here at the WHAT, accessible to anyone in the Lower Cape. The company also sets up a tent in summer for children's shows.

Shopping

Besides more than a dozen galleries—almost all of which are within the triangle formed by Main Street, Commercial Street, and Holbrook Avenue—there are a couple of interesting bookstores; shops stocking items like silk kimonos or Afrocentric art, such as **Off Center + Eccentricity** (Main St., 508/349-7554, www.offcenterwellfleet.com, 11am-4pm); and an exceptional fish market, **Hatch's** (behind Town Hall, 508/349-2810, www.hatchsfishmarket.com, 10am-6pm daily mid-May-June and early Sept.-mid-Sept., 10am-7pm daily July-Aug.).

Food

While a location a step or two off the beaten track has its advantages at the height of summer, off-season it almost guarantees everything is shut tight for the duration. Much of the Outer Cape's dining options disappear after Labor Day, and many more close shop by the end of October.

Moby Dick's (3225 U.S. 6, 508/349-9795, http://mobydicksrestaurant.com, 11:30am-9:30pm daily mid-May-Oct., $18-28, most seafood market price) is one of the summer-only options, a popular stop going to or from P-town that's right on U.S. 6, shortly before the Truro town line. Get big platters of fried fish or seafood, skewered kabobs of blackened shrimp, decent clam chowder, or just a good salad at this casual, bustling eatery. Tipplers take note: this is a BYOB place—bring your own alcohol, and Moby's staff will provide ice and glasses for you.

Closer to Eastham is ★ **The Block and Tackle** (545 U.S. 6, 774/383-3967, www.theblockandtackle.com, 4pm-8pm Wed.-Sun., $18-30) in South Wellfleet, a bit north of the Wellfleet Drive-In Theatre. The hours vary seasonally, but the smoker is cooking up great meats, sausage, and there's buttermilk fried chicken, too, and Cape Cod-themed sauces such as "Whydah Gold" or "Mashpee Mud."

To judge by the plain brown Formica-topped tables in unpretentious elbow-to-elbow rows inside ★ **Mac's Shack** (91 Commercial St., 508/349-6333, www.macsseafood.com, 11:30pm-10pm Wed.-Mon. late May-mid-Oct., $19-32), a barnlike building with a big wooden dory on the roof, you might presume the menu is simply the typical fried and broiled seafood found up and down the Cape. Such traditional fare is indeed available, but the simple preparations showcase just how impeccably fresh the ingredients are. It's not as surprising when you find out that all the fish dishes at Mac's are sourced through the side of the business that runs three eponymous retail fish markets and a regional wholesale operation. The kitchen specials change frequently, and the sushi is generously cut and accompanied by a small but well-chosen selection of cold sakes. The reasonably priced sashimi platter alone is worth a pilgrimage.

Outside Provincetown, ★ **The Wicked Oyster** (50 Main St., 508/349-3455, www.thewickedo.com, 7:30am-noon and 4:30pm-8pm daily late-May-early-Sept., call for off-season hours, dinner $18-37) is about as cool as Cape Cod gets. The casual spot jumps with young well-dressed patrons supping on scallion-infused seafood stew and spinach-and-scallop salads.

PB Boulangerie (15 Lecount Hollow Rd., 508/349-1600, http://pbboulangeriebistro.com, 7am-7pm Wed.-Sun., bistro 5pm-11pm Wed.-Sun.) sets the gold standard for meals as well as morning pastries and coffee in the Wellfleet area. The breads are every bit as good as in France. Artisanal loaves, which sell out, make a great take-home breakfast, but you can eat on the patio as well.

Accommodations

Wellfleet has scores and scores of weekly rental cottages and kitchen-equipped efficiency units, about a dozen B&Bs (most with 1-2 guest rooms), and half a dozen motels, all of which are along U.S. 6. Moderate room rates are fairly abundant in these parts, although minimum-stay requirements are as widespread as everywhere else. Before mid-June and after early September, most motels go straight into their inexpensive off-season rates—ideal for the budget traveler. The **Wellfleet Chamber of Commerce** (508/349-2510, www.wellfleetchamber.com, 10am-4pm Mon.-Fri.) will happily provide you with a brochure that lists every one. Call to request a copy or drop by their seasonal information booth (9am-5pm daily summer, 10am-4pm Sat.-Sun. spring and fall) along U.S. 6 in South Wellfleet, beside the northern end of the Rail Trail.

Among the motels on U.S. 6, South Wellfleet's **Even'tide Resort Motel & Cottages** (650 U.S. 6, 800/368-0007 in Massachusetts or 508/349-3410, www.eventidemotel.com, late Apr.-Oct., $205 d July-Aug., $100 d off-season) is both attractive and reasonably priced. Located near mile marker 98, it's also right on the Cape Cod Rail Trail, which makes it possible to get to local beaches without messing with either highway traffic or resident parking restrictions. In-room mini fridges and all the usual motel amenities are standard, plus there's a 60-foot indoor heated pool. A variety of 2- to 4-bedroom cottages ($1,300-3,000 per week), some with housekeeping, some without, are also available in the woods at the back of the property; rates vary depending on size and season.

For something more like a country inn, with tasteful furnishings, claw-foot tubs, white bedspreads, and amber pine floors, check out the 1813 **The Wagner at Duck Creek** (70 Main St., 508/349-9333, www.thewagneratduckcreek.com, with private bath $240 d late June-Labor Day, less in spring and fall), just off U.S. 6. Overlooking Duck Pond and under 0.5 miles from the center of town, this breezily informal place has its own tavern and is next to two restaurants.

If you're looking for a true getaway, seek out **Gull Cottage B&B** (50 Steele Rd., 508/349-6621, www.gullcottagewellfleet.com, $300 d, 3-5 night minimum), at the end of a two-track carriage road. You'll have your own studio apartment, lovingly furnished and nestled near some of the Cape's most stunning kettle ponds. Their private beach on Gull Pond offers one of the nicest freshwater swims anywhere, and Higgins Pond is perfect for canoeing, fishing, or just finding cool critters in the mud and reeds. The hosts are gracious and helpful, and while the studio is modern (thanks to a renovation of the upper floor of the boathouse, with a gas heating stove and a kitchenette), the main house is over 200 years old. This is a classic example of a Cape Cod house, much of it is unchanged since the 1700s, a rarity these days. It's not hard to imagine Henry David Thoreau wandering these very woodland glades—he actually stayed just across the pond during his visit to this then-desolate land.

Camping

Are you a tenter tired of ending up sandwiched between a pair of patio furniture collectors equipped with enough lanterns and charcoal lighter fluid to outshine a Texas oil refinery? Relief is at hand at **Wellfleet Hollow State Campground** (180 Old King's Hwy., 508/349-3007, massdcrcamping.reserveamerica.com, late-May-mid-Oct.), east of U.S. 6 in South Wellfleet. Located in pine woods a few minutes' ride north of the Cape Cod Rail Trail, most of the 150 sites are strictly for tenters and pop-up trailers. Better yet, they provide wholly separate areas for families, groups, couples, and singles and young couples. Reservations are required.

Prime camping is also possible at the **Wellfleet Bay Wildlife Sanctuary** (508/349-2615, http://massaudubon.com, July-mid-Sept, $330/week), though these limited spots are usually booked up to a year in advance.

Gull Cottage B&B in Wellfleet

Shipwrecks

"'Who lives in that house?' I inquired. 'Three widows,' was the reply."

Henry David Thoreau, *Cape Cod*

As evidenced by Thoreau's quote, throughout its recorded history, Cape Cod has been a dangerous place for mariners. On the journey from Europe, a quarter-point error on the compass in a dead-reckoned course to Boston could put a sailing vessel up against the shoals along the back of the Cape. Before the availability of the mass-produced chronometers that enabled ships to accurately plot their longitude, a course from the southern Atlantic to Boston was well-nigh impossible; instead, to avoid running afoul on the shallow rocks and sandbars scattered around the entrance to Nantucket Sound, vessels had to head toward Long Island and then creep up the coast around the Cape. Bad weather also greatly contributed to the litter of wrecks, with thick fogs that robbed navigators of their bearings and wind-lashed seas that could drive ships aground, if not swamp them outright. An 1864 survey identified nearly 500 wrecks in Cape waters during the 17-year period prior to the Civil War. An even greater number were recorded during the last two decades of the 19th century.

Local fishing fleets have historically been the hardest-hit victims of the weather. The region's 19th-century annals are filled with fierce storms that made widows by the score. The October Gale of 1841, in which 57 fishermen from Truro alone were lost, is among the more infamous examples. Another, the Portland Gale of 1898, was responsible for sinking hundreds of vessels all around the Cape over three days.

Of all the Cape's threats to navigation, Peaked Hill Bar (PEEK-id), about a mile northwest of Truro's back shore, has been the worst. It has claimed more ships than perhaps any other single spot along the Atlantic coast outside of Cape Hatteras. One of its most notable wrecks was that of the HMS *Somerset* in 1778; this was the same British man-of-war that helped blockade Boston's harbor before the Revolution. (Paul Revere was ferried across Boston Harbor right under her nose, so to speak, on that April night in 1775 when the pair of lights in the Old North Church steeple signaled the marching orders of the British Redcoats.) Every few decades, shifts in the sand open up the old ship's grave and let the hull mutely remind beachcombers of the dangers in these waters. There's also a 19th-century ironclad, the *Francis,* that still bares her bones every now and again.

Now that Cape Cod no longer sends the greater share of its able-bodied citizens to labor at sea, the human toll of lost ships and their crews is not nearly as grim as in Thoreau's day. Technology has also helped make navigation safer in fogs and storms. But the risks aren't wholly erased, as high-profile marine accidents over the years have clearly demonstrated. In 1994, for instance, a cruise ship ran aground in Nantucket's South Channel. And in 2003 an oil barge headed to the Cape Cod Canal struck a rock in Buzzards Bay, causing one of the worst oil spills in New England history.

Getting There and Around

Wellfleet is 15 miles (20 minutes) south of Provincetown, 6 miles (10 minutes) south of Truro center, and 8 miles (11 minutes) north of Eastham.

Wellfleet is served four times daily in summer and twice daily in winter by the **Peter Pan bus** (www.peterpan.com), which stops in South Wellfleet at the Marconi Seashore entrance and in Wellfleet center at Bank and Commercial Streets, right near the town green.

Flex bus service (www.capecodrta.org) from the Cape Cod Regional Transit Authority runs along U.S. 6 with up to 0.75-mile deviations for prescheduled pickups, with official stops at Wellfleet Center and Blackfish Variety at Blackfish Creek. Unfortunately, there are no regular stops at any of the Cape Cod National Seashore beaches, which means you'll need to walk, bike, or take a car at least part of the way.

TRURO

When regular visitors to the Cape think of Truro, the image that usually comes to mind is of Beach Point, the nearly treeless low-lying stretch of the bay-side shore visible from the highway. More precisely, the image is of **Days' Cottages** on the beach, classic green-shuttered, white-clapboard, Depression-era rental cottages all in a row right above the tide. These are the most photographed lodgings in the state, some say.

The most sparsely populated town on the Cape, with just over 2,000 year-round residents, Truro is also the most varied topographically. From the Pamet River valley, barely above sea level, it rises to over 120 feet and then back down to its narrow neck in the north, again barely above sea level. In addition to its prominent headlands towering over its backside beaches, Truro has the most visible of the Cape's five major dune systems (best viewed from the Pilgrim Heights picnic area, but also clearly seen from U.S. 6 along Pilgrim Lake in North Truro). The sculpting force of the wind is clearly evident in their form, the centers scooped out as if by a giant bucket. These parabolic dunes also demonstrate the continuing evolution of the Outer Cape landscape as they slowly shift west, invading the waters of Pilgrim Lake.

Truro's splendid isolation and striking seascapes have been a major attraction for artists for much of the past century. Before World War II, artists built a colony of shacks in North Truro's dunes, some of which still remain—preserved only as a historic relic of that era, they are also made available to working artists today under a residency program administered by partners of the National Park Service.

★ Highland Light

Truro's most prominent attraction is Highland Light, also referred to as the Cape Cod Light, built high atop what was once known as the Clay Pounds in North Truro (not to be confused with Nauset Light at Nauset Light Beach in Eastham). Sitting 123 feet above the waves, its light visible for 23 miles out to sea, this important beacon was first lit in 1798, warning mariners away from one of the Atlantic coast's most hazardous shipping lanes: Over one-quarter of all the wrecks on the Eastern seaboard have occurred off the coast of Cape Cod. Moved and modernized 60 years later, the lighthouse was again threatened by erosion in the late 1980s, having lost over two-thirds of its original 10-acre clay hill to the ravages of waves and storms. Local fund-raising to save the structure resulted in the 1996 move to its present location. Although still operated as an automated U.S. Coast Guard aid to navigation, the property is maintained by the National Park Service and the **Truro Historical Society** (508/487-3397, www.trurohistorical.org), which provides access to the very top of the **light** (508/487-1121, 10am-5:30pm daily mid-May-Oct., $7)—though you must be willing to climb its steep winding stairs. This is the only functioning lighthouse on the Cape that's regularly and completely open to the public. The former keeper's house at the base contains the society's gift shop and displays photographs of the 1996 relocation effort.

Back near the parking lot is the society's highly eclectic **Highland House Museum** (10am-4:30pm Mon.-Sat., 1pm-4:30pm Sun. June-Sept., $8 adults, $7 seniors & students, children under 5 free), in what was once a summer hotel on the railroad line to off-Cape. While the lighthouse grounds are free and accessible year-round, separate admission fees are charged for Highland House and to climb up the lighthouse.

Surrounding the lighthouse is **Highland Links** (508/487-9201, www.highlandlinkscapecod.com, $35 for 9 holes, $65 for 18 holes summer), an 1892 descendant of the rough Scottish links.

Beaches

Of the town's several beaches, only those belonging to the National Seashore are open to nonresident day use: **Head of the Meadow Beach** on the Atlantic and **Corn Hill Beach** (parking $15 at both) on Cape Cod Bay. Head of the Meadow is a great spot for seeing seals (which come out on the sand to rest; do not disturb them). Corn Hill has lovely views of Provincetown across the bay.

A couple of hard-to-find little historical plaques testify to the town's small but vital part in the saga of the Pilgrims' brief stay on the Cape at the end of 1620. One is at Corn Hill, namesake for the nearby National Seashore beach, where the hungry immigrants pilfered a Native American stash of buried corn. The other marks Pilgrim Spring, where they first found freshwater, although since the spring was only located in 1920 during the town tercentenary, its authenticity is a matter of trust.

Sports and Recreation

FISHING CHARTER

One of the Cape's many fishing-charter options, and one that some say is the best, **Reel Deal** (508/487-3767, www.fishreeldeal.com; $550 half-day, $925 all-day, tuna trip $1,300) offers custom charters to suit any angler's needs. If catching your own striped bass or tuna is on the agenda, you'll want to check here first.

Food

Perhaps the best meal in Truro proper, **Blackfish** (17 Truro Center Rd., 508/349-3399, 5pm-10pm daily, $26-40) is easy to miss because there's almost no signage. However, those who persevere and find it are in for a treat. The copper-clad tables are a unique touch, and the food is fantastic. Pretty much anything you choose will be delicious, so dive in and enjoy. They also operate a lovely food truck, the Crush Pad, currently parked at the Truro Vineyards winery.

Savory & Sweet Escape (316 U.S. 6, 508/487-2225, 7am-8pm daily Memorial Day-Labor Day, closed Sun. Sept.-late-May, pizzas from $10) is a nice spot, and while pizzas are a bit pricey compared to other parts of the Cape, they're tasty. If you factor in the time and gas required to head to Hyannis or elsewhere for dinner, it's a steal to just grab a pie here.

Nearby, **Bass Tavern** (5 Great Hollow Rd., 508/487-1740, www.whitmanhouse.com, 5pm-8pm Thurs.-Mon., $11-25) at the Whitman House Restaurant is child-friendly, with a casual atmosphere in one of the area's old historic homes; the burgers and steaks are excellent.

Accommodations

Truro has plenty of small motels that look retro because they've barely changed since the days of Buddy Holly, although more and more of them are being used as housing for low-wage seasonal workers in Provincetown's service economy. It also has Spartan cabin and cottage colonies on the highway and all along Beach Point, but most of these are for weekly rentals only, with prime summer weeks often booked a year in advance.

The area's only noncamping budget option is Hostelling International's **Truro Hostel** (end of North Pamet Rd., 508/349-3889 or 888/901-2086, www.hiusa.org, mid-June-early Sept., dorm $45 members, $48 nonmembers). Take the Truro Center-Pamet Roads exit from U.S. 6, and stay to the east of the highway. The hostel is not convenient to any local transit: Both the seasonal local bus shuttle from Provincetown and the P&B bus from Hyannis stop two miles away near the Truro post office, and Provincetown's ferries are a windblown 10-mile trek to the north. But this 42-bed hostel, a former ocean-side Coast Guard station in the Pamet River valley, packs a full house throughout its short 11-week season, and no wonder—it's a two-minute walk from beautiful Ballston Beach, where parking is restricted to residents with beach stickers. It also has plenty of common space, a decent kitchen, and superb second-floor views from the women's dorm. Men share two basement rooms. Have your credit card handy when you call or visit the website. There are no private rooms for couples here, and no family rooms unless space is available. The registration office is open 8am-11am and 3pm-10pm daily.

Horizons Beach Resort (190 Shore Rd.,

Wining and Dining in Truro

Truro Vineyards' iconic welcome is visible from the highway.

Truro Vineyards (11 Shore Rd./Rte. 6A, 508/487-6200, http://trurovineyardsofcapecod.com, 11am-5pm Mon.-Sat., noon-5pm Sun. May-Nov., tasting $15, includes keepsake wine glass) is a lovely family-friendly spot to stop in and spend an hour or a whole afternoon. The relaxed atmosphere, great food, and lovely tastings and tours make it a fun place for anyone heading down the Cape. A gourmet food truck offers guests great eats, there are plenty of lounge chairs to relax in while you imbibe, and in season the tours are held every 30 minutes—$15 includes gustation of 5 different wines, including their signature Cape Cod and Lighthouse. There are tours of the winery as well. Friendly dogs, a low-key atmosphere, and a lovely yard with one of the Cape's oldest mulberry trees add to the ambiance.

Also on the premises is a boutique distillery, featuring the award winning Twenty Boat rum—a lovely amber-colored rum well worth trying after the tour.

508/487-0042, www.horizonsbeach.com, $159-275) has several different units, some just steps away from the beach. All include access to a private beach and their swimming pool, so it's a nice option for those with kids who plan to be in the water all day. The shorefront unit offers amazing sunset views, with a big private deck that seems to be spilling right into Cape Cod Bay. **Topmast Motel & Resort** (217 Shore Rd., 800/917-0024, www.topmastresort.com, $70-185) has motel-style guest rooms, separate cottages ($110-2,200), and actual vacation homes ($230-5,900). Almost all the guest rooms face the ocean, so water lovers will have a lovely view. The units are equipped with private decks, fridges, microwaves, and sitting areas. Many rooms have a two-night or longer minimum stay.

Camping

Truro is about as far from city lights as you can get on the Cape, so clear night skies are always filled with stars. The easiest way to stargaze is just to wander down the beach until you're by yourself. On good days, the Milky Way will seem close enough to touch. You'll certainly be able to appreciate the constellations at the **North of Highland Camping Area** (52 Head of the Meadow Rd., 508/487-1191, www.capecodcamping.com, mid-May-mid-Sept., $48 for 1-2 people, $15 each additional adult, $5 per child), 0.2 miles from

Head of the Meadow Beach on Truro's back shore. Amid the gnarled pitch pine woods are over 200 sites for tents and pop-ups. Peace and quiet is the guideline here, since there are no electrical hookups, no motor homes, no motorcycles, no open fires, and no pets.

Slightly south is **Adventure Bound Camping Resort Cape Cod** (46 Highland Rd., 508/487-1847, www.abcamping.com/abcapecod, year-round, $99 summer, $69 shoulder season), also known as North Truro Camping Area, located between U.S. 6 and Highland Light, which favors RVs with its electrical and water hookups and free cable TV. **Horton's Camping Resort** (71 S. Highland Rd., 508/487-1220 or 800/252-7705, www.abcamping.com/abcapecod, May-mid-Oct., $59 d, $15 each additional adult, $5 per child) is also part of Adventure Bound Camping, so the two campgrounds are both under the same umbrella. Horton's 220 sites include a generous number of tent sites as well as some sites reserved for campers without children. There's also a fully accessible restroom for visitors with disabilities. Reservations are essential during peak season (June 15-Sept. 15), and a three-night minimum is required on holiday weekends. Both are located between Highland Light and the Federal Aviation Administration's big transatlantic air traffic control radomes east of U.S. 6; turn at the blue "Camping" sign about 5.5 miles north of the Truro-Wellfleet line and proceed another mile. June-mid-October, both North Truro and Horton's campgrounds are connected to downtown Provincetown and Herring Cove Beach, as well as to the market in the center of Truro, by the **Provincetown Shuttle,** a seasonal $2-per-ride route of the **CCRTA** (800/352-7155, www.capecodrta.org). The camping area is about one mile from U.S. 6, where the shuttle bus can be flagged down.

Getting There and Around

Truro is 6 miles (9 minutes) north of Wellfleet and 10 miles (13 minutes) south of Provincetown. U.S. 6 is the only connector for all the Outer Cape towns.

Truro, like much of the Cape, has little in the way of public transportation. The good news is that it's small enough that some of the tourist areas are available to anyone with a bicycle.

The **Peter Pan bus** (www.peterpan.com) has two pickup and drop-off spots, one at the Truro Post Office, the other at Dutra's store (North Truro). Only four buses run each day in summer; in winter it dwindles to two.

The Cape Cod Regional Transit Authority runs the **Flex bus** (www.capecodrta.org) along the U.S. 6 corridor from Orleans to Provincetown, with up to a 0.75-mile deviation on either side.

Provincetown

Clinging to the inside shore of the outermost arm of Cape Cod, contemporary P-town is a salty mix of tourists, artists, fisherfolk, and a thriving gay and lesbian community that gives it the nickname "San Francisco of the East." Long before marriage equality was a hot-button issue, Provincetown was a spot where lovers of all kinds could find acceptance and coexist. Rainbow flags are flown proudly here, and it's not unusual to see singing drag queens on roller skates along Commercial Street. The Gay Pride Parade draws so many spectators to this curious tip of the peninsula that traffic slows to a crawl all over Cape Cod.

P-town is a place where the population mushrooms by a factor of 12 between the off-season calm and the high-season carnival. Here is where the *Mayflower* Pilgrims first came ashore, plundered the Native Americans' caches of corn, and then left for the mainland in search of an adequate source of freshwater. Subsequent centuries saw a

Downtown Provincetown

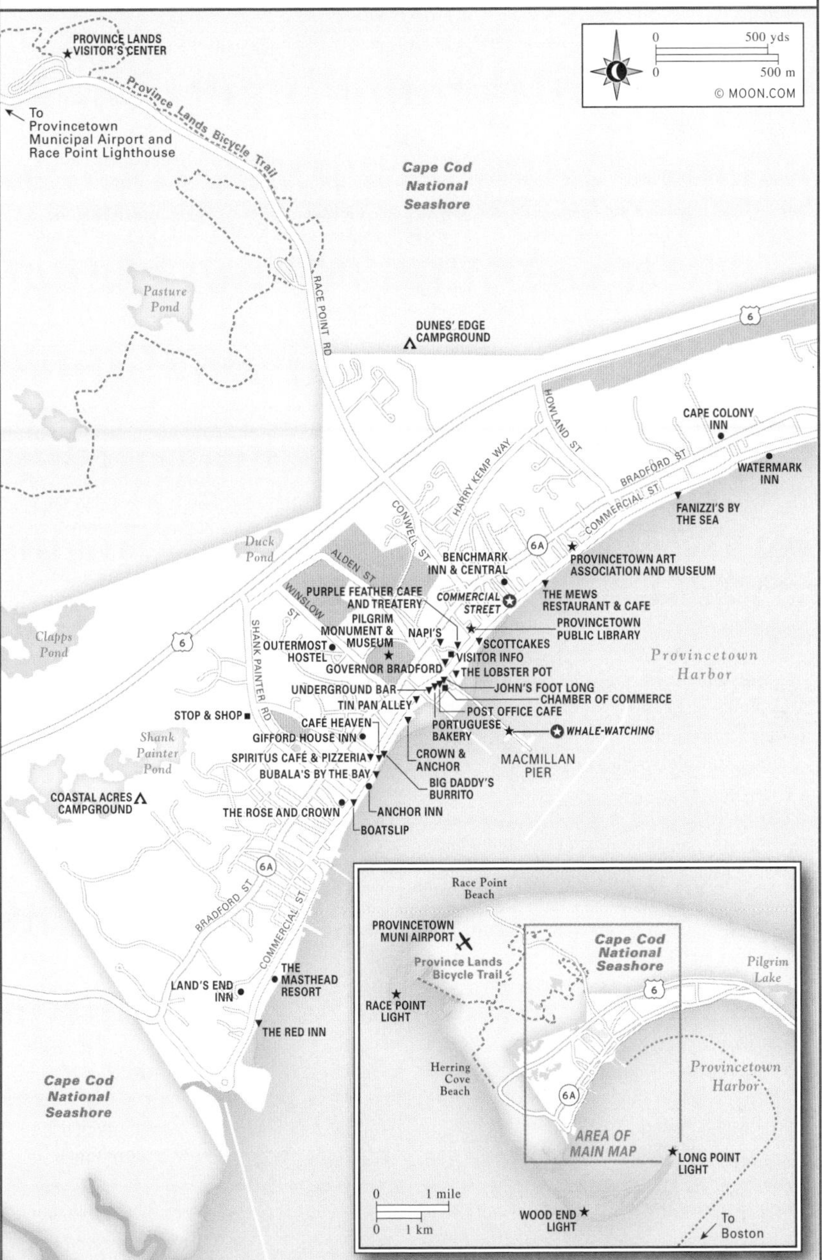

Two Days in Provincetown

From Boston, you can take the ferry to Provincetown, getting two full days to experience the town with one overnight stay.

DAY 1

Arrive in Provincetown Saturday morning, and have lunch at **The Lobster Pot** or another spot on **Commercial Street** that strikes your fancy. Spend a few hours **gallery hopping, people watching,** and perhaps grab a tasty **ice cream** or **fried dough** to munch on. Check into **Land's End Inn,** your hotel for the night. Then get ready for more time on a boat: Head to **MacMillan Wharf** and go on a **sunset whale watch.** Unless it's foggy, you're almost guaranteed to see these magnificent leviathans of the deep feeding, spy-hopping, sometimes even breaching. Come back as the sun sinks down into Cape Cod Bay and eat a late dinner at **Napi's.** Then meander back along Commercial Street, checking out the nightlife scene—the bar at **The Mews Restaurant & Cafe** is always hopping.

DAY 2

Start your day early with **coffee** and something to nibble on as you watch the morning happen from the grounds of Land's End. Then head to **Café Heaven** for an amazing gourmet breakfast (or brunch, if you're a late riser!) before renting a bicycle and heading off for a beautiful pedal through the **Province Lands.** Get up close and personal with pine and beech forests, wild cranberry bogs, dunes, and marshes. This is some of the Cape's most iconic scenery; you won't regret taking it all in. If your calves aren't hurting, come back and visit the **Provincetown Monument** for some spectacular selfies and gorgeous bayside views. Finish with a tasty cupcake at **Scottcakes** (take a few for the ferry ride) or a platter of sizzling fried scallops from **John's Foot Long,** then wait for the ferry, feeding the eager seagulls with a few leftover fries.

hardscrabble fishing village take hold amid the dunes—a place where the bargain cost of living and beautiful light proved a big draw to painters and playwrights in the decades before World War II.

In 1901, Charles Hawthorne, fascinated by the Mediterranean feel of the dilapidated harbor village and all its Portuguese fisherfolk, opened an art school here. Greenwich Village Bohemians followed, a fashionable flock that included the likes of John Reed and Eugene O'Neill, whose Provincetown Players made theater history. John Dos Passos, e. e. cummings, Edward Hopper, Sinclair Lewis, Jackson Pollock, Mark Rothko, and Norman Mailer are some of the other luminaries who have lived here at one time or another.

Because of its proximity to the Marine Sanctuary of Stellwagen Bank, due north, it's also one of the best places to depart on a whale-watching cruise, and boats often see humpbacks breaching, feeding, spy-hopping, or waving their flippers almost as if they're saying hello to their smaller mammalian cousins. Seeing whales is all but guaranteed, the only "if" being visibility. If it's sunny out, go; if it's foggy, pick another day.

SIGHTS

★ Commercial Street

Running the length of town, Commercial Street is made for strolling: One lane wide, with only one sidewalk, it all but requires pedestrians to take command of the road, in turn forcing vehicles to slow almost to a walker's pace. Lovingly tended gardens, gallery windows, and architectural variety ensure that no two blocks are alike. Cape Cod Bay plays hide-and-seek between the houses, sometimes bringing walkers up short in their tracks at the sudden sight of a momentarily perfect composition of light, water, and moored yachts. Discreet, nearly hidden artifacts—the marker for Eugene O'Neill's house, a plaque commemorating the fish shed-turned-theater where O'Neill's playwriting career was launched, the private garden of allegorical creatures and deities, Chiam Gross's potbellied sculpture *Tourists*—are only ever noticed by pedestrians. In short, this is a town where walking one mile merely whets the appetite for one more, and where both may be traced and retraced twice a day for a week without ever growing stale or predictable.

Pilgrim Monument and Provincetown Museum

Also known as the Provincetown Monument, this is the only place in town that combines both a figurative overview of local history and a literal overview of local geography: **Pilgrim Monument** and **Provincetown Museum** (High Pole Hill Rd., 508/487-1310 or 800/247-1620, www.pilgrim-monument.org, 9am-5pm daily Apr.-Nov., 9am-7pm daily late-May-early-Sept., adults $12, seniors and students $10, ages 4-12 $4, under age 4 free). The hill is off Bradford Street behind Town Hall; the iconic monument on top is visible from 40 miles away. Displays remind visitors that Provincetown, not Plymouth Rock, was where the Pilgrims spent their first five weeks in the New World, and modest exhibits range from a model of the original Provincetown Playhouse, which launched Eugene O'Neill's career, to artifacts gathered during the 15 arctic expeditions of native son Donald MacMillan. Take it as a gentle reminder that so-called history is almost invariably less a collection of facts than a point of view. A view that's indisputable is the one from atop the 255-foot granite tower rising over the museum, which in clear weather unequivocally makes up for the lack of an elevator.

Provincetown Art Association and Museum

P-town is chock-full of art, even without counting artist-run boutiques selling unique clothing, jewelry, cards, and other artifacts. Galleries range from experimental spaces to familiar storefronts featuring established local artists, and well-attended openings year-round demonstrate the vitality of the local visual arts. To check out both the deep roots of this community and its emerging new shoots, visit the **Provincetown Art Association and Museum** (PAAM, 460 Commercial St., 508/487-1750, www.paam.org, 11am-5pm or later summer, $10, free after 5pm Fri.) in the East End. Founded in 1914, PAAM has a large permanent collection representing both famous American artists who've worked in P-town over the decades as well as others who've lingered less forcefully in the annals of art history. Changing exhibitions drawing from this repository are staged throughout the year, mixed with exhibits of new work by local working artists.

Provincetown Public Library

Come view the 62-foot half-scale replica of the Grand Banks fishing schooner *Rose Dorothea*, its masts stretching up in to the vaulted ceiling of the landmark home of the **Provincetown Public Library** (356 Commercial St., 508/487-7094, http://provincetownlibrary.org, 10am-5pm Mon. and Fri., noon-8pm Tues. and Thurs., 10pm-8pm Wed., 10am-2pm Sat., 1pm-5pm Sun.), formerly a Methodist Episcopal church built in 1860. The 1907 winner of the regionally renowned Boston-Gloucester Fisherman's Race, the *Rose* provides a glimpse into P-town's long legacy as a commercial fishing port.

Come also for the excellent and free views of town from the top-floor reading areas, within the steeple of the former church; frequent events and a free Wi-Fi hotspot can be found here as well.

SPORTS AND RECREATION

The Province Lands

The **National Seashore Visitors Center** (Race Point Rd., 9am-5pm daily early May-late Oct., 9am-5pm Mon.-Fri. late Oct.-early May), northernmost of three, overlooks the Province Lands, whose name is a reminder of the Province of Massachusetts's explicit title to the area both before and after the town's 1727 incorporation. Now lightly wooded or covered in beach grass, the Province Lands' wind-driven dunes once upon a time threatened to bury the settlement at their watery margin. When the Pilgrims landed in 1620, they found "excellent black earth" when they probed with their shovels, "all wooded with oaks, pines, sassafras, juniper, birch, holly, vines, some ash, and walnut." In defiance of laws enacted as early as 1714 to save it, this tree cover was so thoroughly clear-cut by colonists that the topsoil blew away, freeing the sand to migrate toward the harbor. Two centuries after the Pilgrim landfall, Thoreau claimed there wasn't enough black earth to fill a flower pot, "and scarcely anything high enough to be called a tree." Efforts to stabilize the dunes were begun a generation prior to Thoreau's visits and continue to this day. Along with visitors center exhibits on the landscape's fragility, a variety of ranger-guided activities are scheduled throughout the summer, from beach walks and mountain-bike rides to talks at the **Old Harbor Life-Saving Station** on the back shore; call 508/487-1256 for a schedule. Staff dispense advice and interpretive brochures for trails in the vicinity. National Seashore information is available from the Race Point ranger station at the end of the road. Of particular interest is the weekly live demonstration of the breeches buoy lifesaving apparatus that saved thousands of sailors' lives before the advent of the modern Coast Guard. It takes place at the Old Harbor Life-Saving Station at Race Point Beach; days and times vary.

Most visitors to the Province Lands, like Cape visitors generally, come for the beaches. Mile after mile of coarse sand pounded by the long breakers of the open Atlantic Ocean make **Race Point Beach** a great spot for walking, bodysurfing, and just lazing under a summer sun. Walk far enough west and you'll reach **Race Point Light** (Race Point Beach, U.S. 6, 508/487-9930, www.racepointlighthouse.net), a short cast-iron tower whose steady white flash—now visible for some 11 miles at sea—has warned vessels away from the northern end of the infamous Peaked Hill Bars since 1876. Although its predecessor was undermined by storms, this is the only backside lighthouse not threatened by erosion—instead, P-town's beaches are actually the beneficiaries of sand swept up the coast from the south.

Right at the end of U.S. 6, close to town, is **Herring Cove Beach,** whose westerly orientation makes it the best place to watch the sun setting fire to the waters of Cape Cod Bay. When the sun is up, it's also a nice spot for swimming in gentle surf. Lifeguards are present and bathhouses are open at both beaches July-early September, when the National Seashore charges $20 for parking. The rest of the year, the beaches are free. While unofficial, the area near the rectangular section of the parking lot is a de facto gay beach, although any and all are welcome.

TOP EXPERIENCE

★ Whale-Watching

The southern edge of Stellwagen Bank, a prime feeding area for finback, northern right, minke, and humpback whales, happens to be just offshore of Provincetown's breakwater, making it a top destination for whale-watchers from mid-April through the end of October. Two different outfits offer the three- to four-hour excursions. At the start and finish of the season, you'll find just one or two trips a day, but by summer, operators run as many as nine daily departures from MacMillan Pier. Whale sightings are a sure bet except when it's foggy or visibility is otherwise poor, so plan on seeing some very good close-ups of these amazing animals. It's a special treat, something unique to the area that's always worth the trip. The **Dolphin Fleet of Provincetown Whale Watch** (508/240-3636 or 800/826-9300, www.whalewatch.com, adults $65,

1: a humpback whale feeding off Stellwagen Bank **2:** the Provincetown Monument **3:** Commercial Street

1
2
3
BLISS!
HAND MADE FROZEN YOGURT
PREMIUM SOFT ICE CREAM
FRESH FRUIT SMOOTHIES
PATIO
AMERICAN GRILL & COCKTAIL BAR
True Value
PIG

ages 5-12 $40) originated East Coast whale-watching in 1975 and stands out among local excursion operators for its use of naturalists from the local Center for Coastal Studies—one of New England's handful of cetacean research organizations.

Dune Tours

If you have the appropriate kind of vehicle (and no, a rental car doesn't count), it's possible to obtain an off-road vehicle permit ($50 for 7 days) for driving along the backshore, oversand driving corridor from the National Park Service at the Race Point ranger station. Alternatively, you can not only experience the scenery of the town's Atlantic coastline but also learn about its history and ecology by instead joining one of **Art's Dune Tours** (4 Standish St., 508/487-1950 or 800/894-1951, www.artsdunetours.com, 10am-sunset daily, adults $35, ages 6-11 $22). There's also a lovely sunset dune tour (adults $50, ages 6-11 $28).

NIGHTLIFE AND ENTERTAINMENT

No question about it, Provincetown is the Cape's best place to party, and people watchers will note that the character of Commercial Street shifts the moment dusk hits. Ice-cream-cone-slurping families and whale-watchers are replaced by the LGBTQ+ crowd, skateboarders, buskers, and others who just want to meet, mingle, and hang out. Don't think tourists aren't welcome; it's a friendly, everyone-come-as-you-are scene. You'll see guys wearing leather bondage gear, drag queens in glittery Spandex, the occasional firefighter outfit, bachelorette party girls in matching outfits, and after a few nights hardly anything will seem "outlandish." Most of the time, entry for venues is free, but covers for events and entertainment vary widely. Note: You are not allowed to drink alcohol in public, so be sure to finish that beverage before going outside.

Live shows

The hotel-restaurant-club **Crown & Anchor** (247 Commercial Street, 508/487-1430, https://onlyatthecrown.com, shows 6:30pm-10pm, cover varies) is a mainstay of the P-town drag show scene in a building that dates back to the mid-19th century, with nightly performances (often including dinner that start around 6pm and finish up around 10pm. There's also a popular drag brunch, called Divas by the Sea on weekends, at 11am and 1pm. Come planning to laugh and be wooed by the vocals, the wit, the sass, amid a full house that's got everyone spellbound. After the show they have live piano music, with last call at the bar sometime before midnight.

But in P-town, the venue often isn't as important as the person who is performing. For something a bit different, ask around to find out where **Scream Along with Billy** (www.facebook.com/ScreamAlongWithBilly) is being hosted, currently at **Bubala's By the Bay** (183 Commercial St., 508/487-0773, https://bubalas.com, show 10pm, free). Billy, uproarious and charismatic, belts out tunes, tells tales (often raw, sometimes raunchy) set to music in a way that's almost Arlo Guthrie-esque, if Arlo Guthrie were gay, had platinum hair, wore eyeshadow, and played punk rock on keyboards instead of folksy guitar. Sue Goldberg, of the infamous P-town band Space Pussy, is the bassist. Celebs the likes of Courtney Love and Gordon Gano cameo with him when they're in town, and it's not uncommon to see someone famous in the booth next to you taking in Billy and Sue's show.

Try the **Post Office Cafe** (303 Commercial St., 508/487-0008, https://www.postofficecafe.net, shows and cover varies). It's a relaxed spot, where live jazz might be on the menu, a comedy performance, or (yes, of course!) a drag show. A bar runs most of the length of one side, with cozy tables on the other. The intimate space means you're basically there right with the performers, so it can be nice venue for catching your favorite singer just an arm's length away. **Tin Pan Alley**

1: The Lobster Pot **2:** inside the packed Governor Bradford on a Saturday summer night

LOBSTER
POT
Charcoal Broiled
STEAKS
1
2

(269 Commercial St., 508/487-1648, www.tinpanalleyptown.com, 11:30am-midnight daily), also on Commercial Street, has a grand piano and a rotating series of pianists and vocalists who play. They have a creative drink menu, so cocktail enthusiasts can try things like peanut butter-flavored whiskey and craft cocktails garnished with triple-sec-marinated dried cranberries. Cheers!

Dancing

If you're in P-town to be part of an out and open gay culture, rather than just an onlooker, you'll want to head to the Tea Dance at the **Boatslip** (161 Commercial St., 508/487-1669, https://theboatslip.com cover $5-10), where your evening needs to begin. The Tea Dance is a meet and greet, a chance to mingle with people you plan to party with or hook up with later on. Themes like "Solid Gold" or "Electric Dreams" make it festive, with people arriving in flashy costumes to show their style.

The **Governor Bradford** (312 Commercial St., 508/487-2781, 9am-1am daily) is an old standby for its food, bar, and central location right near MacMillan wharf, but after dark it becomes a fun spot for dancing, with karaoke nights, themed events, and can be packed with all genders on a Friday or Saturday.

The closest thing Commercial Street has to a club scene would be at the **Underground Bar** (293 Commercial St., 508/413-9648, https://theundergroundbarptown.business.site, 6pm-1am, to midnight Sun), with a ping-pong table, a pool table, a good-sized dance floor, and a DJ spinning modern club tunes and popular dance favorites. IDs are checked at the door, but there's no cover.

FOOD

Seafood

Don't leave town without trying some fish stew. **The Lobster Pot** (321 Commercial St., 508/487-0842, www.ptownlobsterpot.com, 11:30am-9pm daily Apr.-Nov., $25-32), just east of MacMillan Wharf, is a fine place to start, especially since it offers two immediate advantages: its waterfront view and the fact that on entering, you must pass the kitchen, inhaling a foretaste of the palate-tickling fare that awaits. Platters of seafood in bread-sopping sauces more than measure up to that evanescent preview, as do the clambakes, lobsters, and vegetarian pastas. If you change your mind about a sweet ending to your meal after walking out the door, step down the street and into the **Purple Feather Café and Treatery** (334 Commercial St., 508/487-9100, www.thepurplefeather.com, 11am-9pm Sun.-Thurs., reduced hours off-season), dedicated to fine homemade chocolates, gelato, fudge, and other confections.

John's Foot Long (309 Commercial St., 508/487-7434, 11am-10:30pm daily), between MacMillan Wharf and Commercial Street, is everything that great Cape fried seafood should be: crispy, not too breaded, tasty, fresh, and steaming hot. Prices are market, but it's always worth it if you're craving a plate of scallops or clams. Even the tartar sauce is yummy.

Fusion

One of P-town's best breakfasts is at **Café Heaven** (199 Commercial St. #10, 508/487-1991, brunch 8am-2pm & 5:30pm-9pm Thurs.-Mon., $12-34). The large windows give you great people watching while you're enjoying tasty meals. Omelets, eggs, pancakes, French toast—it's all here and nicely presented. Dinners vary, but you'll have a nice elegant atmosphere with candles and darkness...a bit better than the typical P-town seafood tavern meal.

Pizza

For a snack, sip, slice, or salad, it's hard not to like **Spiritus Café & Pizzeria** (190 Commercial St., 508/487-2808, www.spirituspizza.com, Apr.-early Nov., 11:30am-10pm daily summer, pizzas $20-29), which is even funkier than its Hyannis progenitor. The chrome proboscis of a cherry-red Caddy pokes out of the ceiling, the tables are adorned with painterly decorations, and the wide front

The Simple Joy of Cape Cod Clams

If "the beach" is the first thing people think of when they come to Cape Cod, then "great seafood" is certainly second. For many, nothing perfects a long day in the sunshine like grabbing a cold beverage and a plate of fried clams, dipping them in tartar sauce as the shadows lengthen and the coolness of evening comes on. It's a Cape Cod tradition, as much a part of life here as fish-and-chips in England and the quesadilla in Mexico.

The taste and quality hasn't changed much in generations, nor have the businesses—it's possible to eat at the same spot where your parents or even grandparents ate 20 or 40 years ago. However, fried clams, which used to cost a whopping couple of bucks, now are "market price," along with squid, scallops, fish, and lobster. So be prepared to shell out $20 a plate or even more for a Cape Cod-style fried dinner.

Fortunately, there are other ways to enjoy the Cape's shellfish bounty. One of the best is to get a clam rake and a shellfish license and go out and get your own bucketful. While it's more work, you're liable to see some amazing marinelife while you muck around for clams, and there's nothing like a great day clamming to make a quahog (KOH-hawg) chowder taste delicious.

Lobster has come down in price substantially these days due to a glut in supply, unfortunately caused by shifting global sea temperatures that are shrinking the Maine lobster's range ever northward, which may soon mean no lobsters at all if the trend continues. Pick up a couple of these lovely crustaceans at your nearest fish market or supermarket and boil them yourself. It's quick, easy, and just as scrumptious as if you ordered them for a premium at a restaurant. (Hint: put them in the freezer for a few hours before boiling to reduce the splash as you put them in.) Make lobster bisque by keeping the shells and boiling them with all the juices and any leftover meat, adding this stock to cream, veggies, and seasonings. Top with sherry, and voilà!

Any time you dine alfresco, remember that any trash you leave will almost inevitably get carried by the wind and end up in the ocean, where it fouls the beaches and harms wildlife. Plastic bags are especially harmful to the Kemp-Ridley sea turtles that frequent the area. So be vigilant about picking up your own waste, and look around to see if there's a way you can leave the beach or picnic area cleaner than when you found it.

steps are perfect for fraternizing. Around closing time in the busy season—when the bars are emptying out and the last pizza slices are being scarfed down by dance-happy clubgoers—the pheromones are nearly as thick as the ice cream.

Mexican

Another satisfying fast-food choice is **Big Daddy's Burrito** (205 Commercial St., 508/487-4432, 11am-4pm or later daily, reduced hours in fall, $7-12) which offers Mexican food with P-town flair, sombreros, wacky decor, and tasty burritos that can be made either with meat or totally vegetarian. Visit Big Daddy's in the Olde Aquarium Building.

American

Other waterfront options worth recommending are found deep in the East and West Ends of town. In the East End is **Fanizzi's by the Sea** (539 Commercial St., 508/487-1964, www.fanizzisrestaurant.com, 11:30am-9pm Mon.-Sat., 10am-9pm Sun. year-round, $23-31), whose dining room is so close to the water that at high tide you may wonder if you'll get your feet wet going back out to the street. It's a casual spot with swift service where you'll eat well—char-grilled burgers, hefty fish-and-chips platters, roasted vegetarian lasagna, seafood over pasta, grilled fresh fish, and even meatloaf with mashed potatoes fill out the menu. The Sunday brunch (all you can eat, $15) is a spectacular value when you consider it includes steamed mussels, fried chicken, and eggs benedict, along with other more typical brunch fare.

Contemporary

At the opposite end of town and a couple of rungs up the foodie's ladder is **The Red Inn** (15 Commercial St., 508/487-7334, www.theredinn.com, 1pm-close daily summer, off-season hours vary, $28-46), a historic lodging property whose elegant contemporary dining room has but two walls of large picture windows between it and the bay. Here you can choose to dress your caesar salad with oyster brochettes instead of anchovies, your mashed potatoes will likely have been laced with truffle oil, the flavorful mushrooms are all wild, and every plate is an edible painting.

★ **The Mews Restaurant & Cafe** (429 Commercial St., 508/487-1500, www.mews.com, 5pm-9pm Tue.-Sun., $21-48) is revered by local residents as a venerable beachfront institution that also happens to serve some of the best meals on the outer Cape. Choose between creative gourmet dining or a casual yet upscale café menu in the always lively bar. Don't miss sampling from New England's largest collection of vodkas: over 300 from 28 different countries.

Portuguese

One of the few year-round stalwarts of the local dining scene is **Napi's** (7 Freeman St., 508/487-1145, https://napisptown.com, 5pm-10pm daily, $19-36), tucked away behind the Tedeschi convenience store on Bradford. The local king of cross-cultural blending, it offers a diverse globe-trotting menu, including spicy Asian noodles, Greek caponata, Thai chicken, Brazilian steak, and, of course, plenty of seafood. Though not cheap ($19 for a veggie alfredo dinner), it's also one of the few spots to please serious vegetarians. Pass on the forgettable overpriced desserts. Decor reflects the owners' passion for objects with a past—from art to construction timber.

For a sample of local tradition, check out the **Portuguese Bakery** (299 Commercial St., 508/487-1803, https://www.provincetownportuguesebakery.com, 7am-6pm Wed.-Sun. Mar.-Oct., $2-6). Despite the impression given by restaurants around town, Portuguese cuisine isn't all tomato, onion, and cumin-flavored fish stews simmered slowly all day. A good dessert tradition exists within the cuisine, as this storefront bakery amply and ably demonstrates. Try the *trutas* (sweet potato fritters) or the almond meringues for a real Portuguese treat.

ACCOMMODATIONS

Provincetown is the only place on the Cape where the accommodations run the gamut from campgrounds and hostels to resort motels, hotels, time-share condos, guesthouses, fancy B&Bs, and romantic spare-no-expense little inns.

If you're on a tighter budget, be advised that during peak season, mid-June-Labor Day, rustic pine-paneled charm is about all you'll be able to find for under $100. Come spring and fall, when the weather still makes being outside—if not in the water—tolerable and restaurant lines have all but vanished, prices everywhere start to come back to earth. A high proportion of places stay open year-round if you need a winter getaway at a good price—and a few even offer in-room fireplaces.

Be forewarned that P-town hosts a number of annual special events that unfortunately inspire innkeepers to demand minimum stays of up to seven days. In addition to the customary Memorial Day, Fourth of July, Labor Day, and Columbus Day holidays, P-town celebrations that routinely cause outbreaks of "No Vacancy" signage include the week-long Portuguese Festival in late June, the week-long Carnival in mid-August, and Women's Week in mid-October. Minimum two-day stays throughout the summer are the rule rather than the exception, and some inns have gone so far as to require four- and five-night minimums June-September.

Under $100

The absolute cheapest choice for summer

There's Only One Kind of Scottcake

Scottcakes, yellow-cake cupcakes with bright pink frosting, are a delicious treat.

If you've got a sweet tooth, you owe it to yourself to get to the one and only **Scottcakes** (353 Commercial St., 508/487-7465, www.facebook.com/ScottCakes, 11am-midnight daily June-early-Sept., 11am-9pm daily early-Sept.-Nov. and May-June, $4): which, yes, has a story so unique and unusual that it has even been made into a musical that played in Boston. You would not think that a simple yellow-cake cupcake with (how appropriate for P-town!) pink frosting would be wildly popular, yet one bite will tell you there's so much more than meets the eye. There'd have to be, because "there's only one kind." No, literally: There is only one kind. No chocolate, no fancy colors or flavors. It's a Scottcake.

It's a yummy cupcake, for sure, and Scott makes a point of reminding everyone that the frosting is made with real buttercream. The place is also open impressively late hours, allowing for that after-the-bars-have-last-call cupcake run before heading home. But more than anything, what you purchase with each cupcake is a chance to eat a piece of the Great American Dream.

Not long ago, Scott was hawking cupcakes on the street. An actor, he'd come to Provincetown temporarily and realized he was meant to stay. But acting gigs are few and far between, and he needed a calling, something that would help him stay there. "Give me my big success!" Scott asked the Universe. The Universe replied, "Make Scottcakes!" Or at least that's what Scott heard. He opened just before Bear Week, and in no time, Scott was known as "the Cupcake Man." After several wildly successful seasons, despite having his vendor's license, he ran into trouble with the town. Not one to accept defeat, he went to court, fighting for the right of the Scottcake, which brought with it a lot of positive coverage from the local newspapers. And when he won, he set to work on a more permanent location than a street corner.

On his birthday, in May 2011, he opened the current store location, and still sells the iconic yellow cupcakes with pink buttercream frosting. Lots has happened since, though—an avid customer brought some friends to the store and then followed up with a note, and that note developed into a relationship that has become a marriage. Hard to believe that selling cupcakes on the corner could start all this.

visitors is the bare-bones **Outermost Hostel** (28 Winslow St., 508/487-4378, http://outermosthostel.com, $55 pp), just past the entrance to the Pilgrim Monument's parking lot. Comprising five historic cabins—epitomizing the height of tourist convenience back before Holiday Inn revolutionized the business—each with six or seven beds and a full bath, the Outermost is undeniably short on frills, but for $55 pp, it's also value in a place where value's hard to find.

$100-150

Throughout the off-season, many of the cozy waterfront efficiencies, suites, and motel rooms at **The Masthead Resort** (31-41 Commercial St., 508/487-0523 or 800/395-5095, www.themasthead.com, year-round, under age 12 free), in the quiet West End, are as low as $96 d with shared bath, $151 d with private bath, making them—and their 450-foot bay-side beachfront—one of the better values in town. The shared-bath rooms remain inexpensive Mid-June-Labor Day weekend; however, most of the other rates nearly triple, going as high as $799 for a three-bedroom cottage.

A painted figurehead greets guests arriving at **The Rose and Crown** (158 Commercial St., 508/487-3332, www.roseandcrownptown.com, $125-300 d), a unique guesthouse located in the center of town. Guest rooms are small but imaginatively designed; one is decked out with fabrics and Victorian antiques, and another features exposed beams and a stately brass bed. Three less expensive rooms upstairs share a bath.

Once the last stop for the stagecoach from Boston, **Gifford House Inn** (9 Carver St., 508/487-0688, www.giffordhouse.com, $125-316) has hosted Ulysses S. Grant and Theodore Roosevelt. The airy guesthouse features spacious guest rooms, and cocktails are served nightly on a wraparound front porch. While the guesthouse goes out of its way to advertise that it caters to gay and lesbian guests (as if that's necessary in P-town), the friendly staff is equally accommodating to everyone. The two-bedroom suites run about $285-389, and all room rates drop in the off-season.

$150-250

If you're looking for a spot that's not quite camping or hostel bunks, why not sleep in the **Race Point Lighthouse's Keeper's House** (855/722-3959, https://www.racepointlighthouse.org, early-May-Nov., $115-230 d)? You'll either need an oversand permit or a ride out to the lighthouse from the friendly keepers, and you'll need your own linens and towels. But what's cooler than spending a night in this iconic idyllic spot out away from everything but the seals and seagulls? There is also Whistle House (rented weekly, or 2-night minimum off-season, $2,000-2,750 per week).

For about the same price, consider a standard motel-style room—and only a two-night summer minimum—at the East End's **Cape Colony Inn** (280 Bradford St., 508/487-1755 or 800/841-6716, www.capecolonyinn.com, mid-May-late Oct., $199-219 d), which has a heated swimming pool.

$250-350

Why settle for a sea-level view of the harbor? At ★ **Land's End Inn** (22 Commercial St., 508/487-0706 or 800/276-7088, Apr.-New Year's weekend, $325-495 summer, $395 off-season), guests have a panoramic view of both Cape Cod Bay and the Atlantic Ocean from the summit of Gull Hill in the far West End. The top-floor loft suite—a 550-square-foot apartment, really—enjoys 360-degree views from its rooftop observation platform as well as private wraparound wooden decks where you can enjoy the complimentary wine and cheese hour while watching sunlight glint off the bay. The shingle-style mansion is tastefully decorated with Victorian art and antiques, much of it from the collection of the Boston merchant who built the place in the early 1900s. To say that all 17 guest rooms and efficiencies are unique is a gross understatement; suffice to say, if you have the slightest affinity for richly ornamented fabrics, arts and crafts wallpapers, stained glass, and carved wood in the fantastical oriental art nouveau style of Aubrey Beardsley, you'll love this place. It's also nicely located, with an easy walk into town or bike to the Province Lands. Pets are welcome.

The **Anchor Inn** (175 Commercial St., 508/487-0432, www.anchorinnbeachhouse.com, $350) is located just west of the center and as such is one of the prime locations to stay. Walk five minutes and you're at MacMillan Wharf; walk 10 feet and you're at the bay. Rooms feel cottage-like, with white paint and wood, beds are firm, and the lounge offers the chance to meet fellow travelers. Some of the rooms have a view of the water, some have balconies—be sure to check first if this is a key aspect of your stay.

$350-500

If the only point to staying in P-town is waking up to water views in luxury, check out the East End's **Watermark Inn** (603 Commercial St., 508/487-0165, www.watermark-inn.com, year-round, $1,660-3,840 weekly, $260-600 daily late June-early Sept.), a harbor-front property that rents exclusively en suite accommodations. Lower rates are for guest rooms facing the street; be sure to inquire about midweek discounts. The bright, comfortable, modern guest rooms each come with a kitchenette, and all but four have access to private or shared sundecks overlooking the water. Prices drop in the off-season.

Adult gratification has never looked better than at ★ **Benchmark Inn & Central** (6 Dyer St., 508/487-7440 or 888/487-7440, www.benchmarkinn.com, late-May-early-Sept. $159-489 d, off-season $99-239 d), a handsome inn that crosses contemporary design with the sensibilities of a cosmopolitan American spa. The Swiss owner has an excellent eye for detail. Drop your libations into the wet-bar ice bucket filled for your arrival, plug your iPod into the stereo next to your bed, watch the flat-screen TVs, and refresh yourself in the sauna or pool before stepping out to one of many fine restaurants within a short stroll.

Camping

Two private campgrounds are on the edge of town: **Dunes' Edge Campground** (U.S. 6, 508/487-9815, www.thetrustees.org, May-mid-Oct., tents $55-75) and **Coastal Acres Camping Court** (508/487-1700, Apr.-Oct., $58-68 d, $18 per additional adult, $6 per child). Reservations at both are strongly

Land's End Inn

recommended July-August. Dunes' Edge is beside mile marker 116 on U.S. 6, at the perimeter of the National Seashore and a short distance from Nelson's Bike Shop, Deli, & Market on Race Point Road, a seasonal rental outfit just yards from the Province Lands bike trails. Among the 100 mostly wooded sites is a secluded tent area and electrical and water hookups for RVs. Rates drop slightly outside peak summer months. Coastal Acres is beside Shank Painter Pond, near the very end of both U.S. 6 and Route 6A; turn at the sign at the Bradford Street exit (Rte. 6A) in the West End, next to Gale Force Bike Rentals, and proceed past the riding stables. Catering more to RVers than tents—almost two-thirds of the 120 sites have power and water hookups—this campground also has one of the longer seasons around.

VISITOR INFORMATION

Get the latest word about goings-on around town at the year-round **Chamber of Commerce** (307 Commercial St., 508/487-3424, www.ptownchamber.com) in Lopes Square, and have a look at their racks of colorful brochures and flyers for information on possible diversions and amusements. Or peruse a copy of ***Provincetown Magazine,*** a free weekly published April-September and found next to many local cash registers. The magazine's restaurant ads, gallery listings, and community calendar page will give you a complete snapshot of the town's commercial, retail, and entertainment possibilities.

GETTING THERE

Car

Provincetown is at the tip of the Cape, the "hand." Provincetown Center is 10 miles (13 minutes) north of Truro, and about 47 miles (67 minutes) from Hyannis Center.

Bus

After stopping at the Hyannis Transportation Center, 1-3 daily selected **Peter Pan buses** (www.peterpan.com) continue to Provincetown and five towns in between (Harwich, Orleans, Eastham, Wellfleet, and Truro)—at least a four-hour trip from the big city all the way to the outermost tip of the Cape. Given the possible connections in Hyannis to Peter Pan buses from Providence and points west, a trip from Manhattan's Port Authority to P-town, with optimum scheduling, would take a little more than eight hours. An intrepid bus rider from Toronto could make it in about 20 hours.

Ferry

Crossing Cape Cod Bay off-season requires a friend in the fishing fleet, but come summer several passenger ferries make the 90-minute dash between Boston and the South Shore to Provincetown, at the tip of the Outer Cape.

Bay State Cruise Company (617/748-1428 or 508/487-9284, https://baystatecruisecompany.com) offers the *Provincetown III or IV,* high-speed catamarans that make the three-hour round-trip ($64 one-way, $96 round-trip) three times daily mid-May-mid-October, daily. Disembark from the Commonwealth Pier in South Boston, beside the World Trade Center, across the street from that building's eponymous Silver Line bus rapid transit station. The Silver Line puts the ferry within minutes of both Amtrak service at South Station and Logan Airport.

Boston Harbor Cruises (617/227-4321, www.bostonharborcruises.com, $64 one-way, $98 round-trip) also makes the Boston-Provincetown run with their flagship 600-passenger high-speed catamaran *Salacia.* It casts off from downtown Boston's Long Wharf, next to the New England Aquarium, every morning early May-early October. For Memorial Day weekend and then mid-June-early September, additional afternoon and weekend evening departures are added to the schedule, with the last boat back to Boston scheduled late enough to allow a leisurely P-town dinner and dessert.

GETTING AROUND

Since P-town is a couple of miles long and just a few blocks wide, one of the best alternatives to driving is using your feet. In warmer weather, bike shops also open for rentals. The best selection is found at **Arnold's** (329 Commercial St., 508/487-0844, http://provincetownbikes.com, 9am-6pm Mon.-Thurs., 9am-8pm Fri.-Sun. May 15-late Oct.), where beach cruisers, 18- and 21-speed hybrid all-terrain bikes, and front-suspension mountain bikes rent on a sliding scale: $15 for up to 2 hours, $22 for 4 hours, $27 9am-6pm, or $95 per week. **Ptown Bikes** (42 Bradford St., 508/487-8735, www.ptownbikes.com, 10am-5pm daily Apr.-Oct.) has similar rates ($14 for up to 2 hours, $24 for 24 hours) and comparable bikes, but longer business hours, plus limited hours into the off-season. If, for some reason, you can't find satisfaction at either of those shops, try **Gale Force Bike Rentals** (144 Bradford St., 508/487-4849, www.galeforcebikes.com, 9am-5pm daily May-Oct., hours vary off-season) in the far West End, whose selection of 3-, 10-, and 18-speed bikes are available for roughly the same rates. All shops provide locks and helmets (free or $2 per day).

If you want someone else to do the driving, look for the **Provincetown Shuttle** (7:15am-12:15am Mon.-Sat., 7:15am-8:15pm Sun., $2 per ride, $6 all-day pass), a seasonal service of the Cape Cod Regional Transit Authority (CCRTA, 800/352-7155, www.capecodrta.org). Between Memorial Day weekend and the third week in October, it loops around P-town, North Truro, and Herring Cove, the nearer of P-town's two National Seashore beaches. Buses run at least every hour, more often in peak-season. Check the website if possible, as schedules vary seasonally. As with all CCRTA buses, the shuttle vehicles are equipped with bike racks.

Alternatively, call a ride-share service or **Cape Cab** (508/487-2222). An in-town ride costs about $7 per person.

Parking

On-street spaces are at a premium in this small town, so drivers should anticipate paying big-city rates to park in one of the flat-rate or per-hour lots within walking distance of all the good stuff. You can slowly circle the Town Hall waiting for someone to give up a precious metered space—if you're patient, you'll circle until winter rolls around, everyone goes home, and you'll get one. If you do, note that most of the town's quarters-only meters run 8am-midnight daily. Yes, midnight! If you are willing to pay for a space in an attended lot, expect anywhere from a flat rate for the day of $5-8 farthest from downtown to $3.50 per hour (up to a daily maximum of $35) at the largest and most central municipal lot on MacMillan Pier. Although they're the most expensive, the city-owned lots are the easiest to find—electronic signs at key intersections point the way, with LED displays to redirect drivers from the pier to secondary lots on Prince Street as necessary. Note that the summer shuttle bus includes nearly every major parking lot on its route, from far-flung lots on Bradford Street to MacMillan Pier, making it doubly convenient for summer visitors to leave the car in one spot and flag down a shuttle for trips around town.

Festivals and Events

APRIL

The bay-side town of Brewster spends three days over the last weekend of April (or the first weekend in May) celebrating **Brewster in Bloom** (Brewster Chamber of Commerce, 508/896-3500, https://brewster-capecod.com), with a parade, a golf tournament, a 5K road race, and a tour of more than a dozen local B&B inns.

MAY

Preseason visitors will find oodles of activities to enjoy during **Cape Cod Maritime Days,** the entire month of May. This local observance of National Historic Preservation Week is celebrated across the Cape with lighthouse tours, slide talks, boatbuilding demonstrations, musical performances, narrated walks, guided kayaking tours, and open houses at historic structures normally off-limits to the public. The busy schedule, sponsored in part by the Cape Cod Chamber of Commerce (508/362-3225, www.capecodchamber.org), kicks off with a day-long symposium on maritime history (register at 508/775-1723 or www.capecodmaritimemuseum.org). A calendar of events is distributed around regional visitor booths, or visit www.capecodchamber.org to print your own.

JUNE

Perhaps the biggest event on all of Cape Cod, **Provincetown Pride** (508/487-2313, https://ptown.org/calendar/pride) happens the first week of June. It's a wonderful, welcoming, high-energy festival with a parade, events, food, musical numbers, drag shows, and more that draws people LGBTQ+ and straight from all over New England. There's even a Pride whale watch you can sign up for.

The side of Provincetown's heritage that is inextricably bound to the glory days of its commercial fishery is on display during the **Portuguese Festival** (508/246-9080, www.provincetownportuguesefestival.com, Thurs.-Sun. last weekend of June). Known primarily for the Blessing of the Fleet that takes place on Sunday afternoon, the festival also includes plenty of live music, dancing (including exhibitions of traditional Portuguese dance), and food, including soups, seafood, and sweets.

JULY

On Wednesday evenings throughout July-August, head down to the Wellfleet Town Pier for free **square dancing** (508/349-0330, ext. 116, 7:30pm-10pm Wed.) under the stars.

The Mashpee Wampanoag Tribe holds an authentic **Powwow** in early July (508/477-0208, https://mashpeewampanoagtribe-nsn.gov/powwow-info), with dances, rituals, Native American food such as fry bread, souvenirs, contests, and more. It's a packed event, with a true multi-cultural feel.

For nine days in the second half of the month, the **Barnstable County Fair** (508/563-3200, http://capecodfairgrounds.com) enthusiastically makes residents and visitors alike forget the fact that Cape Cod has lost nearly all its traditional farmland to development. Barnyard animal displays, beekeeping exhibits, a petting zoo, blacksmithing demonstrations, circus performers, live music, and, of course, a full midway of carnival games and rides round out this charming celebration of agrarian tradition, held every year since the end of the Civil War at the Barnstable County Fairgrounds on Route 151 in East Falmouth.

AUGUST

The first or second Sunday in August marks the return of the Boston Pops Esplanade Orchestra to the Hyannis Village Green for their annual **Pops by the Sea concert**

1: the cranberry harvest, part of Cape Cod autumn
2: pumpkin season, with family fun for everyone

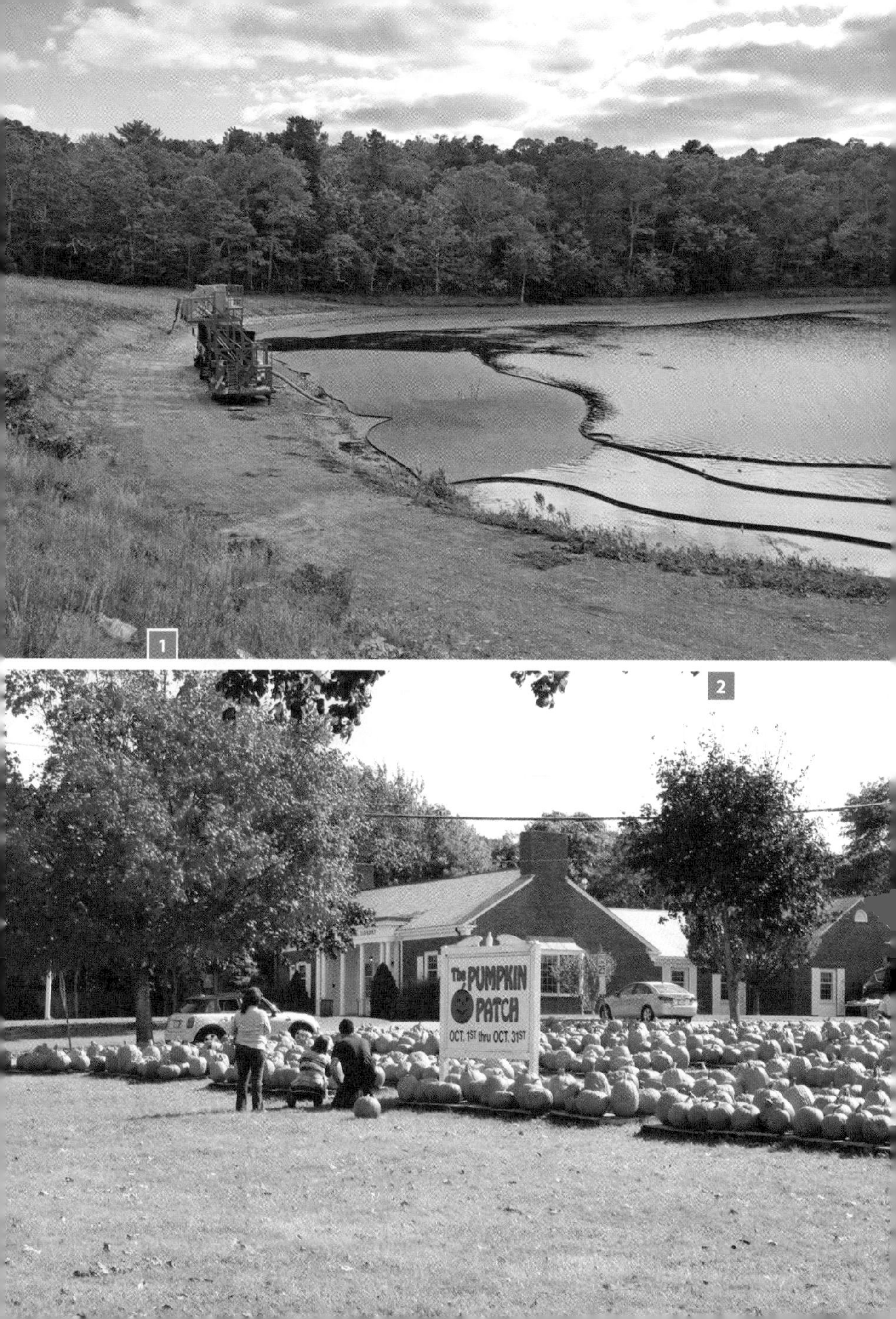
1
2
The PUMPKIN
PATCH
OCT. 1ST thru OCT. 31ST

(508/362-0066, https://artsfoundation.org) to benefit the Arts Foundation of Cape Cod.

The Dennis **Antique Car Parade** (508/398-3568, www.dennischamber.com) happens the third week of August and is an impressive show of cars old and older. Expect everything from Model-Ts to 1970s-era cruisers.

SEPTEMBER

The second weekend of September is when Harwich holds its annual **Cranberry Festival** (HarwichCranberryFestival@comcast.net, https://harwichcranberryartsandmusicfestival.org) in recognition of its leading role in the Cape's cranberry industry.

Around the autumnal equinox—the third weekend of September—the Outer Cape town of Truro ends the summer season with a suitably colorful and eclectic party. **Truro Treasures** (508/487-6464, www.trurotreasures.org) includes live music, arts, crafts, a road race, and a sandcastle competition, as well as an old-time grape stomp and jazz concert at the Truro Vineyard's winery.

OCTOBER

Mashpee Commons, the green beside the Mashpee Rotary at the junction of Routes 28 and 151, hosts **Oktoberfest** (508/539-1400) on the Saturday of Columbus Day weekend. In addition to the requisite beer garden, there are displays of arts and crafts, games for kids, and sidewalk sales at shops throughout the complex. For those who like to earn their beer (or burn those carbs!), there's a 10K road race the same weekend.

DECEMBER

Provincetown's annual—and the world's only—Gay and Lesbian Holiday Festival, better known as **Holly Folly** (508/487-2313 or 800/637-8696, www.ptown.org), livens up the first weekend of December with nightclub dances, open-house tours of local inns, a holiday concert at Town Hall, festive menus at area restaurants, and a "shop hop" among local retailers.

For something a tad more traditional, join Santa and his elves for **Sandwich Holly Days** (508/888-0251, www.sandwichchamber.com/holly-days.html), for the month of December plus the New Year. Enjoy music and caroling, open houses at local museums and inns, glassblowing at the museum and from area artisans, and special treats from local merchants. The historic part of the town already looks the part of the 19th-century New England village, but the holiday decorations make it fit the role even more.

Information and Services

BANKS AND ATMS

Cape Cod towns have numerous banks, and ATMs are almost everywhere (malls, convenience stores, kiosks), so it's no longer necessary to find an actual bank branch just to get some cash. Credit cards and debit cards are also almost universally accepted, without any minimum charges, at any retailer with access to a phone line.

Bank offices are open standard hours—in most cases, 9am-4pm Monday-Friday, 9am-1pm Saturday. Note that only limited foreign currency exchange services are available on the Cape, and only at the largest bank branches.

MEDIA AND COMMUNICATIONS

The Cape region has only one newspaper in wide circulation, the ***Cape Cod Times,*** which has entertainment pages as well as a popular Friday pullout section called *Cape Week,* which highlights live music, performances, and other film or newsworthy events. The ***Barnstable Patriot*** is an even more local paper focusing on the Barnstable area. Most towns have daily rags as well that are essentially advertising pamphlets. With the rise of the internet, many of the more substantial newspapers have gone the way of the dodo.

WBZ (1030 AM) is the region's source for weather, emergencies, and other up-to-the-minute happenings—most of the news is in 10-minute rotation, with traffic "on the threes." As this is a Boston station, only major Cape traffic delays (such as the Labor Day exodus) make it on, but it's a useful tool for planning alternate getaways. **WCAI** (90.1 FM) is the local National Public Radio station, although the Cape's best reception is often **WGBH** from Boston at 89.7 FM. Many stations now have online streaming, both live and recorded, so if your radio isn't getting the signal, you may find that Wi-Fi saves the day.

PUBLIC RESTROOMS

You will see a lot of "No Public Restroom" signs on the Cape and islands, unfortunately for good reason; merchants offering their restrooms to the public often have to deal with vandalism, theft, and filth. Be respectful of these signs, and be aware that on the Cape, public urination is illegal and public exposure is prosecuted as a sex crime. Luckily there's an easy way to avoid getting yourself in trouble when nature calls: Find a convenience store, a gas station, or a fast-food joint, and you'll be saved. Though the trees and bushes are plentiful, public urination is illegal and public exposure can be labeled a sex crime.

Most public beaches also have some kind of restroom, rarely with potable water. Often this is just a portable outhouse—but that's sometimes enough.

MEDICAL EMERGENCIES

If there is a true emergency, call 911 from any cell or landline phone to summon trained EMT or rescue personnel.

Cape Cod Hospital (27 Park St., Hyannis, 508/771-1800, www.capecodhealth.org) is the largest and most central of the Cape's medical options. Located right in Hyannis, it's one hour at most from any part of the Cape and has all services you would expect at a major medical institution. The 24-hour emergency care is probably the most useful for travelers, but they have mental health and addiction services, prenatal and gynecological care, and so on. **Falmouth Hospital** (100 Ter Heun Dr., Falmouth, 508/548-5300) is under the same umbrella as Cape Cod Hospital. Together they serve the majority of on-Cape hospital needs.

A handful of other smaller clinics and medical services are sprinkled around the Cape, along with specialists' offices. **Outer Cape Health Services** (www.outercape.org) has Harwich (269 Chatham Rd., 508/432-1400), Wellfleet (3130 U.S. 6, 508/349-3131), and Provincetown (49 Harry Kemp Way, 508/487-9395) offices. Hours vary based on the care provided and the season, but generally services are not 24 hours.

Martha's Vineyard

Forget about Martha—it's "the Vineyard" to everybody in the know, or simply "the island" to those longtime residents who barely acknowledge the existence of nearby Nantucket.

By any name, it's a peach: big enough to have quiet spots even in the busiest season, small enough that you can get to know it quickly, slightly more democratic than its neighbor in matters of room and board, and far more accessible to day-trippers. This is the island of seaside naps and lazy days in chaise longues, of sailboats and bicycles, lighthouses and gingerbread cottages, artists and professors, carpenters and movie stars, presidential advisers, and occasionally presidents. Water sports, historical exhibits, and nature trails provide alternatives to the beach, while abundant seafood and all manner of sweets

Highlights

Look for ★ to find recommended sights, activities, dining, and lodging.

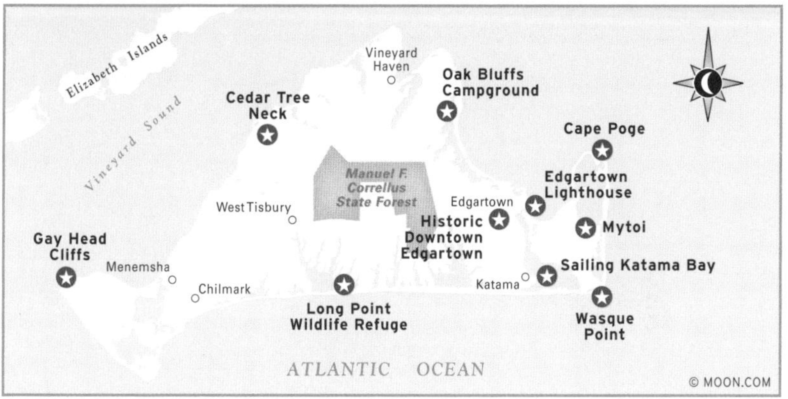

★ **Oak Bluffs Campground:** Stroll curvy lanes amid a postcard-perfect collection of colorful Victorian gingerbread cottages (page 137).

★ **Historic Downtown Edgartown:** Stately waterfront mansions and a stunning Greek Revival church frame the charming shop-filled blocks and narrow garden-lined lanes of the island's oldest town (page 146).

★ **Edgartown Lighthouse:** Beautiful harbor and town views await at this historic 45-foot tower a short stroll from downtown (page 146).

★ **Sailing Katama Bay:** Water rats know nothing is as much fun as lolling under sail aboard one of the Vineyard's beautiful windjammers or wooden yachts (page 149).

★ **Mytoi:** This serene Japanese-style garden is a surprise amid the pines of rural Chappaquiddick (page 151).

★ **Wasque Point and Cape Poge:** Swim, surf-cast, kayak, or bird-watch, all to the steady rhythm of the waves (page 152).

★ **Gay Head Cliffs:** Watch the sunset from the upper cliffs or trek amid the mussel-fringed boulders, mermaid purses, and other marine curiosities along the rough shore (page 163).

★ **Long Point Wildlife Refuge:** Comb the beach, paddle Tisbury Great Pond, or just saunter through the heaths of these ecologically rare coastal grasslands (page 166).

★ **Cedar Tree Neck:** Easy trails through a varied woodland habitat lead to a beautiful scenic shore along Vineyard Sound (page 168).

Martha? Martha Who...?

Martha's Vineyard is generally said to take its name from its abundance of native wild grapes—and perhaps the daughter of Bartholomew Gosnold, the English captain who spent the late spring of 1602 around Buzzards Bay and the Elizabeth Islands (which he named in honor of his queen) in what was then known as "the north part of Virginia." However, given that Gosnold didn't have a daughter named Martha and that his mother-in-law, Martha Goulding, helped finance his voyage, it is more plausible he was honoring her. According to the "Briefe and true Relation" of the voyage by one of its members, John Brereton, Gosnold actually applied "Marthaes vineyard" to a very small, uninhabited island overgrown with various fruit-bearing shrubs and such "an incredible store of Vines . . . that we could not goe for treading upon them." Probably this was what's now aptly called Noman's Land, a naval gunnery range turned wildlife sanctuary off Aquinnah's south shore. By 1610 cartographers assigned the name to the much larger adjacent island. There it remains today, having outlasted "Capawack" (probably from *kuppaug*, the Algonquian word for harbor), which was for decades the most widely used appellation of the first English settlers.

The lure for Gosnold, as for other captains who ranged the New England coast in the early 17th century, was sassafras. The safrole in the leaves is now known to be a carcinogen, but to Gosnold's contemporaries the plant was widely believed to be a cure-all. "The roote of sassafras hath power to comfort the liver," enthused one 1597 herbal encyclopedia, "and to dissolve oppilations, to comfort the weake and feeble stomacke, to cause a good appetite, to consume windiness, the chiefest cause of cruditie and indigestion, stay vomiting, and make sweete a stinking breath." Perhaps more important to the gentry in Europe—whose demand for the stuff kept the price and profitability high—was the belief that it could cure "the French Poxe" (syphilis).

put to rest that austere summer diet you fleetingly considered in order to fit into last year's swimsuit.

The Vineyard's 100-plus square miles are neatly divisible into "up-island" and "down-island." As on Cape Cod, this holdover from the days of whalers and sailors makes sense if you remember that degrees of longitude ascend from east to west.

Down-island is the Vineyard's pedestrian-friendly threshold: Vineyard Haven, Oak Bluffs, and Edgartown. Along with a near monopoly on knickknack shops, sweet treats, and Black Dog T-shirts, down-island is where good food, nightlife, and accommodations are all within walking distance of each other. Car-free visitors also have the flexibility of catching a ferry at almost a moment's notice. While you are more likely to find the comforting glow of streetlights rather than a chorus of crickets outside your bedroom window at night, down-island offers plenty of scenic beauty and is home to more than half of the Vineyard's two dozen public beaches.

Up-island is the island's southwestern corner farthest from the Cape Cod ferries. It comprises the predominantly rural towns of West Tisbury, Chilmark, and Aquinnah, home to only a smattering of small restaurants, stores, and galleries. Many of the area's undulating country roads are lined by great allées of oak, like antebellum plantation driveways, and the woods are filled with the drystone walls of bygone sheep farms. The up-island hills—the Vineyard's highest ground—offer great views en route to their abrupt tumble into the sea beneath the steady sweep of the beacon in redbrick Gay Head Light.

While even this section of the Vineyard heavily depends on "summer people," it also relies on agriculture and fishing. Its working roots are especially visible in picturesque

Previous: entering the harbor of Martha's Vineyard; Gayhead Light; the antique firetruck of the Winnetu Oceanside Resort.

Menemsha harbor—home to more groundfish draggers and lobster trappers than luxury yachts—and at the seasonal biweekly farmers market in West Tisbury. To experience up-island at its best generally requires owning or renting a set of wheels (two or four), although every town is linked to down-island throughout the year by public transit.

PLANNING YOUR TIME

Although the Vineyard is in New England, instead of four seasons to the year there are just two: in-season and off-season. **In-season** is the big mixed-blessing phenomenon of the summer, which has carried the Vineyard economy now for more than a century. It starts on Memorial Day weekend, when in-season does a few light warm-up laps before the real thing starts on the Fourth of July. Everything is crazy through Labor Day, slowing down by Columbus Day—the semiofficial start of the **off-season.**

Lingering momentum and clement weather can prop up off-season weekends through Thanksgiving, but then the island finally again becomes the property of its year-round residents. Off-season living is quiet, sedate, and even boring, but many—if not most—year-rounders will tell you it's their favorite time of year.

The biggest difference between in-season and off-season is, as you might expect, a sudden decrease in the availability of just about everything. By the same token, it's also at this point that the restaurants, buses, ferries, accommodations, and shops all start to scale back their operating hours. Beach buses and hourly public shuttles between up- and down-island are the first to cease, stopping promptly after Labor Day weekend, not to resume until the following mid- to late June (the shuttles still run, but not nearly as often). By mid-October, most up-island restaurants and half the B&Bs in West Tisbury, Chilmark, and Aquinnah have followed suit. By autumn, down-island towns start to roll up the rugs, cover the furniture, and forward the mail—but they have enough year-round residents at least to keep a few restaurants open all year. Last, but not least, there's Vineyard Haven; thanks to four-season Steamship service, it actually retains a passing resemblance to a fully functioning small town, even at the nadir of winter.

The off-season brings with it certain requirements—double-check restaurant hours, for example, and rely more on driving than you would in the longer and warmer days of summer. But these are more than outweighed by advantages such as choosing lodgings upon arrival (rather than sight-unseen three months in advance) and dining when you're ready without waiting in line for an hour or making do with a fifth-choice reservation. While the early off-season (Apr.-June) is most prized, anyone looking for a cozy weekend escape to an austere Winslow Homer landscape shouldn't rule out December, or even February.

What you should not expect from the off-season in the Vineyard is significant savings. Innkeepers' supply costs are as high in winter as in summer, and off-season business is too sparse to be worth a price war. Yes, some room rates may drop almost 50 percent between summer and winter, but that simply reflects the fact that July prices are stratospheric; they return in January to the realm of the average Marriott hotel.

Like resort destinations all over the country, the Vineyard struggles with the pressures of popularity. Realtors talk about three-acre minimum lots as the balm for fears of overdevelopment, but look closely as you come in on the ferry from Woods Hole and you'll see what land conservationists are concerned about—the wooded Vineyard shore is filling with rooftops. The development issue grows ever more urgent as summer traffic in down-island towns approaches your average metropolitan rush-hour gridlock. You can be part of the solution rather than the problem by leaving your car on the mainland, if at all possible, and taking advantage of the year-round public transit, extensive bike paths, taxis, and your feet.

Martha's Vineyard

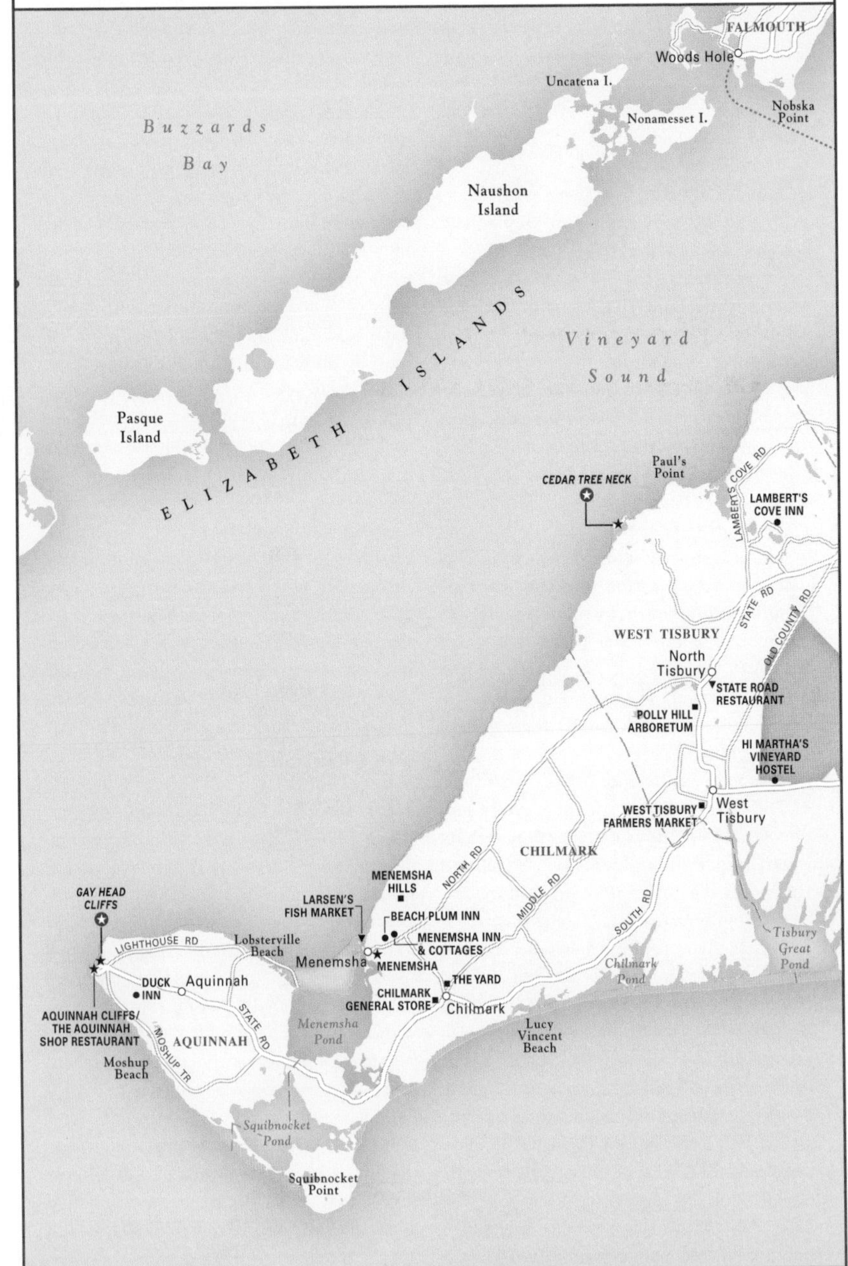

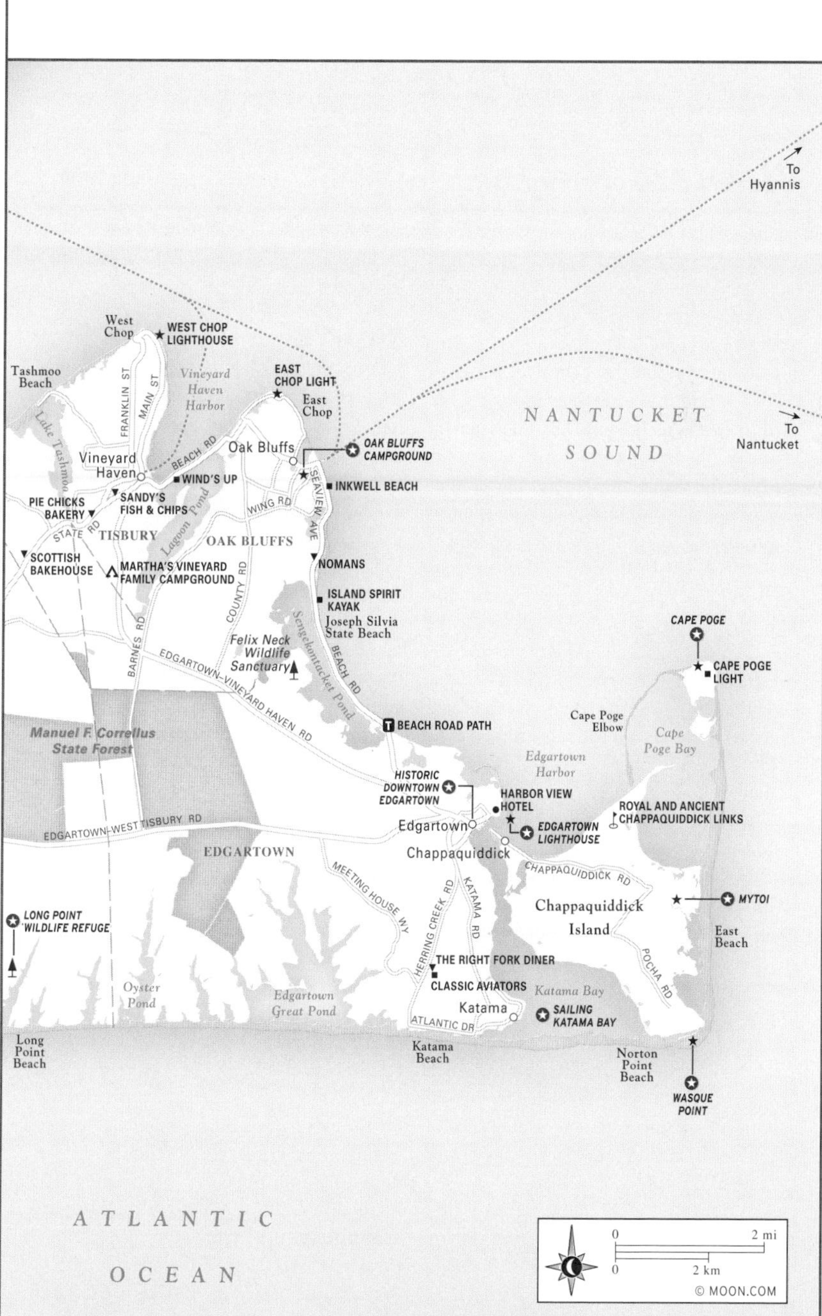

To Hyannis
To Nantucket
NANTUCKET SOUND
West Chop
WEST CHOP LIGHTHOUSE
Tashmoo Beach
FRANKLIN ST
MAIN ST
Vineyard Haven Harbor
EAST CHOP LIGHT
East Chop
Lake Tashmoo
Vineyard Haven
BEACH RD
Oak Bluffs
OAK BLUFFS CAMPGROUND
WIND'S UP
INKWELL BEACH
PIE CHICKS BAKERY
SANDY'S FISH & CHIPS
Lagoon Pond
WING RD
SEAVIEW AVE
STATE RD
TISBURY
OAK BLUFFS
SCOTTISH BAKEHOUSE
MARTHA'S VINEYARD FAMILY CAMPGROUND
NOMANS
COUNTY RD
ISLAND SPIRIT KAYAK
Joseph Silvia State Beach
BARNES RD
Felix Neck Wildlife Sanctuary
Sengekontacket Pond
BEACH RD
EDGARTOWN–VINEYARD HAVEN RD
CAPE POGE
CAPE POGE LIGHT
Cape Poge Elbow
Cape Poge Bay
BEACH ROAD PATH
Manuel F. Correllus State Forest
Edgartown Harbor
HISTORIC DOWNTOWN EDGARTOWN
HARBOR VIEW HOTEL
ROYAL AND ANCIENT CHAPPAQUIDDICK LINKS
EDGARTOWN–WEST TISBURY RD
Edgartown
EDGARTOWN LIGHTHOUSE
Chappaquiddick
EDGARTOWN
MEETING HOUSE WY
HERRING CREEK RD
KATAMA RD
CHAPPAQUIDDICK RD
MYTOI
Chappaquiddick Island
LONG POINT WILDLIFE REFUGE
East Beach
POCHA RD
THE RIGHT FORK DINER
CLASSIC AVIATORS
Katama Bay
Oyster Pond
Edgartown Great Pond
Katama
SAILING KATAMA BAY
ATLANTIC DR
Long Point Beach
Katama Beach
Norton Point Beach
WASQUE POINT
ATLANTIC OCEAN
0
2 mi
0
2 km
© MOON.COM

Those using foreign currency must make their cash exchanges prior to arriving—none of the banks here handle such transactions. You won't ever be far from an ATM in the down-island towns, but up-island is a different story—beyond Beetlebung Corner, there's nothing, so come prepared.

Vineyard Haven

This is the island's largest year-round community and only year-round ferry port. But by all appearances, it's just your average small seaside town of about 2,000 stalwart souls, with a little light industry near the wharf, tree-shaded residential streets overlooking the harbor, and a small commercial downtown. White clapboard and gray shingle descendants of the venerable sharp-gabled Cape-style house rub shoulders with old captains' mansions. The automotive spectrum ranges from rust-flecked American sedans to teenagers in their parents' hand-me-down foreign imports, from oversize pickup trucks that clearly earn their mud flaps to mirror-polished SUVs. Whatever its varied occupations the rest of the year, come summer, the town has its hands full playing host and maître d' to the million-plus visitors swarming through it.

Once known by the Wampanoags as Nobnocket ("place by the pond"), the port was known to later generations of sailors as Holmes Hole, after a 17th-century landowner. Early in the Victorian era, image-conscious citizens changed the name after deciding they preferred living in a place that sounded closer to heaven than hell. Since then, the harborside village has grown indistinguishable from Tisbury, the 17th-century township of which it was once just a part—but aside from legal documents and town stationery, both general usage and the U.S. Postal Service now favor "Vineyard Haven" for the whole.

Visitors coming off the ferries will find restaurants, shops, accommodations, car and bike rentals, ATMs, and public restrooms (in the Steamship Authority Terminal beside the pier and seasonally above the Stop & Shop parking lot across the street)—all within a few blocks' walk.

SIGHTS

Historic Architecture

Since "the Great Fire of 1883" destroyed its center, the town's oldest buildings are found on upper Main Street north of the Bank of Martha's Vineyard building (whose distinctive facade, a cross between craftsman-style stone and Mediterranean tile bungalow, occupies the grounds of the harness shop where the fire may have begun) and a block farther up from the harbor along William Street. Many of the 50-odd houses included in the Historic District along this quiet street were built as a result of the whaling and trade industries. Befitting the wealth of their builders, some of these houses typify the Greek Revival style now most commonly associated with old banks.

Plenty of New England's most attractive civic architecture has been inspired as much by religion as commercial profit, as some of this town's present and former churches attest. Tucked along side streets crossing William Street are three worthy examples: the classically inspired **Tisbury Town Hall,** a former Congregational and Baptist Church on Spring Street that's also known as Association Hall; the newer United Methodist **Stone Church,** on Church Street, built early this century to replace its demonstrably flammable predecessor; and, opposite, the former 1833 Methodist meetinghouse, now **The Vineyard Playhouse,** the island's only professional theater. Association Hall is also home to a performance center, the **Katharine Cornell Memorial Theater,** a fully accessible space

Vineyard Etiquette

The list of past and present Vineyard residents includes Spike Lee, Mike Wallace, Carly Simon, Denzel Washington, Alan Dershowitz, Judy Blume, Diane Sawyer, David Letterman, James Taylor, Bill Murray, Walter Cronkite, Art Buchwald, John Belushi, and Jackie O. Maybe the sun does shine a little brighter on these people, but don't come to the Vineyard expecting to bask in it yourself.

Local wisdom holds that the Vineyard attracts celebrities precisely because locals have either too much Yankee sense or Puritan humility to make a fuss over cultural icons in the flesh. This legendary discretion has become the cornerstone of Vineyard etiquette, which declares that celebrities are to be allowed to go about unmolested by photographers or autograph-seekers. Should you see Somebody, you should feign indifference, instead of, say, crossing the street to get a better look. If Somebody sits at the next table in a restaurant, you are requested to act nonchalant instead of playing paparazzo with your camera.

You can do otherwise, of course, but then many trees' worth of *Vineyard Gazette* newsprint will be expended by local vigilantes clucking their tongues over another tourist who "just doesn't get it." Anyway, you're wasting your time driving Chilmark's back roads hoping to catch some box-office headliners schmoozing over a barbecue; most of those very important people stay so well out of sight that the closest celeb views you'll get will be at the airport.

used by various local groups. During the Town Hall's regular business hours it's worth stepping inside the theater for a peek at the large island-themed **murals** by the late Stan Murphy, a Vineyard artist known for his luminous paintings of people and nature.

Martha's Vineyard Museum

The **Martha's Vineyard Museum** (151 Lagoon Pond Rd., 508/627-4441, www.mvmuseum.org, 10am-4pm Tue.-Sun Sept.-late-May, to 7pm Tues. late-May-early Sept., $18) is fortunate to possess a better-than-average potpourri of historical relics—over 30,000 in all, from scrimshaw and whaling try-pots to costumes, domestic furnishings, and old farm implements. The Martha's Vineyard Historical Society curates the museum, mining this repository of artifacts for its changing exhibits and drawing on the society's vast collection of historical photos, vintage postcards, and ephemera. Genealogists who divine some connection to past islanders should visit the society's library to research the family tree. The library also sells copies of the *Dukes County Intelligencer*, the society's quarterly assemblage of articles on island history and lore.

The museum's most prominent exhibit is a large piece of lighthouse technology over 140 years old—an example of the huge Fresnel lens, whose invention revolutionized coastal navigation. The ground-level view from inside the lens may seem disorienting, but these concentric prisms totally reversed the illuminating efficiency of 19th-century lamps. Whereas before, only one-sixth of a parabolic reflector's light could be seen by mariners, Augustin Fresnel's "dioptric apparatus" concentrated as much light in its high-powered beam as had previously been lost. In a reminder that red-tape bureaucracy is hardly a modern affliction, the U.S. government dithered for 30 years, despite the proven efficiency, making scientific studies and committee reports before finally adopting the French-made lens. One of the earliest Fresnel lenses installed by the U.S. Lighthouse Service, this particular lens faithfully flashed its light over Aquinnah for nearly a century before it was replaced by an electric lamp.

West Chop

Vineyard Haven's V-shaped harbor is protected on either side by jaw-like hunks of land known as East and West Chop. Upper Main Street runs along West Chop to a separate

Island Tours

Sightseeing tours are a great way to see the island.

Want to start off your Vineyard holiday with a 2.5-hour narrated trip around all six towns? The white, pink, and turquoise old school buses of **Martha's Vineyard Sightseeing,** a.k.a. Island Transport (508/693-1555, www.mvtour.com, adults $35, under age 13 $20), rendezvous with all incoming ferries in both Vineyard Haven and Oak Bluffs 9am-4pm daily mid-May-late October, and with the 10:30am and 11:30am ferries April 15-November 1. You can buy your tickets at the Steamship Authority terminal in Woods Hole or aboard the Hy-Line, Falmouth, and New Bedford ferries en route to the island.

The all-island buses pay only a cursory visit to the down-island towns, since the vehicles are too large to negotiate narrow downtown streets, but they do include a 25-minute stop at the Aquinnah Cliffs. The tour guides are typically off-island college students whose knowledge of the Vineyard comes from scripts, so when it comes to identifying celebrity driveways or explaining what happened at Chappaquiddick in 1969, take what they say with a good dash of salt.

Alternatively, consider taking a history-focused tour. **Oak Bluffs Land & Wharf Co.** (508/684-8595, www.vineyardhistory.com, $45, reservations required) conducts air-conditioned van tours around each of the down-island towns—Vineyard Haven, Oak Bluffs, and Edgartown. Call for current departure times and starting points or reserve online.

village of Tisbury, located at the end; East Chop belongs to neighboring Oak Bluffs.

About two miles up Main Street from the downtown shops is the 19th-century **West Chop Lighthouse,** sitting beside the road for photographers' convenience, though not open to the public (it's a private Coast Guard residence). The current 1891 brick tower is the third incarnation in a series of lights at this location that have guided seafarers since James Monroe sat in the White House. The white beacon, visible on the mainland, shows red if you get too close to the shoals off the end of the point.

West Chop Park, near the turnaround loop at the end of Main, is favored for watching the sunsets over Vineyard Sound, but any time on a clear day, it offers a nice view out over what was once one of the world's busiest coastal waterways. Before railroads and the 1914 completion of the Cape Cod Canal siphoned away most of the cargo and passengers, this area was second only to the English Channel in boat traffic. Two hundred years ago, you could have counted scores of sails belonging to coastwise packets bound for Boston or New York and merchant vessels bearing West Indies molasses, South American hides, Sumatran spices, and Arabian coffee. Until the technology enabling precise calculation of a ship's longitude became widely available in the 19th century, most "East-Indiamen" put in at Vineyard Haven or Woods Hole before negotiating the great extended hook of Cape Cod; to set a course for Boston or Salem directly from the Caribbean or South Atlantic would have otherwise risked a fatal snag on Nantucket South Shoals.

RECREATION

Beaches

Vineyard Haven has five public beaches, three of which are within one mile of downtown. Tiny **Owen Park Beach** is only a block from the Steamship Authority (SSA) dock, but it gets more use as a boat launch than as a serene spot for catching rays. Since the breakwater keeps the surf away, it's probably best appreciated by really small kids—but if you have some time to kill before catching the ferry, it's good for soaking tired feet. The area to the left of the wooden town pier is private, by the way. From the SSA, either cut through the parking lot behind the bank, or step up to Main and follow the one-way traffic one block to the bandstand; that's Owen Park. The beach is at the bottom of the hill.

Farther up Main Street, about 0.75 miles from the cinema, is the **Tisbury Town Beach** (also called Bayside), an 80-foot sliver of sandy harbor shoreline between stone jetties at the end of Owen Little Way, from which you can watch the comings and goings at the Vineyard Haven Yacht Club next door. Free swimming lessons are given here in summer. On the other side of the harbor, about 0.75 miles along Beach Road toward Oak Bluffs, is **Lagoon Bridge Park,** on Lagoon Pond. Here too sunbathers are outnumbered, this time by water-skiers and windsurfers. (It's also the only one of the town's four beach parks without any parking.)

Vineyard Haven's most attractive swimming beaches are about two miles from downtown near the west end of Lake Tashmoo. Facing Woods Hole and the Elizabeth Islands across Vineyard Sound (that's big Naushon stretching away to the left and tiny Nonamesset almost opposite), the ocean portion of **Wilfrid's Pond Preserve** is exemplary of the north shore: little to no surf, light if any winds, no audible motorized boats, and water that stays relatively warm and shallow for some distance from shore. It's also quite small, which is why parking (free) is limited to space for five cars. Wilfrid's Pond itself is not open to swimmers, but the bench overlooking its brackish waters is a fine spot to forget worldly cares.

Another 0.5 miles past Wilfrid's, at the end of the same heavily gullied and potholed lane, is **Tashmoo Beach** or Herring Creek Beach (also with free parking, and restrooms). At first glance, it's disappointingly small, but walk back along the sandy lakeshore and you'll find the part favored by regulars. To reach either beach, make a right at the end of Daggett Avenue on the better-maintained of the two sandy tracks there by the fire hydrant.

Water Sports

The island's best all-around source for buying or renting sailboards, sea kayaks, canoes, surfboards and body boards, and just about anything else that can skim across water under power of wind, wave, or paddle is **Wind's Up!** (199 Beach Rd., 508/693-4252, www.windsupmv.com, 9am-6pm daily late June-Aug., call for shoulder and off-season hours), past the big gas tanks on Vineyard Haven's harbor. The friendly folks at this we've-got-everything emporium at Lagoon Harbor Park also offer lessons for nearly all the equipment they stock, provide car racks if you want to try the waters in another town, and for $50 will deliver anywhere on the Vineyard for stuff you rent three days or more. Sailboard rentals range from $50 per hour to $250 per week, more for expert-level boards. A small-group introductory windsurfing lesson is $80, while a five hour package runs $300. Sea kayaks rent for $30 per 2 hours to $150 per week, slightly more for tandem and expedition models; lessons are $50 per hour. Stand-up paddleboard (SUP) rentals run $35 per hour to $190 per week. Half-day (4 hours), full day (24 hours), and three-day rentals are available for most items. Lifejackets are included in the rental prices, as are wet suits, for windsurfing lessons and hourly rentals (they can also be rented separately).

Lagoon Pond is one of the best spots on the island for beginning and intermediate windsurfers. It's great for kayakers too. Good winds and being away from big ships make it a two-mile-long playpen—although it sometimes buzzes with water-skiers. Access is from the adjacent public beaches. If you brought your own rig to the island by car, Sailing Park Camp in Oak Bluffs is the only public access with parking.

SAILING

Local waters are a day-sailor's delight. If you've left your yacht in San Diego, you can rent or charter something here, from a little Sunfish to a big sloop—or catch a scheduled cruise with one of several operators.

The most visible cruising outfit is undoubtedly Coastwise Packet Company, a.k.a. **Black Dog Tall Ships** (Beach St. Ext., 508/693-1699, https://theblackdogtallships.com), owned by Captain Robert Douglas, founder of the Black Dog Tavern and its spinoff merchandising empire. Coastwise has three windjammers dedicated in whole or part to day trips ($80/3 hours, sunset sails available) and charters mid-May-mid-October, with all three in peak service June-August.

The company flagship is the square topsail schooner, *Shenandoah,* a 152-foot (sparred length) motorless wooden ship built in 1964 specifically for passenger service. Only slightly smaller is the meticulously restored gaff-rigged pilot schooner, the *Alabama,* originally built in Pensacola in 1926. The latest addition to the fleet is the *Chantey,* an intimate 38-foot gaff-rigged schooner built in 1927 to a design by William Atkin, whose boats are highly regarded for their seaworthiness.

Both of the bigger ships dedicate several weeks in the height of summer to six-day hands-on cruises for youngsters ages 9-16 ($1,200), so in July-August the only opportunity for adults to catch a scheduled cruise on the *Shenandoah* or *Alabama* may be on Saturday. Fortunately each has room for three or four *dozen* passengers, so it's rare to be turned away even on the day of sailing, although reservations are strongly encouraged.

Day sails on the big vessels last three hours, cost around $80 per person, and, of course, go wherever the wind blows. You'll be able to lend a hand in raising the thousands of square feet of sail, if you want, and can share the wheel with the captain too. Or simply enjoy the salty sea breeze, the slap of waves on the hull, the hum of the wind through the rigging, and the curious gulls overhead while enjoying a complimentary glass of wine. For reservations or information on the fleet's current sailing schedule, drop by the office at the foot of the wharf beside the Black Dog Tavern.

A variety of other options exists for leisure sailing out of Vineyard Haven Harbor during the summer. You could, for instance, call and see if there's a space aboard the ***Ena*** (508/627-0848, $90 pp for 3 hours), a 34-foot John Alden-designed wooden sloop. It is also available for full-day private sailing trips in local waters.

If you want more than just a little half-day cruise on which someone else plays skipper while you feel the wind and spray, you're looking for a **term charter.** ("Bareboat charters," the arrangement whereby you flash your skipper's license and sign a lot of expensive pieces of paper and walk away with a big boat at your command for a week, aren't available on the Vineyard.) Options vary by season and by which boats are there; your best bet is to start asking around for term charters at the docks or the chamber of commerce.

1: West Chop Lighthouse **2:** boys jumping off a bridge **3:** a kitesurfer on Sengekontacket Pond **4:** the ArtCliff Diner

1
2
3
4
The Art Cliff DINER
Est. 1943

Hikes and Rambles

Nearly 1,000 Vineyard acres are available for recreational use, mostly in the form of small preserves with simple trail systems winding through fields and forests, around ponds and wetlands, and along shorelines and streambeds. An excellent, free, island-wide map identifying all accessible conservation properties is available by mail from the **Martha's Vineyard Land Bank Commission** (P.O. Box 2057, Edgartown, MA 02539), or you can pick up a copy in person from their office in Edgartown (167 Main St., 508/627-7141, www.mvlandbank.com).

the tangled forest trail to Cedar Tree Neck

For guidance, pick up a copy of Will Flender's thorough *Walking Trails of Martha's Vineyard* in local bookstores or directly from the **Vineyard Conservation Society** (VCS), an advocacy group headquartered at the **Mary Wakeman Conservation Center** (57 David Ave., Vineyard Haven, 508/693-9588, www.vineyardconservation.org). Two other land-saving organizations, the Sheriff's Meadow Foundation and Vineyard Open Land Foundation, share office space with the VCS at the Wakeman Center.

The **VCS series** (every 2nd Sun. Oct.-Mar.) typically includes at least one hike on privately owned, undeveloped land not otherwise open to the public; the last event of the season is an island-wide beach cleanup on Earth Day in April. The **Land Bank series** (every 1st Sun. Nov.-May) showcases the organization's own fine properties until their culminating full-day cross-island hike on National Trails Day, the first Saturday in June. Both island weeklies, the *Vineyard Gazette* and the *Martha's Vineyard Times,* announce starting times and meeting places a few days before each walk, or you can get the skinny straight from the friendly staff at either organization. Remember that these hikes are often wet or muddy.

The Trustees of Reservations (508/693-7392, www.thetrustees.org) offers off-season hikes and walks, although usually for Trustees members only. Instructions for becoming a Trustees member ($50 individuals, $70 families) can be found on the website.

While some conservation properties ban mountain biking on their trails, the State Forest allows it, and in many cases so does the Land Bank. You'll find each property's policy about bikes—and pets too—at bulletin boards near the trailhead parking areas. And anyone interested in gathering live shellfish at any of the pond or bay-side properties must obtain a town license from the shellfish warden at the appropriate town hall.

Would you prefer solo sailing—or beginners' lessons on something you can haul out of the water without a crane? **Wind's Up!** (199 Beach Rd., 508/693-4252, www.windsupmv.com) rents Sunfish and similar-size boats for $75 per 2 hours, $135 per day; or slightly larger sloops for $115 per 2 hours, $155 per 3 hours. Instruction runs $100 per hour for 1 learner, plus $25 each additional student, or splurge on five private lessons for $400.

ENTERTAINMENT

A variety of groups keep the performing arts alive on the island, often in casual surroundings such as local churches and school auditoriums. Professional theater, however, does have a home of its own: **The Vineyard Playhouse** (24 Church St., box office 508/696-6300, Oct.-June 508/693-6450, www.vineyardplayhouse.org) presents some half-dozen mostly contemporary works by mostly

American playwrights on the main stage between late June and Labor Day (performances 8pm Tues.-Sun.), followed by such perennial off-season events as a fall new-play competition, a winter holiday show, and a spring short-play festival. Rush tickets and previews of all shows are sharply discounted, so if you happen to catch an early dinner in town, it's a cinch to stroll by after and see if there's a pair of good seats left for dessert.

The Playhouse also stages Shakespeare (5pm Wed.-Sat. mid-July-mid-Aug., $25, students and under age 30 $15) in the outdoor **Tisbury Amphitheater,** weather permitting, near the corner of West Spring Street and State Road, beside beautiful Lake Tashmoo.

Named after the local resident and Broadway star whose philanthropy made it possible, nearby **Katharine Cornell Memorial Theater** (51 Spring St.) in Vineyard Haven's Association Hall hosts community theater and chamber music. Consult the island papers or check the display case in front of the building to find out what's currently going on.

The home of the summer blockbuster is the intimate **Capawock Theater** (Main St., 508/627-6689), one of the island's two year-round cinemas showing first-run features and occasional foreign films. Truly independent art-house fare—anything with subtitles, documentaries, and favorites from the Sundance and Cannes festival circuit—is screened on a regular basis throughout the year at the Katharine Cornell Memorial Theater on Spring Street by the **Silver Screen Film Society** (www.mvfilmsociety.com). Schedules are always listed in the weekly papers.

The Vineyard's creative community includes plenty of writers, poets, and scholars who take to the bully pulpit of the **Vineyard Haven Public Library** (200 Main St., 508/696-4211, www.vhlibrary.org) on a fairly regular basis, or pop up for the occasional reading at Bunch of Grapes bookstore. The weekly calendar section of the *Martha's Vineyard Times* (www.mvtimes.com) is the best resource for specific announcements of such upcoming events.

SHOPPING

An abundance of craftspeople and commercial artists consider the Vineyard their year-round home, and Vineyard Haven has its fair share of galleries displaying their work. It has also become the island's center for home furnishings, with an eclectic collection of retailers offering very personal visions of how to beautify your nest, from kilims to English country antiques. There are unique specialty stores too—aromatherapy potions here, Native American jewelry there—and enough apparel shops to keep a clotheshorse occupied for hours. No need to shop on an empty stomach either—you can grab a quick sandwich or snack around almost every corner.

Baked Goods

One of the first sights to greet passengers disembarking from the Woods Hole ferry is **The Black Dog Bakery** (11 Water St., 508/693-4786, www.theblackdog.com, 6am-5pm daily, $2-5), across from the Stop & Shop Market. Although the muffins seem to have shrunk in proportion to their popularity, the Dog is still a mighty contender in the island's baked goods sweepstakes. The related tavern on the beach behind the bakery was famous even before President Clinton and family stopped in for a bite while vacationing here in the 1990s, but the place now seems determined to clothe half the planet in its trademark T-shirts—which is why part of the bakery may at first glance resemble a sportswear store.

Clothing

If you're interested in seeing what, besides clothing, the owners have chosen to put their logo on, from black-lab dinnerware to paw-print drawer pulls, stop in at the **Black Dog General Store** (508/696-8182, 8am-10pm daily in season, hours vary off-season) behind the bakery. If you manage to somehow escape Vineyard Haven without paying this place a visit, don't worry—like an increasing number of other island retailers, the Black Dog General Store has branches in all three down-island towns.

Stina Sayre Design (43 Main St., 508/693-5180, www.stinasayre.com, by appointment Jan.-Mar., 10am-5pm daily Apr.-June and Sept.-Dec., 10am-6pm daily July-Aug.) is a small atelier of women's couture. If you're on the island around Thanksgiving, you can catch Sayre's annual fashion show at the Mansion House, but she also welcomes drop-ins and enjoys meeting potential clients in person.

Housewares

Decorative wares of subtle beauty fill **Nochi** (29 Main St., 508/693-9074, www.nochimv.com, 10am-5pm daily Apr.-Dec., open later in high season), from fine table and bed linens to distressed furniture. European ceramics, selected clothing for women, French soaps, and fresh flowers round out the many items of interest, but this shop is also noteworthy for carrying the delectable and inspired confections of both Vosges Haut-Chocolat and Mariebelle, two of the country's outstanding boutique chocolate makers.

A retro blend of new, old, and new reproductions of the old are found at **Mix** (65 Main St., 508/693-8240, 9am-7pm daily July-early Sept., 10am-5pm daily Sept.-Dec. and Apr.-late-June, erratic hours Jan.-Mar.), a store that more than lives up to its name. There are trays made from recycled magazines, hula-girl highball glasses, old matchboxes, antique cameras, vintage diner signage, and whimsical onesies and other baby clothing. There's colorful melamine and acrylic tabletop goods from Precidio (the Canadian company that brings you Rachael Ray's line of hipster products), sake sets cast from Limoges porcelain, and a broad line of quality ceramics by Mud Australia as well as quilts, scarves, sun hats, floor mats, canisters of gourmet loose teas, and first-edition Golden Books for kids. The gift possibilities are, as you can imagine, virtually endless.

If $80 scarves or $2,000 hand-finished wooden sideboards aren't in your budget, there's always **Chicken Alley Thrift Store** (38 Lagoon Pond Rd., 508/693-2278, www.mvcommunityservices.com, 11am-5pm Tue.-Sat.) between Island Color and Tisbury Printers, a block from the post office. Some surprisingly high-quality merchandise has been known to turn up on the racks amid all the old record albums, used clothing, and household jetsam, making shopping there a little like playing the lottery.

Gifts and Decor

As a port of some renown, Vineyard Haven has the usual complement of marine-related services on Beach Road around the many boat repair shops. It isn't all outboard motors and antifouling paint, though, as illustrated by the flea-market array of consignment material at **Pyewacket's** (135 Beach Rd., 508/696-7766, 11am-4pm daily), in the yellow clapboard house between the shipyards and the Tisbury Market Place mini mall.

If you paid attention to the upper stories of the downtown streetscape, you probably noticed the pterodactyl weathervane adorning the building opposite the Bank of Martha's Vineyard on Main Street. That little woman grasped in the dinosaur's talons is, of course, Raquel Welch, but if you remember the 1960s cult classic *One Million Years B.C.*, you already knew that. If you wonder where that vane came from—and whether you can get one like it—head to the studio-cum-gallery of **Tuck & Holand Metal Sculptors** (275 State Rd., 508/693-3914, www.tuckandholand.com, 10am-5pm Mon.-Fri., or by appt. anytime), about 10 minutes' walk out of town along State Road. There's about a two-year waiting list for the firm's unique repoussé (French for "pushed from the back," referring to how they're made, not how they work) weathervanes, which sell for prices starting in the low five figures for custom designs. But a few stock items are typically for sale in the display room. Browsers are warmly welcomed, and it's always fun just to watch Andy Holand tattooing a good mamba on his latest work in progress,

Vineyard Cuisine

oysters on the half-shell

Most Vineyard eateries compete for either the country-club surf-and-turf set or upscale palates accustomed to fine comestibles at high prices. Local epicures have come to expect fresh herbs, organic greens, bottled water, and meat-free menu selections—so if what you're looking for isn't on the menu, ask. Even delis and fried-seafood shacks cater to health-conscious herbivores with veggie burgers, so in this way the Vineyard offers (for those that can get to it) a variety of healthy eating options that Cape Cod doesn't currently have. If you enjoy wine with your dinner, remember that Oak Bluffs and Edgartown are no longer the only Vineyard communities where you can buy alcohol in stores or restaurants: finally (can you hear the tourists rejoicing?) Vineyard Haven is a wet town too. If you're dining in one of the island's other dry towns, be sure to bring your own—and expect a small corkage fee to be added to the bill.

Most places stay open seven days a week in season, then cut back days and hours when business becomes more uneven. Before or after the June-August season, confirm that your destination restaurant is open before making a pilgrimage.

or to flip through the portfolio books of his and his late partner Travis Tuck's past work. Many of their unique works adorn off-island homes and buildings, from a Steven Spielberg-commissioned velociraptor to the Nittany Lion over Penn State's Beaver Stadium. You'll also find Tuck's designs atop a couple of local town halls, supermarkets, the *Gazette* offices in Edgartown, and the hospital.

FOOD

Seafood

For the ultimate seaside vacation meal, try a bluefish sandwich and soft-serve ice cream from **Sandy's Fish & Chips** (5 Martin Rd., 508/693-1220, 11am-7pm Mon.-Sat. late Apr.-Sept., $7-13), at the corner of Martin Street in the same building as John's Fish Market. While Sandy's can certainly fill your beach basket, picnickers who prefer to play Dagwood and build sandwiches from scratch are best served by the friendly **Tisbury Farm Market,** across from Cronig's Market. You'll find imported cheeses, olives, and other fixings—and high-quality baguettes, focaccia, and other fresh loaves to put 'em on.

American

Easily the most famous Vineyard restaurant is **The Black Dog Tavern** (21 Beach St. Ext., 508/693-9223, www.theblackdog.com, 7am-10pm daily mid-May-Dec., call for hours off-season, dinner $23-34), next to the ferry staging area in Vineyard Haven, behind the Black Dog bakery-clothing store full of Black Dog brand wearables. The T-shirts have been sighted around the world, from Patagonia to Nepal, and if you're grabbing a snack at the bakery counter, you may marvel that global fame hasn't brought tremendous price hikes. The tavern's prices, on the other hand, are more typical of the island's best dining spots, although it isn't one of them—not for dinner, at any rate. Better to come for breakfast, when you can enjoy the harbor view and nautical mementos without breaking the bank. It's absolutely mobbed in summer; reservations are not accepted. While it doesn't have the full menu of the downtown location, the Black Dog's satellite Bakery Café, on State Road at the southern edge of town, nearly opposite the turnoff for the Tisbury Park and Ride, is a good alternative for up-island visitors who want to sample the muffins, chowder, or burgers but avoid the morass of Five Corners traffic.

Named after its original owners, the ★ **ArtCliff Diner** (39 Beach Rd., 508/693-1224, 8am-3pm daily Thurs.-Tue. May-Mar., $8-15) offers hearty choices, from steak and eggs to potato pancakes, although admittedly everything is done up with a Vineyard touch: fresh-squeezed OJ, fine herb and nut breads, plenty of vegetarian options to complement the burgers and lobster rolls, organic yogurt with the granola, and fine Vermont cheddar for the grilled cheese. Breakfast mavens can order their favorite egg dishes right up till closing. There's also a food truck when your meals need wheels. What are you waiting for?

Alternately, if you've got a sweet tooth, try **Pie Chicks Bakery** (395 State Rd., 508/693-0228, www.piechicks.com, 8am-4pm Tue.-Fri., 8am-2pm Sat.), where freshly baked pies, pastries, breads, and other delights await you. It's on State Road as you're leaving Vineyard Haven. They are also at the West Tisbury farmer's market on Wednesdays and Saturdays.

Fusion

When dinnertime rolls around, most diners seem to head to Oak Bluffs and Edgartown, where liquor licenses are in ready supply. Though not in the town center, **Scottish Bakehouse** (977 State Rd., 508/693-6633, www.scottishbakehousemv.com, 6am-7pm daily, entrées $7-14) is a great option. They use local, sustainable, and organic produce to make a scrumptious assortment of baked goods, plus sandwiches, burgers, pasta, and even Thai noodles. This is better as a takeout joint, but there is limited seating and a lawn if you're up for a picnic.

ACCOMMODATIONS

Under $150

The Vineyard's best budget option for overnight stays is camping. Since the island doesn't offer much of a backcountry wilderness experience, fiscal austerity is about the only reason to camp. The only place to do it is **Martha's Vineyard Family Campground** (569 Edgartown Rd., 508/693-3772, https://campmv.com, May 15-Oct. 15). It mostly attracts RV-style campers, but tenters are tolerated. Rates are $59-84 for tent sites for two adults, $15 per additional adult, $5 per additional child, or $70-105 for a trailer or RV and two adults. They rent pop-up campers too. Dogs are only allowed in the off-season, but motorcycles and mopeds are permitted.

Many places, even fancy ones, duck under the $150/night range in the shoulder season. So if you're needing to keep to a tight budget, plan to visit before Memorial Day (late May) or after Labor Day (early Sept.) and rooms that go for $300-400/night during July and August may be within your reach.

$150-250

In summer, the pickings in this price range can be counted on your thumbs, but outside

Advice About Accommodations

Any skeptic who doubts the Vineyard's hot-spot reputation obviously hasn't tried to book a room here in summer, when the island's 100-plus inns, B&Bs, motels, hotels, guesthouses, and resorts are as full as Las Vegas on a Saturday night. Demand is strong enough to keep many innkeepers busy playing their annual game of brinkmanship with visitors, ratcheting up room rates and lengthening minimum-stay requirements to the extreme or ridiculous. So far, most visitors aren't blinking, so scores of the island's rooms now easily top $200, and few accept single-night bookings, not only in high season, but also on weekends and holidays most of the year.

If these stats are troublesome, don't give up hope—just modify your expectations. Staying flexible with your travel dates, sharing a bathroom, accepting smaller quarters, and settling for guest rooms without views are all tactics for maximizing your chance of locating lodging. Leaving kids at home may help too, since most B&Bs and small inns cultivate a kid-free atmosphere. As a rule, the fewer antiques it has or the larger the establishment, the more likely it welcomes families.

Speaking of expectations, traditional B&B lovers should be warned that full breakfasts are possibly the island's rarest amenity. If waking up to eggs Benedict, fresh fruit pancakes, or crepes is why you're choosing a B&B, inquire carefully about what's for breakfast before guaranteeing that three-night reservation with the nonrefundable deposit.

Looking for a place with a private beach? Don't get your hopes up too much, as you can count the number of candidates on your hands. As an alternative, consider up-island accommodations that afford guests the privilege of visiting large, beautiful town beaches restricted to local residents—or try for one of the many guest rooms across the street from Oak Bluffs's or Katama's broad public beaches.

Off-season's popular object of desire—the bedroom warmed by a nice crackling winter fire—is likewise available at just a dozen or so properties, although a score more have hearths in living rooms or other common areas. Can you sit by the fire and watch Neptune hurl waves against the shore outside? Only from a distance. This island is made of sand, not stone; outside of the tranquil confines of Vineyard Haven's inner harbor, any lodging built that close to any coastline not reinforced by concrete would wash away in a year.

high season, many of the pricier larger inns—including nearly all those cited in the higher price categories below—may offer something in this range until at least mid-May and again after late October.

The vast majority of the Vineyard's lodging choices are small inns and adult-oriented B&Bs and finding rooms in this range is next to impossible, especially in the summer peak. Built back when President Jefferson was welcoming Lewis and Clark home from their river trip, **The Look Inn** (25 Look St., 508/693-6893, http://lookinnmv.com, year-round, $175-200 d), at the corner of William Street, offers contemporary prints in tasteful, guest rooms with sinks tucked in corners to make sharing the bath that much easier. The serenity of the breakfast table beside the garden's little ornamental fish pool will make Main Street's bustle seem much farther away than the few blocks it really is.

East of downtown is a quiet residential area occupying high ground overlooking the harbor. Here, just minutes' walk from shops and restaurants, sits **The Nobnocket Inn** (60 Mt. Aldworth Rd., 508/696-0859, www.nobnocket.com, $170-550 d), on two landscaped acres above wooded Cat Hollow. Built in 1906, this chic inn offers seven guest rooms, airy island decor, and great proximity to the streets and treats of the island.

$250-400

The most stylish and luxurious property in town is the ★ **Mansion House** (9 Main St., 508/693-2200 or 800/332-4112, www.mvmansionhouse.com, from $309 d), smack-dab in the center of town. While outwardly resembling a classic clapboard "painted lady" Victorian resort, it is in fact thoroughly modern, having risen from the ashes of the 2001 fire that burned its historic predecessor to the ground. The gables, bays, verandas, balustrades, and lofty cupola are all an architectural tip of the hat to the past, but inside the decor eschews frills and lace in favor of a clean California sun-drenched look. New construction means no creaking 19th-century floors, wafer-thin walls, or plumbing shoehorned into former closets—instead the spacious rooms feature central air, soundproofing, and full-size baths. Some deluxe units and suites ($359-720) also come with oversize plasma TVs, gas fireplaces, and porches that look out over the harbor, and all guests can relax on the rooftop deck with its lovely panoramic views. Rates include breakfast at the inn's restaurant, and there is a full spa and health club on the premises, complete with a 75-foot indoor pool and enough fitness equipment to keep up with your customary cardio or free-weight regimen, which is complimentary for guest use.

If you're a family of four or just prefer free HBO to small talk over breakfast with strangers, make a beeline for the **Vineyard Harbor Motel** (60 Beach Rd., 508/693-3334, www.vineyardharbormotel.us, $360-500 d). It's one of the few properties on the island with its own private beach, a short stretch of sand fronting the boat-filled harbor. All guest rooms have a fridge, and some come with a full kitchen, including the penthouse king-bed suite ($750 in summer).

Lambert's Cove Inn (90 Manaquayak Rd., 800/535-0272, https://lambertscoveinn.com, $399-499) is a secluded, snazzy spot nestled in mature forest with ponds and walking paths, gorgeous flower gardens, and lovely lawns. Some rooms are in the main building, a spotlessly restored farmhouse, and the other rooms are part of two separate cottages. There's a pool for those who prefer to sunbathe without the need for finding parking at the beach. The rooms are light-filled and feature cute photos of farm animals. And did we mention the alpacas? Four fluffy alpacas will endear themselves to you during your stay. It's open May through late October, and it has a restaurant on site.

Oak Bluffs

Although even the meadow voles in the most remote acre of the island must by now recognize the tremors of The Season, possibly no place is as utterly transformed by the summer crowd as Oak Bluffs. From its chaste beginnings as host to great Methodist tent revival meetings, "OB" has evolved into the most hip and happening town on the Vineyard, thanks to its after-dark appeal to the under-25 crowd.

Compared to the rest of the Vineyard, there's no denying that on summer evenings, this joint jumps. Cars prowl along "The Circuit" (Circuit Avenue, downtown's main drag), the small handful of nightclubs and bars pulse with music and pheromones, and even underage kids get giddy in the swirl of yearning, strolling up and down the avenue with gossipy enthusiasm, eyeing members of the opposite sex, and lapping up lots of ice cream. Weekenders and tourists, meanwhile, shop and enjoy the carnival atmosphere. At summer's end, the instigators of all the fun vanish as quickly as they arrived, returning to school yards and campus quads and leaving the town as quiet as a banquet hall after a big wedding. Gone are the gaggles of teenagers, the guitarists gently strumming songs, the cross-legged rows of young sidewalk sitters. Gone are the lines at the two cinemas and the crowds spilling out of the amusement arcade. Although the music still blares and the doors stay open until at least Columbus Day, more often than not it feels as if staff outnumber patrons as the end of summer rolls around. The rapid exodus of the town's spirited lifeblood makes OB the first down-island town every year to roll up its summer finery and shutter its colorful facades. Restaurants and accommodations nearly all close by the middle of October, with the pleasant exception of the least expensive eateries, several of which remain open year-round.

But OB's appeal isn't confined to the young. On the contrary, all but the most rural-minded travelers may find it to be the best base for exploring the whole Vineyard. By bus, car, or bike, it's as favorably connected to the rest of the island as you can get, and has ferry connections to more ports—including Nantucket and Rhode Island—than any other island town. Its restaurants and accommodations fit nearly all price ranges—which is more than can be said of any other place on either the Vineyard or Nantucket. It offers some of the most interesting street fairs and special events, from winter's Chili Contest to summer's Jazzfest. Even the beach and brewpub are but a stroll from most accommodations. All this is wrapped in a fanciful Victorian frame of Gothic Revival and Queen Anne architecture.

SIGHTS

Flying Horses Carousel

It doesn't take a kid or a carousel buff to appreciate the craftsmanship of the landmark **Flying Horses Carousel** (508/693-9481 or 508/627-4440, 10am-10pm late-Jun.-early-Sept., 11am-4pm Fri.-Sun. late-May-late-Jun., rides $3.50), a contemporary of Coney Island's first merry-go-round. The 22 colorful steeds, adorned with real horsehair, were carved in 1876 by C. W. F. Dare. (Although it claims to be the nation's oldest working carousel, Rhode Island has an 1870 contender for the title.) If you grab one of the brass rings at the right time, you get another ride for free. (You can tell which kids have been on-island for a while by the number of rings they're able to grab at once.) The carousel is located on Lake Avenue smack-dab between downtown and the harbor.

★ Oak Bluffs Campground

Just behind the commercial storefronts along Circuit Avenue is a carpenter's jigsaw fantasia of the former Wesleyan Grove, now formally known as the Martha's Vineyard Camp Meeting Association grounds, whose tent revivals begat both OB and the island's tourism industry. Stroll through the Arcade on Circuit

Flying Horses Carousel

Avenue and you'll discover a riot of colorful little cottages encircling Trinity Park and its large open-sided Tabernacle like wagons drawn up around a campfire—hidden from downtown by design.

The tall fence and limited entry points were originally intended to restrict the secular influences of the resort community springing up right in the pious campers' backyard. The closely packed cottages—which truly deserve the name, unlike the extravagances perched on the seaside cliffs of nearby Newport—evoke the intimacy of the tent encampment, whose early years were dominated by big tents shared by whole congregations. The steeply pitched roofs and twin-leaf front doors are deliberate allusions to A-frame tents and their entrance flaps.

If the campground seems too neighborly for comfort by modern suburban standards, remember that in the 1860s, when most of these were built, the average huge hotels in the country's most popular resorts were about as communal as you could get, with just about every waking hour spent in the company of fellow guests. For these happy campers, the mutual lives and close ties to their neighbors were not only customary, they were a source of their security. The ethos of the private car and private bath was still over half a century away when most of these little houses were built, and it shows.

With the exception of the 1879 wrought-iron and sheet-metal Tabernacle, the Campground is a celebration of the power woodworking tools newly available in the latter half of the 19th century. The gingerbread trim, porch railings, and window shutters are a catalog of imagination, from the decorative (arabesques and French curves) to the narrative (a hunter and hound chasing a hare). Stop by the **Cottage Museum** (1 Trinity Park, 508/693-5024, www.mvcma.org, 10am-4pm Mon.-Sat., 1pm-4pm Sun. mid-June-mid-Oct., $3) for some free advice on locating the architectural highlights. You can also check out the museum's collection of furnishings, typical of the Campground's Victorian heyday. Some nights in summer, the Tabernacle is used for musical performances, from Wednesday evening community sings to weekend concerts; if you're visiting in August, check the events listings in the local papers for information.

One of the early secular alternatives to gospel preaching was **Illumination Night,** begun by the Oak Bluffs Company in 1869. Houses in both that company's resort development, outside Wesleyan Grove, and the Methodist Campground itself were bedecked with Japanese lanterns and banners that humorously commingled the sacred and the profane in such messages as "We Trust in Providence, Rhode Island." Now, on the third Wednesday of August, Trinity Park and the surrounding cottages perpetuate the lantern-hanging tradition as part of a community event sponsored by the Camp Meeting Association.

Ocean Park

Fronting Nantucket Sound, surrounded by the turrets and balconies of OB's most spacious mansions, seven-acre Ocean Park is the focal point of many festivities. An ornate bandstand, built in anticipation of President Grant's 1874 visit, sits on the huge lawn like a fancy stickpin on a bolt of green felt; in July-August, **free concerts** by the Vineyard Band are held here on alternate Sunday evenings. Here too are the best seats in the house for August's end-of-season **fireworks display,** which doubles as a fund-raiser for the local fire department. Other times in summer it harbors basking couples, Frisbee players, and small kids running themselves silly. Admirers of **Victorian architecture** can stroll the park boundary and find a textbook of picturesque styles: hints of a Tuscan villa here and a Swiss chalet there, Queen Anne towers and piazzas, craftsman and shingle-style influences, and the ubiquitous fancy roof and porch trim deriving from the town specialty—carpenter Gothic.

In the small portion of the park near the police station stands a monument to the end of

Strawberry Fields Forever

One of the increasingly rare chunks of down-island open land that hasn't been turned into house lots, **Whippoorwill Farm** (Old County Rd., 508/693-4994, www.whippoorwillfarm.org) deserves special mention because it's the only place on the island where you can pick up a basket of succulent strawberries.

Strawberries are usually ready for picking around the second week of June and continue at least until the end of the month; depending on the timing of their crops, some plants bear fruit through July as well. Call ahead to check on the pickings.

Straddling three townships—West Tisbury, Tisbury, and Oak Bluffs—Whippoorwill Farm is most easily reached from the OB side. Don't pay attention to the Private sign at the gates of the fancy Iron Hill Farm housing development, by the way—maybe it helps to justify adding another digit to the value of those pond-side estates or is a minuscule deterrent to the moped-riding, six pack-toting teens who used to hang out here, but the road is most assuredly public.

the Civil War—"The Chasm is closed," begins its inscription. Though it definitely depicts a bronze Union soldier (notice the "U.S." on his belt buckle), the local resident who bestowed the statue as a gift to the town was also a veteran of the 21st Regiment of Virginia, which is why there's a tablet dedicated "in honor of the Confederate soldiers" on the pedestal.

East Chop Light

At the suburban tip of East Chop along East Chop Drive sits the East Chop Light, originally the island's only private lighthouse. In 1869, Captain Silas Daggett ventured his own money to build the navigational aid, then solicited contributions for its support from fellow captains, ship owners, and marine insurance companies. Besides alleged difficulty collecting after vessels had arrived safely, the civic-minded captain's first tower also burned down and had to be replaced—at no small expense. Eventually, the U.S. government bought the whole thing from Daggett. Finding his lantern building to be "little better than a shanty," the Federal Lighthouse Board approved construction of the present cast-iron structure in 1878. The name on the sign, Telegraph Hill, predates the light by a generation. In the early 19th century, a semaphore tower occupied the spot and sent shipping news from the island to Woods Hole for relay to owners and underwriters in Boston. In the middle of that century, that tower was replaced by an underwater telegraph cable.

Leased from the Coast Guard by the local historical society (229 East Chop Ave., 508/627-4441, https://mvmuseum.org), the light is open to the public for **sunset viewing** on summer evenings (7pm-9pm Sun. late June-July, 6pm-8pm Sun. Aug.-mid-Sept., $5).

RECREATION

Beaches

Running discontinuously below Seaview Avenue's sidewalk promenade is the **OB Town Beach,** the most central of OB's four beaches. Except when low tides expose a decent swath of sand, it's narrow and often gravelly—especially at the northern end, between the harbor entrance and the ferry pier at Ocean Park. Near the foot of huge, grassy Waban Park is the most pleasant and popular part, nicknamed the Inkwell, with lifeguards and swimming lessons in summer. South of the Inkwell, the **Joseph A. Sylvia State Beach** stretches in a broad two-mile crescent between OB and Edgartown, which calls its end **Bend-in-the-Road Beach.** Backed by the windsurfing haven of Sengekontacket Pond, facing the gentle kid-friendly waves of Cow Bay, and easily accessible by the paved OB-Edgartown bike path, State Beach is deservedly one of the island's most popular. There is parking and portable restrooms.

Facing Vineyard Haven Harbor is calm, clear little **Eastville Beach** (minimal parking) beside the Lagoon drawbridge and riprap-lined channel underneath. Although lacking the sheer beachcombing breadth of State Beach, it's a good dipping spot for cyclists or neighboring cottage renters and a prized perch for sunset views. The handkerchief-size beach at **Sailing Camp Park** (a former Lagoon Pond Girl Scout camp off Barnes Road in the wooded residential edge of town), is only recommendable as a put-in for windsurfers—despite the diving raft offshore.

Kayaking

Try your hand at paddling around in local inshore waters with **Island Spirit Sea-Kayak Adventures** (508/693-9727, www.islandspiritkayak.com, $35 per hour, double kayak $55 per hour, double touring model $195 per week). Choose from half- or full-day outings, in ponds or the ocean, under the midday sun or the full moon. Everything is provided: quality boats, dry bags for your gear, safety instruction—all you need do, basically, is show up willing get a little wet and have some fun. They also offer SUP rentals and a night-only glow tour ($195 for 1.5 hours).

Parasailing and Power Boating

Got an itch to sail *over* the water? Consider parasailing with **Martha's Vineyard Ocean Sports** (Dockside Marina, Oak Bluffs, 508/693-8476, www.mvoceansports.com, 8am-8pm daily late May-mid-Oct., $150). It's a cinch: You're rigged up on a platform on the back of a turbo-powered boat and towed up 600 feet in the air for a good 10-12-minute ride. Since dips in the water on returning to earth are entirely optional, you can bring your camcorder without fear of submerging it and give the folks back home a satellite view of New England, including the Newport Bay Bridge in Rhode Island on the western horizon, 25 miles away.

If you'd rather stay on the water's surface, MV Ocean Sports can take care of that too, with waterskiing, Jet Skiing, knee-boarding, Bump & Ride inner tubes—you name it. Banana boats are $45 pp. Guided two-hour sightseeing Jet Ski rides to Chappaquiddick are available starting at $285 for one person. Alternatively, outboard-equipped six-seat Boston Whalers may be rented for $210 per 2 hours, $350 per 4 hours, not including fuel.

ENTERTAINMENT

A frequent contributor to summertime cultural performances is Oak Bluffs's octagonal **Union Chapel** (508/338-7420, www.unionchapelmv.org) on the upper end of Circuit Avenue. Free **organ recitals** fill the warmly resonant wooden interior at noon on Wednesday in summer, while a variety of other musical offerings—from Shaker songs to piano jazz—fills up many an evening between the end of June and the end of August.

Nightlife

With one significant exception in Edgartown, nearly all the nightclub action on the island occurs on Circuit Avenue in Oak Bluffs. Try **The Ritz Café** (4 Circuit Ave., 508/693-9851, 4pm-1am Tue.-Sun.), which does its utmost to uphold lower Circuit Avenue's reputation as a party street, against a background of live music by local bands, ESPN, jukeboxes, and loud conversation fueled by cheap drinks. **Nomans** (15 Island Inn Rd., 508/338-2474, www.nomansmv.com, 11am-10pm), is a popular spot between Oak Bluffs and Edgartown, but better than their food is their full bar and their Prohibition-pride: They have a local rum that's quite tasty. Pick up a bottle or just head to the bar and order some drinks that showcase it. Cheers!

Not exactly "nightlife" but certainly entertaining, **Back Door Donuts** is the Hyde to the Jekyll of **Martha's Vineyard Gourmet Café and Bakery** (5 Post Office Square, 508/693-3688, www.backdoordonuts.com, bakery 8am-3pm Wed.-Mon., Back Door 7pm-10pm Wed.-Mon., doughnuts $1.75-5):

1: view of Oak Bluffs Campground's cottages **2:** the iconic exterior of The Oak Bluffs Inn

1

2

This dainty bakery by day opens the back door at night and serves hot fresh doughnuts to hordes of hungry vacationers who swarm around like sharks in a chum trail hoping to get six or a dozen of these delicious indulgences.

Offshore Ale Company (30 Kennebec Ave., 508/693-2626, www.offshoreale.com, 4pm-close Wed.-Mon., from 11:30 Sat.-Sun.) has jazz and other live acoustic performances, with sets usually starting around 9pm.

Note that island-wide ordinances ban smoking in all restaurants and bars.

SHOPPING

Anyone disembarking from the ferries at Oak Bluffs Harbor will be forgiven for initially thinking that T-shirt, postcard, and candy shops are the only retail trade on offer in downtown OB. In spite of the fact that some of the stores contain the word *gallery* in their names, the only art in the Dockside Market Place by the Hy-Line pier is strictly of the tourist variety. Away from the harbor, past the bars and cafés, the main drag becomes slightly more recognizably part of a real town, with diner-like lunch counters and general merchandisers holding back-to-school sales in the fall.

Amid all the shops competing for your attention, it isn't hard to pick out the vivid and whimsical window display at **Craftworks** (42 Circuit Ave., 508/693-7463, www.craftworksgallery.com, 10:30am-5:30pm daily). From bold Marisol-style folk art to the kind of pottery Keith Haring might have kept around his loft, even their functional crafts exude fun.

If brass temple bells, Peruvian woolens, or things made of kente cloth are more your style, check out the **Third World Trading Company** (52 Circuit Ave., 508/693-5550, www.thirdworldtrading.com, 10am-8pm daily), a few doors up the block. There's apparel at **Cousen Rose Gallery** (71 Upper Circuit Ave., 508/693-6656, www.cousenrose.com, hours vary), past the pottery store at the top of the avenue, but it earns its name with its range of mono prints, pastels, watercolors, and other small painterly work. Don't miss the collection of children's books.

Arts District

Located about 0.25 miles from the harbor on Dukes County Avenue, around the corner of Vineyard Avenue, the Arts District comprises a small cluster of artsy businesses, from interior designers to a recording studio. A good first stop is the **Allison Shaw Gallery** (88 Dukes County Ave., 508/696-7429, www.allisonshaw.com, usually 10am-4pm daily, or by chance or by appointment), in a renovated wood-shingled fire station painted a dusky cerulean blue. Inside you'll find posters, notecards, and fine-art *giclée* prints of the owner's striking photography, along with Vineyard-themed books she has illustrated, from coffee-table volumes of sumptuous color to cookbooks celebrating local products.

The adjacent **Periwinkle Studio** (92 Dukes County Ave., 508/494-2433, www.judithdrewschubert.com, by chance or appt.) is a working artist's space where artist Judith Drew Schubert paints primarily landscapes in oils. Across the street is the studio of Michael Blanchard, who runs **Crossroads Gallery** (93 Dukes County Ave., www.blanchardphotomv.com, 10am-5pm Wed.-Sat., 11am-4pm Sun.), featuring inspirational photography that has helped the artist recover from addiction. Find fantastical or uplifting photos in a variety of styles that range from realistic to impressionistic.

Thirsty shoppers and cyclists will find plenty of refreshment in the coolers at **Tony's Market** (119 Dukes County Ave., 508/693-4799), just down the street. Tony's has good pizzas and huge double-stuffed deli subs too.

FOOD

When dyed-in-the-wool Nantucketers threaten their offspring with visions of the bogeyman, chowing down on pub grub on Oak Bluffs's Circuit Avenue is what they have in mind. But bars don't have a monopoly on this island's cheap eats.

American

Make your way to **Linda Jean's** (25 Circuit Ave., 508/693-4093, www.lindajeansrestaurantmv.com, 7am-2pm daily, $10-19), where sturdy breakfasts, lunches, and early dinners transport patrons back to simpler days and square meals, when coffee came only as decaf or regular and Cool Whip had cachet. Linda Jean's may stay open as late as 8pm in peak season.

Pizza and Italian

Hearty, thick-crusted pizza is available at **Giordano's Restaurant** (18 Lake Ave., 508/693-0184, www.giosmv.com, 11:30am-10:30pm daily late May-early Sept., pizza $14-22, slice $3.50, cash only) filling the entire block opposite the Flying Horses Carousel. But the real reason to come here is the robust and inexpensive red-sauce Italian meals.

Mexican

The tasty ★ **Dos Mas** (50 Circuit Ave., 508/687-9271, https://dosmasmv.com, 5pm-10pm daily, $5-8) is a cozy little taqueria that might be as close as you can get to the border here on posh "MV." The sister location of Backyard Tacos, Dos Mas serves up authentic Mexican tacos in a variety of popular flavors along with tequila, margaritas, and other fun beverages, alcoholic and non. A rooftop bar makes things even more happening.

Brewpubs

OB is home to the island's sole brewpub, the **Offshore Ale Company** (30 Kennebec Ave., 508/693-2626, www.offshoreale.com, 11:30am-close daily, $16-30), where a half-dozen house-made beers are always on tap. While the rustic building and peanut shells strewn on the plank flooring set the tone, the food is above average: generous salads, wood-fired brick-oven pizzas, hearty burgers cooked to order, fresh local oysters, beer-battered fish-and-chips, even a kids' menu. Come summer, the Offshore also features live music from 9pm four nights a week, including a weekly Irish session on Wednesday evening.

For a nice view of the harbor, go to **Lookout Tavern** (8 Seaview Ave., 508/696-9844, www.lookoutmv.com, 11am-10pm daily, $15-30) and enjoy fried food staples and beverages as the sun sets and the boats go by. Nice for young families, too; kids can run around here while the adults talk.

Fine Dining

OB has its high-end eateries too, though they tend to be overlooked by the crowds. For a real splurge, try **The Sweet Life Café** (63 Circuit Ave., 508/696-0200, www.sweetlifemv.com, 5:30pm-close Thurs.-Mon. May-mid-June and early Sept.-mid-Oct., 5:30pm-close Mon.-Sat., 11am-2pm Sun. mid-June-early Sept., $31-49) opposite the Oak Bluffs Inn. The elegance and intimacy of the residential interior and back garden provide the perfect backdrop for the kitchen's contemporary approach to classic continental cuisine, pairing fine meats, fresh fish, and pick-of-the-crop vegetables with flavorful herbed broths, glazes, and wine reductions. The menu may feature enticing options such as Maitake mushroom or kurobuta pork—each plate arranged with a painterly flourish. The expertise also extends to the desserts—life doesn't get any sweeter than this.

Sweets

Oak Bluffs has the most ice cream parlors on the Vineyard. Head to **Carousel Ice Cream Factory** (15 Circuit Ave., 508/696-8614, 10:30am-11pm daily July-early Sept., hours vary daily Mar.-Nov.), possibly the best, and across the street, **Ben & Bill's Chocolate Emporium** (20A Circuit Ave., 508/696-0008, 10am-8pm daily, to 11pm Fri.-Sat. July-early Sept., hours vary daily May-mid-Oct.), possibly the most fanciful—try the lobster flavor for proof, or "moose droppings."

ACCOMMODATIONS

$100-150

At first blush, Oak Bluffs visitors are among the island's most fortunate, since a handful of the town's accommodations squeak in under

$150, though not by much, and often not in the high season. What do these lucky supersavers get for their money? B&Bs and guesthouses with shared baths; usually fans in place of air-conditioning; and fewer frilly fabrics, antique furnishings, and soundly insulated walls than typically found at higher rates.

New kid on the block is **Hotel Ginger** (9 David Healey Way, 508/338-2804, https://hotelginger.com, off-season $135, summer $335), with off-season rates at a steal. The distinctive, almost-haunted-looking building has been a hotel for decades and was just recently remodeled. In the peak of summer, alas, the spot leaves this price range and rates go up about $200 (par for the course), but if you're here in the shoulder seasons of May or late September, try Hotel Ginger. Its tastefully decorated with airy rooms, helpful staff, and proximity to everything, which makes it a top Oak Bluffs option.

The side streets off Seaview Avenue, near the town beach and Edgartown bike path, are lined with modest gingerbread cottages, including a number of lodgings. **Titticut Follies** (37 Narragansett Ave., 508/693-4986, www.titticutfollies.com, May-mid-Oct., $135-145 d, cash only) is a prime example: no TVs, phones, or air-conditioning here, just simple wood-floor quarters painted cheery colors a few hundred yards from the beach. Two guest rooms share a cedar shower-house outside. If you have an appreciation—or nostalgia—for the early postwar decades, you may especially enjoy Titticut's trundle-bed, partial-bath apartment units ($165-175, $775-900 per week), whose kitchens wouldn't look out of place on *Leave It to Beaver.*

$150-250

The next step up over the bare-bones guesthouse is one of the neighborhood's rustic B&Bs. Consider, for instance, **The Narragansett House** (46 Narragansett Ave., 508/693-3627, www.narragansetthouse.com, mid-May-mid-Oct., $175-515 d), a block and a half from Circuit Avenue. Built as a hotel in the 1870s, the main building offers 13 guest rooms decorated in summery pastels and painted white wicker, most with a single queen bed, all with private baths and air-conditioning. The most popular guest rooms have private little porches where you can sit and watch the world go by, but the wraparound front porch also has plenty of comfy rocking chairs to coax you into practicing the art of enjoying the moment. The family-reunion atmosphere engendered by regular patrons is quite fitting for such a casual throwback to a pre-Holiday Inn era.

Several options are smack-dab in the center of town. One of the more attractive is the **Madison Inn** (18 Kennebec Ave., 508/693-2760 or 800/564-2760, www.madisoninnmv.com, May-Oct., $189-299 d), which is as centrally located as you could ask for, being surrounded by restaurants and but a block from the Flying Horses carousel and Ocean Park. Six of the 15 guest rooms have two double beds, perfect for families. Clever construction and carefully selected furnishings, such as flat-panel TVs, maximize the available space, and a warm Southwestern palette gives this place a comfortable atmosphere. Peak rates are mid-June-August.

If you want resort activities—tennis courts, a swimming pool, proximity to golf and beaches—without paying a premium for 24-hour staff and room service, consider the Vacasa-owned **Island Inn** (30 Island Inn Lane, off Beach Rd., 800/863-8415, www.islandinn.com, late Mar.-Oct., $200-650 d), about 1.5 miles from downtown. The decor is comparable to modern motel rooms found along every interstate in the country, with comfortable furnishings and forgettable framed art. However, there are also kitchenettes or full kitchens in every room. There is a wide variety of options and decors, and some of the rooms are pet-friendly as well.

At the quiet end of downtown, **The Oak Bluffs Inn** (Circuit Ave. and Pequot Ave., 508/693-7171, www.oakbluffsinn.com, May-Oct., $235-550, d 2- or 3-night minimum) honors the town's decorative pedigree downstairs, but upstairs a soothing lack of

Victoriana reigns, making the comfortable high-ceilinged guest rooms seem even more spacious. A four-story tower with a rooftop cupola gives late-August guests a skybox seat for the town's end-of-season fireworks display (and simply a great view at any time). The rates, which peak mid-June-Labor Day, do not include an 11 percent tax and "gratuity" surcharge.

$250-350

Facing the Hy-Line ferry landing at the edge of the harbor, **The Dockside Inn** (9 Circuit Ave. Ext., 508/693-2966 or 800/245-5979, www.vineyardinns.com, Apr.-Oct., $135-320 d) tips its hat to the Victorian beach resorts of a century ago and the colorful Carpenter's Gothic cottages all around town. Wide wraparound verandas, detailed woodwork, period fabric prints, and furniture styles all allude to the belle epoque (without succumbing to chintz), but modern amenities and spaciousness abound thanks to the inn's true age (it was built in 1989). Put this within just minutes' walk of all of downtown, a beach, and four summer ferries, and its high-season rates (mid-June-Aug.) compare favorably to all the equally expensive places purporting to swaddle their guests in luxuries. Come in the shoulder months, when rates may drop as low as $99, and you'll receive an even better bargain. Pets are welcome in several of the guest rooms.

Edgartown

With more than 350 years of history, staid old Edgartown is the opposite of youthfully energetic adjacent Oak Bluffs, which is why skateboarders and in-line skaters should be aware of the $20 fine for venturing downtown on wheels. Yachting is the only true sport here, and if you can't afford to maintain a boat for the season, you can still adopt the local dress code of ruddy pink pants and brass-buttoned blue blazer—or a full outfit of tennis whites prior to cocktail hour—and pretend one of those sleek-hulled vessels swinging out there on its mooring is yours.

Called Great Harbor by the English, who made it their first island settlement, and then Old Town after a second community was carved out of Native American land to the west, Edgartown was renamed in tribute to the young son of the Duke of York and finally incorporated in 1671, the same year the Duke gave his approval to Thomas Mayhew Sr.'s private Manor of Tisbury. (Getting the ducal wink and nod was crucial—just a few years earlier, the restored Merry Monarch, King Charles II, had sown great confusion by giving the Duke's Manhattan-based colony nominal control over all the dry land off the southern New England coast, from Long Island to Nantucket.) The most enduring legacy of old Mayhew's rule is Edgartown's continuing role as the seat of regional government—named with anachronistic English pomp the "County of Dukes County" and comprising Martha's Vineyard and the Elizabeth Islands. But the Lord of Tisbury might take a pacesetter's pride in the town's per-capita income (highest in the region) and feel a kinship with the town's many registered Republicans (the largest percentage on the island). For the visitor, however, probably more interesting than the modern abundance of country squires is the town's abundant neoclassical architecture—testament to the wealth accumulated by captains and ship owners in the heyday of whaling.

SIGHTS

Landmark Buildings

Three of the town's architectural treasures are owned by the Martha's Vineyard Preservation Trust, which maintains one as a museum and keeps all three open for scheduled seasonal tours. The Trust's headquarters occupy the **Daniel Fisher House** (99 Main St., 508/627-4440, https://vineyardtrust.org), an elegant Federal-style mansion built in 1840 by one of the island's most successful whale-oil tycoons. Superb though its symmetry may be, the good Dr. Fisher's home was upstaged three years later by his next-door neighbor, the **Old Whaling Church,** a Greek Revival eminence whose giant columns and broad pediment evoke the Parthenon's temple front. The Trust-owned building now does double duty as the Edgartown Performing Arts Center, with a broad variety of secular events complementing the Methodist services still conducted each Sunday beneath the graceful chandeliers. Befitting such a true community center, its 92-foot clock tower is also a landmark for boaters out in Nantucket Sound.

In utilitarian contrast to this pair's grandeur is the **Vincent House** (11am-3pm Mon.-Fri. May-early Oct., tour $15), a simple south-facing example of early New England's homegrown "full Cape" style: a steep-roofed, story-and-a-half box with pairs of windows flanking a central door. Built in 1672, it's the island's oldest surviving residence and retains its original masonry, nails, hinges, handles, and woodwork. It's also the Preservation Trust's museum of island life.

Guided tours (508/939-9650, $15 adult, $10 senior, $7 child) of all three Trust properties and a few more are available at 11am, Tue.-Sat., May-early October, starting from (and including admission to) the Vincent House. Private tours can also be arranged.

★ Historic Downtown Edgartown

The streets intersecting Main Street near the center of town—School, Summer, Winter—are all worth roaming for a good look at the full range of island architectural styles, from old saltboxes and half-Capes to spare Congregational meetinghouses and Tiffany-windowed Catholic churches. But Water Street is the island's premiere showcase of Federal and Greek Revival styles. Wander in either direction, north or south, past the shops and the verandas of downtown inns, and you'll quickly come to numerous 19th-century captains' and merchants' houses lined up along the harbor and looking, with their black shutters and white siding, like so many piano keys.

In this street-size textbook of neoclassical architecture, you should have no trouble spotting either the restrained Federal style of the early 1800s (pilasters framing nearly square facades; columned porticos, fanlight windows, and sometimes even sidelights framing the front doors; smaller third-story windows; and fancy turned balustrades crowning flat roof lines) or the bold Greek columns of the successive style, which came into vogue following the widely reported expeditions of Britain's Lord Elgin to Athens's Acropolis.

★ Edgartown Lighthouse

If downtown's concrete expressions of the 19th century's love of Greek and Roman civilization don't inspire noble resolutions to read your Ovid or Aeschylus, perhaps you'd prefer to sit at the base of the 20th-century Edgartown Lighthouse at the end of North Water Street and entertain more modern sentiments about the inconstancy of sun and tide. By early in World War II, when the present cast-iron tower was brought to replace its 111-year-old predecessor, shifting sand had filled in around what was originally a stone pier set a short way from shore; where once the lighthouse keeper had to row to his post, now you can simply stroll through salt-spray roses.

Still an aid to navigation and owned by the U.S. Coast Guard, the lighthouse is maintained by the Martha's Vineyard Museum. Renovated in 2007 to finally outfit the interior with stairs (previously access to the top was only by ladder), the top of the light is open

1: Edgartown Lighthouse **2:** traditional colonial house in Edgartown **3:** views of traditional colonial houses in front of the sea in Edgartown

1
2
3

to the public (10am-5pm daily mid-June-mid-Sept., 10am-8pm Fri. summer, 10am-5pm Sat.-Sun. May-mid-June and mid-Sept.-mid-Oct., $5).

Chappaquiddick

The Wampanoag people's descriptive name for Edgartown's sibling chunk of tree-covered sand means "separated island," but modern inhabitants have no time for all those syllables; it's "Chappy" now to one and all. But the full name endures in infamy after what happened in 1969, when a car accident proved fatal to a young woman and nearly so to the career of the state's then-junior senator, who was behind the wheel, the late Ted Kennedy.

Sparsely inhabited and infused with rural end-of-the-road isolation, Chappy feels far off the map even when the waiting line at the ferry clearly proves the opposite. Visitors are lured by the superb beaches at Wasque and Cape Poge, but canoeing, bird-watching, bodysurfing, surf-casting, hiking, and walking are equally good reasons to join that ferry line.

Means of access to the island, which isn't quite separated anymore, are limited to the **Chappy Ferry,** a.k.a. the *On Time* (508/627-9427, www.chappyferry.com, $13 cars and driver, $8 mopeds and motorcycles and riders, $6 bicycles and riders, $4 pedestrians) or a good 527 foot swim across the narrow entrance to Edgartown's inner harbor. The ferry runs every day of the year from the waterfront downtown, beginning at 6:30am, with on-demand only earlier departures that cost more. Rates and schedule are posted at the landings, but in brief, you can count on continuous service until midnight in season (May 15-Oct. 15) and until 8pm off-season; after 7:30pm off-season, three periods of service are spread out over the evening with the final run leaving at 11pm-11:15pm. All fares are round-trip and are collected in full on first crossing. Because of the maze of narrow one-way streets approaching the Edgartown waterfront, even bicyclists should follow the Chappy Ferry signs.

FARM Institute

The Vineyard is fortunate to have a number of dedicated individuals and organizations trying to raise awareness about the importance of preserving local farms. With homes being built at an annual rate of nearly five per week, there is unceasing pressure to turn the island's remaining agricultural land into house lots. With an eye on changing the perception of agricultural land and labor through education, the **FARM Institute** (14 Aero Ave., 508/627-7007, https://thetrustees.org) uses hands-on activities to teach kids the value of sustainable food production, responsibility for caring for and raising farm animals, and stewardship of land for the benefit of the community. This 160-acre working farm is nurturing a bumper crop of educated consumers and policy-makers for the future, along with chemical-free meat and produce for local restaurants and markets.

The FARM Institute is located on the right side of Katama Road on the way to Edgartown's South Beach, about 1.6 miles from the fork with Herring Creek Road.

RECREATION

Beaches

When it comes to public beaches, Edgartown is arguably the best endowed on the island, with surf of all sizes and miles of sand. Plenty of athletic-looking bronze-bodied young surfers and swimmers make **South Beach** the Vineyard's answer to Southern California, although easy access from town ensures that everybody can see and be seen on this lively three-mile strand. By the way, the security guard at the far western end of the beach should convince anyone skeptical of the idea that some islanders enforce their waterfront property rights rather rigidly; he no longer packs a sidearm, but that's a small improvement. There is parking and pit toilets.

Swimmers who don't want to battle the undertow may prefer the warmer waters of Katama Bay, accessible from **Norton Point,** the narrow barrier that divides bay from ocean at the eastern end of the beach, or **Katama Point Preserve,** a small sandy chunk of Land Bank property adjacent to the town landing on Edgartown Bay Road. County-owned Norton Point, by the way, is the only part of the Vineyard outside of Chappaquiddick that allows driving on the beach. Required oversand vehicle permits ($140 Apr. 1-Mar. 31, county residents $90) are available for online purchase only (https://thetrustees.org).

Facing Nantucket Sound on the combined outer shores of Chappy's Cape Poge Wildlife Refuge and Wasque Reservation, **East Beach** and **Leland Beach** constitute Edgartown's other breathtaking waterfront. Over four miles of austere, unspoiled barrier beach backed by fragile grass-covered dunes, salt marsh, and salt ponds await swimmers and beach walkers. Swimmers should stay far from the Point itself due to the dangerous riptides. Expect to pay admission in season (May 30-Oct. 15, adults $5, under age 15 free), and to find some bird-nesting areas roped off in summer. Each end of the shore has its own access point: the northern end via Dike Road, and the southern end at Wasque Point. Currently there is no oversand access on Wasque Point due to erosion.

Anyone seeking an escape to the water within easy walking distance of downtown should consider **Chappy Point Beach,** a narrow outer harbor strip of sand on Chappaquiddick, within a short stroll of the *On Time* ferry. Flanking the squat tower of Edgartown Light on Starbuck Neck are two more beaches—**Lighthouse** and **Fuller Street**—0.5 miles of mostly sand, weather depending, as suitable for views of the historic Edgartown Inn or close-up portraits of the lighthouse as they are to sunbathing or swimming. There's no designated parking, nor facilities, but it's a lovely spot to dip or stroll.

Private property ownership prevents anyone on South Beach from venturing farther west, but there is in fact a short amount of public beach on the barrier dunes between the ocean and Edgartown Great Pond. Owned by the Land Bank and named, appropriately enough, **Edgartown Great Pond Beach,** the property is only accessible by boat, which can only be put in at the Turkeyland Cove town landing on the Great Pond (all ponds of sufficient size are public waterways). This landing is at the end of an unsignposted dirt turnoff from Meetinghouse Road just opposite the white fence marked "145." From the West Tisbury-Edgartown Road, it's 1.3 miles south on Meetinghouse to the turnoff (the only one with a Y on the right side of the road), and another 0.8 miles to the actual landing; if coming from Road to the Plains, it's 0.2 miles north on Meetinghouse to the turnoff. After you've set out by boat, aim for the left side of the barrier beach and watch for the Land Bank's boundary-marking signs.

Water Sports

Sengekontacket Pond, shared between Oak Bluffs and Edgartown, is an excellent spot for windsurfers, kayakers, and canoers. Although Sengekontacket can get too shallow at really low tides, it typically has steady winds and is free of motorized craft. Access is from the boat ramps off Beach Road. Strong currents and prevailing offshore winds make **Cow Bay** (in front of State Beach) and enclosed **Katama Bay** (accessible from the town boat ramp on Katama Bay Rd. in Edgartown) the province of more experienced windsurfers and paddlers.

Whether you bring your own boat or the means to transport a rental, you'll find several fine saltwater and freshwater ponds worth exploring, including Poucha Pond at Wasque Reservation and Edgartown Great Pond via the Turkeyland Cove town landing off Meetinghouse Road.

★ SAILING KATAMA BAY

Edgartown remains one of southern New England's most popular sailing spots. You too can experience the beautiful bay and adjacent outer harbor waters off Cape Poge with one of the sailing vessels that call this town home.

For scheduled outings, contact **Mad Max Sailing Adventures** (Mad Max

1
2

Marina, 25 Dock St., 508/627-7500, www.madmaxmarina.com, 2pm and 6pm daily late May-early Sept., call for schedule Sept., $100, under age 10 $90), which offers daily two-hour cruises, rain or shine, aboard its sleek 60-foot catamaran, and an evening sail ($110 pp). Another option is the ***Magic Carpet*** (Memorial Wharf, 508/627-2889, www.sailmagiccarpet.com, daily June-early Oct., $85), a beautiful European-built, teak and mahogany, 56-foot Bermudan yawl designed by Sparkman and Stephens, naval architects renowned for their racing yachts. Join this pedigreed former New York Yacht Club flagship for two-hour public sails four times a day from morning till sunset. Calling on short notice—even the same day—is perfectly acceptable, given that you may change your mind about sailing in uncertain weather, although reservations are preferred. Both boats accept bookings for private sails too. Bring your own snacks and beverages, alcoholic or otherwise.

Felix Neck Wildlife Sanctuary

Owned by the Massachusetts Audubon Society, the **Felix Neck Wildlife Sanctuary** (Felix Neck Dr., 508/627-4850, www.massaudubon.org, trails daily dawn-dusk, $4 non-members) lies on a neck of land jutting out into Sengekontacket Pond, a large windsurfer and waterfowl habitat whose saltwater ebbs and flows with the tides in adjacent Cow Bay. A good cross section of the Vineyard's landscape is found here, from open meadows to woodlands. There's a small freshwater pond attractive to black ducks and mallards, and a bird blind to make their nesting and feeding easier to watch. Similarly, patient observers can spy on the spring nesting of fast-diving ospreys—also known as buzzards—atop poles strategically placed in the open margin of the peninsula's pine groves.

Throughout summer and fall, there are various scheduled walks with naturalists to introduce you to the sanctuary's wildflowers, birds, turtles, and marinelife. Other program highlights include canoe trips, stargazing, snorkeling in Sengekontacket Pond, and even cruises to the Elizabeth Islands. Ask at the **nature center** (9am-4pm Mon.-Sat., 10am-3pm Sun. May-Sept., reduced hours off-season) about these and other current activities.

The entrance is a sandy lane signposted on the Edgartown-Vineyard Haven Road.

North Neck Highlands Preserve

One of the least strenuous yet most rewarding hikes is found at this diminutive Land Bank parcel, where one side of Chappy narrows to the point of being just some hundreds of yards in width. From the first parking lot, a short trail west leads to a sharp bluff with panoramic views over Edgartown Harbor, the lighthouse, State Beach, Oak Bluffs, and the long thin arc of Cape Poge Elbow. Wooden stairs descend to the narrow beach below, with benches helpfully placed on the way down. When the beach is in the lee of the prevailing breeze, a remarkable stillness may be found here—and since swimming is not allowed, the quiet is usually only shared with folks casting lines into the narrow gut through which Cape Poge Pond empties into the harbor. The eastern side of the preserve is along the much rougher, rockier pond shore. Both sides afford fine bird-watching, as migrating species take a rest in the preserve's low, scrubby trees after crossing Vineyard Sound. Access to the property is along a very bumpy sand road—North Neck Road—a little over one mile from Chappaquiddick Road, and a total of about 2.5 miles from the Chappy Ferry.

★ Mytoi

Midway along Chappaquiddick's sandy Dike Road, the scaly trunks and tangled branches of pitch pine suddenly give way to the improbable sight of a little Japanese-style garden. The creation of Mary Wakeman, a well-known local conservationist, **Mytoi** (Dike Rd., Chappaquiddick Island, 508/627-7689,

1: rescue station on a Chappaquiddick beach **2:** one of the many bays on Chappaquiddick Island

http://thetrustees.org, sunrise-sunset daily year-round) is now one of the small gems in the crown of the Trustees of Reservations. The garden exudes tranquility. Even at the zenith of summer, the pond inspires philosophical thoughts; cross the arched bridge to the islet at its center and feel them rise up like morning light. In spring—when the slopes are blanketed with bold daffodils, rhododendrons, dogwoods, azaleas, and roses—the windswept, beach grass-covered dunes at the end of the road might as well be halfway around the world. Although entry is free, contributions toward the site's upkeep are encouraged (note the metal drop box before you get to the pond). A water fountain and restrooms provide amenities rarely found on such rural properties; take advantage of the recycling bins for disposing of those empty cans and bottles rolling around your backpack or backseat.

★ Wasque Point and Cape Poge

The Trustees of Reservations also own nearly the entire east shore of Chappaquiddick, from the southern end of Katama Bay to Cape Poge Bay, from whose waters are taken some 50 percent of the state's annual bay scallop harvest. **Cape Poge Wildlife Refuge** encompasses over four miles of this barrier beach, accessible via Dike Bridge at the end of Dike Road, while **Wasque Reservation** (WAY-skwee) protects a few more miles of dunes and grassland around Wasque Point. Admission is charged to either or both ($5, free under age 15, $5 parking June-Sept., free parking Oct.-May). Restrooms, drinking water, and recycling bins for beverage containers are all found at Wasque; at Dike Bridge there is nothing but a pay phone beside the attendant's shack. There is currently no oversand driving permitted, unlike past years.

The summer crowds come mostly for the swimming and surf fishing (beware of the undertow), but any time of year, this shore is unmatched for the simple pleasure of walking until there's nothing but breaking waves and scuttling sanderlings to keep you company. Bird-watching has gained a steady following too, with ospreys nesting on the pole at the northern end of the refuge, great blue herons stalking crabs through the tidal pools behind the dunes, oystercatchers foraging with their flashy orange bills at the edge of the surf, and ragged formations of sea ducks skimming across the winter ocean. The cedar-covered portions of Cape Poge provide browse for deer

Mytoi garden

and small mammals, most of whom remain out of sight but for the occasional footprint or scat pile; if you're lucky, you may catch a glimpse of one of the resident sea otters slipping into a pond on the way up to the 1893 **Cape Poge Light.**

Thanks to the unremitting erosion along Chappaquiddick's outer shore, this is the Vineyard's most transient lighthouse; the present wooden tower has already been moved three times in the last century, most recently in 1986. Before it was automated in World War II, this lonely post was one of the many spoils available to the political party controlling the White House; whenever the presidency changed hands, so too would the nation's lighthouses (Cape Poge's first keeper was appointed by Thomas Jefferson).

Ninety-minute **Lighthouse Tours** (10:30am, 1pm, and 3pm daily Memorial Day-early Oct., adults $25, children $12) are offered. Joining the Trustees gives you discounts, and also makes it possible to sign up for the **self-guided kayak tours** around Poucha Pond (nonmembers $40, members $32, children $25). Special half-price membership is available on the spot for anyone not yet belonging to the Trustees. Preregistration is required for all of these tours; space is limited.

Flying

Katama Airfield, off Edgartown's Herring Creek Road, is the nation's largest all-grass airfield. Established in 1924, its three runways see quite a bit of use from small private planes. Airborne thrills are available from **Biplane Rides by Classic Aviators Ltd.** (508/627-7677, www.biplanemv.com, $349-699 for 2 people, depending on length of ride), offering open-cockpit flights in a Waco UPF-7 acrobatic biplane. Loops, dives, barrel rolls, and other aerobatic maneuvers can be included for an extra fee.

When you return to earth, stop in at the **Right Fork Diner** (12 Mattakesett Way, 508/627-5522, www.rightforkdiner.com, 7am-3pm and 5pm-9pm daily Memorial Day-Columbus Day), the airfield's diner, for a burger and fries, a taste of the owner's sweet rolls from her grandmother's recipe, or just some Ben & Jerry's ice cream.

Golf

The **Royal & Ancient Chappaquiddick Links** (a.k.a. The Royal Chappy, North Neck Rd., 508/627-2729, www.royalchappy.com, 7am-7pm daily, $200-1,500) links are a membership-only affair, but the good news is that their guest pass option (which you can use for yourself) is only $60 per person, which is reasonable when you consider their family membership is $1,500. If you'll play a lot, there's an individual option ($400 for as much golf as you can play), but they may have other specials. The course is a stunning, history-rich nine-hole par-4 and par-3 stunner, with views of the water. For those in the know, there's an off-season "honor" box if you're dying to get some golf in while the course is closed. And yes, Bill Murray has golfed here. Watch out, woodchucks!

ENTERTAINMENT

Diverse is the adjective for Edgartown's **Performing Arts Center** (89 Main St., 508/627-4440, https://vineyardtrust.org), in the Old Whaling Church, whose calendar typically ranges from big names in acoustic and spoken performance to antiques auctions and assorted other community events. One regular on the church schedule is the **Martha's Vineyard Chamber Music Society** (508/696-8055, www.mvcms.org), whose series of weekly concerts in July-August are performed on Monday nights in Edgartown, and then on Tuesday at the **Chilmark Community Center** (520 South Rd., Chilmark, 508/645-9484, www.chilmarkcommunitycenter.org).

SHOPPING

Edgartown shopping is a mix of trendy off-island chains, boutiques that offer the usual souvenirs, and some truly unique island finds. For real art, check out the island's most prominent galleries, and keep an eye out for places that offer the really eye-catching, offbeat, or just plain unique gifts and indulgences.

While you'll find the most interesting gift and souvenir shopping around the harbor, long-term visitors on errands in cars prefer the commercial plazas on Upper Main Street between the Stop & Shop and The Triangle (the local name for the split between Main Street and the roads to Vineyard Haven and Oak Bluffs). The narrow one-way downtown streets are great for pedestrians, but summer drivers should take an extra dose of hypertension medication before trying to do the same.

Foremost among the harbor-front art venues is the **Old Sculpin Gallery** (58 Dock St., 508/627-4881, www.oldsculpingallery.org, 10am-6pm daily late May and Sept.-early Oct., 9am-9pm daily June-Aug., 10am-6pm Mon.-Sat., noon-7pm Sun. early Oct.-Nov.) opposite the ramp for the Chappy Ferry. Housed in a former boatbuilders' workshop, this is the Vineyard's oldest operating gallery, run by the nonprofit Martha's Vineyard Art Association (MVAA). The MVAA also operates a studio school in the building, offering art classes and workshops for kids, teens, and adults throughout the summer; contact the Sculpin Gallery for details. Drop by for a snack and a sip with the artists at the new show openings (6pm-close every Sun.).

A block up from the harbor is the **Christina Gallery** (5 Winter St., 508/627-8794 or 800/648-1815, www.christina.com, 10am-5pm daily Apr.-Dec., hours vary Jan.-Mar.). The paintings and photographs in this two-story gallery range from unique to predictable, but venture past all the sun-drenched beach, cottage, and sailing scenes and you'll find a trove of antique charts and maps, and prices range from affordable on up, so you may find something that fits your budget.

Whaling tales—plus sailing stories and all manner of island-related reading matter—are found across the street at **Edgartown Books** (44 Main St., 508/627-8463, www.edgartownbooks.com, 10am-7pm daily), knowledgeable suppliers of good reading for beach chairs drawn into the shade or armchairs drawn up to the fire.

Stylish eclecticism is at **Mikel Hunter** (11 Winter St., 508/627-1066, www.mikelhunter.com, by chance or by appointment daily year-round), in the large clapboard home of professional fashion stylist Mikel Hunter. Clothing for men and women, from edgy European designers such as Atelier Aura to Japanese-inspired Nippon West, are juxtaposed with home goods—even perfumes and colognes. Toss in contemporary and abstract paintings and sculpture and you have a mash-up of art and apparel unlike anything else on the Vineyard. They even do events and live music; see the website for more info.

FOOD

It's an old bit of folk wisdom that when you come across a botanical hazard in nature, the antidote is always growing nearby. The same principle applies to the cost of eating out on the Vineyard: if something is beyond your price range, go next-door and you may find it's what you're looking for.

Seafood

Fried seafood fans, meanwhile, should head down to the takeout-only **Quarterdeck Restaurant** (29 Dock St., 508/627-5346, 11am-9pm daily May-Oct., $15-25) by the harbor.

Right at the tip of the Triangle itself is **The Square Rigger Restaurant** (225 Edgartown-Vineyard Haven Rd., at Beach Rd., 508/627-9968, www.squareriggerrestaurant.com, 11am-9pm daily year-round, $24-60), the family-friendly home of surf and turf at prices that turn locals into regulars. If you want to sample lobster, make this your first stop (VTA bus 1, 11, or 13). They also offer takeout.

Coffee Shops

The ★ **Dock Street Coffee Shop** (2 Dock St., 508/627-5232, 6:30am-1:30pm daily year-round), also known as the Dock Street Diner, is the island's hole-in-the-wall antidote to wallet-emptying restaurant prices—right in the heart of Edgartown, no less, next to R. W. Cutler's Bike Rentals at the very foot of Main Street. Postcards from customers taped to the soda fountain machine, out-of-date calendars on the wall, newspapers lying around on the counter, tasty breakfasts for two for $10 before tip, and even decent frappes—see? There is good in the world.

Good-quality takeout, sit-down lunches, baked treats, and liquid refreshments are best obtained from **Espresso Love** (17 Church St., 508/627-9211, www.espressolove.com, 7am-5pm daily year-round, coffee $3-5, food $7-14), behind the County Court House on Main Street.

Among the Flowers (17 Mayhew Lane, 508/627-3233, https://amongtheflowersmv.com, 8am-3pm daily Oct.-May, 8am-10pm daily June-Sept., $9-27), is a delightful spot of sunshine (and good omelets!) near the ferry dock. Subscribers to the banana ice cream diet won't want to miss **Vineyard Scoops** (56 Main St., 508/627-4736, noon-5pm daily, to 9pm Fri.-Sat.).

American

Another of Edgartown's most affordable and dependable restaurants is **The Newes from America** (23 Kelley St., 508/627-4397, www.kelley-house.com, 11:30am-11pm daily late May-early Oct., 7am-10am and 11:30am-10pm Mon.-Thurs., 11:30am-11pm Fri.-Sun. early Oct.-late May, closed Christmas, $17-28), in the Kelley House inn at the corner of North Water and Kelley Streets. Reasonable prices doesn't mean inferior food: The Newes's family-friendly menu of soups, sandwiches, burgers, and dinner-size salads keep the casual crowd happy, as does the great selection of microbrews in bottles and on tap, and some tasty craft cocktails. On winter weekends it's the only place for miles that serves food till 11pm, so night owls take note.

Pizza and Italian

Behind one of the porches of the rambling Colonial Inn, where Somerset Maugham sat out World War II, **Chesca's** (38 N. Water St., 508/627-1234, www.chescasmv.com, 5:30pm-10pm daily mid-June-Oct., 5:30pm-10pm Thurs.-Sun. mid-Apr.-mid-June, $25-44) serves up fine Italian-influenced cuisine with a blend of paper-napkin informality and the hardwood, clapboard dignity of an old New England resort. The dining room's contented murmurs aren't due just to the catchy mood music—the food is inspiringly fresh, seasoned with a bold hand, and prettily garnished. The restaurant doesn't stint on the desserts either, as anyone who believes "the more sugar, the better" will happily discover. Though many entrée prices are over $30, there are some relatively good values on the menu, particularly among the pasta dishes.

Fine Dining

When it's time to impress your traveling companion with a fine meal at a local hot spot with the see-and-be-seen crowd—maybe charred *shishito* peppers with fresh Atlantic swordfish or beef tartare—make a beeline for ★ **Alchemy** (71 Main St., 508/627-9999, www.alchemyedgartown.com, 5:30pm-10pm Mon.-Wed. & Thurs.-Sat., $26-46). Specials change nightly. In the off-season months, the bar is a fine place to discover how island life doesn't allow strangers to stay unacquainted for long.

Out-of-the-ordinary touches abound at ★ **Détente** (15 Winter St., 508/627-8810, www.detentemv.com, 5:30pm-10pm Tue.-Sat., $34-48), a hidden gem. Here you might encounter summer peaches in a savory appetizer, autumnal parsnip pierogi paired with a rich osso buco, Sardinian *fregola* to soak up the jus of a rack of lamb, and local monkfish. More inspiration and flavor is packed into the dozen dishes served here than is found on many menus twice as long.

Markets

Get fresh, healthy, locally grown produce at Edgartown's **Morning Glory Farm** (120 Meshacket Rd., 508/627-9003 or 508/627-9674, www.morninggloryfarm.com, 9am-6pm

Mon.-Sat. summer, 9am-5pm Mon.-Sat. off-season) at the corner of Meshacket Road and Edgartown-West Tisbury Road, about a mile from Main Street. It's in a class by itself.

ACCOMMODATIONS

When it comes to accommodations, Edgartown costs more than any of its neighbors—witness the $300 summer rates for standard doubles in the island's only chain hotel. As a result, the only time you will find guest rooms in the $100-150 range or lower is November-April.

$150-250

Located at the quiet edge of downtown, **Edgartown Commons** (20 Pease's Point Way, 508/627-4671, www.edgartowncommons.com, May-mid-Oct., $192-650) targets families seeking affordable lodgings with its 35 guest rooms—ranging from studio units to one- and two-bedroom suites—all featuring fully equipped kitchen areas. There is an outdoor pool and a playground on the premises. Note that there is no air-conditioning in any of the units—fans are provided instead—and there is no maid service.

$250-350

The **Ashley Inn** (129 Main St., 508/627-9655 or 800/477-9655, www.ashleyinn.net, $290-390 d) occupies a shipshape old captain's home opposite small Cannonball Park. Guest rooms in the main house are a comfortable size (no tripping over your traveling companion's belongings) with unpretentious yet tasteful decor and have TVs and phones. Wonderfully friendly innkeepers and a huge yard that invites curling up in the hammock with summer reading, far from the madding crowd, will make you feel welcome. Prices are, of course, lower before June and after early October, bottoming out at $150-205 January-April; the three-night minimum only applies to high-season weekends. One- and two-bedroom townhouse suites with whirlpool tubs are also available by the week for anyone wishing to lie in the lap of luxury.

The **Edgar Hotel Martha's Vineyard** (227 Upper Main St., 508/627-5161, https://edgarhotelmv.com, $319-539 d) has full-size two-bed air-conditioned guest rooms that are comfortable and recently remodeled. Some of the rooms are accessible for both mobility and hearing.

Stately old Edgartown has a number of large, luxurious inns carved out of elegant 19th-century homes. For example, canopy beds abound at **The Christopher** (24 S. Water St., 508/627-4784, www.theedgartowncollection.com, $359-888 d), which captures Victorian spirit, though rooms now have flat-screen TVs with Apple TV. Thoroughly contemporary, however, is the dedication of the hands-on owners and well-trained staff to your comfort and enjoyment of the island, from the complimentary treats to an ever-ready willingness to help make arrangements for whatever sport or diversion suits your fancy. Predictably, rates peak Memorial Day-early October.

Families with young children should seek out the ★ **Winnetu Oceanside Resort** (31 Dunes Rd., 508/310-1733 or 866/335-1133, www.winnetu.com, $995 June-Sept., $350-475 Apr.-May and Sept.-mid-Oct.), a luxury spot that takes extra pains to make families feel at home. That's not to say it doesn't have plenty to offer a couple looking for a romantic getaway—in fact, part of the beauty of it is that because they've paid so much attention to occupying kids with fun activities, couples with or without kids can feel like they're really getting away. The Dunes (the on-site restaurant) has a supervised corner of the room stocked with race car toys, train sets, videos, Legos, and more where children can escape to the moment they're done eating, leaving parents and surrounding diners a rare chance to eat a meal in peace together. Strewn around the vast grounds are boxes with various toys, including several that have pool safety equipment, such as life jackets. The heated pool is smallish compared to tropical resort standards, but when one considers that the biggest pool of them all is a five-minute walk away (it's called the Atlantic), things aren't so bad. The near life-size chess set in the garden is a popular amusement for children and adults alike, as are the nearby Ping-Pong and foosball tables.

$350-500

An atmosphere of relaxed but graceful welcome infuses the parlor registration area of the ★ **Hob Knob Inn** (128 Main St., 508/627-9510 or 800/696-2723, www.hobknob.com, $499-835 d, suites from $699). Thanks in part to the country decor, there is neither starched nor flowery formality here. Instead, these "eco-boutique" guest rooms sport wicker chairs and rockers on the wraparound porch, and comfy seating in the common rooms invite guests to socialize or simply hang out. The staff are clearly pros—warmly courteous, efficient, and prepared at the drop of a hat to help make your stay positively memorable. The individually decorated guest rooms are larger than average and equipped with air purifiers and white-noise generators in addition to such standard amenities as flat-panel TVs, Wi-Fi, terrycloth robes, and high-end bath amenities. Generous made-to-order breakfasts are included, and there are sauna, fitness, and spa facilities on the premises. You can rent bicycles on-site too. Note that in peak times a 3-night minimum stay may be required.

Providing the perfect backdrop to the beachfront view of the Edgartown Lighthouse, the **Harbor View Hotel & Resort** (131 N. Water St., 844/248-1167, https://harborviewhotel.com, June-Aug. $500 d, suites up to $9000, shoulder season as low as $350 d, $500 suite) is the epitome of a classic Gilded Age seaside resort. Built in 1891, its shingle-style sprawl of turrets, wood railings, gables, and wide verandas looks like something out of *The Great Gatsby,* and is a trendsetter in the Vineyard hotel business. In addition to high-end bath products and furnishings in all of its guest rooms and suites, it earns its place at the summit of local luxury properties with an emphasis on concierge services and activities programs for everyone in the family. From breakfast in bed to champagne on ice at arrival, and from Pilates classes on the lawn to fishing charters aboard the hotel's own boat, the Harbor View can pamper like no other.

Up-Island

In a place that's already about as laid-back as New England gets, up-island is where the Vineyard truly goes footloose and fancy-free. Yet the relative seclusion of the up-island villages have traditionally meant that they are the purview more of the summer resident or cottage renter (and celebrities seeking true rural privacy) than day-trippers or weekenders, despite the hordes of bus tourists flocking to the renowned Gay Head Cliffs. "Out of sight, out of mind" seems to be up-island's best disguise—trailheads look a lot like just more private driveways, their flora and vistas hidden from view. Visitors dedicated to maximizing beach time give scant thought to the up-island forests, and people who spend the big bucks to bring their cars across seem most likely to use them to avoid exercise rather than to explore the nooks and crannies where public shuttle- and tour-bus riders can't go. In short, for a variety of reasons, even many up-island regulars never bother to explore the unheralded hilltops, ponds, and meadows virtually in their own backyard. All of which means that if you're able to spare the time and expense to get around up-island at your own pace, you still have the chance to discover the quiet, down-home place that for most down-island residents exists now more in memory than in fact.

WEST TISBURY

Oak Bluffs may boast greater diversity, but the most politically liberal town on the island is this 1896 splinter from next-door Tisbury. Familiarly known as "West Tis" (rhymes with *fizz*), the community had no qualms about allowing hippies to set up camps in the woods back during the first reign of bell-bottoms and the fringed halter. Even today, the area sets the standard for island liberals.

West Tisbury Farmers Market

Although this was one of the fastest-growing towns in the entire state of Massachusetts during the go-go years of the 1980s, agriculture is still a vital part of West Tisbury's economy and landscape. From onions and lettuce to strawberries and cream, ingredients of an island-grown meal are likely cultivated here. Most of the upscale restaurants around the island make a point of using local produce wherever possible, but for a true taste of the Vineyard's gardens, look no farther than the **West Tisbury Farmers Market** (The Grange Hall, www.wtfmarket.org, 9am-noon Wed. and Sat. mid-June-mid-Oct.). The Grange Hall (sometimes still referred to as the Old Ag Hall) is a picture-book 1859 Gothic Revival shingled and gabled barn on State Road in the town center. There are farm stands down-island too, but between mid-June and Columbus Day weekend, The Grange is *the* place to go, as much for the ambiance as for the fruits of the earth. Along with purveyors of affordable vine-ripened tomatoes and enough cruciferous vegetables to make even the surgeon general happy, there are always a few vendors selling fresh-cut flowers, a few masters of the Mason jar selling pickles and preserves, a few bakers with homemade desserts, and perhaps even fresh-spun yarn from the fleece of just-sheared sheep. Thi Khen Tran's famous eggrolls are also a sought-after standard at the Grange.

Up-island's other celebration of its agrarian lifestyle, August's annual **Livestock Show and Fair,** raises the rafters of the New Ag Hall with a Vineyard version of the standard county fair; expect oyster shucking contests and great live music along with horse pulls and tables of homegrown or homemade food. Also known as the Fairgrounds, the new hall is on Scotchman's Lane about 0.5 miles north of the old one.

The Field Gallery and Sculpture Garden

Like a page of Norman Rockwell's sketchbook, the village around the farmer's market is exemplary 19th-century picket-fence New England, from the handsome Congregational Church and well-trod porch of Alley's General Store to the proper old homes on tree-lined Music Street. Once known as Cowturd Lane, this leafy residential way was renamed back in the 1800s for the piano-playing daughters of a resident whaling captain and six of his neighbors. Those old ivories are long silent, but the visual arts live on in and around the **Field Gallery and Sculpture Garden** (1050 State Rd., 508/693-5595, www.fieldgallery.com, 10am-5pm Mon.-Sat., 11am-4pm Sun. May-Sept., call for off-season hours), next door to the Council on Aging center and wonderful town library. As at most other island galleries, exhibits here are condensed for the summer rush, so each Sunday evening is opening night for the new art of the week.

Granary Gallery

Half a mile away, facing the end of Scotchman's Lane, is the large **Granary Gallery** (636 Old County Rd., 508/693-0455, www.granarygallery.com, 10am-5pm Mon.-Sat., 11am-4pm Sun. late May-early Oct., 10am-5pm Sat., 11am-4pm Sun. Easter-late May and early Oct.-Christmas), which has the distinction of being the Time-Life Gallery of Photography's sole New England representative. So, in addition to locally produced artwork in a variety of media (painting, sculpture, and sometimes textiles), you can browse—or buy—limited editions, mostly signed, of museum-quality prints by the likes of Alfred Eisenstaedt, Margaret Bourke-White, Andreas Feininger, Carl Mydans, and others whose contributions to *Life* magazine have become some of the nation's most recognizable cultural images.

North Tisbury

Within 25 years of their arrival, the English outgrew their settlement at Edgartown and moved up-island to this fertile area between Priester's Pond and Lambert's Cove Road. It was known to the Wampanoag as Takemmy ("place where people go to grind corn"), but the name may actually come from *touohkomuk* ("wilderness"). The English shepherds called the settlement Newton (Edgartown then was Old Town) and later Middletown. Now named after the post office station sandwiched into a storefront within a small shopping plaza, this part of West Tisbury township no longer qualifies as very wild, although it's still plenty rural.

One part of the scenery worth stopping for is the **Polly Hill Arboretum** (809 State Rd., 508/693-9426, www.pollyhillarboretum.org, grounds dawn-dusk daily year-round, $5, visitors center 9:30am-4pm daily Memorial Day-early Oct.), about 0.5 miles south of the junction with North Road (to Menemsha). Old stone walls are reminders that these 60 acres were once a sheep farm, but Hill, a famous horticulturist, turned one-third of the property into an open-air laboratory for her work with ornamental trees and shrubs. The rest is kept in natural meadows and woods. Perhaps the most captivating time to visit is mid-June-July, when the lovely kousa dogwoods are in full bloom, but there are numerous rare and beautiful species worth seeing throughout the year, as well as a variety of programs at the visitors center.

North Tisbury's commercial side includes a couple of arty shops along State Road, most notably **Martha's Vineyard Glassworks** (683 State Rd., 508/693-6026, www.mvglassworks.com, 10am-6pm Wed.-Sun., late May-early Oct.), where the art of shaping attractive, functional items out of molten glass is on view daily in season.

Christiantown

Although the Puritan founders of the Massachusetts Bay Colony had obtained their royal patent by promising that "the principall Ende" of their settlement was to convert the indigenous people to "the Christian Fayth," the evangelical magistrates in Boston were so busy prosecuting heretics and building a profitable mercantile trade that it was here on the Vineyard—outside their jurisdiction—that the first New England mission to the Native Americans began. The year after the Mayhews settled their parish in Edgartown, a Wampanoag named Hiacoomes became the island's first voluntary convert to Christianity. Within a decade, over 10 percent of the Vineyard's indigenous population had signed a covenant with the proselytizing Thomas Mayhew Jr.; within a generation, a majority of the Wampanoag on both the Vineyard and Nantucket had not only converted but had also resettled themselves into a series of 15 Christian communities modeled after the English style, a move heralding the profound change colonization wrought on both Wampanoag culture and their relationship to the land.

One such town stood in North Tisbury on what's now Christiantown Road, off Indian Hill Road. With the blessings of Thomas Mayhew Sr., Wampanoag converts consecrated their first Christian church and burial ground here in 1659, on a parcel of land rented from a pair of up-island sachems. Besides the small number of descendants denied federal status as Native Americans, all that's left of Christiantown now is tiny little Mayhew Chapel, an 1829 replacement of the original; the mostly unmarked tombstones opposite; and abandoned 19th-century cellar holes and stone walls along the peaceful loop trail through adjacent **Christiantown Woods Preserve.** A walk about 0.25 miles past the parking lot (follow the road and take the first right; it is not drivable) is a state-maintained **fire tower.** When the tower is staffed—which is only when fire danger is high—you are welcome to go up and enjoy the fine 360-degree views.

CHILMARK

Sparsely populated Chilmark, whose year-round population is less than 850, once resembled a little corner of New Zealand, with more sheep than humans. The resemblance stopped at labor and farm expenses, though; before Down Under's huge sheep stations put the kibosh on profitability, back in the mid-19th century, Chilmark wool had been second only to whale oil in importance to the island economy. The whalers themselves made use of the wool in the form of heavy-duty satinet coat fabric milled in neighboring West Tisbury. Dozens of miles of drystone walls, all built from up-island's limitless supply of glacial till, lie half-hidden in the now-forested hills, quiet reminders of the loose-footed flocks of black-faced sheep that once dominated the local landscape. If you've taken a close look at this kind of wall elsewhere in New England, you'll notice that the Vineyard has a distinctive "lace wall" in its repertoire—a rickety-looking style with big gaps between the stones. The usual explanation has been that these perforated walls were built to accommodate stiff ocean winds raking over the once-treeless up-island hills, but Susan Allport, author of the exceptional *Sermons in Stone,* suggests the design may be a Scottish import. Although there is no written record one way or the other, a nearly identical style of see-through stone wall in Scotland—called a Galloway dike—was built to look deceptively precarious specifically to frighten bold sheep from attempting to leap over them.

Despite having its trees and vegetation shorn to the ground by its early "husbandmen," Chilmark still boasts some of the island's best soil and farms still seem to outnumber retail shops, even if these days artists and telecommuting professionals far outnumber local farmers. The center of the village is the intersection of State Road (alternately known in Chilmark as South Road), Middle Road, and Menemsha Cross Road, named Beetlebung Corner after the stand of tupelo trees whose hardwood was valued by ships' chandlers for making mallets (beetles) and cask stoppers (bungs). On the east side of the intersection is the **Chilmark Library** (522 South Rd., 508/645-3360, www.chilmarklibrary.org, Mon.-Sat.), whose Island Room is an ideal rainy-day destination for anyone whose appetite has been whet by the morsels of history presented here. Also hard by the corner is the **Chilmark General Store** (7 State Rd., 508/645-3739, http://chilmarkgeneralstore.com, 8am-5pm Tue.-Sun. May-mid-Oct.), a worthy pit stop for cyclists and others in need of a sandwich or a slice of pizza. If your consumer impulse runs to something more stylish than groceries and minor housewares, check out the town's popular **flea market** (9am-2pm Wed. and Sat. end of June-late Aug. or early Sept.), on the grounds of the Community Church, where mostly professional craftspeople, artists, and antiques dealers market seconds or blemished wares passed over by regular retail buyers at prices that, while not a steal, are generally well discounted. Locavores will want to seek out **Grey Barn Farm** (22 South Rd., 508/645-4854, farm stand 8am-6pm Wed.-Mon.) for its raw, unpasteurized milk (they have pasteurized too!), along with a varying selection of cheese, pork, veal, and other farm-grown goodies.

With the exception of the village of Menemsha, most of Chilmark is rather leery of visitors. Summer's hordes may pay the bills, but that hasn't alleviated the "not in my backyard" syndrome. (If you've never thought of yourself as the vanguard of the great unwashed, just attend a local town hearing the next time someone proposes creating a public beachfront reserve and listen to the dire predictions of how you'll ruin the neighborhood. You'd think tourists are Hell's Angels in beach wear.) But not all Chilmark's inhabitants are

1: Tisbury's atmospheric Grange Hall **2:** the Menemsha Bike Ferry **3:** Martha's Vineyard Ferry at Tisbury **4:** the beautiful fishing village of Menemsha

GRANGE HALL
1
2
BIKE FERRY
VIA
MENEMSHA
ALTERNATE BIKE ROUTE
TO DOWN ISLAND
9 A.M.- 5 P.M.
BIKE
FERRY
RING BELL ON DOCK
FOR SERVICE
3
4

loath to receive visitors; nothing's going to faze Lillian Hellman or John Belushi, for example, at their eternal residences in **Abel's Hill Burying Ground,** on South Road less than three miles from West Tisbury's town line. While they're probably the most famous tenants, anyone with an eye for good epitaphs and fine stone carving will take greater interest in the many historic 18th- and 19th-century markers.

Menemsha

Anyone who wants proof that some of the people around here make a living off something besides tourism can come to this Chilmark village and admire the Coast Guard station poised above the water in the golden light of a late summer afternoon. But the even bigger attraction is the fishing fleet in Menemsha Basin, whose catch ends up on plates all over the island. Watching guys in rubber boots shovel fish into barrels against a backdrop of buoy-covered shacks crowned with whale-shaped weathervanes is undeniably picturesque—especially compared to down-island's retail barrage—but it resists any use of the word *quaint.* If this place is an anachronism, it's only because so much of the region no longer soils its hands with old-fashioned cash register keys or touch-tone telephones.

Besides watching sunsets framed by the boat basin's thicket of swaying masts, Menemsha's summer visitors come for hiking, swimming, and seafood in the rough. Cyclists looking for a shortcut to Aquinnah—and a chance to avoid some of the hills and punishing headwinds encountered on State Road—won't want to miss the **Menemsha Bike Ferry** (508/645-3511, $5 one-way, $8 round-trip, late Jun.-early Sept.), which shuttles across Menemsha inlet to West Basin, near the east end of Lobsterville Beach. It operates on demand 8am-6pm daily July-Labor Day, plus weekends in the shoulder seasons of June and September-October, weather permitting. Before you make a descent to the Menemsha inlet, check the signs at any of the approaches in Chilmark, West Tisbury, or Aquinnah to confirm whether the ferry is indeed running.

AQUINNAH

The remotest of the island's six towns, rural Aquinnah (year-round pop. 344) seems to stand in sharp relief against the fortunes of its sister communities. Although its population rebounded in the 1990s to keep pace with the rest of the Vineyard's double-digit percentage gains, Aquinnah has an unemployment rate nearly three times the statewide average, and the lowest average household income in Massachusetts. By the numbers, it would seem to belong in Appalachia rather than on one of New England's most star-studded resorts. The numbers, however, don't tell the full story. Most of the town's property owners are summer people whose incomes boost the statistics somewhere else—if their accountants let the government know about it at all. Many other residents thrive on an underground economy of cottage artisanship, cash contract work, or investment income that escapes the attention of labor statisticians. With vacant land selling for $200,000 per acre and town kids tending to go to prestigious colleges and graduate schools, Aquinnah might be called many things, but "poor" isn't one of them.

Along with Mashpee on Cape Cod, Aquinnah is one of two Massachusetts communities with a significant Native American population—almost 30 percent, according to the last national census. Most are Wampanoag people of the Aquinnah (Gay Head) band, one of the remaining handful of the 50 or so bands that once made up the Wampanoag nation; descendants of two other bands, the Christiantown and Chappaquiddick, also live in the community, although their cultural identity hasn't been maintained well enough to receive the same recognition. If every member lived in Aquinnah, they'd outnumber their nonindigenous neighbors by more than four to one, but more than half of the 992-member band live off-island, and most of the rest live down-island.

In the 17th century, this area belonged to the sachem-ship Aquinnah ("high land"). Most of it stayed under Native American ownership until the 19th century, when condescending schemers pressured or duped them into quite literally giving away the farm. After lengthy legal action, a few hundred acres were finally returned to the local Wampanoag people after they obtained federal recognition in 1987, but there's no reservation—the restored acres came with some strings attached. Not surprisingly, accepting less than full control over a parcel of ancestral land much smaller than hoped for was a controversial price to pay for recognition. During most of the 19th and 20th centuries, the community was known as Gay Head, after the high escarpment on which the lighthouse still stands, but in 1997 residents voted to return to their indigenous roots.

For anyone interested in Wampanoag history, the **Aquinnah Public Library** (1 Church St., 508/645-2314, http://www.aquinnahlibrary.org, 11am-5pm Tues. and Thurs., 11am-4pm Sat.), has a room devoted to books about and by Native Americans. Ask the librarian to suggest a few of local relevance.

★ Gay Head Cliffs

The 130-foot-high Gay Head Cliffs were declared a National Natural Landmark in 1966 and have been an attraction for as long as visitors have come to the Vineyard. Cliff-climbing is definitely off-limits—it's dangerous and accelerates the severe erosion of the unanchored clay—but you can admire the antediluvian strata from above or below, depending on whether you take a 5- or 50-minute walk from the parking lot. If the ground could talk, and the fossilized remains of camels are any indication, those multihued layers could tell some mighty interesting stories. On clear or partly cloudy evenings, the cliff-top overlook provides exceptional front-row seats for watching the sun extinguish itself in the ocean off Rhode Island.

Adding to the photogenic view from the cliffs is the 19th-century redbrick **Gay Head Lighthouse** (508/645-2300, www.gayheadlight.org), whose alternating red and white flashes warn ships away from Devil's Bridge, a treacherous line of partially submerged offshore rocks that prompted construction of the original 1799 beacon. Tricky currents and bad weather still sank many a sailing vessel on these rocks, even after the dim lanterns of old were replaced with the

Gay Head Lighthouse and surrounding cliffs

powerful Fresnel lens now seen in the yard of the Vineyard Historical Society; worst among these various disasters was the wreck of the *City of Columbus,* on which more than 100 of its sleeping passengers died within a few minutes on a winter's night in early 1884.

Equally dangerous (to the lighthouse) is the ever-constant process of erosion, which in 2015 required the entire lighthouse's move to a new location farther back from the shore. This difficult procedure was completed without a hitch, and the lighthouse already seems like it's been in its new spot for years.

Although the immediate grounds of the light are fenced off from public access most of the year, on summer weekends (Fri.-Sun.) between June's solstice and September's equinox, the tower and grounds are open for **self-guided sunset tours** ($3, free under age 12, free for everyone on Mother's Day). The gates open 90 minutes before sundown and close 30 minutes after. Tours are canceled if the weather is so poor that the sun can't be seen.

With the exception of a few tacky little gift sheds and fast-food stalls on the path to the cliff-top overlook, Aquinnah is blissfully lacking in commercial attractions. Hungry visitors will find breakfasts, burgers, sandwiches, fried seafood, salads, and diner-style desserts at the seasonal **Aquinnah Shop Restaurant** (Aquinnah Circle, 508/645-3867, www.theaquinnahshop.com, call for hours, as they vary widely due to seasonal needs, but usually open for lunch at least, until about 4pm, $15-42) loftily perched at the cliff edge. Note that if business is slow due to bad weather, the eatery may not remain open past 4pm even in peak season.

RECREATION

Beaches

For the duration of summer, up-island towns restrict most of their beaches to residents or renters who bring a copy of their lease on a local house to the requisite office at town hall. Don't think the permits apply only to cars: Chilmark's beach attendants will check them no matter how many wheels—or feet—you come in on. Guests of Chilmark B&Bs and inns can obtain walk-in beach permits and take advantage of the Chilmark beach shuttle bus that serves the town's handful of lodgings; inquire at check-in. So, **Lambert's Cove** in West Tisbury, **Lucy Vincent** and **Squibnocket Beaches** in Chilmark, and **Philbin** and **Head of the Pond** Beaches in Aquinnah are off-limits to most visitors June-September—although at gorgeous Lambert's Cove, nonresidents are free to come catch the sun's last golden rays 6pm-9pm. But despair not—the publicly accessible alternatives are by no means negligible.

West Tisbury, for example, has a pair of conservation properties along the south shore whose mix of pond and ocean beaches amply reward the effort of reaching them. **Long Point Wildlife Refuge,** another property of the Trustees, has 0.5 miles of dune-backed beach along the Atlantic that rarely gets congested thanks to a strict limit on the number of vehicles admitted. For more elbow room on hot clear days, arrive early and walk west from the parking lot. To get there, turn off the Edgartown-West Tisbury Road onto Waldron's Bottom Road (look for the Trustees sign) and then follow the arrows.

Just west of Long Point is the Land Bank's **Sepiessa Point Reservation,** with a small beach along the edge of Tisbury Great Pond (watch for sharp oyster shells on the beach). The pond itself is a body of saltwater and marsh now hemmed in on the ocean side by barrier dunes (private) that are breached twice a year to augment the pond's salinity, vital to maintaining its shellfish population. This place is virtually unknown even to most Vineyarders, so don't be surprised if you have it to yourself. Though free, parking is extremely limited; beachgoers should use the first trailhead pullout and leave the southerly ones for folks who have boats to schlep. The walk to the beach from the upper trailhead is just over one mile, mostly through woods.

Menemsha Beach is Chilmark's most accessible. A big family-friendly north-shore spot with plenty of parking, food, restrooms,

Beach Basics

Gay Head beach

When it comes to beaches, the Vineyard has a little something for just about everybody, from bodysurfers to wading toddlers. Most, but not all, of the island's more than two dozen beaches are free and open to the public. Several on private conservation land charge seasonal access fees, and five town-owned beaches are restricted in summer to local residents and specific guests. Parking is not a given—some places have little or none, and some charge up to $30 for the privilege.

There's no nude beach per se, although discreet naturists are tolerated in selected areas. Private ownership extends down to the low-water line, however, so please respect beach fences, "No Trespassing" signs, and community standards for shedding your Speedo.

As a rule, the strongest surf is found along the Atlantic-facing south shore, since there's no land between here and Hispaniola to dampen the ocean swells. These beaches are the first to close during foul summer weather, when prevailing southwesterly winds propel huge waves up the shore. In their wake are new underwater sandbars that build the kind of tall breakers beloved by serious boogie boarders but hazardous to windsurfers and their equipment. Parents and timid swimmers should also be mindful of this shore's strong undertow.

Until the onslaught of winter northeasters, the east shore (facing Nantucket Sound) and the north shore (facing the Vineyard Sound) are milder. As a rule, they're also warmer. North shore beaches are reputed to have the clearest water and definitely feature the best sunsets.

and views of the local fishing fleet returning to adjacent Menemsha Harbor, reach it from the village center by following signs for Dutcher Dock. A second concession-free north-shore beach—quite a lovely one—is found at **Great Rock Bight Preserve,** a Land Bank property quickly reached by a short trail accessed off North Road; look for the Land Bank sign a little under four miles south of State Road. By contrast, the Land Bank's **Chilmark Pond Preserve,** off South Road opposite Abel's Hill Cemetery, offers what's tantamount to a private beach club, with the lesser of 10 vehicles or 40 people allowed onto the property at any one time. The preserve's small piece of the south shore is just east of permit-only **Lucy Vincent Beach.** Lucy Vincent is regarded by some as the island's finest beach, but don't get your hopes up—to even reach the ocean dunes, you must bring a canoe or kayak and paddle diagonally across Chilmark Pond (be sure to read the lengthy posted explanations of where you can and cannot land on the opposite shore). As a result, it's one plum that may stay tantalizingly out of reach, despite being free and public.

Arguably the best public swath of south-shore surf and sand is at the Land Bank's **Moshup Beach** and adjacent **Aquinnah Public Beach,** just a scant 0.5 miles or so from the famous Gay Head Cliffs. Limited parking is available, either for permit holders, or for a punitive $30 in summer, in the lot at the State Road loop atop the cliffs, near the public restrooms (where, incidentally, the down-island shuttle bus stops). Cyclists will find free racks down Moshup Trail at the beach itself. The lucky will find one hour parking next to Gay Head Light, or a ticket on their car if they return from an afternoon on the beach.

East of the well-marked Land Bank property line is residents-only Philbin Beach; in the other direction, toward the base of the cliffs, is the island's principal (if unofficial) nude bathing area. Up until the 1990s it wasn't uncommon to see people painting themselves from top to bottom with the richly colored clay from the cliffs, but enforcement of the prohibition against all climbing, digging, and souvenir-taking from this Wampanoag-owned National Landmark has been sharply increased in the years since. The strict rules are not the work of mere spoilsports—clay removal artificially hastens erosion. Simply walking around the base of the spectacular marine scarp and taking photos, however, is perfectly legit.

Aquinnah's only other public shore is sheltered **Lobsterville Beach,** a mecca for surfcasters. The absolute ban on parking on Lobsterville Road makes access difficult, however. Aquinnah house renters and inn guests who obtain town parking permits (and the lucky few who snatch up the three or four spaces available for nonresidents) can park a mile away in the small lot at the end of West Basin Road, just across the narrow channel from the fishing boats in Menemsha Basin; otherwise, it's a two-mile walk from the Aquinnah bus stop up at the cliff-top loop.

By far the best nonautomotive approach is via the Bike Ferry from Menemsha, when it's operating (June-Oct.). Of course, if it's swimming rather than fishing that you want, save yourself a mile's walk or ride and stick to state-owned **West Jetty,** at West Basin. Despite its protection from prevailing southwesterly winds, Lobsterville is generally much too rocky to stretch out a towel on (although it should be pointed out that the offshore eelgrass and crab beds aren't everyone's idea of tactile pleasure).

Manuel F. Correllus State Forest

This forest was originally set aside to protect the dwindling population of the heath hen, a relative of the prairie chicken extinguished on the mainland through hunting and habitat loss. But the gesture was undermined by a big forest fire and continued hunting. By 1932, the hen was extinct. In spite of a legacy of tree farming, a blight that's killing off the remaining stands of red pine, and proximity to the island's airport, some trail-savvy islanders consider the state forest a hidden gem. Hikers interested in the Vineyard's floristic communities won't find any better place to sample the island's pitch pine barrens and scrub oak bottoms, for example, and mountain bikers can crisscross the forest on miles of fire roads. If you happen to visit during a snowy winter, you'll find good cross-country skiing through the property too. Pick up a map and advice from the helpful staff at the forest headquarters (508/693-2540, www.mass.gov), off Airport Road.

★ Long Point Wildlife Refuge

Big waves along an exceptional South Shore beach are the draw for summer visitors to the isolated up-island **Long Point Wildlife Refuge** (508/693-3678, www.thetrustees.org, 9am-5:30pm daily June 15-Sept. 15,

---

1: Lobsterville Beach **2:** Cedar Tree Neck

1
2

sunrise-sunset daily Sept. 16-June 14, $5 pp over age 15 plus $10 parking June 15-Sept. 15, free mid-Sept.-mid-Jun.). Bird-watchers and wild blueberry lovers may prefer the trails around the grasslands and shrub-covered heath opposite the high-season parking lot on Long Cove Pond. Interpretive trail guides to the mile-long barrier beach-and-grassland loop are available year-round at the parking-lot bulletin boards and are downloadable on the website. The other mile-long trail visits the freshwater marsh along the edge of Long Cove, where in spring and summer you might hear frogs singing for sex, see herons stalking their supper, or spot river otters before they spot you.

Spring is also a good time to catch migrating ducks feeding on the ponds and songbirds scouting nesting sites in the woods. Fall is impossible not to enjoy—as the last papery pink salt-spray roses start to fold, the bayberry and huckleberry bushes impart a warm burgundy glow to the heathlands and the waterfowl stop over again on their way south. On good summer swimming days, you'd do well to consider biking in to avoid being turned away when the parking lot fills, but off-season this is a good place to be alone with your thoughts and brisk ocean breezes.

In summer, the Long Point gates are locked an hour after admissions end, so don't expect to hang around watching the sunset over distant Aquinnah or admiring the star-studded carpet of the Milky Way. Summer access is via Waldron's Bottom Road off the Edgartown-West Tisbury Road. Follow the signs to the high-season parking lot by the beach (potable water and restrooms available). Off-season, the gate at road's end is closed; mid-September-mid-June, visitors should then use the heavily potholed single-lane dirt track called Deep Bottom Road (again, follow the signs) to get to the facilities-free parking area near the caretaker's cottage.

Sepiessa Point Reservation

Like nearby Long Point, this Land Bank reservation protects some of the planet's last remaining acres of sandplain grasslands, backed by a large swath of woodlands along the edge of Tiah's (rhymes with *wise*) Cove, one of many slender inlets to Tisbury Great Pond. Since the only public boat access to the Great Pond is via the reservation's cove-side canoe and boat slides, most islanders familiar with this unheralded place know of it by the cove's name instead of the peninsula's. The property sports a short stretch of hard sandy beach along the pond edge, but heed the posted warnings about the broken oyster shells, which are about as friendly to tender unshod feet as discarded metal sardine cans. At a small pull-out near the reservation entrance—the only parking available to hikers and swimmers (each boat slide has its own handful of spaces)—a signboard identifies the trails that loop through pine-oak woods and converge on the grassy meadows about a mile away. Though quite plain for most of the year, the meadows are good wildflower territory in spring—the bushy rockrose, Nantucket shadbush, and other rare sandplain plants blossom throughout May-June. Summer's insects and autumn's berries bring birds out of the woods to forage throughout the rest of the high season, and if you look carefully before they all get eaten, at the end of summer you may spot fruit-bearing creepers of the wild grapevine that supposedly inspired the island's name. Northern harriers, another of the state's rare species, have occasionally been sighted hunting in the meadows for rodents and insects.

Free year-round, Sepiessa Point is signposted with the Land Bank logo along Tiah's Cove Road, a dead-end fork off New Lane in West Tisbury. Only about 1.25 miles from the Edgartown-West Tisbury Road, the reservation is accessible to most bikes and even up-island shuttle riders who request a stop at New Lane, almost across from the volunteer fire station. A downloadable version of the reservation's trail map is available from the Land Bank's website (www.mvlandbank.com).

★ Cedar Tree Neck

Ask your innkeepers or island hosts to

recommend their favorite hiking spot, and nine times out of 10 they'll nominate this property of the Sheriff's Meadow Foundation. Located on West Tisbury's North Shore, it fully earns its reputation with nearly two miles of looping trails through woods, wetlands, dunes, a brook, a morainal ridge, and the beach. A kid-friendly pamphlet—available in the map kiosk at the parking lot—provides interpretive details on one trail; others are summarized on memorandums posted in the kiosk by the property managers. The trails were designed in part by Anne Hale, whose locally published book *From Moraine to Marsh: A Field Guide to Martha's Vineyard* is the best natural history companion for walks around the Neck.

Swimming is prohibited along the property's gorgeous Vineyard Sound shoreline, and a summer attendant enforces this restriction—part of the terms that made the land public. As is the case nearly everywhere on the Vineyard, neighboring houses are never far from sight, but the beauty of the Neck will put them clean out of your mind. In fact, don't be surprised if a scant half-hour of soaking up the views from the beach has you forgetting your own home. Located at the end of Obed Daggett Road, off Indian Hill Road, Cedar Tree Neck is free year-round. A bike rack is provided, but restrooms aren't.

Waskosim's Rock Reservation

Straddling the West Tisbury-Chilmark town line near the headwaters of pristine Mill Brook are nearly 200 acres almost straight out of the 19th century: at **Waskosim's Rock Reservation,** you'll find abandoned farmland bordered by drystone walls, the ever-encroaching forest, and wetlands that feed the brook, a vital tributary of Tisbury Great Pond. The waters of the brook are so clean that they're home to the brook lamprey, a species whose hypersensitivity to pollutants has made it widely endangered.

Presumably named after a local Wampanoag, Waskosim's Rock is a giant cracked boulder that marked a 17th-century boundary between English and Native American lands. Natural forest succession has obscured the views once afforded from the rock, but fine down-island vistas may yet be found by the cleared fields rising out of the Mill Brook valley and from occasional breaks in the hilltop forest. Since much of the abutting private property is equally undeveloped, trails through the reservation's varied habitats are as good for bird-watchers as for anyone looking for a glimpse of Vineyard Haven's water tower. Conspicuous summer visitors include flickers, cuckoos, blue jays, and ovenbirds (in the dry oak forest at the southern high end of the property); cedar waxwings, swallows, song sparrows, and white-eyed vireos (out on the old pastures); and northern parula warblers (around the scrubby red maple swamp near the trailhead).

The reservation's entrance, along with parking for both bikes and cars, is signposted with a discreet Land Bank logo beside North Road a few hundred feet on the Chilmark side of the Chilmark-West Tisbury boundary.

Fulling Mill Brook Preserve

Although drivers on Chilmark's Middle Road will most likely miss its small trailhead parking lot, the relaxing 0.5-mile walk through the Fulling Mill Brook Preserve is worth turning around for. The quiet, lazy trout stream grows garrulous and boulder-strewn as it runs through mixed hardwood forest down the shoulder of Abel's Hill, part of the morainal ridge that runs between Tisbury and Aquinnah. Shrubby savanna interspersed with oaks and a spot of wildflower-filled meadow occupy some of the slopes over the stream.

The brook takes its name from the mill that used its waters in the process of fulling cloth—making it heavier through shrinking and pressing—back in the 1800s. In the 1700s, several tanners treated hides in this neck of the woods too. Today, decaying leaf litter and fresh breezes have replaced the tannic scent of curing leather. In summer, woodland songbirds abound along the brook's path, but proximity to those drier upland habitats means you're as apt to hear mourning doves and song sparrows as the quiet call of the whip-poor-will.

While cars are limited to the Middle Road lot, cyclists can take advantage of a second bike rack, on South Road at the preserve's lower end, beside an impressive stone and wrought-iron gateway.

Peaked Hill Reservation

Three of the island's highest points—including Radar Hill, an old World War II garrison site, and 311-foot Peaked (PEA-kid) Hill—crown a cluster of ridges whose slopes were once nearly girdled with luxury homes at **Peaked Hill Reservation** (Middle Rd. and Tabor House Rd.). The Land Bank's timely acquisition of these Chilmark heights preserved some especially good vantage points for Aquinnah sunsets, views over the Elizabeth Islands to the southeastern Massachusetts coast, and hawk watching. Numerous large moss- and lichen-covered glacial erratics, chunks of granite gouged out of mountains or exposed bedrock farther north and deposited here during the last ice age, dot the wooded trails. Some of the stones form the panoramic ledges; others are distinctive enough to have their own names (such as Wee Devil's Bed) or serve as reminders of the late-18th- and early-19th-century farmers who cleared much of this land (their pin-and-feather technique for splitting huge boulders into gateposts and foundation slabs is writ large on the edges of unused stones).

The military has also left some marks here. They're mostly steel-and-concrete tower footings and broken asphalt, but notice also the mature tree grown up through the old Radar Hill fencing, its trunk indelibly tattooed by the rusty chain link. The reservation now plays host to a large herd of white-tailed deer, whose distinctive bite can be seen in the severed ends of lower branches on small trees and shrubs all over these 70 acres. The rich forest understory and dense thickets also provide vital cover for numerous small mammals and birds, including an array of finches, sparrows, swallows, warblers, and woodpeckers. Conspicuous but locally uncommon species such as yellow- and black-billed cuckoos, killdeer, and bluebirds have been sighted here, and the relatively high elevations attract red-winged hawks and American kestrels during both breeding and migration seasons.

The entrance turnoff is signposted on Tabor House Road, 0.5 miles from Middle Road. Parking, maps, and a bike rack are located 0.8 miles up the potholed dirt lane—always take the right fork, or you'll have to back out of several private driveways.

Menemsha Hills

Part of the reason the vista from the shoulder of Peaked Hill is so attractive is that the wooded hills bordering Vineyard Sound on the other side of North Road are protected by the Trustees' **Menemsha Hills Reservation** (North Rd., Chilmark, 508/693-3678, https://thetrustees.org). Several miles of trails offer walkers oak tree shade, hilltop views, and bracing winds along the lip of the 150-foot marine scarp over Vineyard Sound. Ruminate over the landscape, where sheep once grazed within the property's drystone walls; watch birds gorge themselves on the heath's summer berry crop; or pretend you're Thomas Hart Benton, the Missouri-born painter who summered here in Chilmark for 56 years, and stroll the rocky beach (no swimming) with an artist's eye for the play of light and water on the rough coast. In late fall or winter, you might spot harbor seals basking on the rocks or bobbing in the surf offshore.

A Trustees' white-on-green sign marks the reservation's parking lot off North Road in Chilmark, a little over 0.5 miles west of the junction with Tabor House Road. Admission is free.

ENTERTAINMENT

Modern dance is the bailiwick of **The Yard** (Middle Rd., Chilmark, 508/645-9662, www.

dancetheyard.org) an up-island artists' colony founded in the early 1970s and located in Chilmark, close to Beetlebung Corner. Their Barn Theater hosts a season of dance performances by colony residents at least one weekend a month May-September, often including premieres of improvisational works that will next appear (at much higher prices) in New York City.

Traditional New England **contra** and **square dances,** sponsored by the **Country Dance Society** (Tom Hodgson at 774/392-1056 is the de facto contact), take place in the off-season (Sept.-May). Beginners are welcome; call for a schedule and dates, or consult newspaper calendar listings.

FOOD

Despite having plenty of penny-pinching visitors in its midst, the rural end of the Vineyard is not very kind to budget travelers. The foot-thick topsoil seems to yield not only fresh produce but fancy destination dining. Few places stay open past Thanksgiving out here, and most places start paring back their days and hours after September. Also remember that all three up-island towns—West Tisbury, Chilmark, and Aquinnah—are dry, so stop first at an OB or Edgartown package store if wine is vital to your dining pleasure.

Up-island's only reasonably priced eating is almost exclusively takeout. Worthwhile grocery-store deli counters include **7a Foods** (1045 State Rd., West Tisbury, 508/693-4636, www.7afoods.com, 8am-2pm daily year-round, $8-12), which has deli sandwiches and baked goods, and **The Chilmark General Store** (7 State Rd., Chilmark, 508/645-3739, www.chilmarkgeneralstore.com, 7am-7pm daily July-Aug., 8am-3pm Thurs.-Tues. Sept.-June, $7-8) at Beetlebung Corner.

In Menemsha, options are limited to summer-only, casual spots. For juicy burgers and soft-serve ice cream, check out **The Galley** (515 North Rd., Menemsha, 508/645-9819, www.menemshagalley.com, 11am-8pm daily summer, 11am-3pm off-season, $8-23), at the edge of Menemsha Channel. You can also dine for under $20 at the gift shop-eatery on the top of the Gay Head Cliffs, but come for the view, not the food.

Inquire after the best lobster on the Vineyard and residents will most often steer you to **Larsen's Fish Market** (56 Basin Rd., Menemsha, 508/645-2680, www.larsensfishmarket.com, 10am-6pm daily May-Oct., market price) in the heart of Menemsha. This is a taste of New England, deliciously unadorned. As the name makes clear, it's not a restaurant, but call ahead and order a lobster and they'll boil it for you on the spot to eat out back on the lobster traps at the edge of the dock, at one of the picnic tables nearby, or right on the beach. A variety of seafood soups and snacks are prepared daily too, such as crab cakes, lobster bisque, seafood chowder, spicy stuffies (chorizo-stuffed clams), and seafood salad from the refrigerated cases inside the door. An alfresco picnic of Larsen's sweet tender fresh lobster chased down by steaming chowder as flavorful as fine bouillabaisse and fragrant as the sea, while the sun sets slowly into the ocean and keening gulls wheel in the evening breeze, is an ambrosial experience not soon forgotten.

Simple and rustic, in an uncluttered building decorated with hand-selected antiques, the understated ★ **State Road Restaurant** (688 State Rd., West Tisbury, 508/693-8582, www.stateroadrestaurant.com, dinner 4:30pm-9pm Wed.-Sun., $26-40) offers dinner just a few nights a week. The meals are hearty and balanced, using locally sourced ingredients whenever possible, and while the combinations are not wildly unique (a smoked salmon plate, eggs benedict, breakfast burrito), the flavors are truly special, in part because of the inventive seasonings and in part because everything is so fresh. Limpopos are a popular side for take-out-goers: a brioche bread fried like a doughnut and dusted in sugar. Yum!

Other prime up-island restaurants offer innovative upscale cuisine in settings that range from studiously casual to stylishly contemporary. Several are found on the premises of the elegant inns tucked into the woods, such as West Tisbury's **Lambert's Cove Country Inn** (90 Manaquayak Rd., West Tisbury, 508/693-2298, www.lambertscoveinn.com, 5pm-11pm Thurs.-Sun. June-mid-Sept., hours vary Thurs.-Sat. mid-Apr.-mid-June and mid-Sept.-Dec., $34-49, prix fix $95). Conservative-sounding fare—roast chicken, filet mignon, poached lobster—is paired with rich accompaniments such as butternut squash ravioli, apple madeira wine reduction, and wild mushroom ragout, such that each dish deliciously exceeds the sum of its attractively presented parts.

ACCOMMODATIONS

Up-island may not offer a large quantity of lodging choices, but it certainly has a wide variety, including the island's only hostel, a number of traditional home-style B&Bs, a luxurious inn built around a 1790 farmhouse, and modern lodgings built in the 1970s. Prices, however, are concentrated at the low and high ends, with a big gap between them.

Under $150

The Vineyard's only true budget accommodation is West Tisbury's **Hostelling International Martha's Vineyard** (525 Edgartown-West Tisbury Rd., West Tisbury, 508/693-2665, www.hiusa.org, mid-May-early Oct., HI members $35, nonmembers $38, two-person private room $99, four-person private room $150), a rambling cedar-shingled Cape-style structure at the edge of the state forest on an isolated stretch of the Edgartown-West Tisbury Road. For anyone unfamiliar with the concept, many hostels now offer private rooms for families and couples, but when this one was designed in the 1950s (it's the first American youth hostel built specifically for the purpose), the prevailing ethic called for stacking hostelers like kids at summer camp—20 or more per room. So until someone endows this fine old place with a massive capital renovation budget, its big bunk bed-filled dorm rooms, slightly rustic common spaces, and woodsy locale will remain the archetype of hostel life—especially when the huge downstairs bunk room is filled by some exuberant school group.

The bottom line is that when all 67 beds are full, it's a bit zoo-like despite the staff's superhuman efforts. Off-season, it's one of the most welcoming—and well-run—hostels in the business. Advance reservations are absolutely essential in summer, and strongly recommended off-season. Although accessible by bike path, car, and summer shuttle buses, the hostel is three miles from the nearest decent market, so if you plan to use the spick-and-span kitchen, you may want to shop ahead for groceries. Free Wi-Fi is available 24 hours.

$150-250

Writers searching for inspiration may particularly appreciate the creative vibes around **The Cleaveland House** (620 Edgartown-West Tisbury Rd., West Tisbury, 508/693-9352, www.cynthiariggs.com/cleavelandhouse, $150 s, $175 d, cash only) at the corner of New Lane, home to the author of a series of mysteries set on the Vineyard. The circa-1750 house is chock-full of character, with lots of family heirlooms and stories to tell, and plenty of cozy places to kick back and think up excuses for your editor after the surrounding acres' beauty distracts you from your muse. In addition to a small guest room for singletons, there are two fireplace-equipped guest rooms, one a king and the other with two twin beds. Note that none of these guest rooms have a private bath, and there's a two-night minimum in season.

$250-350

Set way back in the woods at the end of a sandy lane off upper Lambert's Cove Road, West Tisbury's ★ **Lambert's Cove Country Inn** (90 Manaquayak Rd., West Tisbury, 508/693-2298 or 866/526-2466, www.lambertscoveinn.com, June-mid-Oct. $299-639 d) exudes informal sophistication. Fifteen guest rooms are spread among the buildings of what was once a grand residential country estate. The original 18th-century farmhouse, barn, and carriage house have all been completely renovated from the cellar to the rafters to create a secluded oasis of thoroughly modern comfort amid expansive, beautifully landscaped grounds. No two rooms are alike, but the warm palette and tasteful fabrics they have in common would be right at home on the cover of *Elle Decor.* Oriental carpets on hardwood floors here, four-poster and canopied feather beds there, a lot of private decks, marbled baths, abundant pillows, flat-screen TVs and DVD and CD players—you get the picture (and if not, visit the website for photos of every room). This popular inn also features an all-weather tennis court, a modest outdoor swimming pool, and passes to lovely Lambert's Cove Beach (beach umbrellas and chairs provided). Complimentary made-to-order full breakfasts are served in the inn's restaurant, which happens to be one of the island's best choices for dinner.

The **Menemsha Inn & Cottages** (12 Menemsha Inn Rd., Chilmark, 508/645-2521, www.menemshainn.com, May-Oct. $420 d, cottages rent weekly at $650 and up per night, off-season pricing varies) offers a wide range of lodging options, starting at modern motel-style guest rooms with two queen beds to houses that comfortably sleep six and ending with expansive cottages that easily accommodate groups or larger families. The property sits on 14 hillside acres—including a cow pasture—above the cute little village of Menemsha, just off Chilmark's North Road immediately south of the Menemsha Cross Road junction. Contemporary in design and decor, the inn offers a choice of 15 well-appointed doubles and suites, 12 fully equipped one- and two-bedroom housekeeping cottages, and two three-bedroom houses, nearly all facing Vineyard Sound. The beach is a 10-min walk away through a lovely forest and past the friendly cows, turkeys, and rabbits. Rates include a complimentary self-serve breakfast of cereals and baked goods. If you have a group, the Carriage House's six ocean-facing suites and large two-story common room with big cushy sofas around a stone fireplace would serve as an ideal home base. Take advantage of the on-site fitness center, game room, playground, or tennis court. Beautiful sunset views of Aquinnah and Menemsha Bight, luggage-saving extras such as beach chairs and umbrellas, and guest passes to Chilmark's exclusive town beaches (regular shuttle bus service provided in season) make this a deservedly popular place, despite the absence of any air-conditioning

the Menemsha Inn & Cottages

(fans are provided). Book early. Peak rates are mid-July-August, dropping about 20 percent for the three or four weeks before and after, and by about one-third for the first and last four weeks of the season.

Just through the trees bordering the Menemsha Inn, under common ownership but managed separately, is **Beach Plum Inn** (50 Beach Plum Lane, Chilmark, 508/645-9454 or 877/645-7398, www.beachpluminn.com, May-Oct., from $420 d), with five guest rooms in its main house and six adjacent bungalows. The decor is a modern mix of solid summery colors paired with printed fabrics and flocked valances, and some guest rooms feature whirlpool tubs and private decks or patios. The seven landscaped acres include a regulation-size croquet lawn. Guests can use the gym and tennis court next door, and have the pick of Chilmark's beaches, from the public one a short walk down the hill to permit-only Lucy Vincent and Squibnocket Beaches a short shuttle-bus ride away on the Vineyard's south shore. A complimentary full gourmet breakfast is offered at the inn's restaurant, also highly regarded for its evening fine dining.

Festivals and Events

MAY

Ancient pagans helped wake up the earth from its winter slumbers with community rituals on the first of May. Find out for yourself how effective parading around a maypole can be at shaking off the waning grip of cold weather by joining in the **May Day Celebration** at the Native Earth Teaching Farm (94 North Rd., Chilmark, 508/645-3304). A potluck dinner is held following the afternoon of festivities, so bring along something to contribute if you plan on staying until sundown.

JUNE

Midmonth, sup like royalty at **A Taste of the Vineyard Gourmet Stroll** (508/627-4440, https://vineyardtrust.org, $150), on the Dr. Fisher House lawn behind the Old Whaling Church in Edgartown. Proceeds from this food, wine, and beer blowout, extravagantly catered by over 75 island restaurants and fine food purveyors, benefit the Martha's Vineyard Trust.

On June 16, celebrate **Bloomsday** (www.artsandsociety.org, $25) at Vineyard Haven's Katharine Cornell Theater with a night of music, drama, and recitations inspired by James Joyce's *Ulysses*.

JULY

In the middle of July, yachties swarm the Vineyard to race in the **Edgartown Regatta,** sponsored by the Edgartown Yacht Club (508/627-4361, www.edgartownyc.org). The third weekend in July brings a flavor of the Vineyard's Portuguese heritage to Oak Bluffs in the form of **The Feast of the Holy Ghost** (Vineyard Ave., 508/693-9875), held both outdoors and at the Portuguese-American Club.

AUGUST

The first Monday of August finds philanthropic islanders congregating under a big tent on the grounds of Outerland, a nightclub on the airport's entrance road, to take part in the **Possible Dreams Auction** (508/693-7900, www.mvcommunityservices.com). High rollers bid on the opportunity to dine, play golf, go sailing, play tennis, or enjoy other private backstage encounters with Vineyard "dream makers," including many A-list celebrities. Comedian and talk show icon Seth Meyers hosted in 2021. Proceeds benefit MV Community Services, an island-wide social service agency.

For four days ending the third weekend of August, the Martha's Vineyard Agricultural Society sponsors its annual **Livestock Show**

and Fair (508/693-9549, https://marthasvineyardagriculturalsociety.org, $12) at the West Tisbury Fairgrounds (also called the Ag Hall), with old county fair-style fun replete with games, contests, good food, and music.

SEPTEMBER

The first Saturday after Labor Day, Edgartown's nonprofit FARM Institute holds their annual fund-raiser, **Corn-A-Palooza** (Aero Ave., Edgartown, 508/627-7007, www.farminstitute.org, 4pm-8pm Sat., $20). Enjoy foot-stompin' live music, hayrides, games for kids, a giant corn maze, organic burgers and hot dogs, and, of course, fresh corn on the cob.

On the second Saturday after Labor Day, Oak Bluffs takes its final bow of the season with **Tivoli Day,** named for a once-grand but now long-gone Victorian dance hall. Circuit Avenue, closed to all traffic, is filled with a day-long street fair, including a parade, music, food, raffle tables, and such contests as the Waitperson Olympics, in which waiters and waitresses compete in carrying containers of water without spilling.

OCTOBER

The **Martha's Vineyard Food and Wine Festival** (508-939-0199, www.mvfoodandwine.com) is held in mid-October each year, bringing tasty events and tipples to all who attend.

NOVEMBER

The day after Thanksgiving is traditionally reserved for America's national shopping spree. Right after, the tradition continues into the **Annual Thanksgiving Weekend Festival** (Ag Hall, West Tisbury, 508/693-8989, www.vineyardartisans.com, 10am-4pm Fri.-Sun., parking $2), where a cornucopia of locally made crafts tempts browsers into buying something for everyone on their holiday gift-giving list. The entrance fee goes to the local high school's scholarship fund.

DECEMBER

Christmas in Edgartown (508/627-9510), on the second weekend of December, offers cheer, wassail, tinsel, and lights.

On New Year's Eve, Vineyard Haven celebrates **Last Night, First Day** (508/693-0085, www.mvy.com), with arts performances throughout the afternoon and evening, capped off by fireworks over Vineyard Haven Harbor at 10pm.

Information and Services

VISITOR INFORMATION

If you like to peruse racks of promotional flyers or want more accommodations to choose from, drop in on the **Martha's Vineyard Chamber of Commerce** (508/693-0085, www.mvy.com), on Beach Road in Vineyard Haven, opposite the fire station. Place an order from their website or call ahead for a free copy of their visitors guide. In high season, staffed information booths in all three down-island towns are able to give directions, provide dining and lodging information, and answer most general travel questions. Edgartown's booth also sells postcards and stamps, accepts mail, and vends snacks.

BANKS AND ATMS

You won't ever be far from an automated teller machine in the down-island towns, but up-island is a different story—beyond Beetlebung Corner, there's nothing. The deplorable practice of charging fees for cardholders who don't have local accounts infiltrated the Vineyard even before it took hold of the rest of the state, so count on being charged for remotely accessing your money.

Those using foreign currency must make their cash exchanges prior to arriving—none of the banks here handle such transactions.

MEDIA AND COMMUNICATIONS

For the most up-to-date arts and entertainment suggestions, check out Thursday's ***Martha's Vineyard Times,*** which includes nightclub and live music listings in its calendar of events. Last-minute yard sales and estate auctions, on the other hand, are more likely to be found in the classifieds of Friday's more patrician ***Vineyard Gazette,*** regarded as one of the finest small-town newspapers in the nation—and possibly the most quaint. Its oversize page, aphoristic masthead, and columns devoted to bird sightings all recall a bygone era in journalism.

On the radio dial, **WMVY** (92.7 FM) is the local gentle pop-and-rock station and the best up-to-the-minute source for local beach and ferry reports. *All Things Considered* junkies who can't leave NPR behind, even while on vacation, can tune in the Vineyard's own community public radio station, **WCAI** (90.1 FM), an affiliate of WGBH in Boston. Fans of free-form community radio should tune in to the feisty local low-power noncommercial station, **WVVY** (93.7 FM), "radio for the people," dedicated to the rich local music scene plus a dose of Amy Goodman's *Democracy Now* newscasts mixed in every weekday. Although this station's 93-watt transmitter limits audibility to the down-island towns, you can also catch its global beat, blues, "Psychedelarrythmia," and other shows streaming live from www.wvvy.org.

PUBLIC RESTROOMS

The only year-round restrooms open to the public are at the **Steamship terminal** in Vineyard Haven and the **Church Street Visitors Center** in Edgartown. In summer a number of other facilities open up all over the island: in the parking lot next to Vineyard Haven's Stop & Shop market, at the Steamship dock and on Kennebec Avenue in Oak Bluffs, at South Beach in Edgartown, in West Tisbury's Grange Hall on State Road, and at the bottom of the loop drive atop Gay Head Cliffs. Showers are also available (for a fee) at the bathhouse beside Oak Bluffs Harbor and the Manor House Health Club in downtown Vineyard Haven, next to the Chamber of Commerce.

MEDICAL EMERGENCIES

For speedy clinical care of illnesses and minor injuries, **Vineyard Medical Services** (364 State Rd., 508/693-4400), opposite Cronig's Market, accepts walk-in patients (8am-6pm Mon.-Fri., 8am-noon Sat.). For medical emergencies, the island's full-service 24-hour medical center, **Martha's Vineyard Hospital** (1 Hospital Rd., 508/693-0410, www.mvhospital.com), is located off Beach Road at the foot of East Chop, about 1.5 miles equidistant from downtown Vineyard Haven and downtown Oak Bluffs.

Getting There and Around

In summer, all three down-island towns are connected to the mainland by ferries and to each other by shuttle buses and paved bike paths. Here the great concentration of food and lodging, mostly within walking distance of each other and transportation, makes it entirely practical, even eminently sensible, to arrive without a car.

GETTING THERE

Ferry

Ferries from Woods Hole are the most common way to reach the Vineyard, but there are other options, most of them seasonal between late May and early September.

- **Steamship Authority** (508/477-8600,

Taxi Services

VINEYARD HAVEN

- **Stagecoach Taxi** (508/627-4566, www.mvstagecoachtaxi.com) 10 generations of drivers have served Martha's Vineyard, since the horse and buggy days.
- **Bluefish Taxi** (508/627-7373, www.bluefishtaxi.net)

OAK BLUFFS

- **Atlantic Cab** (508/693-7110, www.atlanticcabmv.com)
- **Martha's Vineyard Taxi** (508/693-8660, www.marthasvineyardtaxi.com)
- **All Island Taxi** (508/693-2929)
- **Your Taxi** (508/693-0003 or 800/396-0003)

www.steamshipauthority.com, adults $9.50, 45 minutes, cars allowed) runs year-round between Woods Hole and Vineyard Haven, seasonally to Oak Bluffs.

- **Falmouth Ferry Service** (508/548-9400, www.falmouthedgartownferry.com, adults $36, 60 minutes, no cars) runs seasonally between Falmouth and Edgartown.
- **Martha's Vineyard Fast Ferry** (508/548-4800, www.vineyardfastferry.com, adults $56, round-trip $89, 2-4 trips daily, 100 minutes, no cars) runs seasonally between North Kingstown (Rhode Island) and Oak Bluffs.
- ***Island Queen*** (508/548-4800, http://islandqueen.com, adults $15, round-trip $23, 4-7 trips daily, 45 minutes, no cars) runs seasonally between Falmouth and Oak Bluffs.
- **Hy-Line Cruises** (800/492-8082, http://hylinecruises.com, adults $32, round-trip $62, 2-6 trips daily, 60 minutes, no cars) runs seasonally from Hyannis to Oak Bluffs.
- **Seastreak** (800/262-8743, http://seastreak.com, from New Bedford adults $40, round-trip $70, from New York City adults $165, round-trip $240, 1 hour from New Bedford, 5 hours from New York City, no cars) runs seasonally between New York City, New Bedford, and Oak Bluffs.
- **Patriot Party Boats** (508/548-2626, www.patriotpartyboats.com, adults $14, 6-8 trips daily, 45 minutes, no cars) runs year-round between Falmouth and Oak Bluffs.

Air

Martha's Vineyard is served by a number of airlines, most of them seasonal. Cape Air flies year-round out of Boston, with seasonal flights from Hyannis, New Bedford, Nantucket, and White Plains (New York). American Airlines has seasonal service to the Vineyard from La Guardia (New York City) and Washington DC. Delta runs seasonal service from New York City's JFK. Tradewind Aviation has a seasonal shuttle Thursday-Monday out of White Plains (New York).

GETTING AROUND

Public Transit

Year-round island-wide public transportation is provided by the **Martha's Vineyard Regional Transit Authority** (VTA, 508/627-9440, www.vineyardtransit.com). It's entirely possible to visit every village on the island, connect to the Steamship docks in Vineyard Haven, get to town—any town—from the airport, and ride to the beach, all via one of the VTA's dozen different routes. Most of the buses run on a fixed hourly schedule, although off-season some routes have less frequent service, and the trolley to South Beach is only seasonal. In summer—from the third Saturday in June to the end of the Labor Day holiday weekend in early September, to be exact—system-wide frequency of service increases significantly. For instance, buses start rolling among the three down-island towns at 6am, with half-hourly service from around 7am until after midnight, and service every 15 minutes 10:30am-6:45pm. All fares are $1.25 per town, including the town of origin—meaning $2.50 between towns, and $6.25 for full cross-island rides. One-, three-, seven-, and thirty-one-day passes for unlimited travel are available from the drivers or at the Edgartown Visitors Center on Church Street for $8, $18, $25, and $40, respectively. Yearly and school-age student passes are available too, although only from the Edgartown Visitors Center. Cyclists who underestimate the strength of the island's headwinds will be gratified to know that all VTA buses have bike racks mounted on the front.

Two of the VTA routes provide nearly continuous service mid-May-mid-September to their respective downtowns from free peripheral parking lots on State Road in Vineyard Haven, by the Triangle in Edgartown, and at the Edgartown elementary school on West Tisbury Road.

Alternately, ride-share services such as Lyft and Uber are commonly used.

Bike Rentals

Vineyard Haven, Oak Bluffs, Edgartown, and parts of West Tisbury are linked by more than 15 miles of paved bike paths, so cycling around the island is a snap even for riders normally intimidated by traffic. The only major portion of the island lacking segregated bikeways is the southwest corner, but the beautiful tree-canopied roads there make for lovely riding nonetheless. And what better way to work off those calories from last night's dinner?

Over a dozen shops rent bikes—three on Circuit Avenue Extension next to Oak Bluffs's ferry docks, three within a block of Vineyard Haven's Steamship terminal, two within a stone's throw of Edgartown's central Main Street-Water Street intersection, and a couple more at the Triangle on Upper Main Street in Edgartown. Guests of B&Bs and inns away from the town centers can take advantage of the free bike delivery and pickup offered by such outfits as **Martha's Vineyard Bike Rentals** (1 Main St., Edgartown, 800/627-2763, www.marthasvineyardbike.com, 9am-6pm daily Apr.-Nov.); or **Wheel Happy** (opposite the Harborside Inn, S. Water St., Edgartown, 508/627-5928, Apr.-mid-Nov.). Most rental fleets are trendy mountain bikes and hybrids, but retro three-speeds, tandems, lighter road bikes (perfectly adequate if you intend to stick to pavement), and trailers for towing kids are also widely available. Wheel Happy also caters to corporate outings, with fully guided cycling tours from Edgartown to Oak Bluffs. Rates are about $30-35 per day.

If you've brought your own wheels and need repairs, several rental shops double as fix-it stops: simply visit Vineyard Haven's year-round **Cycle Works** (351 State Rd., Vineyard Haven, 508/693-6966, 9am-6pm daily May-Oct.); **Anderson's Bike Rental** (Circuit Ave. Ext., Oak Bluffs, 508/693-9346); **Edgartown Bicycles** (212 Upper Main St., Edgartown, 508/627-9008, www.edgartownbicycles.com, 9am-5pm daily); or **R. W. Cutler Edgartown Bike Rentals** (1 Main St., Edgartown, 508/627-4052 or 800/627-2763, www.marthasvineyardbike.com, 9am-5pm daily Apr.-Oct.).

Taxis

For island-wide convenience, choose from among the many available taxi companies. Since each town has its own set of regulations for taxi companies based within their borders, fares vary somewhat from one company to the next, particularly when it comes to the extras—fees for extra passengers, luggage, pets, late-night drop-offs, and driving on dirt roads. So if the same cab ride you took yesterday ends up suddenly costing more today, don't jump to the conclusion that you're being cheated.

Car Rental Agencies

VINEYARD HAVEN

- **A-A Island Auto Rentals** (Five Corners, 4 Water St., 508/696-5300 or 800/627-6333, www.mvautorental.com)
- **Adventure Rentals** (19 Beach Rd., 508/693-1959, www.islandadventuremv.com)
- **Budget** (45 Beach Rd., 508/693-1911 or 800/527-0700, www.budget.com)

OAK BLUFFS

- **A-A Island Auto Rentals** (31 Circuit Ave. Ext., 508/696-5211, www.mvautorental.com)
- **Budget** (9 Oak Bluffs Ave. Ext., 508/693-1911 or 800/527-0700, www.budget.com)
- **Sun-N-Fun Rentals** (28 Lake Ave., 508/693-5457, www.sunnfunrentals.com)

EDGARTOWN

- **A-A Island Auto Rentals** (196 Main St., 508/627-6800 or 800/627-6333, www.mvautorental.com)
- **Auto Rentals of Edgartown** (141 Main St., 508/627-7241)

MARTHA'S VINEYARD AIRPORT

- **A-A Island Auto Rentals** (508/627-6800, www.mvautorental.com)
- **Budget** (508/693-1911 or 800/527-0700, www.budget.com)
- **Hertz Rent-A-Car** (508/693-2402 or 800/654-3131, www.hertz.com)

Rates for up to two people from the Steamship docks in either Vineyard Haven or OB can run as high as $65-75 to Aquinnah, $35-40 to the hostel in West Tisbury, and $15-20 between down-island towns. Additional passengers are usually $3-5 each, and in the timeframe of 1am-7am expect the fare to be doubled.

Car and Moped Rentals

If you're staying down-island in summer, you really want to avoid driving. You may not think so, as you imagine all the luggage you have to carry and all the shopping you want to do—but if it's a vacation you're after, seriously reconsider your determination to drive; you're letting yourself in for a slow stop-and-go crawl through intersections packed with 20,000 other cars, not one of which will yield to your left turn. If you're coming in the off-season or intend to spend most of your time up-island and have never ridden a bicycle, driving is a slightly better idea. Just mind all those cyclists, and the deer at night—particularly on curvy, shoulderless up-island roads.

If you decide to rent a car, be prepared for rates that fluctuate wildly. Ever-popular Jeeps and convertibles that rent for over $200 a day on any midsummer holiday, for instance, may drop by half off-season, unless the weather is spectacular and demand is strong. Don't expect anyone but the major chains to quote prices over the phone—the independent operators prefer not to commit to anything that may scare off potential business. Remove any diamond jewelry you may be wearing and don't introduce yourself as a doctor, and you'll find these indie outfits are prepared to haggle—so long as you're mellow and not too pushy, and they can see that the competition across the street still has a car or two in the lot. By the way, before you pay a massive premium for renting one of those macho four-wheelers, remember that driving on Vineyard beaches is restricted to privately owned vehicles (not rental cars) with valid permits. **Oversand vehicle permits** for Chappaquiddick are $160 from the Trustees (508/627-7689); for Norton Point—the only other part of the Vineyard's coast open to off-road vehicles—the requisite permits are $80 from the Treasurer's Office (9 Airport Rd., 508/696-3845), or at South Beach in the summer.

Hitchhiking

While it's never really the case that hitchhiking is safe, in Martha's Vineyard it's at least more common than on the mainland, and people are accustomed to both giving and getting rides. It's a vestige of the 1970s preserved here thanks to the island's small size (no need to worry about making conversation for just a couple of miles). If you've never tried thumbing a ride and want to, this is a good place to start; if you mourn the passing of good ol' hitching in the rest of the country, you'll find this a welcome time warp. Which isn't to say you shouldn't trust your instincts; if you aren't comfortable with someone who's stopped to offer a lift, decline the ride, and be cautious (as always) with strangers. Conversely, if you've got room in your car and see someone in need of a lift, consider doing them a favor and stop when they wave their thumb.

Nantucket

This fog-shrouded shoal defies easy definition, and as such, it should make its way onto any vacationer's "To Do" list. It is steeped in some of America's oldest and most vibrant history (much of it carefully, even strictly preserved).

Visiting the Whaling Museum, touring the old houses, or even just walking down the cobblestone streets make you feel like time has somehow been dialed back a few centuries. In the center of Nantucket town, you'll feel a little like you're in a movie set—the houses still look like they might have back at the turn of the century, as if not that much has changed since whaling days. While not all of this is as authentic as it looks, and in many cases the authenticity ends the moment you step inside, it's still unequivocally more attractive than the acre after acre

Highlights

Look for ★ to find recommended sights, activities, dining, and lodging.

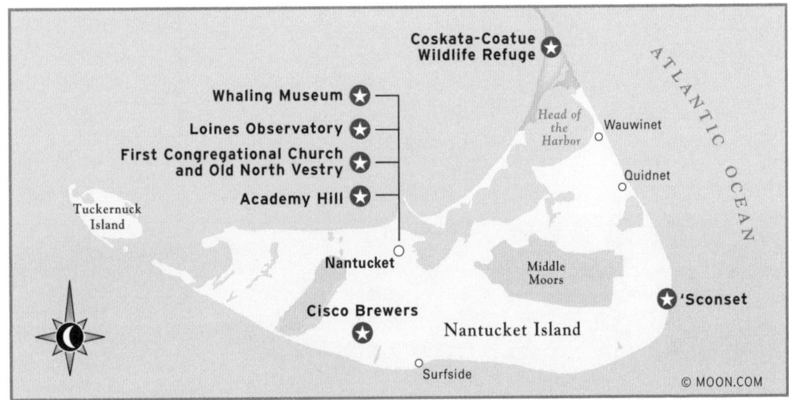

★ **Whaling Museum:** Learn the story of the island's whaling industry, artfully told through artifacts and engaging gallery talks (page 185).

★ **Loines Observatory:** Marvel at the night's starry wonders in weekly seasonal programs that highlight the features of a Nantucket nightscape (page 188).

★ **First Congregational Church and Old North Vestry:** Climb to the top of the church steeple for incomparable panoramic views (page 190).

★ **Academy Hill:** Admire this collection of intact historic homes and museums, many of which have looked like this for centuries (page 190).

★ **'Sconset:** Enjoy one of Nantucket's finest beaches, whether you come for the crowd scene in summer or wait for fall to have it all to yourself (page 193).

★ **Cisco Brewers:** Fresh pints, tours, live music, and Nantucket trivia await at the island's only brewery (page 194).

★ **Coskata-Coatue Wildlife Refuge:** Nantucket's largest barrier beach offers amazing photography, birding, seal-watching, hikes and tours, and even a lighthouse (page 196).

of condominiums, strip malls, or golf courses that one associates with other resort areas.

The island of Nantucket has a unique vibe that changes almost as quickly as New England weather. It all depends on the season and what events are—or aren't—happening. Come here during the Figawi race or the lovely Nantucket Wine Festival and you'll find throngs of people. Lines will go out the door for coffee or breakfast. Bars will be full of the very "merry." Beaches will be packed—and parking? Well, you can forget it. But the bright side is that Nantucket is a walking town and a biking island—it's easy to get around without needing four wheels. And unlike the nearby Cape, so close and yet so far away, the Nantucket party vibe is welcoming (perhaps just because it's that much closer to Margaritaville?).

Visit Nantucket in the off-season, and it's as calm and peaceful as it must have been in the days of old, when the whaling ships had set off for foreign waters while the wives waited. Shops close, streets are empty, and beaches turn back into wave-sculpted deserts where you can walk for hours without needing to say "hi" to anyone. The lighthouses, salt-sanded clapboard walls, old-timers, and the almost tropical color to the ocean make it an entrancing, captivating place to search your soul or walk hand-in-hand with someone special.

It's easy to shrug off Nantucket as being only for the very wealthy, but if you're not planning to buy land here, it's still worth a day trip or a weekend. Whether you come at the peak of a tourist event or a desolate day in late fall, Nantucket will refresh and surprise you.

PLANNING YOUR TIME

One of the best things about Nantucket is that it's truly a walking and biking town, which means you don't need to have a vehicle. In fact, people often bypass the Cape entirely and take a bus to Hyannis, walk to the ferry, and zip to Nantucket, where they spend a weekend or weeks without ever needing more than their feet to get around. Others find that they can rent a moped for the longer trips to the other side of the island. But certainly a car—whether rented or your own—makes it easy to take in all sides of Nantucket, not just the town.

Any time of year, anyone with the least bit of appreciation for American history or historic architecture will find a surfeit of both. Start with the **Whaling Museum** and then simply spend time strolling around the diminutive lanes and alleyways of downtown. Throughout the high season the whole island is served by excellent public transit, so there's no excuse not to venture out to **'Sconset** to experience quaint residential Nantucket at its most picturesque. Or just go there to stroll the **Bluff Walk** and view the beautiful **Sankaty Head Light** presiding over the wild eastern shore, where Mother Nature annually exposes the impermanence of the earth beneath your feet.

Whatever your taste in beaches, there is one here with your name on it, so visitors spending more than a day should certainly sample the local waters. Mostly level terrain and an extensive network of paved bike paths make getting out to any of the major beaches a cinch on a bike; rental shops are all easily found within steps of the ferries. If more time is available, it becomes possible to slip into the casual rhythm of island life. Make an impromptu picnic for a walk to **Brant Point Light** out of fresh-picked Bartlett's Farm berries sold right off their daily truck stand on Main Street, sample several different praiseworthy restaurants, catch a sunset at **Madaket Beach,** rent a kayak to poke around the inner harbor, learn about the constellations at **Loines Observatory,** and, of course, browse through the galleries on Old South Wharf. A week would be ideal, but a long weekend is a good start on sampling all that the island has to offer.

Previous: Brant Point Light; 19th century brick building on Centre Street; flower garden in Nantucket.

Nantucket

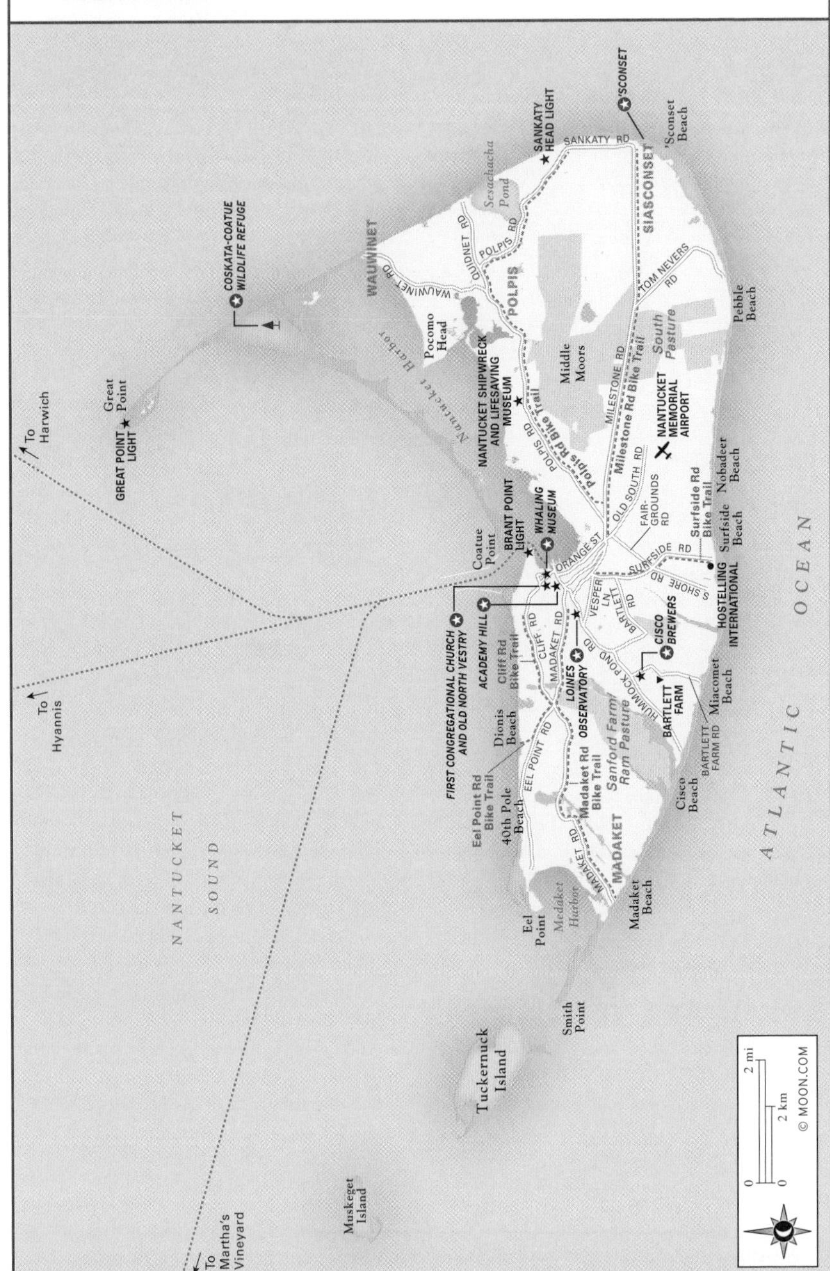
To Harwich
To Hyannis
To Martha's Vineyard
NANTUCKET SOUND
ATLANTIC OCEAN
Great Point
GREAT POINT LIGHT
COSKATA-COATUE WILDLIFE REFUGE
Nantucket Harbor
Pocomo Head
WAUWINET
WAUWINET RD
QUIDNET RD
POLPIS RD
POLPIS
Sesachacha Pond
SANKATY HEAD LIGHT
SANKATY RD
'SCONSET
'Sconset Beach
SIASCONSET
TOM NEVERS RD
Pebble Beach
South Pasture
Middle Moors
NANTUCKET SHIPWRECK AND LIFESAVING MUSEUM
Polpis Rd Bike Trail
MILESTONE RD
Milestone Rd Bike Trail
NANTUCKET MEMORIAL AIRPORT
OLD SOUTH RD
FAIR-GROUNDS RD
Surfside Rd Bike Trail
Nobadeer Beach
Surfside Beach
SURFSIDE RD
S SHORE RD
HOSTELLING INTERNATIONAL
Coatue Point
BRANT POINT LIGHT
WHALING MUSEUM
ORANGE ST
FIRST CONGREGATIONAL CHURCH AND OLD NORTH VESTRY
ACADEMY HILL
VESPER LN
BARTLETT RD
CISCO BREWERS
Cliff Rd Bike Trail
CLIFF RD
MADAKET RD
LOINES OBSERVATORY
HUMMOCK POND RD
BARTLETT FARM
Miacomet Beach
BARTLETT FARM RD
Dionis Beach
EEL POINT RD
Eel Point Rd Bike Trail
40th Pole Beach
Sanford Farm Ram Pasture
Madaket Rd Bike Trail
MADAKET
Cisco Beach
MADAKET RD
Madaket Harbor
Madaket Beach
Eel Point
Smith Point
Tuckernuck Island
Muskeget Island
0 2 mi
0 2 km
© MOON.COM

High season in Nantucket has a little bit of the feel of a big game of musical chairs, with seemingly far more people searching for places to eat, seats on tours, or guest rooms to stay in than can possibly accommodate them all. With patience and flexibility, you need not be disappointed in whatever you seek, but it helps to anticipate that everything from meals to transportation inevitably will take more time than you might have thought.

Sights

Ferry passengers disembarking from the Steamship Authority at Steamboat Wharf are greeted a block off the gangway by hints of Nantucket's two principal attractions—recreation and history. With the exception of a couple of the island's lighthouses, all the historic sights and museums are within walking distance of one other.

★ WHALING MUSEUM

Steps away from the Steamship ferry dock on Broad Street is the **Whaling Museum** (508/228-1894, www.nha.org, 11am-4pm Sat.-Sun. early Feb.-late Apr., 10am-5pm daily late Apr.-mid-Oct., 11am-4pm Thurs.-Mon. mid-Oct.-late Dec., $23 adults, $20 seniors, $5 child/student 6-17, under 6 free), the flagship property of the Nantucket Historical Association. Meander through the exhibits under a giant, beautifully preserved whale skeleton and see highlights such as a Fresnel lighthouse light, scrimshaw carvings, photographs, displays, and educational films. Additional rotating exhibits are on special loan from other institutions, so there's always something new and fresh to see.

Appropriately, the museum partly occupies a former candle factory, whose tapers were made from that most prized of whale oils, spermaceti. There are wonderful views over the town and harbor from the rooftop deck, usually accompanied by evocative sea chanteys gently piped through speakers in the walls. If the try-pots and whale tales whet your appetite for related books, toys, or even scrimshaw, be sure to visit the well-stocked museum shop.

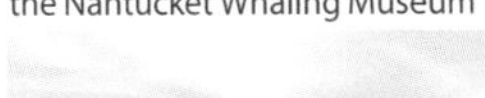

the Nantucket Whaling Museum

Gone Whaling

humpback whale "waving" at awed passengers

Nantucket island is synonymous with whaling even to this day. Herman Melville's most famous character, Captain Ahab, was a Nantucketer for good reason, as from this tiny port hundreds of ships left for voyages that lasted as long as five years (if they returned at all). The 2015 movie *The Heart of the Sea* is based on the true story of the ship *Essex*, which left from Nantucket and met its doom at the hands of a whale. Fortunes were made and lost, boys left its shores and were men by the time they returned, and countless whales were slaughtered in what has been called the "cruelest of all hunts" so as to return with precious and expensive whale oil.

MARIA MITCHELL ASSOCIATION

In 1831 the King of Denmark offered a prize to the first discoverer of a comet by telescope. Sixteen years later, Maria (ma-RYE-ah) Mitchell, daughter of a multitalented local educator, won the gold medal with the aid of a telescope she and her father shared on the roof of the former Pacific National Bank. At a time when, as she mused to her diary, "the needle is the chain of woman, and has fettered her more than the laws of the country," Mitchell quickly became an international celebrity.

She learned astronomy from her father, whom she aided in his sideline business of calibrating navigational chronometers (note the inscribed stone markers used for this work at the curb beside the bank at 61 Main Street, and a block south on Fair Street). After being lionized for her discovery—she became the first woman elected to the American Academy of Arts and Sciences—Mitchell undertook a career in mathematics and astronomy, eventually spending 20 years on the faculty at Vassar College before ultimately retiring to Nantucket, where she lies buried in Prospect Hill Cemetery.

Today, the **Maria Mitchell Association** (MMA, www.mmo.org) promotes the study of astronomy and the natural sciences through lectures, classes, field trips, and a handful of public attractions.

MMA Aquarium

Located in the former Nantucket Railroad ticket office and a pair of adjacent buildings on Washington Street near the Town Pier, the **MMA Aquarium** (508/228-5387, 10am-4pm

For centuries Native Americans sought the right whale, so named because it was the "right whale to hunt"—it was slow, unafraid of boats, and floated after it was killed due to its thicker-than-normal layers of blubber. One or two animals would feed hundreds for months. To survive during the long winter months when food was scarce, the Nauset would make pemmican, a mixture of calorie-rich fat such as whale blubber, meats, and the dried blueberries, cranberries, and bearberries that were all found in abundance here. Stored in a cool place, this precursor to the granola bar would last for months.

Only when the hunt changed in purpose from subsistence to profit did whale species really start to dwindle. Ships pursued whales in every possible corner of the ocean, and in less than a century, species that had numbered hundreds of thousands were reduced to less than 1 percent of that. Right whales in particular suffered the most: They remain on the brink of extinction, their numbers so depleted that a localized disaster (such as an oil spill in the right place or a leak at Pilgrim Nuclear Power Station, close to Stellwagen Bank) could wipe them out completely.

Bowhead whales, a relative of the right, have recently been discovered to be one of the longest-living mammals. These shy whales are native to the frigid waters around the arctic coasts, and scientists have discovered recently deceased carcasses with spearheads from the 1800s still embedded in them. These whales are so old that they remember—perhaps in crystal clarity—the whaling days, and those survivors have remained cautious about humans ever since. These amazing creatures may live up to two hundred years.

Whale killing today has been eclipsed by whale watching in most of the world, although people in Iceland, Norway, and Japan still hunt using technologies that, while far more effective, are as or even more cruel than the way whales were hunted centuries ago. One can easily spend an afternoon or even a weekend immersing oneself in this fascinating bygone era's museums and historic houses; however, there are no whale-watching vessels that leave directly from the island. If you want to get up close to these gentle giants, your best bet is to head to Barnstable or Provincetown, as Nantucket is quite far from Stellwagen Bank, the primary viewing zone.

Mon.-Fri., 10am-1pm Sat. mid-June-Labor Day, $10) features a score of saltwater tanks displaying such denizens of the local marine ecosystem as squid, whelks, and shellfish. There are also a couple of touch tanks where you can get your hands wet making the acquaintance of live sea creatures up close. This is a deservedly popular place for kids.

Natural Science Museum

Live reptiles such as turtles and snakes are among the leading attractions at the **Natural Science Museum** (508/228-0898, 10am-4pm Mon.-Sat. mid-June-Sept 30, $5, children free), in the 19th-century Hinchman House on the corner of Vestal and Milk Streets. Collections of shells, preserved wildflowers, and small stuffed critters are used to illustrate island flora and fauna. Among the prizes of the museum herbarium is the great amateur naturalist Eugene Bicknell's exhaustive unrivaled collection of Nantucket plants, meticulously gathered around the turn of the 20th century.

The building houses the association's gift shop, an excellent place to pick up field guides to everything that blossoms or breeds on the island. Or, for expert guidance in the flesh, join one of the many association-sponsored nature walks held weekly through the June-September season. Choose from early-morning bird-watching trips, beachcombing strolls, wildflower walks, and more.

The MMA campus also includes a **Science Library** (2 Vestal St., 508/228-9219, 10am-4pm Mon. year-round) open by appointment to professional researchers and anyone else naturally curious about the universe.

Mitchell House

Across Vestal Street from the Natural Science Museum is Maria Mitchell's birthplace, **Mitchell House** (508/228-2896, 10am-4pm Mon.-Fri., 10am-1pm Sat. mid-June-mid-Oct., $10). It has been restored with family possessions and other artifacts to illustrate the domestic life of a 19th-century Quaker family such as the Mitchells.

Vestal Street Observatory

The historic 1908 **Vestal Street Observatory** (3 Vestal St., 508/228-9273), adjacent to the Mitchell home, offers a guided tour (2pm Mon.-Fri., $5) that may include a talk about the association's contributions to astronomy as well as sunspot observations, if the clouds are cooperative. Among the permanent exhibits are photos from an extensive collection created over the course of nearly a century by MMA astronomers, plus a scale model of the solar system in the observatory's garden and a calendar of astronomy-related events.

★ Loines Observatory

If you've tired of the nightlife but not of the night's lights, **Stargazing Nights at the Loines Observatory** (59 Milk St. Ext., 508/228-9273, 9pm-10:30pm Mon., Wed., and Fri., $10), the MMA's research-oriented facility, a short distance beyond where the town's sidewalks end, may be just the solution. You'll need clear skies, but because of Nantucket's distance from the mainland, the clarity of the cool atmosphere over the local ocean, and efforts by town planners to eliminate unnecessary streetlights, star-gazing conditions here are excellent.

Dr. Vladimir Strelnitski, the observatory's gregarious director, typically leads these events, discoursing on fundamentals of astronomy as he identifies constellations, visible planets, features of the moon, or whatever other celestial bodies are appropriate to the evening's conditions. You'll get to peer through the eyepiece of one or both of the observatory's optical telescopes, the largest of which (a 24-inch reflector) is used in the organization's ongoing research into variable stars.

HISTORIC HOUSES

In addition to the Whaling Museum, the **Nantucket Historical Association** (NHA, 508/228-1894, www.nha.org) maintains a number of carefully restored old buildings, from one of the island's oldest surviving houses to the early-20th-century summer residence of a pair of Nantucket's most picaresque bohemians. Most are free, but the four that offer interpretive tours, each of which is outlined here, require purchase of either the NHA's all-inclusive combination ticket ($23, includes Whaling Museum admission) or the Historic Site Pass ($6, historic houses only).

Guided tours of the four are offered daily in season. All are open briefly for Memorial Day weekend, then reopen a week later and stay open 10am-5pm Monday-Sunday through Columbus Day in early October. Hours then change to 11am-4pm Saturday-Sunday until late November. For inquiries about any of the properties, call the NHA's main office or visit its website.

The other structures of the NHA's collection, where visitors guide their own tours, are the **1805 Old Gaol,** off Vestal Street past the Maria Mitchell complex; the **Macy-Christian House** (12 Liberty St.), an 18th-century merchant's home; the island's **first public school,** on Winter Street; the **Fire Hose-Cart House,** an 1886 neighborhood fire station with antique equipment related to the Great Fire of 1846, on Gardner Street; and the restful **Greater Light Garden,** a former pig and cow barn turned summer home on Howard Street.

The Oldest House

This is a required stop for anyone interested in Nantucket history. Pick up a museum guide from any of the staffed NHA properties and follow its suggested half-day walking tour for a thorough stroll through the ages, starting with the 1686 **Jethro Coffin House** on Sunset Hill, 10 minutes' walk from the center of town. While there are other houses that can vie for the title of "oldest," this is the oldest unmoved, unmodified house that's still on its original foundation.

The house was a wedding gift for a marriage that helped end a major family feud on the island. Its design (with its central chimney, hall, and parlor) marks an ambitious improvement over that of the First Period dwellings (with one or two rooms and chimneys on the ends of the buildings) more typical of the region. Extensive refurbishment was required in the 1870s thanks to early tourists' practice of carving their names in the walls and stealing souvenir shingles.

A kitchen garden with a raised beds of herbs and medicinal plants typical to the colonial period is maintained on the property, along with a small orchard planted with an antique variety of apple tree.

Hadwen House

At the other end of the spectrum from the Coffin House is one of the NHA's youngest properties, **Hadwen House** (96 Main St.). Commissioned by William Hadwen, a silversmith turned whale-oil dealer, this handsome 1845 mansion embodies 19th-century ostentation as much as the Coffin House, in its rudimentary way, had set the standard for high living 160 years earlier. The Ionic-columned Hadwen and its Corinthian-columned neighbor are known as "The Two Greeks," in counterpoint to "The Three Bricks," an exceptional trio of transitional Federal-style homes built across the street by Hadwen's father-in-law.

The little dated wooden markers that identify the pedigree of many buildings on either side of the Hadwen House are the work of the **Nantucket Preservation Trust** (NPT, 11 Centre St., 508/228-1387, www.nantucketpreservation.org), one of the several island nonprofits dedicated to the protection of local historical structures, including their interiors. The NPT hosts regular **guided architectural walking tours** (3pm Tue. & Thurs. July-Oct., $10) of these historic blocks of upper Main Street between the Pacific National Bank and the Civil War monument, starting in front of their office.

Quaker Meeting House

In the early Bay State colony, under the theocratic rule of the Puritans, membership in the Society of Friends—also known as Quakers—was punishable by banishment or even death. By the time the English crown revoked the Puritan colonial charter in 1692 and established the province of Massachusetts, Puritan authority had waned enough so that Quaker preachers could travel around the region with relative freedom.

The Quaker community on Nantucket originated from the visit of such an itinerant preacher in 1701. Within a century Quakerism had become the island's dominant religion, with adherents among all the most prosperous families and business leaders. As the interpretive guide at this site will explain, eventually sectarian divisions split the community; the 1838 Quaker Meeting House was thus originally erected by one of the splinter groups as a school.

While here, be sure to take note of the current exhibit in the one-room Whitney Gallery inside the entrance of the **Fair Street Research Library** (7 Fair St., 508/228-1894, https://nha.org, 10am-4pm Mon. and Thurs.-Fri., 11am-4pm Tues.), drawn from the NHA's extensive photography and print archives adjoining the back of the Meeting House. The gallery, which is free, shares the library's hours. Library access, for all you genealogists, writers, and ephemera enthusiasts, is free.

The Old Mill

The photogenic 1746 windmill on South Mill Street is the last survivor of a collection of such grist mills that used to occupy the high ground on the outskirts of town. The oldest windmill still in operation in the United States, its practical mechanical design allows the cap of the mill to be rotated with a great wooden spar so that the blades can face the wind from any direction. The wind-driven millstones are still put to work producing cornmeal for sale in season whenever the weather allows.

★ FIRST CONGREGATIONAL CHURCH AND OLD NORTH VESTRY

Outside of a trip to Altar Rock in the Middle Moors, the best panorama of the island is found atop the steeple of the 19th-century **First Congregational Church and Old North Vestry** (62 Centre St., 508/228-0950, www.nantucketfcc.org, 10am-4pm Mon.-Sat. mid-June-mid-Oct., suggested donation $5). The hike up all the stairs is amply rewarded by the view over rooftop widow's walks, a vantage from which weathered shingles, rose-covered trellises, and "catslide" roofs (shorter in back than in front) can be appreciated as textures of the landscape rather than as architectural details.

★ ACADEMY HILL

The visual elements that define Nantucket are certainly abundant in the downtown area, from the brick sidewalks and undulating cobblestones to the dignified wood-columned facades of library, bank, and church buildings salted amid the intimate commercial blocks and one-way streets. To truly immerse yourself in the essence of ye olde Sherburne (as the town was originally known), step away from the bustle of shoppers and steamship traffic and stroll the residential Academy Hill neighborhood around the First Congregational Church.

Spared the ravages of the 1846 Great Fire, the delightfully quiet lanes and narrow, well-shaded streets in this area—Church, Academy, Westminster, Gay, and Quince—are lined with fine shingle and clapboard homes, many retaining the character of their 18th- and early-19th-century origins. Some houses were dressed up over the years with Greek Revival entrances, Victorian porches, or bits of fancy decorative woodwork around the facades. Others sport the traditional roof walk, large chimney, and fully enclosed front entrance that typify what is locally known as the Quaker style, named after the denomination to which so many of the shipmasters and other well-to-do families who built this neighborhood once belonged.

To the left of the Academy Hill Apartments on Westminster Street—site of the private school for which the area is named—is one of the town's few remaining historic footpaths, once called Breakneck Alley for its steep pitch down to Lily Street. Use it to reach **Lily Pond Park,** a public property of the Land Bank that offers a pleasant oasis for a picnic or snooze in the sun. Despite the name, there's no pond, but if it's late summer, there may be fresh edible blackberries to be found along the paths—if the large variety of resident and migratory birds haven't gotten to them first.

AFRICAN MEETING HOUSE

By the early 19th century, the area around "Five Corners"—the intersection of York Street, Pleasant Street, and Atlantic Avenue—became the heart of the free Black community on Nantucket. Nicknamed New Guinea, it was similar to other Black neighborhoods in towns and cities elsewhere up and down the Eastern seaboard, and it included Black-owned stores, homes, inns, and churches.

While houses remaining from that era have been extensively modified, the **African Meeting House** (508/228-9833, www.maah.org, call ahead for hours, generally 10am or 11am-2pm or 4pm daily, $5), at the corner of York and Pleasant, has been restored by Boston's Museum of African American History as an interpretive exhibit center. Built in the 1820s as a school for children denied access to segregated public schools, this modest, shingled, single-story structure went on to serve New Guinea's residents as a Baptist church and social center after a lengthy legal challenge finally opened the white schools to all island children in 1848.

1: the First Congregational Church and steeple **2:** the bell inside the First Congregational Church's belfry **3:** Great Point Light **4:** Nantucket Harbor

1
2
3
4
NANTUCKET

The Meeting House is the centerpiece of the **Black Heritage Trail,** whose nine stops are described in a handy brochure available at the Whaling Museum or the Visitor Services office (25 Federal St.), among other places. You can also download a copy from the Museum of African American History's website (www.maah.org). **Guided walking tours** of the trail (11am and 3pm Sat. and by appointment) are offered during the height of summer, departing from the Whaling Museum.

NANTUCKET SHIPWRECK AND LIFESAVING MUSEUM

It's hard to imagine today, what with GPS, radar, sonar, and cell phones, but the stretch of sandbars from Provincetown down past Nantucket once accounted for one-fourth of all the shipwrecks on the entire Eastern seaboard. Shifting sands and strong currents carved up the shoreline and deposited fresh sandbars in places where channels used to be. It wasn't until the Cape Cod Canal was built in 1931 that ships had genuinely safe passage on their way to and from Boston.

Prior to the U.S. Coast Guard was the U.S. Life-Saving Service, a hardy corps who manned the remote, often desolate lifesaving stations that were spaced out all along the coast. The **Nantucket Shipwreck and Lifesaving Museum** (158 Polpis Rd., 508/228-1885, https://eganmaritime.org, 10am-5pm Mon.-Sat., noon-4pm Sun., late-May-early Oct., $10) pays tribute to this service and its staff with displays of equipment, numerous photos, and descriptions of their exploits—which often seemed to entail rowing out to foundering ships in open boats during brutal winter storms. When rowing was impossible, a cannon with a rope attached was fired over the bow of the sinking vessel and sailors were rescued one by one in a contraption called a breeches-buoy. Although it is located about three miles east of the Milestone Rotary, the museum is right on the Polpis Road bike path and the Nantucket Regional Transit Authority (NRTA) 'Sconset-via-Polpis-Road shuttle route.

The original **Surfside Life Saving Station,** of which the museum building is a replica, still stands about a block behind Surfside Beach. It's now the seasonal home of the local branch of Hostelling International.

NANTUCKET LIGHTSHIP BASKET MUSEUM

Attempts were also made to keep passing ships from getting into trouble in the first place. One 19th-century solution was to anchor lightships—essentially floating lighthouses—near various hazardous shallows. Many crew members relieved the boredom of their stationary duties with handicrafts—basket weaving in particular. In time a distinctive wood-bottomed bowl-shaped utility basket became the namesake style of the lightship crews, who supplemented their income selling them to fellow islanders and, eventually, Victorian-era tourists. In 1949, a Filipino immigrant, José Formoso Reyes, reinvented the nearly forgotten tradition for a new generation of tourists by adding decorative lids to the baskets and transforming them into women's purses. The rest, as they say, is history.

The evolution of this indigenous art form is chronicled in the **Nantucket Lightship Basket Museum** (49 Union St., 508/228-1177, www.nantucketlightshipbasketmuseum.org, 10am-4:30pm Tues.-Sat. late May-mid-Oct. $7), less than a 10-minute stroll from Main Street. The NLBM is currently undergoing a merger with the Nantucket Historical Society, so displays and locations are in a state of flux. The permanent collection is complemented by changing annual exhibits, live demonstrations, and Reyes's complete workshop, right down to the handwritten "Gone Fishing" sign he'd often hang outside his door. The small garden, by the way, has been planted with varieties that would have been contemporary to the 1821 construction of the building, including herbs, antique roses, and heritage apple trees.

LIGHTHOUSES

Three lighthouses grace Nantucket's coast, and if you're keen on seeing all three, you'll have your work cut out for you. Turn-of-the-20th-century **Brant Point Light** is the easiest to visit. It's the diminutive wooden nubbin at the end of Easton Street, the one around which the ferries arc into the harbor. At only 26 feet, it's the nation's shortest lighthouse, but being small hasn't spared it the ravages of the elements. Recurring fires and storms have forced the original 1743 light to be rebuilt nine times.

About six miles to the east, at the end of the Milestone Road bike path, is **Sankaty Head Light,** both the island's oldest and the only one that hasn't had to be rebuilt, although it had to be moved in 2007 to avoid being fatally toppled by erosion of the scarp on which it sat. Erected in 1849, the distinctive red-belted light towers 150 feet over some of the region's most treacherous waters, its flashing beacon nearly reaching Cape Cod, 30 miles away. Although it kept mariners away from the beach, during the 50 years after its construction many of the 2,000 ships that went aground on Nantucket's shoals did so off this shore—on Rose and Crown, Great Rip, Old Man, and many of the other named hull-scraping rocks and shallow bars. These days, it makes a prominent target for landlocked navigators cycling across the hummocky Middle Moors, suspended on the windblown horizon like a tantalizing heat mirage.

Most difficult of all to see close-up is **Great Point Light,** way out at the northernmost tip of Nantucket, requiring a 4WD vehicle. The newest of the island's lights, the present youthful incarnation is the replacement for the historic stone tower utterly destroyed by a violent winter tempest in 1984. So that this one may possibly beat its predecessor's 166-year tenure, its reinforced concrete walls are five feet thick at the base.

★ 'SCONSET

This charming little village sits at the lip of Nantucket's eastern edge. Once a collection of fishing shanties barely more substantial than the beach from which the fisherfolk launched their dories, the village has evolved into a summer cottage colony whose grand oceanfront homes buffer the island's most exclusive golf courses from the hungry Atlantic. Pretty and serene, during the brief high season it comes alive with short-term residents and visitors who appreciate outdoor activities over shopping.

From the rotary in the village center, all of 'Sconset's attractions are within walking distance: restaurants, galleries, Sankaty Light, and the seemingly never-ending beach. Start by strolling among the dainty little "dollhouses" along residential Front Street, a narrow grass alley with century-old vehicle tracks of crushed shell and sandy soil. In summer, the local palette of weathered gray shingle is brightened by roses climbing up trellised walls and roofs and hydrangeas grown wherever there's enough room for a garden. Midway along the street, a side path angles down to Codfish Park, the tiny neighborhood at the foot of the bank facing the public beach. A second, steeper path descends to Codfish Park from the street's north end, just past the "Footpath Only, No Bicycles" sign.

This path's left fork is also the beginning of the **Bluff Walk,** a public way skirting the very edge of the heights above the beach, hat-tipping distance from the back porches of the large Queen Anne shingle- and stick-style mansions that face Baxter Road. Here is where the sun rises on America; to the east is nothing but water until Portugal. The undertow along this stretch of shore is fierce, which is why the beach far below is usually sparsely populated, even in the heat of summer. If the bluff's seaward edge is cliff-sharp and bare of vegetation rather than having a stable angle of repose covered in wild beach rose, you are looking at the latest loss of land to Mother Nature. These ever-eroding acres are among the most transitory on the island, relentlessly

Drink Responsibly; Drink Locally

Living on an island far away from the mainland inspires a lot of ingenuity and self-reliance. And living on an island where the long quiet winters leave you with a lot of time on your hands inspires a lot of crazy ideas. Perhaps that's partly why Nantucket has for some time now been proud home to a winery, a microbrewery, and a small-batch distillery—**Nantucket Vineyard, Cisco Brewers,** and **Nantucket Triple Eight Distillery**—combined now under one metaphorical roof at 5 Bartlett Farm Road (508/325-5929, www.ciscobrewers.com, 11am-7pm Mon.-Sat., noon-6pm Sun).

The vineyard was started in 1981, but summer conditions on the island were not good for the vines. Since the late 1990s, the company's nine different red and white wines have been carefully blended from varietal grapes primarily imported from the West Coast.

Cisco's brewing operations began in the 1990s, and thanks to the great taste of the flagship English-style amber Whale's Tale Pale Ale, have expanded rapidly. Summer selections like The Gray Lady (a lemony wheat beer named in honor of the island's nickname) and seasonal fall brews mean there's always a tasty surprise. The microbrewery now produces over half a dozen standards, including ales, lagers, porters, and barley wine. From there it was a short leap to making fine spirits—as the owners realized, whiskey is basically just distilled beer. Premium single-malt bourbon whiskey also takes a helluva long time to make, so the inspired crew at Cisco turned to distilling vodka and other spirits like gin and rum.

The results of the microdistillery experiment, begun in 2000, can be tasted at bars and restaurants all over the island as well as on the mainland for the lucky residents of some dozen states, mostly in the northeast. The namesake Triple Eight vodka, triple distilled from a base of organic corn and Nantucket sand-filtered well water, has acquired a devoted following for its smooth taste and slightly sweet finish. Ever the upstart, it has beaten far better-known international brands at the annual World Spirit Championships. Their flagship beers are now so popular that they are brewed off-island, allowing the small-town vibe of Cisco to remain.

Tours of this "alcohol amusement park," just off Hummock Pond Road midway between town and Cisco Beach, are offered by appointment ($20). They are also open for tastings and direct purchases. A free shuttle runs continuously from the brewery door to the tourist info center in town. If you want to anchor your drinks with some good food, turn right out of the driveway and follow the road for about 0.5 miles to **Bartlett's Farm** (33 Bartlett Farm Rd., 508/228-9403, http://bartlettsfarm.com, 7:30am-7pm daily), where you'll find great made-to-order sandwiches and paninis, plus salads, soups, and freshly baked desserts.

gnawed away by winter storms that swallow up to a dozen feet a year, on average, and have at times suddenly reduced house lots to sandbars in the surf.

The **Nantucket Preservation Trust** (55 Main St., 508/228-1387, www.nantucketpreservation.org) conducts periodic **walking tours** of the village with a focus on the architectural heritage of its houses, some of which predate the American Revolution. Call or check the website for the current schedule.

★ CISCO BREWERS

Cisco Brewers (5 Bartlett Rd., 508/325-5929, www.ciscobrewers.com, tasting room 11am-7pm Mon.-Sat., noon-6pm Sun.) is the island's microbrewery, with some flagship ales that have caught on even on the mainland. They've added spirits to the menu, making it the area's only micro-distillery as well. Stop by, taste some of the brews and liquors, and take a bottle home as a liquid keepsake. Tours are offered Saturday or by appointment, but more frequently in summer.

Sports and Recreation

For visitors and locals alike, "outdoors" often means the beach. However, you can get tanned in a host of other ways as well, and Nantucket has some of the area's most interesting topology. The moors and marshes teem with migrating birds, while fields and forests have everything from scenic wildflowers to a gamut of wildlife (deer, foxes, and raccoons are the three largest mammals you're likely to see). If your legs are tired, find a boat and head out for scores of seals, dolphins, basking sharks, and pelagic birds.

MIDDLE MOORS

It's important to note that these are not moors in the European sense: despite a resemblance, they're primarily not peat, and therefore host quite different flora and fauna. When the settlers first arrived here, the area was hardwood forest that was quickly exhausted for firewood and boatbuilding. Only then did the moors appear, as grasses were one of the few things that could grow on the salty nutrient-poor sand.

The Middle Moors, a great expanse of undeveloped land between Polpis and Milestone Roads east of town, is a good example of this grass and heath mixture—and it shows how this distinct ecosystem is in a constant state of change. Look closely, and you'll see that scrub oak is beginning to grow up through the grasses. This sort of plant succession is entirely natural and would eventually return the island interior to the wooded state it was in when Europeans arrived. But prior to colonial settlement, the heaths flourished close to shore—where salt air put trees at a disadvantage—and in forest openings created by fire. Homeowners covetous of ocean views cleared much of that away, and fires are now suppressed to prevent property damage, so the heaths and their dependent ecosystem of insects, birds, and small mammals are headed toward extinction.

Altar Rock, a glacial erratic embedded in the overgrown ridge called Saul's Hills that defines the moor's northern edge, affords the best panorama over the huckleberry, false heather, and intruding scrub oak barrens. Though a mere 100 feet above sea level, this viewpoint and the four other hills in the ridge that share the same elevation are among the highest points on the island. Only Sankaty Bluff (at a skyscraping 109 feet), Folger Hill (108 feet), and part of the $28 million Rees Jones golf course to the east are higher. Altar Rock also offers one of a declining number of island vistas whose foreground isn't speckled with vacation homes. The most direct route to the rock is via the easy-to-miss sand track off Polpis Road, exactly opposite the Quaise Road turnoff; head toward the funky-shaped building that's actually a radio antenna.

To identify other trails through the moors, pick up an all-island *General Information and Properties Map* from the **Nantucket Conservation Foundation** (NCF, 118 Cliff Rd., 508/228-2884, www.nantucketconservation.org, 9am-5pm Mon.-Fri.). Thirty miles of sandy roads accommodate mountain bikers—although to reduce erosion, bikers are requested to stay off trails blocked by posts or that are obviously narrow and suited only for walkers. Like all NCF holdings, the Middle Moors are distinguished from private land by the organization's gull-waves-hills logo, affixed to maroon posts at the boundaries.

CRANBERRY BOGS

Cranberries are as native to Nantucket as the thick morning fogs, but only since the mid-1800s have they been cultivated. To keep the island's remaining cranberry bogs from becoming summer cottages, they were purchased and donated to the Nantucket Conservation Foundation. Through the NCF, **Windswept Cranberry Bog,** off

Polpis Road opposite the Wauwinet turnoff, and **Milestone Road Cranberry Bog,** about five miles east of town along the 'Sconset bike path, remain open to active cultivation, with hundreds more acres of marsh, ponds, and forest open to the public. These bogs make for excellent bird-watching throughout the year. Look closer and the curious botanist will find sundews, lobelias, Saint-John's-wort, monkshood, and a host of other blossoms (including the crane-like cranberry flowers). A trail map specifically for the Windswept property is available at the NCF office on Cliff Road.

When wholesale prices make the harvesting economically feasible, come mid-October the fruits of these acres are reaped with mechanical "water reels" that plow through submerged bogs beating the cranberry vines, creating great crimson oceans of floating berries in their wake. The crop gets vacuumed up for shipment off-island, where the berries are turned into the jellies and sauces you may be buying for Thanksgiving. (Wet-harvested berries are never sold fresh because the water breaks down their natural waxy coating, eliminating any chance of a viable retail shelf life.) As you'd expect, local bakeries and restaurants often demonstrate the versatility of these tart treats in all manner of sweet and savory dishes during the late fall—although not necessarily with native-grown berries.

★ COSKATA-COATUE WILDLIFE REFUGE

One of The Trustees of Reservations' many fine properties, **Coskata-Coatue** (ko-SKATE-ah ko-TWO, 508/228-5646, gatehouse 508/228-0006, www.thetrustees.org) encompasses Nantucket's longest barrier beach, largest salt marsh, a cedar forest, and—at the far north end of that beach—Great Point's lighthouse. Tide pools hold plenty of shellfish, such as scallops, clams, and mussels, while wild roses, the elusive beach plum, and even prickly-pear cactus grow amid the dunes. Hundreds of terns from a summer nesting colony wheel and dive over the surf, northern harriers ride thermals rising from the sun-heated sand, and the occasional shearwater, a pelagic visitor more commonly found far out at sea, can be spotted resting on shore. Fiddler crabs scurry away from your approach, oystercatchers stalk the surf line for fiddler crabs, and beneath the sweep of the lighthouse beacon, cocky young seals sun themselves on the beach between bouts of play in the strong fickle currents of the offshore rip.

harvesting of the cranberry crop

Despite the temptation, do not climb on the fragile dunes. There is almost nothing to protect them from wind erosion, and even a few footsteps can kill the grass or microscopic patina of algae and lichens that hold the sand in place. Swimming isn't recommended either due to dangerous riptides. With over 10 miles of shoreline on three bodies of water—the Atlantic, Nantucket Sound, and the enclosed harbor—this is the place to take long meditative walks on the beach. This is a prime fishing spot as well, so count on some company when the bluefish and stripers are running.

May through October, the Trustees offer three-hour **narrated excursions** out to the lighthouse (9am and 1pm Fri.-Sun., adults $60, discounts for Trustees members) via a comfortably air-conditioned SUV. Your driver is a naturalist who has lived on the island year-round for over two decades. She provides well-informed commentary as well as binoculars. On Tuesday in July-August there's an additional sunset trip, and if you have a group of six (or are prepared to buy six seats) you can arrange a custom excursion.

Tours depart promptly from the gatehouse in the Wauwinet Inn parking lot at the end of Wauwinet Road, the access point for the property. Call 508/228-6799 for reservations, which are required. The tours typically sell out ahead of time, so booking in advance (a week or more for weekends and sunset trips) is definitely advisable. Although insect repellent is customarily recommended for any visit to the refuge due to the prevalence of biting greenhead horseflies, the only time you'll be outside the tour vehicle is at the lighthouse, where stiff ocean breezes keep the insects firmly at bay.

When not restricted for beach-nesting plovers and terns, 4WD vehicles with the proper permits may also use designated roads out to the lighthouse. Permits ($160 per year for private off-island vehicles, or $75 per day), information, and maps are all available late May-mid-October from the gatehouse.

THE SANFORD FARM

On Madaket Road, about two miles west of the waterfront on the Madaket shuttle route, are a small parking area and trailhead for the former Sanford Farm, now one of several contiguous parcels of public conservation land stretching nearly three miles to the South Shore's Cisco Beach. Several miles of trails traverse a varied set of habitats bounded on one side by Hummock Pond, whose waters fill a narrow glacial outwash valley. Swamps and sloughs where you might see turtles napping in the sun, old fields surrendering to bayberry and wild grape, grassland meadows known as the Ram Pasture, woodlands browsed by white-tailed deer, and plenty of wild blueberries are among the treats for walkers and cyclists (others are described on the 26 interpretive markers spread along the six-mile loop to the ocean). If you can't spare a few hours to go the whole way, at least go as far as the barn—about 30 minutes' walk from the Madaket Road gate—for great views to the ocean.

MIACOMET GOLF COURSE

There are several nice courses on Nantucket but many require an expensive membership and thus aren't ideal for the "here for a few days" traveler. If you'll be here more than a week and golf is a key part of why you're on the island, check out some of the exclusive clubs. Otherwise, you may want to opt for a lovely round or two at Miacomet (12 Miacomet Rd., 508/325-0333, www.miacometgolf.com, 5am-7pm daily, 18-holes $50-160), which has a nice option for day-use visitors. The course is a medium-level par 3-4, with pretty inland views. It's close to Bartlett Farm and Cisco Brewery too—so the family can do some sightseeing while you get in a few rounds.

BEACHES

Over 20 named beaches dot the island's shore, from remote windswept ones shared only with gulls to a handful that are fully catered with food concessions, bathhouses, and lifeguards. In general, beaches facing south or east receive the big breakers, strong currents, and fine sand, while those facing Nantucket Sound to the north are warmer and calmer, but also more pebbly.

Sometimes sustained windy conditions will propel flotillas of the stinging jellylike Portuguese man-of-war into local waters from its normal habitat in the Gulf Stream a dozen miles to the south. Lifeguards post warnings at the entrances to the major public beaches when this occurs, and the local media quickly issue advisories too, since touching the creatures, even after they have washed up on shore, can be painful enough to require medical attention. North shore and inner harbor beaches are less prone to closure due to Portuguese men-of-war than southern and eastern ones.

While the vast majority of Nantucket's 80-plus miles of shoreline have historically been open to public use, most beach frontage is actually under private ownership. Leaving no trash behind on any beach and being courteous to adjacent homeowners are thus not just good manners, but also greatly appreciated by all the future beachgoers who would suffer if "No Trespassing" signs were erected at every private property line.

In Town

Kid-friendly **Children's Beach** wins the popularity contest for beach-going families seeking to avoid an all-day excursion out of town on account of its location a few blocks north of Steamboat Wharf, as well as all its extras: a playground, a snack vendor, restrooms, and showers. It's also a perfect spot to watch the ferries and other boats come and go.

Other harbor swimming spots include modest **Francis Street Beach,** as placid as a pond, out toward the end of Washington Street Extension; and **Brant Point,** by the lighthouse, with a stiff current (swimmers beware). Neither beach is staffed by lifeguards, and only Francis Street has a restroom.

North Shore

Generally calm conditions prevail at all the north shore favorites. With its windsurfing concession, beach volleyball, snack shack, adjacent public tennis courts, and shuttle bus service, **Jetties Beach** is not the place to seek splendid isolation, and the seaweed and shells can make for some odiferous summer days, but it's also deservedly popular precisely for its convenience (you can even walk to it from downtown), amenities, and just-right water conditions. It has seasonal lifeguards, restrooms, and changing rooms.

A short distance west, past the private stretches of shore belonging to the Galley Beach Restaurant and Cliffside Beach Club, is **Steps Beach,** accessible from a long wooden staircase at the end of Lincoln Avenue. There is no lifeguard or restroom here, but the water is relatively warm, the surf is light, and the views are worth millions—just ask the owners of the big mansions above.

At the end of the 3.5-mile bike path along Madaket and Eel Point Roads is 0.5-mile-long **Dionis Beach,** which can also be reached by a combination of the NRTA's Madaket route to the Eel Point Road stop and walking the final 1.5 miles. It's well protected from shore breezes by high dunes, and it's large enough so anyone unburdened by kids and coolers will likely find some elbow room. Like Jetties, it features seasonal lifeguards and a bathhouse with changing facilities and restrooms.

Farther west along Eel Point Road is **40th Pole Beach,** owned by the Nantucket Land Bank and named for the number of telephone poles between Madaket Road and its parking lot. Although it shares the generally warm and calm conditions of Dionis, unfortunately it is also exceedingly popular with the "I can't live without my SUV on the beach" crowd.

South Shore

The island's main magnet for sun-worshipping blonds and the bronzed (and anyone else who hasn't heard about the holes in the ozone layer) is **Surfside,** at the end of the eponymous road and bike path.

Restrooms, showers, and food are all available in season, as is shuttle-bus service from downtown. Surfside is huge, but it still fills up, so get here early if you don't want to fight for a spot against a horde of SUVs.

Walk east one mile and you can join the lighter ranks of surfing enthusiasts who favor the big breaks at **Nobadeer Beach,** virtually under the end of the airport runway. Here too the Expeditions and Navigators sometimes seem to outnumber actual people, and the high school vibe is loud and strong. If "beach" isn't synonymous with "parking lot" in your dictionary, then walk west from Surfside. Just be aware that if you walk far enough you'll eventually arrive at the one part of Nantucket's shoreline frequented by the clothing-optional crowd. Strictly speaking, nude sunbathing is illegal, but this is the one spot where it is overlooked—at least by authorities, if not by prurient guys with binoculars.

Although it has neither lifeguards nor restrooms nor any other amenities, **Miacomet Beach,** at the end of West Miacomet Road, is a family favorite because behind the beach is Miacomet Pond, whose warmer, shallow, and calm waters are ideal for small children. Meanwhile, the ocean side drops off deeply underwater, creating strong surf close to shore; swim with care.

At the end of Hummock Pond Road is **Cisco Beach,** a.k.a. End of the Road Beach, a favorite of surfers. To the west, past the foot of Hummock Pond, is a sparsely frequented stretch of beach generally referred to as **Clark's Cove** after the body of water it divides from the ocean. This so-called cove, which once included the western third of a much larger Hummock Pond until shoreline shifts bisected the two, is surrounded by rural conservation land, including Sanford Farm, which adds to the sense of splendid isolation. Offshore rips can be quite strong in this vicinity, so know your strength as a swimmer—there are no lifeguards to come to your rescue here, and there may be no other swimmers within earshot either.

The other beach with southern exposure is the vast sweeping expanse of **Madaket Beach,** as far west as the island's shuttle buses and bike paths go. Besides invigorating waves that leave you feeling like a sock in the spin cycle, Madaket is the best place on Nantucket for lovely ocean sunsets. And, unlike Cisco, it has restrooms.

Jetties Beach, with heaps of slipper shells

Shark Sense and Safety

Warning signs are posted on many beaches on the Cape and islands.

While movies have been filmed on, near, or about Cape Cod for decades, none comes close to the fame of that Spielberg classic, *Jaws*. The idea of a man-eating shark coming into placid Nantucket beaches sends chills into even the most avid swimmer. And who doesn't remember the look on Chief Brody's face as he stares out at the water and prophesies, "We're going to need a bigger boat"?

It's not all Hollywood fancy. Those great apex predators of the deep regularly cruise Cape waters looking for seals. Unfortunately, as the seal population has grown, so too has the proximity with sharks and area beaches. In 2018 a swimmer was killed by a Great White—the first death due to sharks in the region since the mid-1930s.

Despite the perceived danger, sharks like the great white deserve our admiration, respect, and help, and you can easily minimize your risk of being bitten by following a few key steps and being "shark sensible" rather than "shark silly."

- Avoid swimming in the early morning or at dusk, when there is less visibility.
- Avoid swimming near seals.
- Be alert to your surroundings and heed any warnings and shark advisories.

Surfers joke that you don't have to swim faster than the shark, just swim faster than the nearest surfer next to you. Joking aside, don't let the fear of sharks prevent you from enjoying the waters. These incredible creatures have been here—for decades—and the incidents of human-shark interaction (let alone fatal ones) are extremely rare. Despite the fact that you stand a better chance of getting hit by lightning than being bitten by a great white, the phobia and stigma remains—and it has needlessly taken a huge toll on the world's shark populations. Shark-fishing contests are a popular sport all over the globe, including the Cape and islands. Worldwide, tens of thousands of sharks are caught, have their fins cut off, and are then thrown back into the water to suffocate, all in service of the shark-fin-soup industry. As a result, one of the ocean's most amazing creatures is being hunted in part due to a misconception of them as dangerous man-eaters. Peter Benchley, the author of *Jaws,* spent the last decades of his life trying to dispel some of this fear, which he in part caused with his work of fiction. Taking a few precautions can greatly reduce your risk.

East Shore

In summer, there are shuttle buses to 'Sconset from Nantucket town (on Washington St. at the corner of Main St.); from the bus stop at the Main Street Rotary, it's just a short stroll down to **'Sconset Beach.** Known for its rough breakers, the most swimmable portion lies between the village and the Coast Guard's LORAN navigational radio masts to the south. For sustenance after arriving in the village, consider a box lunch from Claudette's, whose shady patio faces the Rotary across from the bus stop, or fetch take-out fare from the small 'Sconset Market next to the post office, since there are no food concessions at the beach. There aren't any toilets at the beach either, but public restrooms are located off Pump Square (site of the old village pump) just north of the market.

One of the island's least well-known swimming spots is **Quidnet Beach,** north of Sankaty Light on shorefront property owned by the Massachusetts Audubon Society. While the open ocean is on one side of the dunes, on the other is Sesachacha (SACK-a-juh) Pond, a favorite of kayakers. To get to this overlooked spot, follow Quidnet Road nearly to its end, then turn right on Sesachacha Road to the parking area near its end.

WATER SPORTS

Surfing

While New England doesn't stand in the company of traditional surfing meccas like Hawaii, Baja California, and Australia, Nantucket offers fair surfing when conditions are right. During late summer and early fall, hurricanes in the Caribbean and mid-Atlantic region can produce overhead or even higher waves for several days—and Nantucket's south-facing beaches are the first part of New England to get good groundswell when it's out there.

Surfers who have left the board back home can rent one from the **Nantucket Island Surf School** (Cisco Beach, 508/560-1020, www.nantucketsurfing.com, $90 private lessons, $65 group lessons) for a complete door-to-beach, gear-included, guided surfing experience.

Throughout the summer, windsurfers have only one place to keep in mind: Jetties Beach. That's where **Nantucket Community Sailing** (508/228-5358, www.nantucketcommunitysailing.org, mid-June-Labor Day, sailboats $150 per 2 hours) staffs its seasonal concession for sailboard lessons and rentals, youth windsurfing clinics, adaptive windsurfing lessons for disabled athletes, and other sail- and paddling-related activities.

Paddling

Canoeists and kayakers will love Nantucket's stretches of protected waters, tidal estuaries, and secluded beaches. Several of its ponds are also large enough to warrant putting in.

Kayaks may be rented from friendly **Sea Nantucket Paddle Sports** (Francis St. Beach, 508/228-7499, www.seanantucketkayak.com, Memorial Day-Labor Day, $25 per hour, $55 per day, $40 hour for double kayaks). Their nonrollable singles and doubles are ideal for beginners, who have the entire protected length of Nantucket Harbor to play around in—from Coatue's gull rookeries east to Wauwinet. The company also handles deliveries, if you want to row around inland waters like long narrow Hummock Pond, west of town, or large Sesachacha Pond, on the eastern shore by Quidnet Beach.

Sailing

It's a fair bet that if you're hanging around anyone who grew up here, they already know how to sail. Few things beat a lazy afternoon spent sunning oneself on a deck as the water laps against the hull. If you're making yourself at home on the island for the whole summer, **Nantucket Community Sailing** (508/228-6600, www.nantucketsailing.com) can help you learn how to sail. If you prefer a boat with an engine, try **Island Boat Rental** (508/325-1001, www.nantucketboatrental.com). All-day rental and fuel starts at $700.

Island Fishing

It should come as no surprise that the islands constitute an angler's heaven. Whether fly-fishing for "funny fish" (bonito) or "albies" (false albacore); trolling deep waters for mackerel, tuna, and swordfish; or jigging for flounder and pollack near coastal rocks, there's plenty of variety to keep beginners and experts occupied. Sometimes the warm Gulf Stream even brings southern exotics like mahimahi into local waters. But most prized by local fish fanciers are two species favored by surfcasters—striped bass and bluefish.

Stripers are nocturnal feeders, though they can be caught any time of day, depending on conditions and the tides. They school up in local waters starting around mid-April. Blues tend to start their runs past the islands in mid-late June. Blues are like oceanic attack animals, making slash-and-run moves on anything in their paths—from flesh to fishing tackle (use extreme caution when removing hooks or attending a loose fish on deck to avoid a painful, even dangerous bite). Schools of blues are easily detected by terns and gulls diving into the water to catch smaller baitfish as they try to escape the blues' high-speed attacks.

Both species have felt the impact of overfishing and pollution—stripers, in particular, were nearly wiped out in the region a decade and a half ago—so strict regulations have been set on the size and quantity you can take home. Consult local tackle shops for current restrictions on keepers. There are no regulations on bluefish, although it's common to see these scrumptious fish being tossed back (or, worse, left for the gulls) because some people only eat stripers.

On Nantucket, anglers can choose among half a dozen sportfishing boats ready and waiting down on Straight Wharf, such as the **Althea K** (508/325-2167, www.altheaksportfishing.com, 3 hours $800, 5 hours $1300, 10 hours $2,500). If you're staying out on the west end of the island, ring up **Capt. Tom's Charters** (508/228-4225, www.capttom.com, inshore and offshore trips start at $150, rates vary by boat) or Captains Corey or Bill at **Bill Fisher Outfitters** (508/901-9087, http://billfisheroutfitters.com; 4 hours inshore $850, $100 per extra hour, 8 hours inshore $1,700, full day offshore $2,000, shorter trips possible, prices cheaper Sept.-mid-June), both of which depart from Walter Barrett Pier, the public landing at the end of F Street in Madaket.

Indoor Swimming

It's almost silly to think of swimming inside when so many amazing beaches are just steps away. But the waters are never exactly warm and, in all but the summer months, they require a wetsuit for anything more than a quick dip. Year-round you can swim at the **Nantucket Community Pool** (508/228-7285, ext. 1353, day-use $10 adults, $6 youth 6-17) at the intersection of Atlantic and Sparks Avenues, next to the high school (reachable on the NRTA South Loop shuttle). The Olympic-size heated indoor facility offers a varied schedule of adult, senior, and youth lap swims, water aerobics classes, open family swims, and other organized programs. Bring your own towel and a lock for your belongings.

ORGANIZED TOURS

Walking and Driving Tours

A good way to get a broad overview of Nantucket is by taking one of the small van tours available in season. Both **Gail's Tours** (508/257-6557, 10am, 1pm, and 3pm daily, $35) and **Ara's Tours** (508/221-6852, www.arastours.com, $50 adult, $25 child) offer informative all-island tours lasting around 90 minutes several times a day. Up to 7 people can charter a tour privately for $350-450. Both pick up from any in-town guesthouse or inn (or from the ferries, if you let them know when you'll be arriving). Both operate year-round, with up to three tours daily in season. They let their phones ring through to an answering service while conducting tours, so the best time to reach them in season is before 9am or after 5pm; usually calling a day in advance is sufficient for finding a space, although if you have one of their specific departure times in mind, you would be well advised to book at least a few days ahead. **Val's Tours** (508/280-1300 or 508/221-7640, $40/person, reservations required) offers a two-hour tour around the island's historic sites, including a visit to both Brant Point and Sankaty Head lighthouses, with lots of history stops along the way.

If you'd rather experience local history at a pedestrian's pace, both the Nantucket Historical Association and the Nantucket Preservation Trust offer seasonal **walking tours** of the town historic district. The tours of town (11:15am and 2:15pm daily May-Oct., $10) are guided by NHA interpretive staff and originate at the Whaling Museum, while the NPT tours (9:30am daily June-Sept., $10, $35 including a copy of their coffee-table book about the area covered by the walk) commence from in front of their office (55 Main St.).

Sailing Tours

You'll be missing out on some of Nantucket's best vistas if you never leave the land. For a reasonably priced outing aboard a classic traditional wooden boat, try the ***Endeavor*** (508/228-5585, www.endeavorsailing.com, daily May-Oct., $80-110), a gaff-rigged Friendship sloop that makes trips of up to 90 minutes around the harbor and Nantucket Sound. Drop by their slip at Straight Wharf to check the latest list of departure times. The *Endeavor* also offers "pirate adventures" for kids, cruises accompanied by a traditional fiddler or singer of sea chanteys, and private charters.

Cruises

The tiny islet of Muskeget (mus-KEE-git), a half-dozen miles off Nantucket's western tip, is home to a year-round colony of gray seals. The only way to observe these fat fellows—they're mostly bachelors—is by boat. If you don't have your own, join one of the two fun-lovin' guys who do: Captain Blair Perkins's **Shearwater Excursions** (508/228-7037, www.shearwaterexcursions.com, year-round, $95 pp).

Shearwater offers various other excursions too, from a cruise around Nantucket Harbor while snacking on ice cream (60 minutes, $55) to cocktail cruises ($55 person for 3 hours, private tours for up to 49 people also available) and whale-watching trips (6 hours, mid-June-mid-Oct., private tours only). While Stellwagen Bank, north of Cape Cod, is the actual sanctuary and the most well-known, whales can be spotted in other places as well. Nantucket's Great South Channel has the right combination of depth, currents, and water temperatures to make for decent whale spotting.

Shopping

Locals joke that Nantucket is where billionaires hire millionaires to mow their lawns, so it should come as no surprise that cheap and funky shopping is in short supply. (In how many other places might you overhear someone complaining about stooping to rent a jet because the one they own is being serviced?) Nor will you find the usual national chains in downtown Nantucket, thanks to a ban enacted in 2006 after a Ralph Lauren Polo store opened up on Main Street. While plenty of windows discreetly announce sister locations in equally fashionable resort towns around the world, the parent companies must have fewer than 14 outlets. Since the law wasn't retroactive, the Polo store remains.

There's no shortage of shops filled with apparel and accessories for women with a six-figure credit line. If you're seeking gold jewelry and couture clothing, you've definitely come to the right place.

Plenty of shopping opportunities are also

found along the waterfront, with Straight Wharf holding the edge on cute little boutiques and Old South Wharf taking the lead in sculpture and painting galleries.

GIFTS AND SOUVENIRS

There are a handful of singular shops that sell inimitable goods particular to the island or region. One leading example is **Murray's Toggery Shop** (62 Main St., 508/228-0437, www.nantucketreds.com, 10am-5pm Mon.-Sat., 10am-4pm Sun., hours may differ in off-season), whose very name captures a bygone age of local retailing. Murray's is best known as the fount of all Nantucket Reds, the brick-red cotton canvas clothing for both men and women that, on fading to a pinkish tomato-bisque hue, has become emblematic of the island.

FURNITURE AND DECOR

For home furnishings, step into the showroom of **Stephen Swift—Furnituremaker** (23 Federal St., 508/228-0255, www.stephenswiftfurnituremaker.com, 10am-5pm Mon.-Sat.). Designed and built with real Yankee craftsmanship, the hunt boards, desks, chairs, dressers, tables, and other beautiful handmade furniture you'll see are all available custom-made to your specifications.

Antiques are also frequently featured at the regular **Rafael Osona Auctions** (508/228-3942, www.rafaelosonaauction.com) held in the American Legion Hall (21 Washington St.) at 9:30am every Saturday late June-mid-September, plus once more each month October-December. Whether or not you join in the bidding, it's well worth a visit to glimpse whatever museum-quality sampling of memorabilia, paintings, and crafts associated with Nantucket are currently on offer, usually along with exquisite furnishings consigned to sale by the changing fancies or fortunes of the island's more affluent residents.

More ephemeral beauty can be found at **Flowers on Chestnut** (1 Chestnut St., 508/228-6007, www.flowersonchestnut.com, 10am-5pm Mon.-Sat.), a flower boutique filled with stunning arrangements of both cut and faux flowers, along with flower-related books, decorations, gift baskets, vases, tools, and furnishings. It's a visual feast and if you're planning a Nantucket wedding, these are the folks to talk to.

BOOKSTORES

Beach-blanket or fireside reading material abounds at both **Nantucket Bookworks** (25 Broad St., 508/228-4000, www.nantucketbookworks.com, 10am-9pm Sun.-Thurs., 10am-10pm Fri.-Sat.), and **Mitchell's Book Corner** (54 Main St., 508/228-1080, www.mitchellsbookcorner.com, 10am-5pm daily) on downtown's cobblestoned main square diagonally across from the Pacific National Bank. True to form for independent bookstores, the staff of both shops are knowledgeable about everything they carry and as helpful as you could want. Mitchell's has a particularly impressive quantity of titles related to all things Nantucket. The Bookworks, as a member of Book Sense, the national association of independent booksellers, honors gift certificates from that organization. Both stores are happy to ship books worldwide.

Additional selections of local-interest books can be found at the Whaling Museum and the Maria Mitchell Association gift shops.

Food

True to its nature as a high-end resort island, Nantucket has many small, upscale restaurants serving fine food and drink. It's still going to be on the pricey side due to what this quirky market can command, but it's quite easy to stop in somewhere for a meal and be pleasantly surprised. Don't be afraid to do it yourself for this part of your visit, but if you're looking for suggestions, consider the ones below.

BREAKFAST AND BRUNCH

Fortunately, eating well in the morning on Nantucket doesn't have to break the bank. That's especially true if you step on over to ★ **Black-Eyed Susan's** (10 India St., at Center St., 508/325-0308, www.blackeyedsusans.com, 7am-1pm and 6pm-10pm Mon.-Sat., 7am-1pm Sun. mid-May-Oct., closed Nov.-mid-May, $11-28, cash only). The food is creative, fresh, and filling, and the ambiance is closer to that of a college town café than a fussy old Nantucket institution. No reservations are accepted and lines form on weekends, so arrive early to put your name on the list, and they'll assign you a time to come back to eat up.

Ask anyone local where to have breakfast and they'll mention **Island Kitchen** (1 Chin's Way, 508/228-2639, www.nantucketislandkitchen.com, 7am-2pm, 5:30pm-9pm daily, $10-18), slightly outside the town center. It does dinners, too, but most of the time people are craving the Panko-crusted Eggs Benny or the mouthwatering Turkey Hash. It can get crowded at peak times (even outdoors), but you won't go away disappointed.

If great cinnamon sugar donuts sound yummy, head over to the **The Corner Table** (22 Federal St, 508/228-2665, www.cornertablenantucket.com, 7am-6pm daily, $10-13), for soft, pillowy freshness that's irresistable. If they're not still warm when you get them, it's worth asking them to heat them up for a few minutes. They also do prepackaged takeout food for eating on-the-go or at one of the self-serve tables or outside on the lovely patio.

Decidedly higher-end is **Proprietors Bar & Table** (9 India St., 508/228-7477, www.proprietorsnantucket.com, 5pm-close Thu.-Sat. & Mon.-Tue., brunch 11am-2pm Sun., $12-28), which has a Sunday brunch that foodies shouldn't miss. Served in a casual yet elegant mix of white tablecloths and rough-wood decor, brunch includes typical options like herbed eggs benedict with lobster or more unique courses like seared tuna on a bed of greens and caviar. If you want something a little different from the typical mimosa with your brunch, ask the bartender to make you something special, like a glass of prosecco and Luxardo liqueur, garnished with a tart cherry.

If you're staying on the fringes of town, you needn't go all the way into the center for good chow: **Something Natural** (50 Cliff Rd., north of the Oldest House, 508/228-0504, www.somethingnatural.com, 9am-4pm daily late Apr.-mid-Oct., sandwiches $7-26), **Nantucket Bake Shop** (17½ Old South Road, 508/228-2797, www.nantucketbakeshop.com, 6:30am-5pm Mon.-Sat. Apr.-Thanksgiving), and **Provisions** (3 Harbor Square, 508/228-3258, http://provisionsnantucket.com, 7am-5:30pm daily May-early Oct.) are all worthwhile stops for takeout coffee and breakfast bakery goods.

When longtime residents speak of "real" restaurants—as opposed to all those tourist joints—it's usually the ★ **Downyflake** (18 Sparks Ave., 508/228-4533, www.thedownyflake.com, 6am-2pm Mon.-Sat., 6am-1pm Sun. mid-Apr.-mid-Jan., $10-15, cash only), across from the Stop & Shop plaza, that they have firmly in mind. It offers diner food with a Nantucket twist: Chowder and codfish cakes are on the menu alongside burgers, dogs, BLTs, and tuna salad, all at genuine diner prices. Consequently, it's hugely popular. It's also super casual, just as you'd expect from a place with a giant doughnut out front. Jeans-clad waitresses banter with the regulars, patrons at the Formica-top counter read papers or watch the cable TV slung on the back wall, and kids in high chairs eat cereal with their hands. Those doughnuts are legendary, and the light fluffy omelets are worth the 20-minute walk from in-town lodgings.

CASUAL DINING

If you'd prefer to hoist a few cold ones over a burger plate or fish-and-chips rather than deciding between smoked tomato broth and truffle butter sauce, check out **The Rose and Crown** (23 S. Water St., 508/228-2595, www.theroseandcrown.com, 11:30am-midnight Sun.-Wed., 11:30am-1am Thu.-Sat. daily Apr.-Dec., $14-18). After a square meal at a great price, hang out at the lively bar with scads of young seasonal workers.

For something a little different, check out **The Beet** (9 South Water St., 508/680-1857, www.thebeetnantucket.com, noon-9pm Tue.-Sat., noon-9pm Mon.-Sat. July-Aug, $17-42), which offers unique fusion combinations that make the tastebuds pop. There's a little of everything here, from Hawaiian-style Poke to spaghetti carbonara to vegan and vegetarian dishes to tasty chicken and lobster rolls. Great cocktails (most with punny names that will make you groan) are another reason to stop by.

Instead of a TV in the background, **The Sandbar at Jetties Beach** (4 Bathing Beach Rd., 508/228-2279, https://jettiessandbar.com, 11:30am-7pm daily year-round, $12-34) offers the lovely soft feel of sand between your toes. You can't get much closer to the beach, and if you're just looking for a nice view with breezes off the bay, and food and cocktails that won't disappoint, this is a great spot. It's also got easy access by bus for those who aren't driving. No surprise, this can make it quite popular at peak times.

Finally, since most of the pizza passed off on tourists down by the ferry piers is a waste of your time and money (you're much better off waiting until you get back to Hyannis), impatient pizza lovers would do well to bike out to **Pi Pizzeria** (11 West Creek Rd., near the Milestone Rotary, 508/228-1130, www.pipizzeria.com, 11:30am-2:30pm and 5:30pm-9pm daily Apr.-Sept., 11:30am-2pm and 5pm-9pm Wed.-Mon. Oct.-Mar., $12-25). The classic thin-crusted Neapolitan flavor combinations are made with organic flour and fresh ingredients and baked in a wood-burning brick oven. The prices are also just like on the mainland.

Not every restaurant in town is pricey. Good value for your dining dollar may be found at ★ **Black-Eyed Susan's** (10 India St., at Center St., 508/325-0308, www.blackeyedsusans.com, 7am-1pm daily, 6pm-10pm Mon.-Sat. mid-May-Oct., hours vary Apr.-mid-May and Nov.-early Dec., BYOB, dinner $27-31, cash only). Like the breakfasts, the dinners reflect the chef-owners' appreciation for fresh veggies and international spices—it's world music for the mouth. Seafood lovers and vegetarians who care about taste more than candlelight and starched linen will be enchanted. Susan's also boasts a commendable policy of offering dishes in generous but money-saving half-portions.

Thanks to Nantucket's high-priced dining, sushi is actually one of the less expensive meals to be had here. **Bar Yoshi** (22 Old South Wharf, 508/228-1801, www.bar-yoshi.com, 11am-11pm daily Apr.-Oct., $8-44) is the newest incarnation of a 25-year-old sushi standby, now with a full bar (yes, the alcohol kind!) to accompany that sushi. *Maki* rolls prepared by the Tokyo-born and trained chef and his crew are the mainstay, but Yoshi also offers inexpensive noodle dishes, cooked salmon and veggies over rice, shrimp tempura, chicken teriyaki, and even ceviche, among other items.

FINE DINING

Reservations are typically recommended in peak season for nearly all the fine-dining restaurants in town. If you prefer to put your trust in serendipity, just be prepared for the likelihood of a long wait, although waiting for your table at the bar is a good introduction to a major part of Nantucket society. Or consider dining early: Since most reservations will be for 7pm or later, parties of two who promise hostesses not to linger for hours over a meal usually have no difficulty being seated promptly at the very start of the evening dinner service.

Elegance and good eating can both be found at **Dune** (20 Broad St., 508/228-5550, www.dunenantucket.com, 5:30pm-9pm Mon.-Sat. May-mid-Oct., $34-45), but without making you feel you have to whisper or wear a black tie. Personable, attentive service and conversation-friendly small rooms in a beautiful old house—or breezy tables on the patio—are a perfect match for the flavorful fish and seafood dishes. A creative cocktail menu adds to the fun.

Open year-round is the **Boarding House** (12 Federal St., 508/228-9622, www.boardinghousenantucket.com, 5:30pm-close daily, brunch 11am-2pm Sun. late May-early Oct., hours vary in shoulder seasons, $27-38). The bar and bistro scene here is a cornerstone of gay island social life, and the relaxed dining room is at the forefront of contemporary farm-to-table cuisine with light but intensely flavored stocks and sauces, perfectly prepared fresh vegetables, and presentations as wonderful to view as to eat.

Sharing the same space as Boarding House is **Pearl** (12 Federal St., 508/228-9701, 5pm-close, $29-45), an Asian-fusion spot with tantalizing entrees such as Korean rice gnocchi or Massaman curry or lemongrass and cilantro BBQ—all tastes that are better experienced than described. The outdoor patio, the intimacy of the inside dining with its starched linens and candlelight, and the warm, attentive service all make it a lovely spot to dine, be it a family gathering, a special night with a special friend, or a spontaneous splurge.

Inspired cooking is front and center at ★ **The Nautilus** (12 Cambridge St., 508/228-0301, www.thenautilus.com, 5:30pm-9:30 daily June-Aug., bar till 1am, hours vary Oct.-May, $25-42), set in a rustic house several streets away from the ferry terminal. The Nautilus is both a great dining spot and a fantastic bar, serving a hip, young crowd locally sourced foods and boutique cocktails. A

grilled asparagus at The Nautilus

variety of small plates make it almost tapas-style, but there are larger noodle dishes and some meals meant to share as well. Drinks range from seasonal specials based on in-season fruits to speakeasy-era classics that are (finally) coming back en vogue.

Tucked up on the second floor of a house facing the harbor, ★ **Òran Mór** (2 S. Beach St., 508/228-8655, www.oranmorbistro.com, 6pm-9pm Tues.-Sat. late Apr.-early Dec., 6pm-close daily late Apr.-early Oct., $30-44) is a delightful example of a contemporary American bistro. At first the menu reads like a slightly exotic garden and pantry tour, with various wild mushrooms, pickled vegetables, unusual chutneys, Asian spices, and uncommon grains and legumes. But while the top-grade ingredients may be unfamiliar, these are dishes that you do in fact know—grilled steak, roasted fowl, sautéed fish; you just get to rediscover them in deceptively simple yet novel new guises, the recognizable flavors coming together in unexpected and utterly captivating combinations. It's the sort of place where the initial thought of, "Why didn't I think of that?" is quickly followed by, "Who would have ever thought of that?"

Sitting virtually in the harbor, ★ **Straight Wharf Restaurant** (6 Harbor Square, 508/228-4499, www.straightwharfrestaurant.com, 11:30am-2pm and 5:30pm-10pm daily, brunch 11am-2pm Sun. June-early Sept., 5:30pm-10pm Tues.-Sun. mid-Sept.-mid-Oct., $25-40) has been a fixture of Nantucket dining for about as long as anyone can remember, but was reborn in 2006 as one of the state's top dining spots after new ownership. Under barnlike beams draped in midnight blue cloth sprinkled with stars, enjoy classic seaside fare—chowder, clam bake, grilled chicken and fish, ice cream floats—served with unparalleled gourmet flair. The seafood positively sings with freshness, fruit and produce is as passionately ripe as summer itself, and the desserts are dreamy.

OUTSIDE THE HISTORIC DISTRICT

Off the day-trippers' beaten path is a reliable local favorite: **The SeaGrille** (45 Sparks Ave., by the Milestone Rotary, 508/325-5700, www.theseagrille.com, 11:30am-2pm and 5:30pm-9pm Mon.-Sat., $29-43), about a 20-minute walk from Main Street. It's a family-friendly surf-and-turf place specializing, as the name suggests, more in the surf, but the pasta and veal dishes are handled as well as the offerings of lobster, fillets, chowders, and steamers.

If you're out the Madacket direction and don't fancy a trek back into town, **Millie's** (326 Madacket Rd., 508/228-8435, www.milliesnantucket.com, 11am-9pm Mon.-Sat., 8:30am-9pm Sun. May-Sept., $19-30) is a great stop for lunch, dinner, or the afternoon tipple. Cocktails come in canning jars and the place has an easy "I'm on the island" vibe. A nice menu of sandwiches, salads, quesadillas, and Mexican-American fare can be washed down with fresh local Cisco brews on tap. Sit down or grab takeout and a glass of frosty Nantucket pride and watch the sun go down in style. The popular food truck is also available for events and catering.

'SCONSET

Nearly hidden from the street by ivy-draped trellises, **The Chanticleer** (9 New St., 508/257-4499, www.thechanticleer.net, 11:30am-1:30pm & 5:30pm-9:30pm daily late-May-mid-Oct., $31-49) has long been a Nantucket icon. It has changed owners more than once since it first started serving meals in 1909, and it just keeps getting better. In keeping with the latest trends in Parisian dining, the brasserie menu updates traditional French cuisine with a modern awareness of the health and worldly tastes of today's well-traveled food lover. That means fragrant savory broths, aiolis, rémoulades, and ragouts are favored over artery-seizing cream sauces, and great care is given to sourcing ingredients at the peak of their natural season. The tables under the rose-draped arbor in the flower-filled garden are rightly ranked among the most romantic on the island.

Alfresco dining doesn't get much more casual than **The Beachside Bistro** (16 Ocean Ave., 508/257-4542, www.thesummerhouse.com, 10am-10pm daily late June-mid-Oct., $35-40), right on the sandy margin below the Summer House cottage resort. Its location beside the resort's outdoor pool, within the sight and sound of the Atlantic surf, means patrons are more likely to be in T-shirts and flip-flops than dinner jackets and designer dresses. Since this is Nantucket, though, casual doesn't mean cheap in any sense of the word. Burgers are made from specialty beef, salads are composed from the freshest local mixed greens, fish is all sushi-grade, and the lobster-roll bun is actually a brioche. Large umbrellas over the tables provide shade when the sun's up, and the ever-attentive, well-tanned staff will fire up space heaters and break out blankets if the air turns too cool. Whether the food lives up to the prices is highly debatable, but the setting is truly delightful. At the very least, let the bartenders mix you one of their rejuvenating elixirs in the golden glow of late afternoon and watch all earthly cares ebb away with the tide.

Accommodations

Many of Nantucket's 18th- and 19th-century houses have been converted to inns that are in keeping with general New England B&B decor. Double and four-poster beds, lace curtains, and flower-pattern quilts and wallpaper prevail, along with antiques and curios that may or may not be authentic to the island. Truly inexpensive housing is hard to come by, so prepare to pay a premium for overnighting here. Another important thing to keep in mind is that many B&Bs require 2-3-night minimum stays. Guest rooms with shared baths (look for "semiprivate") can easily run more than $150. A handful of simple guesthouses offer some relief, but, in general, be prepared to wait until the season ends if you want a good deal.

It should come as no surprise that spending the night (or week, or month) here is going to cost substantially more than if you were on the mainland, so if you are on a budget, you'll want to spend the majority of your nights off-island. There are some lovely places to stay, however, and if you're not watching your wallet, you'll be fine with paying a bit more for the convenience of being in the thick of things. Be aware that old houses do have quirks: Sometimes that means thin walls and other times a lack of space or amenities. But at a certain level this market is simply a question of supply and demand—just as real estate prices have soared, so too has the cost of rentals and hotels. Unless you want to commute via ferry and leave by 6pm each night, you'll want to be here overnight.

Of course, there are many places where impeccable taste, authenticity, consummate professionalism, and sincere attention to your comfort justify every dollar charged. For aid in booking a room or renting a cottage, consider a reservation service such as **Nantucket Accommodations** (508/228-9559, www.nantucketaccommodation.com).

Nantucket Visitor Services and Information (25 Federal St., 508/228-0925, www.nantucket-ma.gov/visitor), downtown, keeps a list of availability within the upcoming 1-3 days and is happy to furnish you with the relevant contact numbers, if you call, or even to place the phone call themselves and then hand you the receiver, if you show up in person at the bureau's office. However, the bureau's desk staff will not discuss prices—you'll have to make that judgment call yourself when you follow up directly with the hotel.

BED-AND-BREAKFASTS AND INNS

As on the Vineyard, bed-and-breakfast homes and inns almost all serve basic continental breakfasts, so if you want more than cereal, muffins, and fruit without leaving the premises, you'll have to stay at one of the dozen luxury-priced full-scale hotels with restaurants, or at the exceptional Union Street Inn (value-conscious travelers will want to take advantage of the off-season drop-in rates at such upscale places). The Union Street Inn offers a complete meal cooked to order and a menu that changes daily, in addition to a lovely assortment of pastries and such if you only want to grab a bite for the road—but why do that when you'd miss such a fantastic beginning to your day?

For really great waterfront views, your best bet is to head to **The Cottages** at the Boat Basin on Old South Wharf. Finally, if you're after a romantic off-season getaway curled up in front of a crackling fire, keep in mind that because of the liability insurance for historic wooden buildings, most places restrict guests to using compressed fire logs rather than real roaring wood fires. A notable exception is the Union Street Inn.

Under $100

The only truly budget option on the island is **Hostelling International Nantucket** (31 Western Ave., 508/228-0433 or 888/901-2084, www.hihostels.com, late May-mid Sept., weekends through Columbus Day, $39-45 HI members, $42-48 nonmembers) out at the end of the Surfside bike path. Common rooms, dining rooms, and kitchen facilities occupy a handsome 1873 former lifesaving station with Victorian gingerbread trim; guests have a choice of separate single-sex dorms or large (often full) family rooms. Despite the perpetually full house, the staff's good humor more than makes up for nights in a room full of snorers. Reservations are essential most of the season. U.S. citizens can purchase the $18-28 membership outright on arrival.

The nearest markets are back on the edge of town, so pick up groceries before arriving.

$150-250

This price (if you can find it!) during the high season will get you a single or double room with a shared bath, without a wide selection or much in the way of frills. They're still hard to come by, so make your reservations early.

The Periwinkle Guest House (7 and 9 N. Water St., 508/228-9267, https://periwinklenantucket.com, year-round) is in the quiet blocks behind the Whaling Museum. It actually comprises a pair of adjacent properties, the second of which, The Scallop Inn, has no private baths or air-conditioning and thus stands out for its high-season affordability ($119-165 d June-Sept.). While this is one of the better deals price-wise, be aware that it does have thin walls, and the guest rooms are small.

$250-400

One block south of Main Street is **The Ships Inn** (13 Fair St., 508/228-0040, www.shipsinnnantucket.com, mid-May-late Oct., from 325 d), occupying a mansion built in 1831 by one of Nantucket's more prominent whaling captains, Obed Starbuck. Starbuck is credited with the discovery of several small islands in the Pacific, including one that still bears the name of his cousin and fellow whaler Valentine Starbuck. Operated as an inn since 1913, it is filled with a dozen guest rooms that capture the essence of a traditional historic village inn. No two are alike, although most have at least a queen bed and a private bath, including one guest room with a classic lion's claw-footed tub. Solo travelers will find this inn has a pair of the most comfortable single guest rooms available in town, sharing a good-size and well-maintained bath. Besides the customary amenities that typify this price range—in-room mini-fridges, blow-dryers,

1: The Union Street Inn **2:** spectacular succulent gardens at the Pippa Hotel **3:** the old fire truck at The Nantucket Hotel & Resort

1
2
3
Massachusetts
V 13286
LIVERY

ironing boards, beach towels, Wi-Fi, continental breakfast—there are a few extras, such as umbrellas for both the beach and bad weather, beach coolers, a guest pantry stocked with refreshments, and a complimentary 5pm cocktail reception in the unpretentious colonial-themed Dory Bar, beside the low-key fine-dining restaurant in the basement.

On a quiet block just minutes' walk north of downtown is **The Carlisle House Inn** (26 N. Water St., 508/228-0720, www.carlislehouse.com, year-round, $349-700 d). Built in 1765, this large inn has a relaxed summer-by-the-sea ambience imparted by the friendly staff and the used books in every room, perfect for taking to the beach. Guests favor the pleasant garden as the breakfast room, weather permitting. Hallway carpeting helps deaden traffic from the 13 guest rooms and suites in the main house; all have TVs, and some have DVD players. Four guest rooms come with huge fireplaces, and all come with mini-fridges. Single rooms start around $229.

$400-500

Right on Chestnut Street is the aptly named **Chestnut House** (3 Chestnut St., 508/228-0049, www.chestnuthouse.com, year-round, $495 d). Four of its five guest rooms are actually two-room suites, superior in price and size to many other offerings in the area. The fifth room is a king double. All are much cheaper during the off-season. Original owners Jeannette and Jerry Carl were both artists (their children now run the place), and their paintings, ceramics, and baskets and his hooked rugs are found throughout the premises, complementing the arts and crafts fixtures and furnishings. If the cozy library doesn't erase the disappointment of waking up to thundershowers (or snow, in winter), the decanter of sherry in each guest room surely will. Guests are given a coupon toward breakfast at either of a pair of popular downtown eateries. For such a central location, Chestnut Street is remarkably quiet, and the property's garden only adds to the serenity.

Between downtown and the NHA's Hadwen House stands the **76 Main Street Inn** (508/228-2533 or 800/876-6858, www.76main.com, mid-Apr.-mid-Oct., $375-575 d), occupying a large captain's mansion built 1876-1883. The Victorian style of the first floor—with its original inlaid wood floor and double-width vestibule doors—is carried through to the reproduction furnishings in both the main house and the six-room patio annex. While first-floor guest rooms are best suited to morning people who won't be awakened by the foot traffic to and from the kitchen and front entryway, upper floors are quiet and solidly constructed after having been rehabbed down to the joists and wiring. Rates drop in the off-season, and include continental breakfast. A number of guest rooms have multiple beds, making this one of the few inns to genuinely welcome families, as opposed to merely tolerating them. Puzzles and games are available, and breakfasts include plenty of sugar-laden Kellogg's cereals. The sheer size of the premises makes it possible for couples in search of a romantic getaway to coexist with Monopoly-playing kids without friction. Additional amenities include central air-conditioning for unobtrusive summer comfort and bathroom heat lamps for chilly spring and fall days, a secluded backyard patio with an arbor, and a separate bath for guests who have checked out but spend the remainder of the day on the island before leaving.

Near Lily Pond Park is **Life House** (10 Cliff Rd., 866/466-7535, www.lifehousehotels.com, Apr.-Oct. $371-890). The guest rooms here are chic without being ostentatious, and this brand aims at being a perfect blend between affordability and style. Common areas such as the kitchen and garden make it possible to meet fellow travelers while you stay, yet it's got the privacy and amenities of a classy hotel, too. The posh bar and lounge keep the relaxing going after the sun goes down.

Occupying a large gray-shingled home a block off Main Street is ★ **The Union Street Inn** (7 Union St., 508/228-9222, www.unioninn.com, Apr.-Oct., $139-399 off-season, $439-1200 in season). Attractively restored and furnished with antiques, as befits its colonial heritage, the inn is professionally managed with a thoroughly cosmopolitan dedication to comfort. The crisp white duvets, tasteful fabrics, and restrained wallpaper designs create an air of understated elegance that surely would earn approval from the Quaker captain who built the place circa 1770. (He might also appreciate that the owners have respected the builders' lack of leveling tools: No doorframe is square at the corners, and no marble will roll across the floor in a straight line.) Half of the 12 guest rooms include working wood-burning fireplaces, and all have fully modern private baths. It's the only B&B-style property on the island to provide an honest-to-goodness made-to-order hot breakfast with the bed. It can even be served in bed, if you fancy. The inn's refreshingly hyperbole-free website deserves special mention for clearly showing the size, shape, and character of every guest room, as well as the in- and off-season prices.

At ★ **The Veranda House** (3 Step Lane, 855/652-0137, www.theverandahouse.com, May-mid-Dec., $499-700 in-season, from $159 off-season), "retro-chic" muted contemporary elegance is accented with bold splashes of color, flat-screen DVD-playing TVs, and rainfall showers. The three-story building, greatly expanded over the centuries from its original incarnation as a 17th-century farmhouse, stands (literally!) head and shoulders above its neighbors, giving its namesake triple tier of wraparound porches unparalleled views over town and harbor. But this place isn't just about good looks and a great lookout. The owners pride themselves on their consummate professional service, in particular their ability to assist you in planning, booking, or procuring just about anything on the island. Gourmet breakfast and home-baked treats for afternoon tea are included, and beach gear is available.

The Pippa Hotel (5 Chestnut St., 508/228-5300, www.hotelpippa.com, year-round, $429-905 d) offers light, airy decor that makes even the smaller rooms feel sunlight-filled. Free breakfast is included. Several of the guest rooms are small, "for affectionate couples," as their website says—and one of the doubles has a private bath that's outside the room (not shared, just not in-suite). They offer online discounts and deals, so check the website for offers before you book – off-season rates can be down to $219. Most in-season rates require a minimum 3-night stay.

Over $500

While other properties put the word *beachside* in their names despite being blocks from the water, **The Cliffside Beach Club** (46 Jefferson Ave., 508/228-0618, www.cliffsidebeach.com, May-Oct. $615-1270) genuinely lives up to its moniker. Bright and airy, with cathedral ceilings and casual yet classy wood-accented decor, the club's waterfront guest rooms (some fashioned out of the early-20th-century bathhouses in which patrons traded their formal street attire for bathing costumes) all have views of Nantucket Sound and access to the beach.

When the late humorist Art Buchwald wrote, tongue in cheek, "I had simple tastes and didn't want anything ostentatious, no matter what it cost me," he might have been referring to **The Summer House** in 'Sconset (17 Ocean Ave., 508/257-4577, www.thesummerhouse.com, Apr.-Dec., $695-945, $270-570 in the off-season). Comprising a collection of 16 small, plain, wood-beamed tourist cabins refurbished with a white-on-white minimalism accented by hand stenciling, modern tile baths, and flat-panel TVs, this property proposes that perhaps the greatest luxury is none at all. This, of course, will not be to everyone's taste. Given what the same nightly tariff will buy in the way of sensory-overloading glitz in Las Vegas, Miami Beach, or Waikiki, it may seem faintly ridiculous that so much less can cost so much more. But if you feel that over-the-top bling is fast becoming America's lowest common denominator, then you will probably recognize the bygone simplicity of 'Sconset and the Summer House as priceless rarities. Or you can simply reckon that you're paying a premium for location, exclusivity, privacy, and service: it's steps from a vast beach, as well as a pool if you prefer, far from the in-town crowds of summer, with more twinkling stars for company at night than you'll see almost anywhere else in the country, a manager-concierge who hides her Germanic efficiency behind an affable Southern drawl, and good dining on the premises.

If you came to Nantucket aboard a private yacht and snagged a slip at one of the wharves, congratulations for having the best location for enjoying the tranquility of the harbor and the excitement of supping and drinking in town, just steps away. For everyone else who wants to share in the same experience without investing in a floating mobile home, there is **The Cottages** (1 Old South Wharf, 508/325-1499 or 866/838-9253, www.thecottagesnantucket.com, May-Oct., $900-2,000) at the Boat Basin. These shipshape little studio, one-, two-, and three-bedroom units, all with kitchens and most with decks, are perched right over the water on the same wharves at which yachts are berthed. The net result is like being on a boat but with more headroom and no rocking when the tide turns. Some are pet friendly. In a word, it's unique.

Steeply discounted Sunday-Thursday rates for the weeks before Memorial Day and after Columbus Day are usually posted to The Cottages' website in the spring; early birds who can take advantage of these special offers can land a room at a fraction of the high-season rate.

HOTELS

The following are the Nantucket equivalent of standard mainland motels and hotels, albeit wrapped in locally appropriate shingle or brick. Instead of idiosyncratic guest rooms nestled in every corner of an 18th- or 19th-century mansion, these places have guest rooms with private entrances, TVs and phones, internet access, private baths, and sometimes two double beds. Many have outdoor swimming pools, and some have full-service restaurants. All those listed here offer a complimentary continental breakfast in high season. The quality of in-room and on-premises amenities varies with price, of course, although the relationship isn't always as direct as you would hope.

Prices at the following places peak almost in tandem with the calendar summer—that is, late June-mid-September, with slight differences of a week or so at most. Rates often drop by up to 75 percent in the off-season.

$200-400

The **Nantucket Inn** (1 Miller's Way, at Macy's Lane, opposite the airport terminal, 508/228-6900 or 800/321-8484, www.nantucketinn.net, $237-590) is the closest thing to a modern hotel in ambience, amenities, and decor. It has a pool, a restaurant (full breakfast included), an hourly downtown shuttle, and courtesy pickups for Steamship Authority passengers available in season; it's open daily April-October and Friday-Monday the first weekend of December. Off-season rates drop substantially; kids under 18 stay free in their parents' room any time.

Jared Coffin House (29 Broad St., 508/228-2400 or 800/248-2405, www.jaredcoffinhouse.com, year-round, $335-585 d summer, as low as $145 off-season) is a relative steal for its center-of-town location, historic decor, and restaurant. Rooms vary in size and beds, with one single room and mostly doubles or kings.

$400-800

The Beachside at Nantucket (30 N. Beach St., 508/228-2241 or 800/322-4433, www.thebeachside.com, mid-Apr.-early Dec., $454-633 d), a 90-room 1960s-era motel renovated in 2000, is a five-minute walk to Jetties Beach. Room rate varies based on variables such as the view, poolside or no, and so on, but it's one of the few places that, even in summer, can sometimes dip (especially online discounts) below $200.

The Nantucket Hotel & Resort

(77 Easton St., 508/310-1734, www.thenantuckethotel.com, $369-595, discounted off-season) offers resort-style accommodations with service and atmosphere that will make you feel more like you're staying with a kind relative. The building wraps around a spotless pool, offering sunbathers a seclusion that belies the hotel's right-in-the-center-of-things location. The ferries, beach, restaurants, and shops are all an easy walk from the front steps. The rooms are sunlit and cottagey and feel like home away from home. There are even weekly clambakes in summer for that true New England vibe.

Over $800

The White Elephant (50 Easton St., 508/228-2500 or 800/475-2637, www.whiteelephanthotel.com, May-Oct., $1,170-1,920, lofts $2,300-2,500) is a classic deluxe seaside hotel beside the harbor boat basin, with patios and porches under striped awnings, a pool, a fitness room, a library, croquet, jitney service to beaches, a shuttle to the ferry, an upscale cosmopolitan restaurant, and lounge entertainment. What sets it apart from the other high-end places is the sense that you're joining a family each time you stay. If they recognize a guest caught out in the rain, a driver will pull over and ask if they want a lift or need an umbrella. There's a fantastic port and cheese hour in the afternoon, and many of the rooms have views of the harbor. They have also added two stunning lofts and the White Elephant Village, which offers White Elephant's signature service and luxury, but in an upscale resort-style setting. Prices drop by more than half in October.

The Wauwinet (120 Wauwinet Rd., 508/228-0145 or 800/426-8718, www.wauwinet.com, early May-Oct., $1,050-1,700 d), under the same ownership as the White Elephant, is a grand Great Gatsby-era seaside inn offering sophisticated casual relaxation amid antique-filled luxury. There's a concierge, a video library (order a title and it's delivered with hot popcorn), tennis, croquet, bicycles, water sports, jitney service to town, two private beaches on Nantucket Bay and the open ocean, and a restaurant with the island's top wine cellar. The Wauwinet regularly woos travel magazine editors (no, not me!) with freebies, and coincidentally gets rave reviews all over the place. Come the chilly months, the prices drop to something that resembles a domestic airline ticket, rather than an international one.

Festivals and Events

APRIL

On the last full weekend of April, Nantucket trumpets the real arrival of spring with its annual **Daffodil Festival** (508/228-1700, www.nantucketchamber.org). Garden Club and Art Association events, inn tours, an antique and classic car parade, a tailgate picnic, and some three million daffodils are among the highlights.

MAY

Around the middle of May every year, the **Nantucket Wine Festival** (39 Commonwealth Ave., Suite 11, Chestnut Hill, 617/527-9473, www.nantucketwinefestival.com, mid-May, $100-125, Grand Fete $500) brings in big-name chefs and a full stable of international wine sellers, pouring and serving for a grand tent full of revelers. Increasingly popular, the festival is a weekend-long celebration that includes a formal gala, seminars and tastings galore, and plenty of parties.

Each Memorial Day weekend the **Figawi Race** (508/221-6891, www.figawi.com) covers the waters between Hyannis and Nantucket with the largest sailboat race on the East Coast. The race's current size and respectability belies its rum-soaked origins, the only remnant of which is the name, an homage to the slurred morning-after query of hungover racers: "Where th' Figawi?"

JUNE

June is a delightful time to be on the island. Buoyed by spring sun and fair breezes, islanders enjoy the island without the droves that arrive post-4th of July. What better time to celebrate **National Historic Preservation Month**? Sponsored by the Nantucket Preservation Trust (508/228-1387, www.nantucketpreservation.org), it's observed locally with tours of historic island properties and public lectures about preservation projects.

Another June highlight is the annual **Nantucket Film Festival** (646/480-1900, www.nantucketfilmfestival.org), an intimate and casual celebration of the art of screenwriting held over the third weekend of June, when people actually have a chance of finding both lodging vacancies and restaurant reservations. For a precise schedule, call or visit the website.

JULY

Fourth of July on Nantucket is celebrated in traditional style: races and games in the late afternoon, a band concert in the early evening, and fireworks at dusk. Jetties Beach is the center of the fun; for details, call the Parks and Recreation Commission (508/228-7213).

AUGUST

If you like browsing through other folks' old furnishings, mark August's first weekend in your calendar: Friday-Sunday, the Nantucket Historical Association (508/228-1894, www.nha.org) sponsors the **Annual August Antiques Show** at Nantucket High School.

Among the most highly anticipated events of the summer calendar is the annual **Boston Pops on Nantucket** benefit performance by the Boston Pops Esplanade Orchestra, outdoors at Jetties Beach, usually the second Saturday of August. Proceeds support the Nantucket Cottage Hospital, whose online gift shop starts selling tickets early in the spring (www.nantuckethospital.org, click on the Events link in "Ways to Get Involved"). General admission simply lets you pick a spot on the beach, so plan on bringing a beach chair or blanket.

On the third weekend of August, Nantucketers turn out for the **Annual Sand Castle and Sculpture Day** (508/228-1700, www.nantucketchamber.org) at Jetties Beach on that Saturday, while sailors

common sight at Nantucket's Daffodil Festival

A Week of Wine

What started as a simple get-together of a few wine aficionados has turned into the island's—and the area's—biggest wine event. At the **Nantucket Wine Festival,** over 200 exhibitors come to purvey artisanal breads, delicate chocolates, new liqueurs, soups, sandwiches, and, of course, wines from all regions of the globe. The event is well-planned, and despite the crowds, it's relatively easy to get to the tables you most want to taste. The problem is that there are just so many lovely vintages—and so little time.

The lovely Grand Tasting sessions aren't the only reason to reserve your tickets early for this incredible weekend: There are lectures, seminars, wine pairings, and other wine-related events throughout the four-day extravaganza, often with enticing names like Drink Pink (of course it was all about rosé) or the oh-so-scrumptious Champagne Brunch.

glasses at the Nantucket Wine Festival

The gourmet in you may want to snag tickets to the Harbor Gala, as it is the biggest event to offer food and wine pairings. Restaurants from as far away as Boston participate, so in a few hours you can sample every high-end classy joint the Cape and islands have to offer.

To reserve your tickets, visit www.nantucketwinefestival.com or call 617/527-9473.

compete that Sunday in the East Coast's oldest wooden boat race, the **Opera House Cup Regatta** (508/228-6600, www.nantucketcommunitysailing.org), outside Nantucket Harbor. Join race-watchers at Brant Point and admire the regatta cheerleading squad, a band of small sloops with bright-hued sails known as the Rainbow Fleet.

A few days before the end of August, the local Arts Council kicks off its **Arts Festival,** a week-long extravaganza involving a prodigious display of resident creativity. Gallery exhibits in all media, live music in the streets, staged readings, and daily author kaffeeklatsches run right up through Labor Day. For details, contact the Arts Council (508/325-8588, www.nantucketartscouncil.org).

OCTOBER

On the first Saturday of October, the Nantucket Conservation Foundation (508/228-2884, www.nantucketconservation.org) holds its annual **Cranberry Festival** at the Milestone Cranberry Bog on Milestone Road. Watch harvesters suction up the acres of ripe berries, enjoy hayrides and other family diversions, and snack on cranberry-themed treats.

DECEMBER

During the first full weekend of December, shoppers are lured out to Nantucket by its annual **Christmas Stroll,** sponsored by the Chamber of Commerce (508/228-1700, www.nantucketchamber.org). In conjunction with contests for best shop-window and residential-door display, the Whaling Museum exhibits trees decorated by the community. Don't miss the Town Crier welcoming Santa to the island (he gives his reindeer a rest and comes on a Coast Guard cutter).

Information and Services

VISITOR INFORMATION

The downtown **Visitor Services and Information Bureau** (25 Federal St., 508/228-0925, www.nantucket-ma.gov/visitor) should top your itinerary if you're looking for brochures. Many of the same brochures and lodging listings are also available at the **Nantucket Chamber of Commerce** (Zero Main St., 508/228-1700, www.nantucketchamber.org), whose very polished *Official Guide* makes an attractive free keepsake (or you can call ahead and order a copy for $10 postage and handling within the United States) and also helps in scoping out accommodations.

ATMS

Automated teller machines with 24-hour access are found at 20 Federal Street opposite the visitor services building; at the Nantucket Bank offices (2 Orange St., just around the corner from Main St.; 104 Pleasant St., out near the Milestone Rotary; 1 Amelia Dr.); on the left side of the Pacific Club building at the foot of Main Street; and in the Steamship Authority terminal (except when the night watchman is out doing his 15-minute rounds). During regular business hours, additional ATMs are found in the Pacific National Bank on the main square, at both the Grand Union and Stop & Shop supermarkets, and at the airport.

MEDIA AND COMMUNICATIONS

To immerse yourself in local news, pick up Thursday's ***The Inquirer and Mirror*** (www.ack.net), known to some as the "Inky Mirror," founded in 1821 and now owned by a subsidiary of News Corporation.

Are you one of those public radio listeners who suffers withdrawal if you go a week without *Morning Edition, Fresh Air,* or the *BBC World News*? No worries; you should have no trouble tuning in to your favorite NPR shows broadcast over the local transmitter for **WNAN** (91.1 FM), part of the Cape and islands radio network affiliated with WGBH in Boston, even from the terribly cheap little bedside radio alarm clocks found in many local accommodations.

PUBLIC RESTROOMS

Restrooms are found behind the **Visitor Services and Information Bureau,** around on the East Chestnut Street side of the building; on **Straight Wharf** by the Hy-Line ferry dock; and in the **airport terminal.** During the summer season, facilities are also open at Children's, Dionis, Jetties, and Surfside Beaches.

MEDICAL EMERGENCIES

The island's only 24-hour year-round full-service health-care provider is **Nantucket Cottage Hospital** (57 Prospect St., 508/825-8100, http://nantuckethospital.org), just west of the Old Mill.

Getting There and Around

GETTING THERE

Ferry

Both high-speed and regular ferries run year-round to the island from Hyannis, Massachusetts. There is seasonal service as well from May to early September.

- **Hy-Line Cruises** (800/492-8082 or 508/228-3949, www.hylinecruises.com, 1 hour, up to 9 trips daily, $44 one-way, $81 round-trip) offers year-round fast ferry service.
- **Steamship Authority** (508/228-0262, www.steamshipauthority.com, up to 6 trips daily, traditional $19.50/$39, fast ferry one-way/round-trip $39.50/75) has both traditional (2.25 hours) and fast ferry (1 hour) service year-round.
- **Freedom Cruise Line** (508/432-8999, www.freedomferry.com, 80 minutes, $50 one-way, $80 round-trip) runs to Nantucket from Harwich seasonally, with at least one trip daily late May to mid-October and up to three trips daily mid-June to September 1.
- **Seastreak** (800/262-8743, www.seastreak.com, 100 minutes, 2-3 trips daily, $50 one-way, $90 round-trip) runs from New Bedford seasonally.

Air

CapeAir (www.capeair.com) flies year-round from Hyannis, Boston, Martha's Vineyard, and Nantucket, with seasonal service from White Plains (New York), New Bedford (Massachusetts), and JFK airport (New York City). **Jetblue** (www.jetblue.com) has seasonal service from Boston, New York, and Washington DC. **Delta** (www.delta.com) offers seasonal Nantucket-to-La Guardia (New York City) flights. United (www.united.com) has seasonal flights to and from Newark (New Jersey). **American Airlines** (www.aa.com) has seasonal Nantucket flights from Washington DC's National Airport, La Guardia (New York City), and Charlotte (South Carolina). **Tradewind Aviation** (www.flytradewind.com) has seasonal flights from White Plains (New York) and Teterboro (New Jersey).

GETTING AROUND

Public Transit

Before you even check bus schedules, keep in mind that Nantucket is a walking town and a biking island. You may be better served with a two-wheeled rental than by planning your day around the bus. That said, buses are frequent enough to make it possible to avoid renting anything if you so choose. Between the third Saturday in May and the end of Columbus Day weekend in October, the **Nantucket Regional Transit Authority** (508/228-7025, www.nrtawave.com) revs up regular public bus service around town and to 'Sconset. From June through early or mid-September (depending on the route) service increases in frequency, and additional routes are added to the airport, beaches, and the western end of the island.

Buses out to Madaket depart hourly (every half-hour daily end of June-Labor Day weekend) from Broad Street in front of the Peter Foulger Museum, while all other inland routes depart from Salem Street at the corner of Washington Street, around the back of the Main Street building with the famous compass rose painted on the side.

Those other routes include three different 'Sconset shuttles; Miacomet and Mid-Island Loop shoppers' shuttles, which run every 15-30 minutes to various peripheral commercial and residential areas; and an airport shuttle, running every 20 minutes 8am-6pm daily. Find route maps almost everywhere tourist brochures are displayed. Shuttle stops are marked with gray poles with red and maroon stripes. Except for the airport route, all shuttles operate until 11pm or even later, depending on the route.

Fares are $2 in town and $3 for long-distance destinations. If you intend to hop on and off a half-dozen times a day over a long weekend, purchase a one-, three-, or seven-day pass ($7-30) from any bus driver. Thirty-day, full-season, senior, commuter, and student passes ($75-135) are also available from the NRTA office (3 E. Chestnut St., directly behind the visitor services building) during weekday business hours. Tired or out-of-shape cyclists will be happy to know all the NRTA buses are equipped with bike carriers.

Warm weather also prompts the NRTA to commence its **beach shuttles** to Jetties and Surfside Beaches from in front of the Peter Foulger Museum and Salem Street stops, respectively. These are weather-dependent: Rain storms keeps them grounded, and a cold spell may delay their start times. Ideally, however, shuttles run every 30-40 minutes 10am-5:30pm daily mid-June-Labor Day.

A complete Rider's Guide is available on the NRTA website (www.nrtawave.com).

Bike Rentals

Assuming you don't mind a little sunshine as you tootle around, bicycles are a great way to see all that Nantucket has to offer. You don't have to wait for buses, you avoid traffic jams, and the island is bicycle-friendly in other ways too: From the steamship piers, every beach is within a nine-mile radius, and most lodgings are within just a mile or two. Level terrain and five paved bike paths radiating in all directions from town are added incentives. Headwinds and other weather issues are the main concern. Sunblock and a weatherproof shell are key items to pack. Cobblestone streets quickly give way to pavement too.

Rentals are available right off the boat: visit **Young's Bicycle Shop** (Steamboat Wharf, 508/228-1151, www.youngsbicycleshop.com) and **Nantucket Bike Shop** (on Steamboat and Straight Wharves, 508/228-1999 or 800/770-3088, www.nantucketbikeshop.com). Ever-friendly and helpful, Young's is open March-December, while the Nantucket Bike Shop is open mid-April-mid-October. Both offer a standard 24-hour day rate or, for day-trippers, "shop day" rate (bring it back before the shop closes). Rentals by the week, month, or season are also available; the longer the rental, the greater the discount off the daily rate. A couple of blocks from Steamboat Wharf is **Cook's Cycle** (6 S. Beach St., 508/228-0800, www.cookscyclesnantucket.com), a small friendly shop next to, and affiliated with, Affordable Rentals car rentals. If you're staying out near the airport, you may find it most convenient to rent from **Island Bike Co.** (25 Old South Rd., 508/228-4070, www.islandbike.com). Another option if you're not downtown is to call **Easy Riders Bicycle Rentals** (508/325-2722, www.easyridersbikerentals.com) for island-wide delivery of top-notch bikes at very competitive prices, particularly for a week or longer (delivery is free with multiday rentals).

No matter where you rent, anticipate shelling out $35-40 for 24 hours rental of either a hybrid fat-tire touring bike or an all-terrain mountain bike. Full-seat and front-post suspension systems and ergonomic or gel seats have also become standard at island rental shops. Local law requires all riders age 16 or under to wear a helmet, but you're well advised to wear one no matter how old you are. Especially in the era of texting while driving, anything can happen, and it's better to be safe than sorry. All these vendors also carries kids' bikes, child seats for adult bikes, baby trailers, jogging strollers, Trail-A-Bike attachments, and, of course, tandem bicycles. Most also offer free road service if you get a flat, and Young's offers discounts for Hostelling International members.

Taxis

Taxi fares are based primarily on a flat-rate system based on specific point-to-point routes: $8 for a single passenger traveling anywhere within town, for instance, or $16 from downtown to the airport, several fare zones away. Fees to and from the airport to fare zones are higher than from town. So, a trip from the airport to Massasoit Bridge costs $32, while that same destination from town only costs $24. Each additional passenger costs another $2. Mileage fees are charged only for cross-island trips that exceed the established base rates. After 1am surcharges are added (up to an extra $5 until 6am). Drivers are also allowed to charge for more than two pieces of baggage, bikes, pets, and driving on dirt roads, if they want.

If you need to be fetched from outside of town, it wouldn't be uncommon to find yourself waiting for an hour, so schedule pickups as far in advance as practical. You'll find cab stands at the airport and both ferry piers; a list of over 30 taxi operators—including those that take bikes—is available from visitor services.

Car and Moped Rentals

If you arrive by ferry, you'll find all the downtown bike shops also offer car or scooter rentals, or both. **Affordable Rentals** (6 S. Beach St., 508/228-3501 or 877/235-3500, www.affrentals.com) offers cars, Jeeps, convertibles, and mopeds April-October. **Young's Bicycle Shop** (Steamboat Wharf, 508/228-1151, www.youngsbicycleshop.com) offers cars, Jeeps, and SUVs March-December. **Nantucket Bike Shop** (on Steamboat and Straight Wharves, 508/228-1999 or 800/770-3088, www.nantucketbikeshop.com) offers single- and double-seat scooters.

If you arrive by plane or are staying out by the airport, the rest of the island's rental agencies are found in the airport terminal or on Macy's Lane between the airport and adjacent Nantucket Inn. These include **Hertz** (508/228-9421 or 800/654-3131, www.hertz.com), **Nantucket Island Rent-A-Car** (508/228-9989, www.nantucketislandrentacar.com), and **Nantucket Windmill Auto Rental** (508/228-1227 or 800/228-1227, www.nantucketautorental.com).

All of the companies mentioned here offer to pick you up almost anywhere on the island for no charge. Summer rates hover from around $150 a day for a compact car to $380 or higher for a day for a 4WD sport utility vehicle; off-season, everybody drops their prices. Rentals are generally off-limits to anyone under 25. Some companies include oversand permits with the 4x4 rental; others do not.

Beach Driving

Four-wheeling on any beach requires a permit May-October, either from the local police at the Public Safety Facility on 4 Fairground Road (508/228-1212, 8am-4pm Mon.-Fri., $200 in season for rental vehicles, $150 for off-island vehicles, $50 discount for non-rentals if purchased before May 31), or, for driving within the Coskata-Coatue Wildlife Refuge, from The Trustees of Reservations ($160 per year, $75 per day). Trustees permits are available online only (www.thetrustees.org). Even with all the proper permissions, beach driving is heavily restricted and may even be completely denied in some areas through mid-August, when endangered shorebirds finally leave their nests. Always drive on the marked areas, and never over the beach grass.

Some rental vehicles capable of driving in sand come with one or both of the necessary beach permits, but if that's why you're renting in the first place, be sure to ask. And don't drive recklessly. These are fragile, scenic areas that should be appreciated and preserved.

Background

The Landscape

The land beneath Massachusetts has suffered a lot of abuse over the last billion years, having been thoroughly folded, spindled, and mutilated by the forces of plate tectonics. Throughout the Paleozoic Era, 350-570 million years ago, continental plates carrying the bulk of the present North and South American, European, and African landmasses alternately split apart and rammed together, finally fusing into the supercontinent known as Pangaea. At the beginning of the Mesozoic Era, some 225 million years ago, the tectonic convection that once smooshed Massachusetts into Scotland and Morocco shifted gears,

opening up a rift in Pangaea that eventually became the Atlantic Ocean. Ever since then, Massachusetts has remained on the trailing edge of this big planetary demolition derby. As the Atlantic widened, mountains were born in Nevada and California; New England simply eroded.

In recent geological time—the last couple of million years—a score of ice ages have come and gone, abetting the erosion process by grinding away the peaks of the old Paleozoic mountain ranges. But the glaciers were only borrowers, not thieves. When they retreated north, they left behind everything they'd taken from these central uplands, and then some. Cape Cod's long limb of glacial drift and the offshore islands of Nantucket and Martha's Vineyard are partially such remnants, fashioned 14,000-21,000 years ago by the great Laurentide ice sheet of the Wisconsin glacial stage.

Compared to the billion-year-old landscape of most of Massachusetts, Cape Cod is thus a veritable newborn. It also has a relatively short life expectancy for a landmass—the Atlantic Ocean may erase the Cape from New England's rocky coast within another 5,000 years. That's based on an extrapolation of today's rate of loss, but rising sea levels caused by global warming could cut that figure dramatically. In fact, rising seas currently claim nearly three times as much acreage every year as surf erosion, and predictions are that storm tides will produce increasing flooding in such low-lying areas as downtown Provincetown.

As for the erosion, if it happened any faster, it would be like watching Alaskan glaciers calving icebergs; the 14-mile stretch of cliffs and barrier beaches along the Cape's outer shore already recede an average of several feet a year. For a graphic illustration of how dynamic these shorelines really are, check out the short film presented at the Cape Cod National Seashore's Province Lands visitors center, or the Cape Cod Museum of Natural History's before-and-after photos of Chatham's storm-punctured outer bar.

MORAINES

The advancing and retreating glacial lobes of the last ice age are responsible for giving the region its current topography. Three discreet lobes from this continental ice sheet covered Cape Cod and what's now the surrounding continental shelf; Nantucket, Martha's Vineyard, and the Elizabeth Islands around Buzzards Bay are evidence of these lobes' farthest advance. Like a carpet wrinkled by sliding heavy furniture across it, sedimentary layers up to 100 million years old in the glacier's path were folded into ridges, or moraines, that now form the backbone of these islands.

The rocky spine of unsorted stone and sediment along the upper and middle Cape is another such end moraine, bulldozed into its present location during a brief southward push in the thick ice sheet's 15,000-year meltdown. Known to geologists as the Sandwich moraine, the ridge is now topped by the Mid-Cape Highway (U.S. 6), and in selected conservation areas its uneven slopes provide the region's most challenging mountain biking. South of the moraine, the landscape is characterized by outwash plains formed after the glacier resumed melting, releasing everything from fine-grained clay to gravel and larger boulders.

OUTWASH PLAINS

When the two-mile-thick glacier finally began to melt faster than the cold weather up north could replenish it, the runoff spread outwash plains of glacial drift—all the rocks, sand, and soil scraped up and ferried southward in the great ice sheet—like skirts around the hips of these terminal moraines. (Think of a 1,000-foot-thick ice sponge that's been wiped across all of New England, sopping up

Previous: Seagulls on the beach may help themselves to your belongings while you swim.

a sample of every bedrock surface it crosses. When that ice melts, it's just as if you gave that sponge a squeeze.) Some of the material deposited has been matched to unique bedrock formations, such as the Brighton volcanics—igneous rocks dating back to the ancient heyday of a Boston-area volcano. These are good indicators of the path of the original glacial advance, southeast from Canada.

Probably the best way to experience these glacial features is by bicycle; you can actually feel them in your leg muscles. On Martha's Vineyard, for example, most of the paved bike paths inscribe the great level outwash plain filling the island interior, but ride out of the port of Vineyard Haven and you can't miss the slope of the plain's eastern edge, collapsed after the retreat of the glacial ice like a row of books that has lost its bookend.

Outwash deposits give Nantucket a low, flat profile as well. But there's actually a big difference between the island's oldest plain, spread evenly in front of where the glacier's leading edge used to be (a clear shot on a bike from Nantucket Town east to Siasconset), and the dips and curves of the younger plain on the western end of the island, along the bike path to Madaket. This more varied terrain was formed as the receding Laurentide glacier shed enormous chunks of ice and then buried them in glacial drift too heavy to be borne out to the coastline (then some 70-80 miles south) by meltwater streams.

As these big ice cubes melted, the surface of this newly formed plain was left with kettles—holes or pockets of subsidence, sometimes many acres in size. When deep enough to reach the water table, these depressions form distinctive, nearly circular ponds. Gull Pond in Wellfleet, Cliff Pond in Nickerson State Park, Nantucket's Head of Hummock Pond, and Uncle Seth's Pond on Martha's Vineyard are all prime examples.

RISING WATERS

As the ice age ended, rising oceans swollen from melting ice inundated the conifer- and tundra-covered continental shelf around the Cape and islands, submerging habitat once roamed by mastodons and mammoths, according to dental records dredged up offshore. By about 6,000 years ago, the ocean had filled Nantucket Sound and Cape Cod Bay and begun biting away at the islands' moraines, creating prominent marine scarps at Nantucket's Sankaty Head and the Vineyard's Aquinnah Cliffs. The geologic record revealed at these sites is hardly as accessible as in the walls of the Grand Canyon, though—at Sankaty Head, the Laurentide glacial deposits are tossed with sands a good 100,000 years older, while Aquinnah interleaves folds of Tertiary and Cretaceous strata 5-75 million years old.

Although the rate at which the oceans are rising has slowed considerably over the last few thousand years, the water is still creeping upward and may in fact accelerate if predictions about human-induced global warming prove accurate. The shorelines of Nantucket and Martha's Vineyard already lose an average of about 30 feet to the tides and winter storms annually; by some estimates, tiny Nantucket will be a mere shoal under the waves within the next 700-800 years.

Land loss isn't even or gradual, by the way: Some shores may be stable for years, and then lose a hundred yards in a single storm season. In the meantime, the islands are migrating slowly toward Cape Cod as northbound currents relocate a portion of the material eroded from beaches and shore cliffs. This "longshore drift" is most visible in the lengthening of the fingerlike sandbars at Nantucket's Great Point and the Vineyard's Cape Poge.

CLIMATE

Weather on both Cape Cod and the islands is governed by the ocean. Slow to heat up, and equally slow to cool down, the surrounding saltwater acts as a vast heat sump that keeps local temperatures from hitting the extremes recorded around the rest of the state—much the same way that the air in your home dilutes the effect of either your freezer or oven when the door is held open. The briny reservoir is itself warmed by the 50-mile-wide Gulf Stream current, which comes pouring up the eastern seaboard from the Caribbean and brushes within a few dozen miles of the islands' southern shores en route to northern Europe. Despite the islands' being surrounded by water, humidity is kept at bay by the sea breezes that both residents and innkeepers rely on to make even August heat waves quite tolerable—which is why many island lodgings offer no air-conditioning.

Remember that since the wind in this region is always cooler coming off the ocean, this means that if you go out sportfishing on a broiling 90°F August afternoon, you'll probably regret it if you don't dress for 68°F. In winter, when the prevailing wind shifts around to the northeast, a simple waterfront walk can become downright painful.

Spring, a quiet season of daffodils and days that call for a sweater, comes earlier and lasts longer on the islands than on the Cape, with average temperatures in the upper 40s and low 50s. **Summers** are ideal, with the average high for July-August pegged at only about 80°F on the Cape and Martha's Vineyard, and in the mid-70s on Nantucket, although increasingly stifling traffic conditions will make drivers feel anything but cool and relaxed.

Early **fall** is valued not for its foliage but for its tranquility, as the hectic hordes of summer visitors return to school and jobs. Discerning or contrarian folks who don't mind that restaurants may be short-staffed or that some public shuttles no longer run will find their stay rewarded with warm weather (in the 60s and low 70s), slightly fewer rain days than in the rest of the year, and water temperatures nearly unchanged from balmy August.

After October, cool nights become downright chilly, and short days usher in brisk lashings of **winter.** December boasts the lowest lows—down to 0°F. While January features a brief warm spell, it and February are overall the coldest months, with temperatures dipping down to the 20s through early March. Though usually spared the heavy snowfalls that routinely blanket roadways from Boston to western Massachusetts, the Cape and islands receive rough compensation from ferocious northeasters ("nor'easters" in the parlance of folksy meteorologists) and their accompanying storm surges. These huge waves—amplified by winter's high tides and the storm's own low-pressure center—can turn beachfront homes into beached rafts, punch holes in barrier beaches, take mammoth bites out of shoreline dunes and cliffs, and otherwise demonstrate the impermanence of oceanfront real estate. Needless to say, even the 400-ton island ferries tend to batten down in their snug Cape Cod harbors when these North Atlantic Valkyries come calling.

Newspapers from Boston to the Cape print daily forecasts year-round. Although there is no recorded weather information specifically available for the islands, the Mid-Cape forecast from the website of **WQRC-FM** (www.wqrc.com) at least apprises you of the general weather in the vicinity. Just bear in mind that temperature and humidity on the islands are typically lower than at this Hyannis radio station. Online, www.accuweather.com summarizes weather conditions based on local meteorological stations and offer extended forecasts.

Stormy Weather

Hurricanes occasionally hitch rides up the Gulf Stream between July and October, the fast-moving columns of rising air sustained by the current's warm waters, but the cold-air phenomenon known as the "Bermuda High" keeps most of these Caribbean interlopers from ever making it this far north. The downside of this neighboring high-pressure cold is that it can also keep summer thunderstorms stalled over the islands for a few days at a time. Otherwise, storm fronts blow quickly out to sea, so while precipitation is evenly spread across the calendar (with most months averaging 10-12 days of rain or light snow), it's unusual to have more than a couple of days in a row spoiled by wet weather.

Given the risk from northeast storms, any circumnavigating sailor crazy enough to winter over in this region rather than farther south should haul his or her boat into dry storage—unless it's a weather-tight Great Lakes trawler with enough bow and stern anchors to keep it from becoming a waterborne bulldozer in a gale. But for temporary refuge from passing summer depressions, Hadley Harbor (at the northern end of the Elizabeth Islands, facing Woods Hole) and Vineyard Haven Harbor are as well protected a pair of hurricane holes as you could ask for in these parts.

Beach Tips

Since clouds, fog, and lower temperatures are more prevalent where the cool sea breezes come ashore, bathers may wish to keep in mind that the prevailing winds in summer are southwesterly, which means that the protected beaches on the lee side of the islands—the north shores—are apt to be sunnier and warmer than those on the windward side. Sometimes the differences are quite sharp: Passengers disembarking from the ferry in Vineyard Haven can be squinting in the sun and reaching for their shades at the same time that frustrated beachgoers on the other side of the island are wondering who brought the pea-soup fog.

When the wind swings around to the northwest in summer it brings sultry, sticky weather from the mainland, and in winter it delivers blasts of Canadian-chilled air known as "Alberta clippers." Swimmers should note too that no matter what the provenance of the offshore Gulf Stream, local waters are warm compared to the Gulf of Maine, not to Miami Beach. While Cape Cod Bay, Nantucket Sound, and Vineyard Sound are diminutive enough to heat up a good 10-20°F more than the open ocean in summer, swimming in this latitude of the Atlantic is otherwise guaranteed to cool you off, often quite briskly. The goose bumps raised by waves in the mid-60°F range lapping on each island's southern shores, for example, can be the perfect antidote if you or your children have overheated.

Plants and Animals

PLANTS

Thanks to the temperate ocean-warmed climate, growing conditions on the Cape and islands differ from those elsewhere in southern New England. Plants more common to Chesapeake Bay, for instance, flourish here at the northern limit of their range. Examples include Maryland meadow beauty, Eastern silvery aster, St. Andrew's cross, and post oaks, which in these latitudes grow only knee-high to their stout Dixie cousins. Even more unusual are arctic species, such as broom crowberry and caribou moss, that advanced ahead of the ice age glaciers and then adapted sufficiently to survive after the big thaw. The moss will be familiar to architecture students and model railroaders; when dried, its tiny treelike branches often serve as Lilliputian shrubbery.

Along the Coasts

Great grassy meadows once flourished along southern New England's sandy margins, but coastal development has all but eradicated this globally rare ecological community. Most of the planet's remaining acreage of this **sandplain grassland** is found on the islands—an estimated 90 percent on Nantucket alone. Sandplain grasslands are geological twins of the sandplain pine barrens found between Rhode Island and Cape Cod, but visually and botanically they resemble Midwestern prairies. **Asters, wild indigo, goat's rue,** and **bluestem grass** are typical of these oft-overlooked meadows; so is **Nantucket shadbush,** a feathery-white May bloomer common to both islands but a rarity anywhere else.

Sandplain grasslands are rich in other rare or endangered wildflowers such as **bird's foot violet, sandplain flax, New England blazing star,** and **bushy rockrose**—and insects such as the tiger beetle, American burying beetle, and moths so uncommon that they are known only by their Latin names. The terrain is also vital habitat for northern harriers (marsh hawks), short-eared owls, and grasshopper sparrows—ground nesters made rare on the mainland by territory lost to housing subdivisions and eggs lost to raccoons, skunks, and other mammals. (Consider yourself particularly lucky to catch sight of the owls; only a few dozen breeding pairs remain in all of New England.)

Human activity hasn't been exclusively detrimental to the grasslands, however. At Katama Airfield—a historic 1929 grass-strip "airpark" on Martha's Vineyard, once visited by Charles Lindbergh—the sandplain grasses have been unwittingly perpetuated by the mowing and burning used to keep runways clear of invasive shrubs and seedlings; now conservationists on both islands practice controlled burns to try to aid the survival of this diminishing landscape.

Heaths are another distinctive feature of the regional landscape, primarily on Nantucket and parts of the Outer Cape. A shrub-dominated plant community, it's disappearing across the region, like the sandplains, due to forest succession and habitat loss.

In the Forest

The ancient oak, cedar, and beech trees whose huge proportions amazed the earliest English explorers to these shores were long ago felled by settlers' axes. Their successors have largely been fast-colonizing species able to thrive in depleted soils and desiccating salt air, which "burns" most deciduous trees' fragile leaves where they are unprotected by topography or other trees.

The most abundant survivors are the salt- and fire-resistant **pitch pine** (native to the Cape and Vineyard, introduced on Nantucket), well adapted to the task of securing sandy ground laid bare by overgrazing and firewood gathering, and the even more salt-tolerant **scrub oak,** which seeds rapidly and germinates in even the poorest soil.

With its superior growing conditions, the Vineyard has reacquired some of the diversity described by 17th-century English settlers. Both islands have also acquired a whole host of introduced species: ornamentals such as **cockspur thorn, Russian olive,** and **purple loosestrife;** seafaring souvenirs or old-country natives including **Japanese black pine, Scots pine,** and **English oak;** and others, such as the **red pine,** planted for their economic value in reclaiming damaged land and providing a source of new timber.

ANIMALS

This region routinely ranks among the nation's top bird-watching destinations, thanks to active local bird-watchers; a closely packed array of diverse habitats, from shore and marsh to woodlands and meadows; and its location on a migratory flyway used by more than 300 species of songbirds and shorebirds. Plenty of **terns, cormorants, gulls, herons, ospreys,** and other seafood eaters are resident in both summer and winter, as are **cardinals, woodpeckers, mourning doves,** and some **finches.**

Spring and fall see the largest number of migrants pass through, from **Canada geese** and **gannets** to **song sparrows** and **warblers.** Some—particularly shorebirds like the **plover** and **sandpiper**—come all the way from Mexico specifically to spend the season munching fly larvae on the islands' beaches.

Winter brings large flocks of sea ducks down from Canada: **scoters, scaup, mergansers, goldeneyes, buffleheads,** and thousands of mollusk-loving **eiders** (North America's largest duck). Some years, when their winter food supply in northern New England gets skimpy, even **snowy owls** from the Arctic put in an appearance on local shores.

The Lifesaving Horseshoe Crab

a horseshoe crab molt, drying in spartina grass

Since the early 1970s, a simple 15-minute chemical test has been the regulatory standard for identifying whether drugs and medical devices are contaminated by endotoxins, a common bacteria of the type that produces toxic shock syndrome, typhoid, and spinal meningitis. The key ingredient in this test, which requires nothing fancier than a test tube and the ability to see the color blue, is Limulus amoebocyte lysate (LAL). This compound is found in just one place on earth: the blood of the horseshoe crab, a veritable living fossil whose 500-million-year-old Paleozoic family *(Limulidae)* is considered more closely related to spiders than to true crustaceans.

Before the LAL test was discovered by marine biologists working in Woods Hole, detecting bacterial contamination in drugs required injecting live rabbits with samples from each batch produced and then waiting to see if the rabbits developed fever. By making the in vivo rabbit test obsolete, LAL revolutionized drug manufacturing. Science writer William Sargent, author of *Crab Wars: A Tale of Horseshoe Crabs, Bioterrorism, and Human Health,* estimates that millions of lives have since been saved by the discovery of LAL.

Rapid growth in pharmaceuticals and biotechnology has in turn made the LAL industry worth several hundred million dollars. The safety of vaccines, intravenous devices, and surgical instruments everywhere, from the nation's top hospitals to rural Third World clinics, now depends on an undiminished supply of horseshoe crab blood. You would think, then, that the horseshoe crab is an extremely valuable commodity, protected with the same diligence that is reserved for strategic stocks of minerals or oil. Alas, not so.

With proper handling, crabs bled for LAL can be returned to the ocean alive, but hundreds of thousands of crabs continue to be harvested as bait for the politically astute mid-Atlantic conch and eel fisheries, whose economic value is less than one percent of the LAL industry's. Habitat loss on coastlines and pollution from shoreline development also puts pressure on crab populations, which have been steadily declining all along the East Coast. Even some of the major LAL producers have shortsightedly resisted efforts at regulating horseshoe crab collection.

Cape waters, which include sanctuaries in both the Monomoy National Wildlife Refuge and the Cape Cod National Seashore to protect crab spawning grounds, supply about one-quarter of the horseshoe crabs used by the biomedical industry. On the other hand, Massachusetts also used to have the second-highest harvest quota among the 12 Atlantic states that regulate horseshoe crabs. But in 2008, the commonwealth cut that allowance in half after stocks in some Cape estuaries were depleted by bait collectors driven north by stricter limits in the mid-Atlantic states, where population declines have been the most dramatic.

Since it takes about a decade for the crabs to reach reproductive maturity, many more years must pass before it will be known whether conservation efforts are succeeding. Hopefully greater awareness of its vital importance to humanity will keep us from carelessly wiping out a critter that has been crawling along the continent's shores since before the first dinosaur.

The increase in off-road-vehicle use in the last 20 years has made **piping plovers** and **least terns** the most endangered beach nesters, although protection programs on the Cape and islands have caused their numbers to rebound. Curiously, the very success of the beach-driving restrictions has brought pressure to relax them. Adopting the kind of weird logic that would suggest seat belts and airbags are no longer necessary now that they've saved so many lives, periodically proponents of off-road recreation try to open up beaches to plover-squashing Jeeps and dune buggies again.

White-tailed deer are the largest animals in the region. You may catch them at dusk browsing in fields, munching tulip buds in the backyard of your B&B, or risking a dash through your high beams on some back road far from town. **Harbor seals** also frequent some coastal areas, and signs of elusive **river otters** and **muskrat** can be found at certain ponds, even on the Vineyard.

Note that there are no poisonous snakes or spiders on the Cape or islands—none—so don't head to the tool shed for a weapon when you see a "rattler," "cobra," "black widow," or any other such "vermin." This area needs all the reptiles and spiders it can get, since they cut down on the real pests: mice and other rodents, which are a far larger vector for Lyme disease, along with mosquitoes, which carry West Nile virus and eastern equine encephalitis virus (triple E).

Lyme disease, spread by being bitten by the deer tick (the smaller of the area's two tick species, only about the size of a pencil point), has become a recognized threat over the past few decades. While this is an easily treatable disease and locals know to pay attention to tick bites, visitors often brush off a bite and don't realize it could be carrying Lyme disease. The long-term effects of this virus can mimic arthritis and cause debilitating pain, so it's worth wearing long sleeves and being aware of any bites or ticks.

West Nile virus, a recent arrival to the area, is mosquito-borne, so always bring bug repellent and, if possible, avoid staying out late in the evening in areas where mosquitoes are prevalent.

ISLAND DIFFERENCES

Although 5,000 years of separation from the mainland have given rise to some endemism on the islands—there's a species of vole on Nantucket's Muskeget Island, for example, that is found nowhere else—there are more noticeable differences in what's missing. Mammals such as the red fox and the wily coyote, which has even trotted across the Cape Cod Canal bridges and swum to the Elizabeth archipelago, haven't yet figured out the ferry schedules to Nantucket or the Vineyard. Nantucket doesn't even have raccoons or skunks. As on Cape Cod, there are no poisonous snakes on the islands either—the shy little red-bellied *Storeria occipitomaculata* you may chance to see are dangerous only to slugs and worms.

Anyone interested in plant and animal identification will be disappointed to find that most regional nature guides treat the islands almost as an afterthought to the more heavily visited Cape Cod. Island-specific field guides for trailside flora and fauna are so rarely stocked by Massachusetts bookstores—even on the Cape—that your best bet is to simply do your book-buying after you arrive on the islands. The independent retail bookstores in Nantucket, Edgartown, and Vineyard Haven are particularly worth visiting, although for the widest range of natural history titles you would do well to check out Nantucket's Maria Mitchell Association gift shop; for the Vineyard, stop by the store at the Massachusetts Audubon Society's Felix Neck Wildlife Sanctuary.

History

NATIVE AMERICANS

At the time of first contact with 16th-century Europeans, southern New England's indigenous Native Americans are estimated to have numbered in the thousands in the region now within Massachusetts's borders. At least 100 villages have been identified as having belonged to bands of some half-dozen groups: the Massachusett, Wampanoag, Nipmuck, Pawtucket, Pocumtuck, and Mahican. Each group comprised many bands, some more loosely allied than others. All shared the language of the Eastern Algonquian, the linguistic group encompassing most of the people on the East Coast between the Carolinas and the Iroquois Confederation. Although effectively a dead language (the last native speaker died in the early 1900s, and in 1995 a Wampanoag speaker who had spent some 21 years working to revive it died too), several Algonquian nouns have made their way into English, including *skunk, chipmunk,* and *powwow.*

The Europeans brought with them, among other things, diseases against which Native Americans had no resistance. These afflictions, particularly smallpox, proved disastrous for New England's indigenous people. An epidemic in the years just prior to the arrival of the Pilgrims at Plymouth virtually depopulated the entire Boston basin (Squanto, famous for serving as both a friend to and interpreter for the Pilgrims, was kidnapped from his village on Plymouth Bay in 1614, and by the time he returned from Spain and England, the Patuxet band to which he belonged had been utterly wiped out by disease). A second major epidemic swept the New England Native Americans again after the Puritan migration in the 1630s, and smaller scourges took place periodically well into the 1700s. But despite the depredations of disease, loss of ethnic identity through acculturation, and two devastating wars with the English, the Native Americans did not entirely vanish. Indeed, they're still here: Several bands of the Wampanoag and Nipmuck people reside in Massachusetts, and two—one each at Cape Cod and Martha's Vineyard—have even obtained federal recognition.

EARLY EXPLORERS

After the Pilgrims had desecrated a few Native American burial mounds in their explorations of their landing spot on Cape Cod, they decided that it was "odious unto [the Native Americans] to ransack their sepulchres." But one mound was uncommonly large, which made them curious enough to dig into it. What they found was a double grave, containing a child and a blond-haired man—who had been buried with belongings that included a knife, "a saylers canvas Casacke, and a payre of cloth breeches." The following spring, a solitary Native American strolled into the settlement at Plymouth and greeted the surprised Europeans in clear English. Plainly, the Pilgrims were not the first Europeans to have visited these shores.

Royal Ambitions

The English claim to North America is based on John Cabot's 1497-1498 voyage along the Atlantic coast in search of the fabled Northwest Passage to Asia. It's unlikely that Cabot, a.k.a. Giovanni Chabotte (Giovanni the Coaster), an Italian navigator sailing under the patronage of England's King Henry VII, ever actually laid eyes on New England. But given the prevailing climate of political and economic rivalry with other European powers, his voyage was a convenient pretext for giving the first royal sanction to a New England colony in 1578. The lucky fellow who obtained Queen Elizabeth I's permission to try housekeeping on the Maine coast was Sir Humphrey Gilbert, author of an influential treatise that used classical Greek cosmography to prove the Northwest Passage's existence. In addition to searching for the passage, Gilbert intended to use his New World manorial estate (he was a lord, after all) as a base for attacking Spanish treasure galleons in the West Indies. Unfortunately for captain and crew, Gilbert's ship sank on its first voyage to claim his prize.

Far East or Bust

In the decades between Cabot and Gilbert, the English devoted themselves more to trying to find a way around the new landmass to their west—that Asia obsession again—and to fishing offshore than to exploring the land itself. The realm of the Great Khan was also the goal of the first European who can reliably be said to have laid eyes on Massachusetts, Giovanni da Verrazzano, the Italian navigator sailing on behalf of the French crown. He passed by Cape Cod in 1524 on his way from Narragansett Bay to the Gulf of Maine.

Estevan Gómez, a Portuguese mariner who moved to Spain and won the patronage of that nation's sovereign, sailed along the same shores in the opposite direction in 1525. Two years later, an Englishman, John Rut, cruised by en route from Labrador to the West Indies. Before the end of the century, at least a handful of other explorers, sailing on behalf of various European maritime powers, at least observed Cape Cod as they sailed between Newfoundland and Florida searching for passage to the Sea of Cathay.

With the possible exception of Rut, who vaguely alludes to going ashore someplace along his journey, and various anonymous fishermen who traded trinkets with local Native Americans while curing their catch on the coast, none of the others saw any reason to set foot on Massachusetts soil or to meet any of its indigenous people.

This is not to say that Europeans were disinterested in the Americas. The codfish-rich waters off the New England coast became well known to whole fleets of Portuguese, Basque, and Bristol fishermen by the early 1500s. And England's competitors actively pursued resources elsewhere on the continent. Thus, by the end of the 16th century, Spain's lucrative South and Central American conquests had already spun off permanent settlements in both present-day New Mexico (San Juan Pueblo, founded 1598) and Florida (St. Augustine, founded 1565). France, meanwhile, had established a steady fur trade in the Gulf of St. Lawrence by the 1580s and attempted permanent settlement in Canada as early as 1542.

Most of the English, on the other hand, still dreamed of a northern route to the Spice Islands. With the exception of Sir Gilbert and his half-brother, Sir Walter Raleigh (who tried twice to establish a foothold for his sovereign on North Carolina's Outer Banks in the 1580s), England at the end of the Elizabethan age was at risk of being left out of the New World by trying so hard to get around it.

England Plants the Flag

The start of the 17th century brought significant changes in Old World attitudes toward "Norumbega," as New England was then known (possibly derived from Indian usage—nobody knows for sure—Norumbega made its debut as a place-name in 1529). Highly embellished maps and journals published during the prior century's rush of exploration fanned the notion that Norumbega was a fruit-filled Garden of Eden whose capital city rivaled London.

A temporary lull in wars among the major European powers enabled the French, English, and Dutch to stake overlapping claims to this tantalizing new destination and dispatch expeditions to back them up. It hardly mattered that exploratory voyages by England's George Weymouth in 1605, Samuel de Champlain for France in 1603-1609, and the Netherlands' Henry Hudson in 1609, among others, dispelled the more outrageous Norumbegan myths. By making much ado about what they did find—from the best fishing they'd ever seen to soil more fertile than any overworked farm back home—they contributed to the momentum for imperial expansion.

English territorial ambitions finally made

The Norsemen Cometh... or Not

Amateur historians and local mythmakers have been beguiled for generations by the idea that Vikings were the Bay State's first European visitors, arriving sometime around AD 1000. The most basic justification for these conclusions relies on a conflation of the Norse and English languages: the Vikings' mentions of "Vinland" within the sagas of their voyages, the argument goes, must refer to what is now Martha's Vineyard (or any other wild-grapevine-covered beach between Maine and New Jersey, depending on where the person advancing this argument is from). But despite gaining a measure of credibility from various less-than-scholarly museum displays and tour guides in the region, there is no real evidence to distinguish such claims from pure theory.

For a start, linguistic research suggests the Old Norse word *Vÿnlâd* may refer to grasslands, not grapevines. Moreover, although almost 50 years have passed since archaeological traces of a Norse settlement were discovered at L'Anse aux Meadows in Newfoundland, there's never been incontrovertible proof of any settlement farther south. This isn't to say that Vikings didn't venture up the Charles River, through Vineyard Sound, or around Narragansett Bay, but lines from Norse sagas describing days longer than those in Iceland and wood resembling oak aren't enough to support the assertions of most modern theorists.

their first mark on the New World during the reign of King James I, who succeeded Queen Elizabeth on her death in 1603. Two pro-colonial cartels backed by wealthy financiers and aristocrats were each awarded land grants and patents—royal permissions—in 1606. With their new king's blessing, these companies invested in settlements from the Kennebec River in Maine to the James River in Virginia.

The initial results were decidedly mixed. While the London Company, a.k.a. the First Virginia Company, did well with its Jamestown colony, most of the Plymouth Company's efforts fell far short of their founders' aspirations.

For Money and Country

Ships laden with cod, sassafras, and beaver pelts were what motivated the deep-pocketed speculators—along with continued dreams of finding that elusive northwest shortcut to the riches of the Orient—but domestic problems in England made colonization as important as profit-making. An exploding population, crop failures, and the societal shift from self-sufficient villages to a market society created a large migrant pool of tenant farmers and landless artisans willing to emigrate to wherever they might be able to eke out a living. Thousands had already gone to Europe in the decade before the *Mayflower* set sail. Any risks in the New World—violent clashes with Native Americans, for a start—were conveniently dismissed by colonial promoters.

English nationalism also fueled the promotional rhetoric. Although the French also had more failures than successes—only Quebec, founded in 1608, lasted more than a single winter—their attempts at settling the Maine coast posed a great financial and theological threat to Protestant England. Even the Dutch were getting into the act, setting up year-round shop on Long Island in 1617 after several years of seasonal trading voyages to the mouth of the Hudson. Given the urgent need to build bulwarks against the expansion of these economic rivals, it's hardly surprising that English writers gave positive spin to their descriptions of what lay in store for would-be colonists.

PILGRIMS AND PURITANS

Captain John Smith, now remembered primarily as the founder of Virginia's successful Jamestown, was one author of glowing reports on New England's bountiful resources. It was Smith, in fact, who gave New England its name, partly in an attempt to stimulate financial support at home for his voyages. Among the audience for his public relations campaign was a small group of "separatists," disaffected Protestants repeatedly harassed by King James's campaign against religious nonconformity. James picked up where the reign of "Bloody Mary" left off, jailing and terrorizing the Church of England's critics after a half-century of Elizabethan compromise.

The separatists, by choosing to contest the whole purpose of the Anglican hierarchy, took a seditious step farther than their fellow dissidents, the Puritans, who merely sought to "purify" the Church of England of its pagan-based rituals—such as Christmas and Easter—and other allegedly Catholic pomp. King James rightly detected that separatist reformers, hostile not only to the "Roman rites" of Catholicism but to the very existence of English bishops, would someday reject his authority too. Scorned by their king and most compatriots, scores of separatists—or "Saints," as they called themselves—fled to Holland, where all manner of religious practices were tolerated.

The principal separatist congregation grew discontent with Dutch life after a decade of self-imposed exile in Amsterdam and Leyden. Their unhappiness stemmed partly from unshakable poverty—most of the group had never been more than simple working-class villagers and journeymen, even in England. But the group's members were also concerned that Holland's permissive society would corrupt their impressionable young children. In short, Dutch freedom of religion became almost as odious as England's lack of it.

The Saints Come Marching In

Once they resolved to establish their own private theocracy someplace in the New World, where they half-believed that they might be united with the Lost Tribe of Israel, a quick process of elimination brought the Leyden Separatists to consider New England, which was conveniently out of reach of any Anglican authorities. Captain Smith, still trying to find customers for his "planting" schemes, offered to guide them to their proposed new colony, but the separatists declined, frugally preferring to simply buy his book and sea chart and try their luck on their own. Financial backing came from a middle-class group of London venture capitalists known to history as the Merchant Adventurers.

Fear, hardship, dissent, and family responsibilities whittled the final number of emigrating Saints down to 41, less than one-sixth of the full Leyden congregation. To meet the needs of establishing a colony, the Merchant Adventurers hastily rounded up an equal number of new recruits, dubbed "Strangers" by their self-sanctified shipmates. Both groups also brought along indentured servants, manual laborers who would work for seven years in return for room and board.

Finally, after three years of preparation, weeks of last-minute delays, and two aborted departures, the tiny *Mayflower,* with 102 passengers and an unknown number of crew, leaving behind its leaky companion, the *Speedwell,* made its solo crossing of the stormy Atlantic in late 1620. Nearly 10 weeks later, landfall was made at present-day Provincetown, on the tip of Cape Cod. Over a month after that, having failed to locate a suitable source of freshwater, the emigrants moved across Cape Cod Bay and established their "plantation" at Plymouth.

Half of these settlers died during their first winter in the new land. But eventually, with infusions of new blood from home and lifesaving agricultural lessons from their new Native American neighbors, these separatists, "Strangers," and their servants, all lumped together under the rubric of "Pilgrim" only after 1840, did well enough to both completely repay their investors and attract a slew of new homesteaders to burgeoning outposts from Boston Harbor to Cape Cod.

Puritans Pull a Fast One

Eight years after the arrival of the Pilgrims, a small group of Puritan "lord brethren" arrived in present-day Salem, on the northern shore of Massachusetts Bay, and seized control of

Myths About the Pilgrims

Myths about the Pilgrims and the Puritans run rampant; here are a few ways to set the record straight:

Myth: The Pilgrims made landfall at Cape Cod only because they were lost.

Facts: The Pilgrims had originally been given a grant to settle in northern Virginia, but the royal grant for "Virginia" initially comprised everything between the Jamestown settlement and the 41st parallel (around present-day New York City). There's plenty of evidence that the Pilgrim leaders never intended to subject themselves to the Old Dominion authorities in Jamestown, and merely took a patent from them as a precaution in the event that their other plans failed to materialize.

As soon as the newly empowered Council had word of the success of the *Mayflower,* the charter the Pilgrims probably hoped to have all along was dispatched without any negotiation, granting the autonomy the Pilgrims desired.

Myth: The Pilgrims landed in a howling wilderness with nothing but their wits and industriousness to save them.

Facts: The *Mayflower* contingent chose for their settlement the site of an abandoned Native American village—one not at all unknown to Bradford and others. Champlain had thoroughly charted it 15 years earlier, when it and the surrounding bay was still occupied by some 2,000 Patuxet people (before they were wiped out by an epidemic of a European disease).

The village site included fields cleared for cultivation, overgrown only two or three years. Paths through the woods were well maintained by regional Native American bands engaging in constant social and trading activities. Thanks to their forest-management practice of setting small fires in order to improve game hunting, much of the forest understory was so clear that the settlers remarked on how easy it was to ride through the woods.

One hardship they did encounter was the weather; their arrival was ill-timed with the start of winter. Probably the greatest obstacle they faced, however, was their own lack of skills appropriate to building a coastal colony. As villagers and artisans, none of the settlers were very proficient at fishing or farming, for example. And they were so incurious about their new surroundings that it took some three months to venture even as far as two miles from their settlement (and then only because one young Pilgrim, having climbed a tree, thought he saw an inland sea, which turned out to be a large pond).

Myth: After difficult beginnings, the Pilgrims celebrated their first harvest with a big Thanksgiving feast, including turkey and all the trimmings.

Facts: Pilgrim theology permitted but three holidays: Sabbath, Fast Day, and Thanksgiving, and Thanksgiving proclamations were essentially random events. The warring American colonies joined in the first common Thanksgiving in 1777 to celebrate victory over the British at the Battle of Saratoga. It took President Lincoln to finally make it an official holiday after Gettysburg, in 1863.

As for the practice of including turkey in the meal, that most likely derived from the English custom of a turkey Christmas dinner, established some 35 years before the Pilgrims departed for the New World. The meal the Pilgrims ate that first fall was more venison than wildfowl. While there were wild turkeys in New England, the Pilgrims preferred domesticated European breeds, which are, in fact, the progenitors of the turkeys we eat most commonly today.

an English fishing community, a remnant of a failed settlement farther up the coast. Within two years, these zealous brethren's simple land grant was converted into a royally chartered trading organization called the Massachusetts Bay Company. This set the stage for John Winthrop, an influential autocrat, to come a-calling in the *Arbella* and a fleet of over a dozen other ships. This huge flock, dissatisfied with their first landfall and seeking something better, moved twice before settling on the hilly peninsula they named Boston.

Like the Pilgrims, the Puritans eluded direct English control by design. Winthrop, a well-trained lawyer, recognized an omission in the text of his company's charter. While stockholder meetings to direct the company had to be held where the charter was kept, nothing required the charter to be kept in England. This loophole made it possible to simply pocket the document and bring it along to America—putting the whole wide Atlantic between the colony and oversight by parliament and the crown.

Unlike the hereditary or proprietary (i.e., feudal) royal charters given to Maryland's plantation owners or the Duke of York, the Massachusetts Bay political framework of "freemen" (stockholders) assembling in a General Court established the basis for representative government by a company of equals. This may sound democratic, but only shareholders could vote, and out of 1,000 emigrants, exactly four were first enfranchised in the Great and General Court. Only mutinous threats forced revision of the court's composition, creating a bicameral chamber—one part elected by all freemen, the other appointed by Bay Company officers—and expanding voter eligibility to other men of property.

Back home, dissent against the Anglican bishops and economic stagnation from farm shortages proved so widespread that within a generation, 20,000 English—predominantly from East Anglia—joined the Great Migration to the Bay Colony.

Intolerance

Despite legal documents that seemed to institute a measure of democratic rule, the early Puritan colony, under Governor Winthrop, was as harsh a theocracy as that of Iran under the Ayatollah Khomeini. Religious and social dissenters faced serious censure, cruel punishment, or even death for disagreeing with or denying the will of church leaders. Since Puritans equated change with sin, the status quo justified the most abominable abridgments of what we now call civil and human rights.

The Pilgrims in the adjacent "Old Colony" were no better. You could get part of your ear sliced off if you were caught eavesdropping. Doze off during the many hours of sermonizing on the Sabbath and your tongue might be impaled on a sharp stick. Notwithstanding such cruelty—and the liberal application of both banishment and the death penalty—the authorities of both colonies left records rich in reports of what they officially considered sins: drinking, incest, adultery, homosexuality, bestiality, and plain old crooked business dealings.

These early English settlers were often a disputatious lot and frequently dragged each other into court. Despite an apparent love of legalisms and litigation, actual justice was in short supply—particularly with regard to relations with various indigenous peoples. After enduring epidemics and the consequent destruction of their alliances, Native American populations around Massachusetts had managed to stabilize. But this increased the potential for cultural misunderstandings over all sorts of issues, especially as the English became hungry for more land. Tensions quickly escalated after the 1661 death of the Pokanoket (Wampanoag) chief Massassoit, a steadfast Pilgrim ally, and after the subsequent death of his son and successor, Alexander, who died of an illness after being forcibly detained by the English on suspicions of conspiring against them.

Unfortunately for all concerned, the colonists' fears became self-fulfilling. Alexander's brother, Philip, known to his people as Metacom, strategized with various allies across Massachusetts to boot the Anglos back across the Atlantic.

King Philip's War

Philip came close, but not close enough. His rebellion began prematurely, in 1675—after the colonials had gotten wise to his intent—and without the vital cooperation of a couple of other Native American groups in central and western New England. So the "Red King" missed his mark, though not without inflicting serious setbacks on both Pilgrim and Puritan colonies: 50 of 90 existing towns were destroyed, many more were abandoned by fearful settlers, and the colonial militia was given a run for its money. Ultimately, however, victory over Metacom's coalition brought uncompromising and indiscriminate revenge and reprisals against Native Americans throughout the region.

The colonists paid a heavy toll in the war besides lost lives and abandoned towns. The cost of arming and operating its military force financially crippled them. Plymouth's share of the debt exceeded the value of all its real estate. A further consequence was that the troubles called into question the colonies' ability to conduct their affairs outside the purview of English authority, which ended their prized independence. Parliamentary demands for security after the war reinstituted imperial dominion. Thus, in 1684, the Restoration Monarch, Charles II, officially dissolved the Puritan charter. Seven years of political suspense followed, filled with jockeying by various scheming factions, the death of the Merry Monarch, the brief reign of his brother James II, and England's Glorious Revolution. Finally, in 1691, a new charter was issued by England's imported coregents, William and Mary. With that, at long last, Massachusetts became a true royal province.

INDEPENDENCE

During the century following the crown's imposition of control over its wayward colony, the bond between the English colonists and their king deteriorated as ineluctably as had the earlier generation's relations with the Native Americans. Some scholars point out the influence of mercantile interests, which effectively used propaganda to sway the colonists in what was actually a struggle to practice unfettered capitalism. Others suggest that this is a simplistic view, especially in light of evidence that antipathy toward England's bullying tactics cut across social and economic classes. Even subsistence farmers, who made up the vast majority of the colonial population, became radicalized by the unfolding tug-of-war between the crown and the colonial middle class. But the notion of the aggrieved American yeoman putting aside his plow to fight a parasitic monarchy in defense of some inalienable rights—an indelible part of the nation's founding self-image—is an oversimplification too. As subsequent events clearly demonstrated, farmers were equipped and encouraged to serve as soldiers only as long as it was in the interests of the colony's moneyed men.

Push Comes to Shove

Revolution finally erupted in Lexington and Concord on April 19, 1775, when a makeshift force of British regulars and their fellow German soldiers (hired by the shorthanded English from their Prussian allies) fired on local militia while searching for a stash of munitions. Colonial forces harassed the retreating infantry in a running battle all the way back to Boston. The British occupiers were forced out of the city after an eight-month siege by newly commissioned George Washington and his fledgling Continental Army; thereupon the land war moved to New York and the mid-Atlantic states.

By the time independence was declared on July 4, 1776, Massachusetts had shifted from a central to a supporting role, furnishing the war effort with soldiers, sailors, and military stores. Although a large contingent of the British Navy was stationed throughout the war in next-door Newport, Rhode Island, its commanders preferred the comforts of their busy social lives ashore over armed action against the sparsely populated Cape and islands.

Within this region, the major action of the war was a four-day raid on Martha's Vineyard in September 1778 by a fleet of 82 ships, led by British Major-General Charles Grey. It resulted in a loss of some 10,000 sheep and 600 oxen as well as the destruction of every cornfield and root crop within two miles of the British landing. During the harsh winter that followed, the populace nearly starved to death.

British landing parties also attempted to harass the town of Falmouth in 1779, but local militia repelled the effort. Other than more thefts of cattle from the islands, where no attempt could seriously be mounted to oppose them, the British mostly confined themselves to maneuvering their fleet offshore. By the end of the war, fears of a major invasion by sea had never fully materialized.

GROWING UP ON SALT AND FISH

The 50-some years between the Revolutionary War and the Industrial Revolution witnessed steady population growth across the region, despite the depletion of terrestrial resources. The abundant forests that greeted the earliest "old comers" had been largely used up for construction materials and fuel during the colonial era, which had the corollary effect of hurting agriculture, since unprotected topsoils were then free to be blown or washed away. As Henry David Thoreau observed on one 1850s visit, "All an inlander's notions of soil and fertility will be confounded by a visit to these parts, and he will not be able, for some time afterward, to distinguish soil from sand." Cape Codders and their island neighbors thus sought to make a living from the surrounding ocean, from which they harvested crops of salt, fish, and whales.

All across the Cape, windmills were erected to pump seawater into evaporation vats to produce salt, which was then used for curing locally caught fish and tanning leather or shipped to urban markets. Until serious competition arose from both imported and domestic salt producers by the 1850s, hundreds of saltworks occupying mile upon mile of shoreline annually produced tens of thousands of bushels of table and industrial salt.

The transportation of salt and dried fish by packet vessels plying coastal trade routes from nearly a dozen regional harbors helped sustain other related industries, such as boatbuilding, ship fitting, and fish processing. Recognizing the navigational needs of this increased maritime traffic, the nation's young federal government paid for a dozen new lighthouses to be built around the region.

Lighthouses alone couldn't reduce the navigational hazards posed by dangerous shoals and constantly shifting sandbars in the waters surrounding the Cape and islands. Thus throughout the early 19th century there were periodic outbreaks of "canal fever" as proponents of various shortcuts between Cape Cod Bay and other bodies of water pitched their proposals. Most projects were abandoned before barely turning a spade of dirt, although in 1804 a short, swampy trench known as Jeremiah's Gutter, large enough for shallow-draft boats carrying salt, was successfully dug in Eastham between Cape Cod Bay and the Atlantic.

A TRUE MELTING POT

Throughout the 18th and early 19th centuries, the regional population was quite racially and culturally mixed. The local whale fishery, with its extended international voyages on which captains filled out their crews in overseas ports, brought back an assorted cast of men from the Azores, Cape Verde, South America, the Caribbean, Hawaii, and various South Pacific islands. These men established residences in local port towns, joining Native Americans and free blacks (Massachusetts abolished slavery in the 1780s) similarly drawn to maritime occupations.

The region also subscribed to an unusual degree of religious pluralism. Throughout the decades of Puritan control over the Massachusetts Bay colony, doctrinal freethinkers who upset the Boston-based ecclesiastic authorities often relocated to the Cape and islands, which were too sparsely populated and too distant to be tightly supervised. While Massachusetts towns were required by law to construct meetinghouses and hire ministers who then customarily served for life, clergymen on the Cape were routinely dismissed if they weren't pleasing to their parishioners. Quakers, Baptists, and Methodists who were deemed heretics to Puritan orthodoxy all found willing congregations in the region, fostering a tolerance for freedom of religious expression.

Such liberal-mindedness set the stage for embracing the evangelical Protestantism of the Second Great Awakening, which swept the nation from 1800 through the 1830s. Itinerant preachers had already been proselytizing in the region since immediately after the end of the Revolution, but starting in 1819 large Methodist tent revivals began to be held each summer from the outer Cape to Martha's Vineyard. In concert with the antiwar and antislavery teachings of local Quakers, the revival movement is widely recognized as having spawned a variety of social reform movements before the Civil War, from abolitionism to temperance. Locally, it also helped usher in a trend that would eventually prove to be equally momentous: tourism.

TOURISTS TO THE RESCUE

Traveling to the Cape and islands for purely recreational purposes dates back to the late 1600s, when the Elizabeth Islands, an archipelago off the western shore of Martha's Vineyard, were stocked by a wealthy Bostonian with deer and fowl in the tradition of the English private hunting estate. Hunting and fishing for sport remained nearly the sole draw for outsiders up through the early 1800s, although Nantucket's "bracing air" and "excellent water" were also being promoted as treatment for invalids as early as 1792.

Regular visitors from outside the region became a much more widespread phenomenon with the establishment of regular ferry service in the first half of the 19th century. The ferries enabled people to attend the large revivalist camp meetings convened on the Vineyard throughout the mid-1800s.

During the same period the region suffered from major population loss, beginning with the 1849 gold rush. Thousands of local "Argonauts" were lured westward to try their luck in the California mineral lottery. The following decades also saw the collapse of local industries undercut by large-scale competitors from outside the region. The rise of tourism couldn't stanch the dramatic exodus precipitated by these events, but it took the sting out of the economic decline that accompanied them.

By the late Victorian era, speculators were thoroughly capitalizing on the fresh sea breezes and quaint seaside villages to market relaxation to urbanites from every teeming metropolis between New York and Boston. The exclusive little hunting lodges accessible by stagecoach at the beginning of the 1800s were, by century's end, superseded by grand resort hotels served by coastal steamers and regional rail lines.

In 1890, the region attracted national attention when President Grover Cleveland purchased a fishing lodge in Bourne between his first and second terms in the White House. The social cachet of summering on the Cape and islands brought wealthy seasonal residents whose property taxes helped swell small-town treasuries.

But the real boom in tourism came by car: The Depression-era public investment in improved roads started to pay off even before the end of the New Deal, putting much of the Cape within reach of "day-trippers" from off-Cape. On the eve of World War II, fully three-quarters of the region's towns were reliant on tourism for up to 75 percent of their income.

These days those numbers have changed somewhat, as the region becomes home to a growing number of both long-distance commuters who work in the Greater Boston area and second-home owners who spend their weekends here. Besides contributing to increasing suburbanization, these trends have helped the Cape become the fastest-growing part of the state. But tourism continues to be the region's top economic engine, hands down. And its influence on lifestyles, people's livelihoods, and even the very landscape remains profound.

Essentials

Getting There

Massachusetts may seem to sit on the edge of any U.S. map, but it is thoroughly connected to the rest of the country and much of the world by air, rail, road, and water. What follows is a general outline of your transportation choices to get to the Bay State from wherever you live.

AIR

Off-Cape Gateways

The major point of entry into New England for commercial airline passengers is **Logan International Airport** (800/235-6426, www.

massport.com/logan-airport) in Boston. With no single carrier dominating, there is a fair amount of competition. But don't assume that's true for all routes. Budget carrier Southwest Airlines flies into **T. F. Green Airport,** a relatively short distance due west of Cape Cod in neighboring Providence, Rhode Island, so selected fares within the markets they serve may be significantly cheaper than if you fly into Boston. Other regional airports—particularly **Manchester-Boston Regional Airport** in Manchester, New Hampshire, about an hour north of Boston—may also offer enough outright savings to offset the greater distance and cost of ground transportation. The bottom line is this: When using your favorite online flight search engine, be sure to include other nearby airports in your search before settling on arriving at Logan.

Neither should you overlook the potential savings offered by small, cut-rate, no-frills carriers you might not have heard of and whose budget-friendly fares stay low because they don't pay for placement in any of the major travel comparison websites.

At any hour of day or night, you can obtain the latest fares and schedules of all the buses and boats that will be available to you after arriving at Logan—plus up-to-the-minute traffic reports on airport roadways—by calling the automated **Logan Information Service** (800/235-6426).

Flying Direct to the Cape and Islands

The leading year-round airline to the Cape is **Cape Air** (508/771-6944 or 800/227-3247, www.capeair.com), whose fleet of nine-passenger Cessnas flies to Barnstable Municipal Airport in Hyannis (the middle of the Cape), Provincetown Airport at the very tip, and both islands. A regional code-sharing partner of JetBlue Airways, Cape Air offers discounted one-day round-trips on nearly all its routes and joint fares with nearly all major foreign and domestic airlines flying into Boston and Providence, its principal gateways to the region, as well as year-round direct flights from New York City's LaGuardia Airport.

In summer, service to Hyannis and Nantucket expands to include **JetBlue** from New York City (JFK and LaGuardia). Some small air charter services also offer regular summer flights.

Thrifty international passengers from countries with ridiculously cheap direct flights to New York City may be tempted to think that the relatively short distance between New York and Cape Cod can be bridged more cheaply by ground than by air. Think again. For someone originating travel from New York, the answer would generally be yes (internet-only airline specials or student fares are potentially an exception), but anyone flying to the United States from overseas can ordinarily get that last domestic leg from their U.S. port of entry to their final destination at a steep discount if it's booked as a continuation of your international flight. Unless you want to make a Manhattan stopover that's otherwise strictly forbidden, the ground connection will not be a painless alternative to paying that extra airfare.

Airport Car Rental

You'll have your pick of a handful of car rental agencies and taxis at Barnstable Municipal and both island airports. (There are taxis at the Provincetown Airport, all of which charge the same flat fee to town, but no car rentals.) All air terminals except Provincetown's are also on the route of public transportation, although on Nantucket the airport shuttle only operates late June-early September, and in Hyannis the local bus service only swings by the terminal at the request of departing passengers, not arriving ones.

Previous: The Hyannis trolley is a great way to get around car-free.

Airline Contact Information

DOMESTIC

- **Alaska Airlines** (800/252-7522, www.alaskaair.com)
- **American Airlines/American Eagle** (800/433-7300, www.aa.com)
- **Cape Air** (508/771-6944 or 800/227-3247, www.capeair.com)
- **Delta/Delta Connection** and **Delta Shuttle** from New York's LaGuardia Airport (800/221-1212, www.delta.com)
- **JetBlue Airways** (800/538-2583, www.jetblue.com)
- **Southwest Airlines** (800/435-9792, www.southwest.com)
- **Spirit Airlines** (855/728-3555, 800/772-7117, www.spirit.com)
- **United/United Express** (800/864-8331, www.united.com)

INTERNATIONAL

- **Aer Lingus** (800/474-7424, www.aerlingus.ie)
- **Air Canada/Air Canada Jazz** (888/247-2262, www.aircanada.com)
- **Air France** (800/237-2747, www.airfrance.com)
- **Alitalia** (800/223-5730, www.alitalia.com)
- **British Airways** (800/247-9297, www.britishairways.com)
- **Cabo Verde** (866/359-8228, https://caboverdeairlines.com)
- **Cayman Airways** (800/422-9626, www.caymanairways.com)
- **Finnair** (844/218 6391, www.finnair.com)
- **Iberia** (800/772-4642, www.iberia.com)
- **Icelandair** (800/223-5500, www.icelandair.com)
- **JAL** (800/525-3663, www.jal.com)
- **KLM** (800/618-0104, www.klm.com)
- **Lufthansa** (800/645-3880, www.lufthansa.com)
- **SATA** (351/296-209-720, www.sata.pt)
- **Swissair** (877/359-7947, www.swiss.com)
- **Virgin Atlantic** (800/862-8621, www.virginatlantic.com)

BETWEEN THE CAPE AND ISLANDS

All flights depart from Barnstable Municipal Airport (HYA). Cape Air flies to Martha's Vineyard (MVY) and Nantucket (ACK).

- **Cape Air** (800/227-3247, www.capeair.com)

Other Regional Airports

The following two airports are listed in order of proximity to Cape Cod. T. F. Green has direct daily bus service to Cape Cod and the ferry terminals for Martha's Vineyard and Nantucket; Manchester has services daily to Boston's South Station bus terminal.

T. F. GREEN AIRPORT (PVD)

Warwick, Rhode Island, www.pvdairport.com

- **Airlines:** Major domestic carriers, a handful of regional commuter lines, Air Canada, and SATA International. Direct daily nonstop service from Atlanta, Baltimore, Charlotte, Chicago, Cincinnati, Cleveland, Detroit, Fort Lauderdale, Las Vegas, Minneapolis, Nashville, Newark, New York, Orlando, Philadelphia, Tampa, Toronto, and Washington DC.

- **Car rentals:** Alamo, Avis, Budget, Dollar, Enterprise, Hertz, National, Payless, Thrifty, and Zipcar.

- **Transit to Cape Cod** (83 miles to Hyannis; 80 miles to Woods Hole): Peter Pan Bus Lines (888/751-8800, www.peterpanbus.com) makes a handful of daily runs to Hyannis from downtown Providence (2 hours 20 minutes to 2 hours 40 minutes, not counting the required airport-downtown Providence transfer via local public bus), with connecting service in Bourne to Falmouth and Woods Hole ferry (2 hours 35 minutes to almost 4 hours, depending on the connection layover). It's $58 round-trip to either Woods Hole or Hyannis.

- **Transit to the Vineyard:** 15 minutes' shuttle ride from the airport is the embarkation point for the seasonal Vineyard Fast Ferry to Oak Bluffs (www.vineyardfastferry.com, adults $56-66 one-way, $89-109 round-trip, children under 12 $44-54 one-way, $66-86 round-trip).

MANCHESTER-BOSTON REGIONAL AIRPORT (MHT)

Manchester, New Hampshire, www.flymanchester.com

- **Airlines:** Three major U.S. carriers or commuter airlines, with daily nonstop service from Atlanta, Baltimore, Charlotte, Chicago, Detroit, Las Vegas, New York, Orlando, Philadelphia, Tampa, and Washington DC.

- **Car rentals:** Alamo, Avis, Budget, Dollar, Enterprise, Hertz, National, Payless, Thrifty, and Zipcar.

- **Transit to Boston** (60 miles): Until recently, the airport operated a free van service, the Manchester Shuttle. Alas, there really is no such thing as a free ride. The shuttle service was replaced by a private operator, Flightline (603/893-8254 or 800/245-2525, www.flightlineinc.com). Flightline shuttle service offers door-to-door rides to many locations in New Hampshire and Eastern Massachusetts. Quotes vary based on the number of passengers and distance to/from the airport, starting around $111 pp for a trip to Boston's South Station.

RAIL

It's possible for **Amtrak** (800/872-7245, www.amtrak.com) riders to connect from Boston and Providence to Cape-bound transit. Providence is accessible from the south by Amtrak's coastal line through Rhode Island, Connecticut, and New York City—a line served by *Acela Express,* North America's fastest trains. From the west, Boston may be reached via Amtrak through Albany, Buffalo, and Chicago. From the north, there's a short Amtrak line to Boston from Portland, Maine, and southern New Hampshire.

The Amtrak station in Providence is walking distance to the intercity bus platforms in downtown Kennedy Plaza. In Boston, trains from the south and west arrive at the intermodal South Station, from which all buses to the Cape depart. Trains from northern New England arrive 1.5 miles away at North Station, a short taxi or subway ride from South Station (switch at Park Street from the Green or Orange Line to the Red Line).

The ***Cape Flyer*** (508/775-8504, www.capeflyer.com) has seasonal rail service from Boston's South Station to Hyannis Friday-Sunday.

In summer, Amtrak riders bound for Martha's Vineyard have the added option of connecting to the **Martha's Vineyard Fast Ferry** from North Kingstown, Rhode Island, whose dock is only 15 miles from the Amtrak station in Kingston, Rhode Island. A list of taxi services that can connect the two is available at www.vineyardfastferry.com.

BUS

The most affordable year-round alternative to driving to the region is to take a bus. No matter where you're coming from in the United States or Canada, you can reach Cape Cod and the islands using a major interstate bus company, such as Greyhound or a member of the Trailways network, in conjunction with the two regional companies that cover the final New England leg of the journey.

Don't assume buses to the island ferry terminals coordinate their schedules with the boats; long layovers are more the rule than the exception, and some buses from both Boston and New York arrive in time to miss the last ferries of the day entirely. Even when bus arrival times do appear to be perfectly synchronized with boat departures, don't bet on it: Traffic conditions routinely make buses just late enough to foil an attempt at avoiding a layover. Therefore, it is never worth purchasing passenger ferry tickets in advance online if you are arriving by bus, despite the recommendations that the ferry companies make about doing so for their high-speed services; don't worry, they never sell out.

To the Upper Cape and the Vineyard

Direct bus service to the Steamship Authority dock at Woods Hole, the year-round gateway to Martha's Vineyard, is provided by **Peter Pan Bus Lines** (888/751-8800, www.peterpanbus.com) from New York City, Albany, and Boston (both Logan Airport and the South Station bus and train terminal). The Manhattan route runs via coastal Connecticut, while the inland route from Albany runs through western Massachusetts. These two New York routes converge in Providence and make stops in southeastern Massachusetts (Fall River and New Bedford) before arriving on the Cape. All routes make stops in Bourne and Falmouth en route to Woods Hole.

To the Mid-Cape and Nantucket

Peter Pan also provides service from New York via Providence, Fall River, and New Bedford to Hyannis, the year-round gateway to Nantucket, as well as to destinations further down Cape, all the way to P-town. To reach Hyannis from Logan Airport or Boston's South Station you can also take one of the frequent daily buses of the **Plymouth & Brockton Street Railway** (508/746-0378, www.p-b.com). The Hyannis Transportation Center at which all buses arrive is about a 15-minute walk from either the Hy-Line or

The Air Charter Option

flying to Chatham

If you've ever wished you could call on an airplane like a taxi (and skip the trip to the big metropolitan airport), if your transcontinental arrival comes in too late to meet the last scheduled commuter flight, or if you've just heard a report that the traffic jam down to the Vineyard ferry landing is five hours and growing, maybe you should consider chartering a plane. Sound pricey? If you're traveling with another couple or a group, chartering a plane to the Vineyard or Nantucket from Long Island, Philadelphia, Washington, or New Bedford might actually be cheaper than flying the scheduled big-name alternative. Even when nothing can beat the price of that 21-day advance internet fare with the hour-long layover in Boston, the sheer convenience of a direct flight that leaves right when and where you want may make up for the difference.

Charters charge by the hour, and the meter's running from the minute the plane leaves its home field to the minute it returns. Obviously, the most cost-effective method is to use an outfit whose home base is the beginning or end point of your trip.

Several charter companies routinely make summer round-trips by turboprop to the islands from the Boston and New York metropolitan areas. Passage aboard these fixed-schedule "shared charters" is sold on a per-seat basis just like typical airfares, and it is competitively priced against the major scheduled airlines. Other options include **Linear Air** (781/860-9696 or 877/254-6327, www.linearair.com), serving Nantucket from Bedford (Massachusetts) and White Plains (New York) with four-person flights that range $1,700-4,500. **Tradewind Aviation** (800/376-7922, www.flytradewind.com) also serves Nantucket and Martha's Vineyard from White Plains.

Steamship ferry docks. A free Steamship Authority shuttle van swings by the transportation center as it makes its rounds between satellite parking lots and the South Street ferry terminal, but frankly, walking is often just as quick.

To the Outer Cape and Provincetown

After stopping at the Hyannis Transportation Center, 1-3 daily selected Peter Pan buses continue to Provincetown and five towns in between—at least a four-hour trip from Boston all the way to the outermost tip of the Cape. Given the possible connections in Hyannis to Peter Pan buses from Providence and points west, with optimum scheduling, a trip from Manhattan's Port Authority to P-town would take about eight hours. An intrepid rider from Toronto could make it in about 20 hours.

FERRY

Ferries are the year-round lifeline for the islands, transporting passengers, vehicles, and cargo from the Cape to both Martha's Vineyard and Nantucket several times daily, every day of the year. Of course, the greatest variety of service blossoms in high season, between May and October. That's when additional passenger-only service plies the waters between New York, Rhode Island, and southeastern Massachusetts and the Vineyard; between the Vineyard and Nantucket; between secondary ports along the Cape's south shore and both islands; and between Boston and Provincetown at the tip of the outer Cape.

To the Vineyard

Vineyard-bound travelers have two year-round choices: the **Steamship Authority** at Woods Hole (508/477-8600, www.steamshipauthority.com, 45 minutes) and **Patriot Party Boats** at Falmouth (508/548-2626 or 800/734-0088, www.patriotpartyboats.com, 25 minutes). The Steamship Authority has the greatest number of daily sailings—over a dozen even in the dead of winter.

Only the Steamship Authority vessels take vehicles; Patriot Boats operates a small traditional monohull. Both take bikes and pets.

If you find yourself stranded after missing the last scheduled ferry, Patriot Boats also offers 24-hour water-taxi service. Since the Vineyard depends on Patriot for the daily newspapers from the off-island world as well as some express parcel-delivery services, you can also count on them to continue operating during the kinds of stormy conditions that force the large ferries to cancel trips. Call 508/548-2626 for more information.

Between spring and fall, several other companies weigh anchor with their own passenger-only services, departing from Falmouth, Hyannis, New Bedford, Rhode Island, and Long Island, New York. Most competitive with the Steamship Authority's Vineyard run in both price and speed is the ***Island Queen*** (508/548-4800, www.islandqueen.com, 35 minutes), from Falmouth's Pier 45, on the east side of the harbor on Falmouth Heights Road, to Oak Bluffs. If you would rather be strolling around Edgartown within the hour, head over to Pier 37, on the west side of the harbor at 278 Scranton Avenue next to Falmouth Marine, and catch one of the daily departures of the **Falmouth Ferry Service** (508/548-9400, www.falmouthedgartownferry.com, late May-mid-Oct., 60 minutes). They also have ample—and expensive—parking.

From the Mid-Cape, **Hy-Line Cruises** (800/492-8082, www.hylinecruises.com, mid-May-mid-Oct.) operates a fast cat between Hyannis and Oak Bluffs (55 minutes) and supplements it in summer with a more leisurely and less expensive traditional ferry, albeit just once a day (100 minutes).

Seastreak (800/262-8743, www.seastreak.com, mid-May-mid-Oct., 60 minutes) runs a high-speed catamaran seasonally from New Bedford's downtown State Pier to Oak Bluffs. They also depart for Martha's Vineyard (and Nantucket) from Highland, New Jersey, and 35th St., New York City.

From Rhode Island, the high-speed **Martha's Vineyard Fast Ferry** (401/295-4040, www.vineyardfastferry.com, late May-early Oct., 90 minutes) departs to Oak Bluffs from south of Providence at Quonset Point in North Kingstown, just minutes from I-95, up to four times daily. For anyone coming up I-95 from Connecticut or New York, this means you can be sauntering around the Vineyard in about the same time it would otherwise take to get to any of the Cape ferry terminals and park your car.

To Nantucket

The sole year-round gateway for Nantucket is Hyannis, where travelers may select from either the **Steamship Authority**'s

Vineyard Ferries

All fares are one-way unless noted. Only the Falmouth-Edgartown ferry requires passenger reservations; for the rest, just show up before they lift the gangway. Tickets for children ages 5-12 are generally half the regular adult price, and the discount on high-speed services is about 30 percent; younger kids generally ride free. Senior discounts are offered by the Steamship Authority, but only for local Cape and island residents. Parking rates are per calendar day, so an overnight on the islands will cost two days' worth of parking. Steamship Authority parking lots accept credit cards.

FROM WOODS HOLE (UPPER CAPE)

Steamship Authority (schedule and advance auto reservations 508/477-8600, on-island terminal questions 508/693-0367, www.steamshipauthority.com)

- **To Vineyard Haven:** daily year-round, passengers $9.50, bikes $4, cars $91-115 April-October, $59 November-March; parking $13-15 mid-May-mid-October, $10 mid-October-mid-May
- **To Oak Bluffs:** daily late May-mid-October, passengers $9.50, bikes $4, cars $91-115 April-October, $59 November-March; parking $13-15 mid-May-mid-October, $10 mid-October-mid-May

FROM FALMOUTH (UPPER CAPE)

Patriot Party Boats (508/548-2626, www.patriotpartyboats.com)

- **To Oak Bluffs:** daily year-round, passengers $14, bikes free, no cars; parking $15

Island Queen (508/548-4800, www.islandqueen.com, cash and traveler's checks only)

- **To Oak Bluffs:** daily late May-early October, passengers $15, round-trip $23, bikes $4, no cars; parking $20

Falmouth Ferry Service (508/548-9400, www.falmouthedgartownferry.com)

- **To Edgartown:** Friday-Sunday late May-mid-June and early September-mid-October, daily mid-June-early September, passengers $36, bikes $8, no cars; parking $30

poky car ferry (508/477-8600, www.steamshipauthority.com) or **Hy-Line Cruises'** deluxe, passenger-only, high-speed catamaran (800/492-8082, www.hylinecruises.com). Weather permitting, the Authority has at least three daily slow ferry crossings in winter (twice that number in summer) from its South Street docks on Hyannis Harbor to Nantucket's Steamboat Wharf (135 minutes), as well as a fast ferry (60 minutes). Hy-Line's fast cat, the *Grey Lady,* makes at least five round-trips between Ocean Street in Hyannis and Straight Wharf daily year-round (60 minutes), as well as offering a slow ferry in summer.

From mid-April through the end of December, the Steamship supplements their car ferry with daily trips aboard the swift catamaran *Iyanough*, departing from the same dock (60 minutes). In summer, Hy-Line Cruises does just the reverse and supplements its zephyr-like catamaran with a slower traditional boat from Hyannis to Nantucket (110 minutes).

If you want to avoid the crush of traffic around the Hyannis docks, consider Harwich Port's **Freedom Cruise Line** (508/432-8999, www.nantucketislandferry.com, late May-mid-Oct., 80 minutes), with three daily round-trips to Nantucket in summer, and one a day in both spring and fall, from Saquatucket Harbor on Route 28.

FROM HYANNIS (MID-CAPE)

Hy-Line Cruises (schedule, tickets, and parking info 508/693-0112 or 800/492-8082, www.hylinecruises.com)

- **To Oak Bluffs:** Standard: daily mid-May-mid-October, passengers $29.50, bikes $7, no cars; parking $17

INTER-ISLAND

Hy-Line Cruises (schedule 508/778-2600 or 800/492-8082, on Nantucket 508/228-3949, on the Vineyard 508/693-0112, www.hylinecruises.com)

- **Nantucket to Oak Bluffs:** daily mid-June-early September, passengers $38, bikes $7, no cars

FROM NEW BEDFORD, MASSACHUSETTS

Seastreak (800/262-8743, www.seastreak.com)

- **To Oak Bluffs:** daily mid May mid October, passengers $40, bikes $7, no cars; parking $15

FROM NORTH KINGSTOWN, RHODE ISLAND

Martha's Vineyard Fast Ferry (401/295-4040, www.vineyardfastferry.com)

- **Quonset Point to Oak Bluffs:** daily late May-early October, passengers $56, round-trip $89, bikes $8, no cars; parking $15

FROM NEW JERSEY AND NEW YORK

Seastreak (800/262-8743, www.seastreak.com)

- **Highlands, NJ, to Oak Bluffs:** one weekly round-trip, passengers $165, round-trip $240, bikes $20, no cars; parking free at Highlands only
- **35 St, NY, to Oak Bluffs:** one weekly round-trip, passengers $165, round-trip $240, bikes $20, no cars; no parking

Alternatively, use **Seastreak** (800/262-8743, www.seastreak.com, mid-May-mid-Oct., 100 minutes) from New Bedford's downtown State Pier to reach the island.

To Provincetown

Crossing Cape Cod Bay off-season requires a friend in the fishing fleet, but come summer, several passenger ferries make the 90-minute dash between Boston and the South Shore to Provincetown, at the tip of the Outer Cape.

Bay State Cruise Company (617/748-1428, www.baystatecruisecompany.com) offers the *Provincetown II-IV*, high-speed catamarans that makes the three-hour round-trip three times daily mid-May-mid-October and once or twice daily weekends the rest of the year. It disembarks from the Commonwealth Pier in South Boston, beside the World Trade Center, across the street from that building's eponymous Silver Line bus rapid transit station. (The Silver Line puts the ferry within minutes of both Amtrak service at South Station and Logan Airport.) Tickets are $64 one-way, $96 round-trip.

Boston Harbor Cruises (617/227-4321, www.bostonharborcruises.com) also makes the Boston-P-town run with their flagship, the 600-passenger high-speed catamaran *Salacia*. It casts off from downtown Boston's Long Wharf, next to the New England Aquarium, every morning daily early May-early October.

Nantucket Ferries

All fares are one-way unless noted. Only high-speed ferries (and Hy-Line's first-class lounge on its standard service) accept passenger reservations; for all other boats, just show up prior to departure. Steamship tickets for children age 5-12 are half the regular adult price; younger kids are free. For the Hy-Line, children ages 5-12 are 30 percent off for the high-speed ferry and free up to age 12 on the traditional ferry. Senior discounts aboard Steamship Authority vessels are only available to local Cape and island residents. Pets are not allowed on the high-speed boats. With one exception noted below, parking rates are per calendar day, so an overnight on the islands will cost you two days' worth of parking. Steamship Authority parking lots accept credit cards.

FROM HYANNIS (MID-CAPE)

Steamship Authority (schedule and auto reservations 508/477-8600, information only 508/228-0262, www.steamshipauthority.com)

- **Standard service:** daily year-round, passengers $19.50, bikes $7, cars $246-275 April-October, $166 November-March; parking $15-20 mid-May-October, as low as $5 in winter, and $10 all other times (the Brooks Road lot by the airport is $12-15 in both shoulder and high seasons)
- **High-speed service:** reservations 508/495-3278; passengers $39.50, bikes $7, no cars; parking rates as above

Hy-Line Cruises (schedule, tickets, and parking info 508/228-3949 or 800/492-8082, www.hylinecruises.com)

- **High-speed service:** daily year-round, passengers $44 ($81 round-trip), bikes $7, no cars; parking $10-28

FROM HARWICH PORT (LOWER CAPE)

Freedom Cruise Line (508/432-8999, www.nantucketislandferry.com)

- **From Saquatucket Harbor:** daily late May-mid-October, passengers $50, round-trip $80, bikes $10, no cars; parking $25 per night, free for same-day return

FROM NEW BEDFORD, MASSACHUSETTS

Seastreak (800/262-8743, www.seastreak.com)

- **High-speed service:** daily mid-May-mid-October, passengers $50 (round-trip $90), bikes $10, no cars; parking $15

INTER-ISLAND

Hy-Line Cruises (schedule 508/778-2600 or 800/492-8082, 508/228-3949 on Nantucket, 508/693-0112 on the Vineyard, www.hylinecruises.com)

- **Oak Bluffs to Nantucket:** daily mid-June-early September, passengers $38, bikes $7, no cars

For Memorial Day weekend and then mid-June-early September, additional afternoon and weekend evening departures are added to the schedule, with the last boat back to Boston scheduled late enough to allow a leisurely P-town dinner and dessert.

Tickets for BHC catamarans are $67 one-way or $100 round-trip (with discounts for seniors and children), and they may be purchased in advance on their respective websites. Bikes are an extra $9 each way.

Whichever boat you choose, call to confirm departures if the weather is unsettled—occasionally, trips are canceled due to rough seas.

Taking a Car to the Islands

Although all the slow Steamship Authority vessels carry vehicles, car owners—particularly those bound for Nantucket—are strongly urged to leave them behind on the Cape if possible. If you actually enjoy spending your vacation in what by summer often resembles the roll-off line of a Detroit assembly plant, by all means fork over that $200-280 to the Vineyard or $500-550 to Nantucket (summer round-trip price based on vehicle size, over and above the cost for driver and passengers), and you too will be able to savor life in a quaint seaside parking lot. On the other hand, for less money and hardly any less convenience, you can hire taxis as necessary on Nantucket, or choose between a couple of weeks' worth of shuttle bus tickets, several days of bike rentals, and a couple of cross-island cab rides on the Vineyard. Sure, a car-less vacation in the United States is almost worthy of *Ripley's Believe It Or Not!*, but unless you're traveling in winter, staying at a rural Vineyard B&B, or carting around toddlers, there's little need to add to the congestion of the islands' roadways.

If, after all this, you still can't be parted from your car, at least do yourself the favor of planning ahead. Auto reservations are mandatory for Vineyard-bound traffic the Thursday-Tuesday of Memorial Day weekend, every weekend (Fri.-Mon.) during the summer high season (late June-early Sept.), and the whole week before and after July 4. They're accepted up to 30 minutes before sailing, but keep in mind that some popular weekends have been known to sell out months in advance.

The **Steamship Authority** starts accepting summer car reservations via mail or on their website (www.steamshipauthority.com) on the second Friday of January, and by phone two weeks later. Though not mandatory, car reservations for the spring season (through mid-May) are accepted after New Year's.

Prices are based on vehicle length, so if you are planning on taking a rental car but don't have the actual vehicle in hand when making reservations (you need to give a license plate number to complete the reservation process), the agents may initially charge you for the maximum car length (the SUV rate). When you show up at the dock to pick up your ticket, make sure the rate accurately reflects the size of the car you actually have. Reservations also incur a fee if canceled, so making multiple speculative bookings is inadvisable.

Whenever reservations are not required, show up and try your luck in the daily **standby lines.** Call 508/548-3788 to inquire about the length of the wait for the Woods Hole boats. Call 508/771-4000 for standby conditions in Hyannis, or go to their website and follow the link from www.islandferry.com to Operation/Parking Info. Since neither port has unlimited space, there are caps on the number of vehicles that can wait on standby; preference is given to anyone staying on-island more than five days. Up-to-the-minute service bulletins—plus the latest schedule and fare information—are also available from websites such as **Sigalert.com,** a traffic monitoring and mapping website.

As a further disincentive to car owners with inflexible schedules, be warned that if the ferry for which you hold a reservation is canceled due to bad weather, you'll be stuck on standby with the exact same status as someone driving up without reservations. Depending on how many vehicles get bumped, how heavily booked the boats are when they start moving again, and whether you're willing to sit in parking lots for hours on end, even after routine service resumes you can easily get stranded on-island for a couple of *days*. When it happened to me, I just chalked it up to research, but will your boss be as understanding?

Leaving Your Car Behind

Island-bound passengers sensibly leaving their cars behind should allow some extra time. For example, Woods Hole is so small that in high season, ferry parking is usually available only in one of the five satellite lots in Falmouth and Cataumet, a few miles away. (Electronic signs posted along Route 28 coming from the Bourne Bridge will direct you to whatever lot has space available.) Free bike-rack-equipped passenger vans shuttle from these outer lots to the docks daily, and a van specifically for bicycles and baby carriages is provided Friday-Sunday in the late spring preseason and daily through the summer. Cyclists may enjoy a beautiful four-mile ride along the paved **Shining Sea Path** from Falmouth direct to the ferry landing.

If you spend the night in Hyannis before or after catching one of the ferries there, be sure to inquire from your motel or innkeeper about reduced-rate parking—it can cost appreciably less than the ferry company lots. And if you arrived at either Hyannis or Woods Hole by bus—and intend to return the same way—don't forget that the ferries and buses are not fully synchronized; be careful not to end up marooned for the night after getting off the boat.

Ferry Tips

Friday and Sunday in summer see the most sailings from Cape and island ports, with evening or nighttime departures (as late as 9:45pm for the Steamship Authority, arriving at Martha's Vineyard at 10:30pm) added to regular weekday schedules. The reason for the extra boats, of course, is the extra demand; be prepared to face larger crowds, shorter tempers, and less parking if you choose to travel on these days. Phone reservations are not accepted for passengers on the so-called traditional boats (with the exception of certain early and late sailings on the Falmouth Ferry), but they are accepted for all the high-speed services, although tickets purchased in advance don't always guarantee seating. All sailings are, of course, dependent on the weather—if in doubt, call ahead.

YACHT

If you're coming on your own boat, you'll find nearly every Cape harbor has at least a couple of anchorages or berths for visitors. Marinas and yacht yards able to accommodate at least a few dozen cruisers are found at Cataumet on Buzzards Bay; Falmouth, Osterville, and Hyannis, on the south shore; and Provincetown.

The islands are among the world's yachting centers, so book a mooring in advance. For an extended anchorage, consult the local town harbormasters, who generally deal in season-long leases; transients, meanwhile, are better off calling the private mooring rental companies. The cost of an overnight mooring to sober up from shore leave before braving the infamous rips and shoals of Nantucket Sound ranges from a low of $45 per night in Edgartown Harbor to $65-100 per night at Nantucket.

In Nantucket, the Town Pier's harbormaster (508/228-7261) can either help you directly or refer you to an appropriate private marina. On the Vineyard, you can choose between anchorages in each of the bustling down-island towns or a more sedate berth amid the small up-island fishing fleet at Menemsha. Here are the numbers for their respective harbormasters: Vineyard Haven (508/696-4200), Oak Bluffs (508/693-4355), Edgartown (508/627-4746), and Menemsha (508/645-2846). Transients visiting the Elizabeth Islands should call Cuttyhunk's harbormaster (508/990-7578) for advance information on public moorings.

Since all fuel sold on the islands has to be shipped in, budget-conscious cruisers will want to top off their tanks at a mainland marina if at all possible. Launch services, haul-out, dry storage, and all manner of repairs are available on both islands, but don't count on public showers or dockside pump-out facilities at all moorings.

No cruiser should venture into local waters without a proper reference book near the chart table. In addition to the don't-sail-from-home-without-it *Eldridge Tide and Pilot Book* (sold at marine stores from Maine to Florida), the traditional companion for sailors heading to Massachusetts is the latest edition of *Cruising Guide to the New England Coast,* by Roger F. Duncan, Paul W. Fenn, W. Wallace Fenn, and John P. Ware (New York: W.W. Norton).

An equally valuable work, more specific to the islands, is Lynda and Patrick Childress's *Cruising Guide to Narragansett Bay and the South Coast of Massachusetts* (Camden, ME: International Marine). Despite its obvious appeal to powerboaters and amateurs, die-hard yachties shouldn't overlook *Embassy Cruising Guide: New England Coast,* from Richardson's Charts (www.richardsonscharts.com). With its NOAA coastal charts, GPS waypoints, extensive anchorage descriptions, and marine service summaries for every harbor in the state, the latest spiral-bound edition puts Google Maps to shame.

Getting Around

Shaped like a flexing arm, Cape Cod is just over 60 miles long from the canal to the tip of Provincetown, a deception that can get many first-time visitors in trouble. In theory, one could drive (and driving is by far the most convenient way to get around) end to end in just over an hour, but locals know to multiply that driving time by two or even three depending on the time of day. At midnight you might leave P-town and be crossing over the Sagamore Bridge 90 minutes later. But during the day, at rush hour, or on any major weekend, with the long stretches of stop-and-go traffic between Orleans and Provincetown, slow traffic in Harwich on "Suicide Alley," and the often miles-long backups at the bridges, one can expect it to take twice that.

Though long, the Cape is not wide: Even in the dead center of the thickest part of "the arm," one can reach the ocean either north or south in twenty minutes or less, not counting the numerous lakes and freshwater ponds.

Both Nantucket and Martha's Vineyard have a network of roads that brings one around or through the island, though again, congestion in town centers can make for longer travel times. With lots of bike shops, good bus routes, and far less distance to cover, going carless makes a lot more sense on these islands than on Cape Cod.

AIR

Island visitors looking for alternatives to the ferries between the Cape and Martha's Vineyard or Nantucket—or fans of the kind of flying where you can watch the wheels leave the ground, or even look over the pilot's shoulder—have **Cape Air** (508/771-6944 or 800/227-3247, www.capeair.com).

CAR

All three locations are well-suited for travel by car, and in summer the out-of-state license plates outnumber the local ones by 3 or 4. To bring a car to the islands one will need to reserve a spot on the ferries, weeks in advance. Cape and Islands roads are usually pot-hole-free, and most have a shoulder or emergency lane. However, hazards such as sand or bicyclists mean drivers have to be alert.

On most interstates and some state highways within Massachusetts, the speed limit is 65 mph, but along the Mid-Cape Highway—U.S. 6—it's 55 mph or less. You'll soon see—from traffic in most areas—that these are more polite suggestions than true limits. Still, don't push it: When the selective dragnet finally picks you, the tickets will make you wince (for speeding violations along the two-lane portion of U.S. 6 between Dennis and Orleans, fines are doubled). Buckle up; it's the law. Driving with a non-hands-free cellphone in use is also illegal. While driving with less than 0.08 BAV is legal in Massachusetts, driving while exceeding that entails automatic license suspension, among many more serious risks.

Speeding tickets may be paid by phone with a call to the Registry of Motor Vehicles' Customer Phone Information Center (617/351-4500); have the citation number and a valid credit card handy. You can also pay

Cape Cod Public Transit

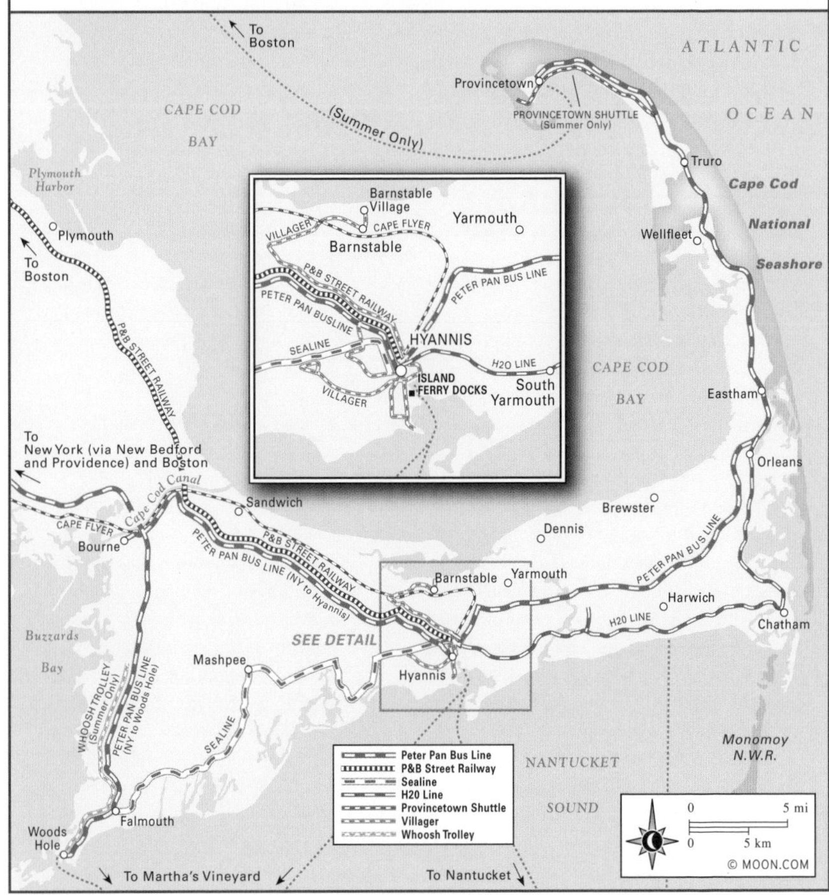

online at www.mass.gov/rmv. Treating tickets as souvenirs—not to be taken seriously once you're safely back home or across the border—is inadvisable, since Massachusetts shares outstanding ticket data with many states and several Canadian provinces.

PUBLIC TRANSIT

The Cape doesn't have the best public transportation, particularly in comparison to the islands. While the region is served by public buses and (in places) tourist park-and-ride trolleys, many of the drop-off spots on the routes are far from the actual tourist spots (like beaches), so you may have to wait for the bus and then still walk 0.25 miles or more until your feet are actually in the beach sand. Many operate year-round (Nantucket excepted), although of course the greatest quantity of service to the widest number of destinations is offered in summer. It's a two-edged sword: with a car, you'll have independence, but may fight (and pay up the nose!) to find somewhere to park.

Bike Routes

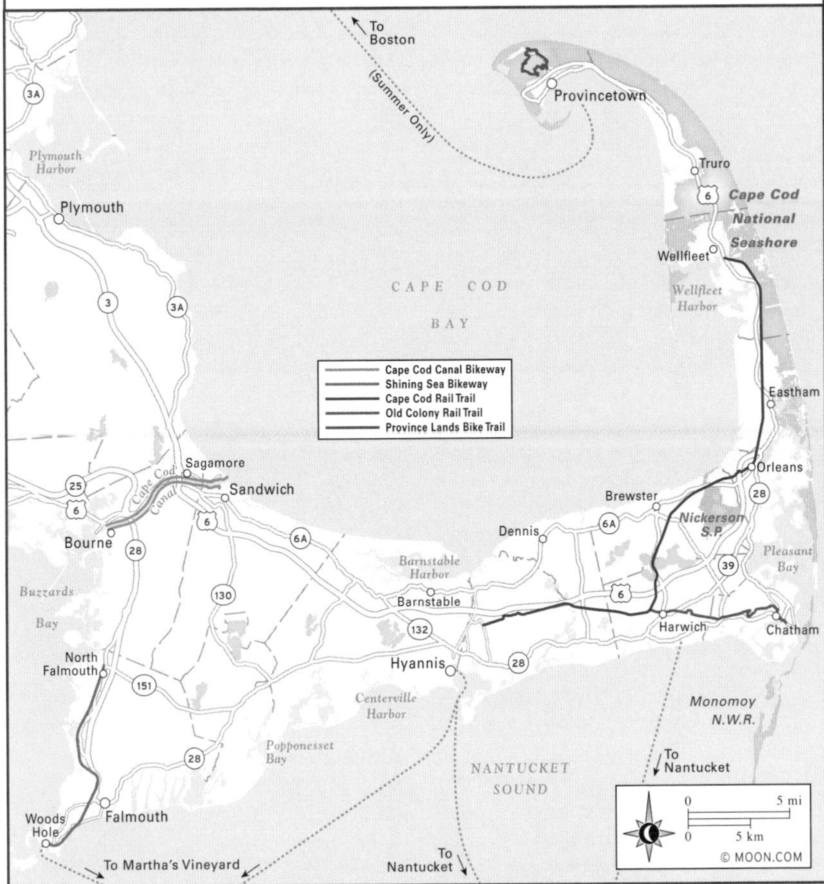

With patience and a few dollar bills, it's possible to reach almost every town on the Cape with the **Cape Cod Regional Transit Authority** (800/352-7155, www.capecodrta.org) and its collection of year-round bus lines and summer trolleys—in combination with the all-season **Plymouth & Brockton** (8 Industrial Park Rd., Plymouth, 508/746-0378, www.p-b.com) and **Peter Pan** (888/751-8800, www.peterpanbus.com) buses. But the down side is that the buses usually just run the length of the Cape, stopping at central points along U.S. 6, while most of the tourist draws such as hiking, scenery, or beaches are at the edges. The CCRTA does have a door-to-door pickup service in all 15 towns, but this must be arranged in advance and you must be ready for pickup within a 1.5-hour window. So the bottom line is that it's relatively easy to get here and leave by public transit, but getting around is harder and requires more time than should be necessary. If you've got the resources for a car and any associated parking stickers, Cape Cod's a good place to rent one.

Peter Pan provides local service from the Mid-Cape (Hyannis) to Provincetown via U.S. 6, with stops at all the Outer Cape communities from Orleans north, as well as local stops in towns along the Buzzards Bay side of the Upper Cape, from the Cape Cod Canal down to Woods Hole. Every south shore and backside town between Woods Hole and Orleans is served by a combination of the **Hyannis-Falmouth/Woods Hole Sealine** and **Hyannis-Orleans H2O** bus routes, which operate daily late June-early September and Monday-Saturday otherwise, plus **The Shuttle** between North Truro and Provincetown, which runs seven days a week right through mid-October. Although Hyannis is the hub of the system, connections in Orleans make it feasible to do a circle trip around most of the Mid-Cape-Outer Cape area.

Fares on the Hyannis-area routes and both summer shuttles are $2 per ride or $6 for an all-day pass. While the shuttles run well past sundown—past midnight, in some cases—year-round buses favor daylight hours. Pick up a complete system timetable at the Hyannis Transportation Center, town information booths, or almost anywhere you see racks of tourist brochures, or visit the website (www.capecodrta.org). You can also call the CCRTA directly (508/385-8326 or 800/352-7155) and press the appropriate buttons to get prerecorded schedules.

The Hyannis Transportation Center serves as an endpoint for all three year-round CCRTA bus routes: the **Sealine,** running west to Falmouth and Woods Hole; the **Villager,** heading north to Barnstable Harbor via the Route 132 malls; and the easterly **H2O Line,** connecting Hyannis to Orleans via Route 28 through Yarmouth, Dennisport, Harwich Port, and Chatham. Saquatucket Harbor in Harwich Port, the departure point for the Freedom Cruise Line boat to Nantucket, is one of the possible stops along the H2O route. All routes operate daily late June-early September, and then mostly Monday-Saturday the remainder of the year. Call the CCRTA (800/352-7155) for schedule and fare information, pick up their system timetable at the bus terminal, or download everything you need to know at www.capecodrta.org.

Cyclists should note that all the CCRTA vehicles are equipped with bike racks—unlike the Peter Pan and P&B buses, which only take bikes as last-priority baggage (if there's room and as long as no risk is posed to other luggage). All buses and shuttles are also wheelchair accessible.

Getting around each of the islands is thoroughly detailed within the relevant chapters themselves.

BICYCLE

On the islands of Martha's Vineyard and Nantucket, short distances, relatively flat terrain, an established network of bike paths, and the high cost and scheduling hassles of ferrying a car from the mainland all combine to make bicycles a thoroughly appropriate transportation alternative. Rental shops are found in all the gateway towns within minutes' walking distance of arriving ferries. Public buses on both islands are also equipped with bike carriers on the front, making it doubly easy to get yourself back to whence you started if either fair weather or willpower abandon you.

Recreation

Summer recreation here is synonymous with at least some time in or on the water. Luckily, the Cape and both islands are well equipped to offer aquatic fun-seekers a busy time aboard a wide variety of human-, wind-, wave-, and engine-powered inventions. Underwater sports are another matter—the marinelife of the temperate zones is too monochromatic to interest most casual snorkelers, and only one outfitter currently offers a dive boat to any of the worthwhile shipwrecks in the vicinity. Hard-core dive rats may be able to get a fix by making friends with local boat owners knowledgeable about the local waters (there are dive shops on the Cape and both islands), but most recreational scuba and snorkel divers should probably leave the fins and masks at home and use the luggage space for something else.

Don't want to get wet? Dry land offers plenty of diversions, almost none of which will cause vertigo. Bird-watching is a major activity—the region is smack-dab on the migratory route of numerous North American bird species, but you don't have to know or care that the nearby songster is a rufous-sided towhee to enjoy the backcountry walks through local conservation lands. Bike riding is another favorite activity for visitors, especially on Martha's Vineyard and Nantucket, both of which have extensive paved bike paths for safe and comfortable family cycling.

As for sports, golf is Cape Cod's secular religion—it's one of the most golf course-saturated regions of the United States, with dozens of clubs welcoming the public to their courses. Public tennis courts are also widely available.

PARKS

Easily one of the most influential events in the last century of Cape Cod's history occurred in 1961, when President Kennedy signed into law the legislation that created the **Cape Cod National Seashore.** That pen stroke protected a huge 40-mile chunk of the Outer Cape from future development, including almost all of Provincetown, most of Wellfleet and Truro, and portions of three other towns. The Seashore is unequivocally one of the region's crown jewels, not only in terms of things to do and see there, but also in terms of what can't be done and seen: You can't shop at malls built on paved-over salt marshes or exhaust your allowance in video arcades overlooking the ocean, and, unlike on much of the Cape's south shore, rich people can't buy up all the best beachfront real estate to build ostentatious mansions fringed with security fencing and No Trespassing signs. Under the terms of the park's creation, private property holders were grandfathered in, but property improvements are limited to maintenance, not expansion. As a result, the Seashore preserves not just natural habitat and endangered ecosystems but also a view of Cape residential life circa 1959—possibly an instructive contrast to what has evolved elsewhere in the region over the intervening decades.

The other major federal presence is the U.S. Fish and Wildlife Service, custodian to the 2,750-acre **Monomoy National Wildlife Refuge** off the coast of Chatham, and the **Mashpee National Wildlife Refuge** on the south shore of the Upper Cape, whose current 2,000-plus acres may eventually triple in size if proponents and refuge partners succeed in their conservation goals. Like the unique **Waquoit Bay National Estuarine Research Reserve** located nearby, all these refuges are accessible to one degree or another for passive recreation and are, of course, outstanding places to experience firsthand Cape Cod's reputation as a bird-watcher's delight.

The **Department of Conservation and Recreation** is the keeper of the state's public lands. It has only a modest presence in the region, most notably with the 25-mile **Cape Cod Rail Trail, Nickerson State Park** in Brewster, and **Manuel F. Correllus State Forest** on Martha's Vineyard. All state parks and forests—particularly those with fishing and camping—are reasonably well signposted from adjacent major roadways.

PRIVATE LANDS FOR PUBLIC USE

Complementing the national and state holdings are a number of sanctuaries and conservation properties owned by private organizations, most notably **The Trustees of Reservations**—perhaps the oldest land protection organization in the world. Founded in 1891 (with a charter that became the model for England's National Trust), the Trustees' mission is to acquire for public enjoyment lands of "uncommon beauty and more than usual refreshing power, just as the Public Library holds books and the Art Museum pictures." By any measure, their nearly 100 Massachusetts preserves are among the state's finest open lands. Among this remarkable collection of properties are wildlife refuges on Cape Cod, Martha's Vineyard, and Nantucket, outstanding island beaches, and historic lighthouses. A few of these regional properties charge admission for nonmembers in high season, so if you want a good discount on beach parking and various ancillary services—including summer canoe rentals and natural history tours—consider becoming a member. Join online at www.thetrustees.org, or call the membership office at 978/921-1944. The website also offers information about individual reservations, including directions and upcoming events.

The other major conservator of nature here is the **Massachusetts Audubon Society,** whose sanctuaries showcase the diversity of the region's habitats, from Wellfleet Bay's saltwater marsh on Outer Cape Cod to the heaths of Nantucket. Several of the Audubon sanctuaries offer programs much of the year, including canoe trips, after-hours stargazing, butterfly watching, reptile talks, and nature walks. The frequency of the offerings increases with warm weather and demand. Advance reservations are usually required; for current calendars, call the individual properties or check out the society's website (www.massaudubon.org). All Audubon sanctuaries charge a nominal admission to nonmembers, so here too you may find membership quickly pays for itself, especially if you go on a binge at any of their gift shops—members get discounts on cash purchases. (Note that members of the national Audubon Society have no privileges with Mass Audubon; the two are wholly separate entities.) Become a member online at www.massaudubon.org or call 800/AUDUBON—800/283-8266.

CYCLING

When it comes to building bike paths or enhancing existing roadways and bridges to more safely accommodate cyclists, Massachusetts trails nearly the entire nation. Tens of millions of dollars in both federal appropriations and state-authorized bonds are available, and towns across the commonwealth have a long list of popular proposals in need of funding. Yet for some inexplicable reason, the Massachusetts Highway Department seems determined to keep bike-related projects from ever seeing the light of day—even going so far as taking control of millions of federal dollars that legally may go directly to local planning agencies, and then leaving three-quarters of it unspent. Despite such unfortunate circumstances, the Cape and island region leads the state in designated bikeways and converted railroad beds, including the state's premier rail-to-trail conversion, the 25-mile **Cape Cod Rail Trail.** Moreover, scores of back roads are simply perfect for exploration by cyclists.

No need to lug your own bike along either; inexpensive rentals are found throughout the region and are almost ubiquitous on both Martha's Vineyard and Nantucket. A searchable database of bike shops can be found online at www.capecodbikeguide.com, along with detailed descriptions of both paved bike paths and off-road trails. Jane Griffiths' *Short Bike Rides on Cape Cod, Nantucket & the Vineyard,* one of many fine guides published by Globe Pequot Press, is a recommended addition to your pack. You'll find it in any cycling shop, bookstore, or recreational outfitter around the region.

A mountain bike or a slick-tired hybrid comes in handy for negotiating sandy back roads—and Nantucket's cobblestones—but given all the miles of well-paved roads and bike paths, there's little reason to rent fat tires if you have your own skinny-tire touring cycle at hand. Serious mountain bikers won't find this terrain all that challenging; with a few exceptions, off-road island cyclists face more deep sand than steep grades. The fragility of the open land also means that the damage done by even one or two bikes lasts an entire season or longer, so heed restrictions where

Massachusetts Beach Access: No Trespassing

In nearly every coastal state in the United States, you have the legal right to walk along the beach. This simple right is wholly independent of who you are, where you live, or what you own. Four states have placed all tidal land in "public trust" (a legal arrangement dating back to the Roman Empire), thus preventing any private property ownership below the high-tide line. Seventeen other states let owners of waterfront property build wharves and otherwise exercise "franchise rights" in the intertidal zone—the area between high and low tides—only so long as beach users aren't impeded from passing over or under whatever is built. Only Massachusetts and Maine (which was part of Massachusetts until 1821) allow private ownership of the coast to extend all the way down to the mean low-water line. With over 70 percent of the Massachusetts coast in private hands, it should therefore come as no surprise that you'll often encounter No Trespassing signs at both ends of nearly all public beaches.

This sad state of affairs is a relic of a 1647 colonial ordinance enacted to promote maritime industry. However, that same 1647 law enshrines three exceptions to these exclusive property rights. The public, it says, has the right to use the intertidal zone for "free fishing and fowling"; also, the public may not be prevented from freely passing by "boats or other vessels . . . to other men's houses or lands." In general, this means that you can walk across otherwise private beaches (always below the high-tide mark, usually indicated by a wrack line of organic debris) only if you're engaged in surf-casting or bagging blackbirds with a blunderbuss (simply carrying a fishing rod doesn't count). Massachusetts courts have upheld certain modern activities as natural derivatives of one or another of the allowable uses—sport hunting and windsurfing, for example—but many coastal towns have their own restrictions concerning both guns and sailboards, so don't get your hopes up. On the other hand, courts have been unequivocal about most other beach pastimes. The law in no way allows you to set down a towel or a chair, stop for a picnic or sunbathe, or practice beachcombing or bird-watching.

Back in the 1970s, an attempt was made to amend the colonial statute to include walking as one of the legal uses of privately owned beaches, but it took 17 years to finally arrive at wording that wouldn't violate the Massachusetts Constitution. When finally passed in 1991, the law simply said that since it would be a good idea to give the public access to the state's entire coast, the state's Department of Conservation and Recreation has a mandate to acquire the necessary rights for trespass on the intertidal zone. In other words, the state authorized one of its agencies to dicker with landowners to let the unwashed masses take a walk by the water. Given that shoreline property tends to belong to the wealthier and more influential of the state's citizens, the execution of this mandate is an extremely contentious issue.

The bottom line is this: Posted restrictions should be taken seriously. Ignoring them doesn't just put you at risk of arrest but also jeopardizes the entire effort to persuade beach owners that people won't abuse the right to trespass, if that right is ever granted. Someday, the amendments found on a few signs—Walkers Welcome—may become more widespread.

they exist, and be sure to use established trails wherever you go.

BEACHES

Free, public, warm-weather swimming is a rarity in Massachusetts. In summer (June-early September), most bodies of water—either fresh or salt—are restricted to local residents and summer renters or saddled with stiff parking fees. Thankfully, pedestrians and cyclists are usually exempt from parking fees or resident-sticker requirements, but not always; selected resident-only beaches check the status of everyone who attempts to enter during daylight hours all summer (caveats are included where necessary in these pages). About the only place where public beaches are free and unrestricted is offshore, on Martha's Vineyard and Nantucket. Needless to say, while beaches on both are free, the boats to reach them are not.

Scores of beautiful beaches line Cape shores, and from the end of June through Labor Day, in early September, hardly a single one has free parking. In most instances, you pay a daily fee to a gatekeeper to gain entrance, but some beaches reserve parking exclusively for residents or for guests who purchase special weekly stickers or season passes at the appropriate town hall (bring your vehicle registration as well as proof of local property rental or motel or B&B stay). Since applicable fees are collected only until 5pm but most beach parking is kept open in summer until at least sunset (and as late as midnight in some towns), there's a nice window of opportunity for those who care more about catching a quick swim or a good sunset than a day of tanning. Individual town information kiosks (all prominently placed at strategic highway junctions or right downtown) can provide a fairly thorough list of local beaches, but the ones most welcoming of nonresidents are also well-signed from major roads, such as Route 28 and Route 6A.

The heaviest and coldest surf is from the Atlantic Ocean piling up along the backside beaches of the **Cape Cod National Seashore.** Summer's prevailing southwesterly winds can fatten up the waves on the south shore too, but in general the Nantucket and Vineyard Sound beaches (and Buzzards Bay) are either more sheltered, shallower, or otherwise kinder and gentler than those on the Outer Cape. By virtue of the great tidal flats extending far from shore, bay-side beaches are most serene in summer and relatively tepid. Offshore, the Bay is actually colder than the surrounding Atlantic Ocean, because the northern Labrador current, coming down along the coast of Maine, gets embayed by the Cape's hook, while the Atlantic is warmed by the Gulf Stream 100 miles to the southeast.

Before undertaking certain shore hikes (at the Namskaket Sea Path in Nickerson State Park, for example, or Great Island in Wellfleet), digging clams, windsurfing, or ocean kayaking, it would be wise to check for the high and low tides. Consult the tide tables printed in any of the local Cape daily papers, or pick up a handy free chart from the outdoor enthusiast's year-round friend, the Goose Hummock Shop, located at the Town Cove in Orleans on Route 6A, and at Route 28 and Main Street in Hyannis.

SAILING

The Cape is a sailor's joy—steady winds mean great sailing throughout the warmer months. There are plenty of opportunities to rent boats, since nearly every village and town along the coast has a marina and many host various charter services during the summer season.

GOLF

If you ever needed proof that Cape Codders saunter to the beat of a much more relaxed drummer than most of the rest of us, you need only know that the Cape has scores of golf courses—one of the highest number per capita in the nation, right up there with Florida and Myrtle Beach. With almost twice as much real estate given over to golf than to agriculture, golf courses are indeed *everywhere,* from championship layouts designed by the most famous names in the business to the scenic rough heathland links of the Outer Cape, where you can go back to the game's Scottish roots at one of the nation's oldest golf courses still in operation. Most are open year-round, and in typical years—when lingering snowfalls are a rarity—there are die-hard players squeezing a few rounds of practice into even the chilliest midwinter afternoons.

A good place to start planning your tour of the region's fairways is with a visit to www.golfcapecod.com, a commercial website with links to many of the 30-some public courses in the region. The Cape Cod Chamber of Commerce (508/362-3225 or 888/332-2732, www.capecodchamber.org) also has information about hotels in the area that specialize in golf vacation packages.

Food and Accommodations

FOOD AND DRINK

Fortunately for visiting food mavens, Massachusetts cookery over the past couple of decades has the embraced salutary influences of, among others, former resident Julia Child, raising awareness of good food throughout the state and firmly putting to rest comparisons to the infamous cuisine of New England's namesake across the Atlantic. Century-old ties to Manhattan's social and artistic elite also ensure that restaurateurs in Wellfleet, Provincetown, and the islands must routinely satisfy palates accustomed to New York's finest dining.

Admittedly, mediocre meals are by no means an endangered species (Cape Cod swims in them), and plenty of the national fast-food chains or their local imitators are only as far away as the next strip mall on Route 28. But if you aren't indifferent to what you eat, you won't have to look far to find stellar food, whether in trendy chef-owned bistros that draw customers from clear across town lines (the true measure of success among parochial Bay Staters), homey neighborhood holes-in-the-wall where natural-born cooks hold court, or, at its most elemental, in the roadside stalls of the region's few remaining farms.

The rampant resort pricing endemic to the Cape and islands makes for a fine line between mediocrity and robbery—such as a gourmet café charging $12 for yesterday's stale dessert, or a B&B inn shamelessly serving a supermarket doughnut and coffee as continental breakfast to guests paying $325 a night. Every attempt is made in these pages to highlight establishments offering good value, but neither this nor any other guide can predict the rapid shifts in quality from one year to the next—the result of extremely high turnover in staff and even ownership, particularly among restaurants.

From Land and Sea

Massachusetts is no California or Tuscany, but the movement epitomized by California cuisine, with its firm emphasis on super-fresh regionally grown ingredients, is one that's strongly evident among the better restaurants around the region. Enjoying meals prepared from the cornucopia of Massachusetts farms usually (but not always) carries a premium price, since small-scale and organic farmers with short growing seasons can't hope to compete in price with America's agribusiness giants. When it comes to taste, of course, there's no competition whatsoever. As every back yard gardener knows, nothing picked when immature and artificially ripened while in storage or during transcontinental shipping can compare to the flavor of fresh, picked-when-ready local produce. If getting a taste of New England is important to you, come during the summer or fall and visit local farm stands. Or leave room on your credit card for a small splurge at the kind of restaurant that respectfully pays homage on every plate to those of our neighbors who have chosen to keep farming and dairy farming alive.

Most out-of-state visitors to Massachusetts come looking for seafood. It's an expectation easily met, from humble clam shacks and family-friendly chowder houses to the sushi bars and upscale restaurants highlighting exotic or underutilized fish species. Luscious quahog clams, fresh oysters, mussels, scallops, lobster, monkfish, halibut, bluefish, striped bass, shad, yellowtail flounder, bluefin tuna, and yes, even cod are all worth the tariff on local menus. (Scrod, it should be noted, isn't actually a species of fish—it's a catchall term at the Boston fish auction for baby cod, haddock, and any other flaky white-flesh fish under 2.5 pounds in weight.)

Do not, however, fall into the common trap of assuming that waterfront restaurants are the best places to dine on the bounty of the sea—some of the finest seafood meals to be had in the state are hours from any coastline. Given that Massachusetts is a net importer of seafood (overfishing has caused offshore fisheries to collapse, rendering numerous species commercially extinct), you may also be disappointed to learn that even here in seaside towns with local fishing fleets, there are restaurants whose scallops are more likely flash-frozen and then shipped from Asia or Iceland than they are fresh out of the water off Martha's Vineyard. Even worse, a restaurant's delicious-sounding special salmon is probably raised on the same aquaculture farm up in Maine that express-ships its product to Atlanta and Chicago. But don't worry—plenty of places cited in these chapters do serve tonight something caught this morning by that picturesque boat at the end of the working pier.

In this age of overnight cargo, don't let my caveats obscure the more relevant fact that Massachusetts draws on such a deep tradition of seafood preparation that you could give many of its chefs a frozen fish stick and they'd still make something so wonderful and tasty of it that you'd never know or care what it looked like or where it came from before ending up on your fork.

Specialties of the House

Like Memphis ribs, Cincinnati chili, or the olallieberry pies of the Pacific Northwest, Cape Cod has its own set of recipes and restaurant specialties that, while not necessarily unique to the state or the region, are definitely idiomatic. Lobster rolls, for example: A basic commodity at beachfront concession stands and other indigenous fast-food stalls, these resemble tuna salad served on a hot dog bun, except that lobster meat is used in place of the tuna.

Clam chowder (made with quahogs, pronounced "KO-hog") is equally ubiquitous, and though it's never, ever made with tomatoes (that's Manhattan's recipe), diligent chowderheads will find almost no two versions alike. Chain restaurants that come in from outside the region often mistakenly assume that New England clam chowder should have the texture of wallpaper paste, but don't be fooled—proper "chowda" never requires a spackling knife. Cod cakes have been getting a boost from creative chefs who dress them with garlicky aiolis, peppery Asian spices, or other multicultural exotica—but at their most traditional, these deep-fried patties of minced white fish are served for breakfast.

Though the national franchising of sandwich shops has diluted regional differences in food terminology, sub sandwiches in this region are often still called "grinders," as they are in New Hampshire and Rhode Island (it's a "hero" to New Yorkers, a "hoagie" to Philadelphians).

Indian pudding (a cornmeal and molasses concoction) and Grape-Nut custard aren't as common as they used to be, but you'll still find them on diner menus here more often than elsewhere in the country. Saltwater taffy and homemade fudge are summertime standards throughout the region, and super-premium ice cream, though found nationwide, achieves perfection at summer ice cream shops around the Cape. If you want a milk shake from any of these places, be sure to order a "frappe" (rhymes with trap) or you'll get nothing more than milk flavored with syrup.

Finally, chocolate lovers will be gratified to learn that Massachusetts has a serious addiction to sinfully rich chocolate desserts. Even local ice cream parlors typically have a core selection of 6 or 10 variations on dark chocolate, white chocolate, chocolate mousse, chocolate fudge, chocolate chips, or some combination of chocolate and coffee.

International Cuisine

As is the case throughout much of the United States, Italy and China are the most common contributors to the region's ethnic dining, although the influences of both are in general rather heavily Americanized. The Portuguese who dominate the fishing industry—particularly in Provincetown, where many Portuguese historically settled—have made the Cape one of the best places in New England for a taste of their robust seafood stews, kale soup, and spicy sausages known as *chouriço* (pronounced shur-REES, not chor-REET-zo; that's the Spanish version).

In more recent years the most pronounced influence on local dining has been the seasonal influx of immigrant service-industry labor from the Caribbean and Brazil. Jerk seasonings show up on a number of otherwise staid American surf-and-turf menus, and Brazilian-style *churrascarias* (steak houses featuring all-you-can-eat rotisserie-grilled meats) have appeared in Hyannis and on Martha's Vineyard.

Drinking

If you seek a tipple, there are several wineries in the region; two on Cape Cod, one on Nantucket, and one on Martha's Vineyard, all of which offer tours and tastings at least during summer. Aficionados of craft beer should keep an eye out for the logos of the Vineyard's Offshore Ale Co., Nantucket's Cisco Brewers, and Hyannis's Cape Cod Beer in liquor stores and at selected restaurants throughout the region. Several distilleries have sprung up, often best sampled at wineries. 20 Boat Rum and Triple 8 brand spirits (particularly the vodka) are available from Provincetown to Pocasset and on both islands.

Minimum legal drinking age in the state is 21. Valid identification (state-issued ID, a passport or international driver's license along with your home country license) is required to purchase alcoholic beverages in stores or bars. Many clubs won't admit anyone under the legal drinking age. At these places, you'll be asked for photo ID at the door. Nightclubs that advertise "18-plus" shows provide fluorescent wristbands to patrons who can prove they're 21 or over, without which the club bartenders will refuse to serve you alcohol.

Happy hours are illegal in Massachusetts, and bars close at 2am or earlier. Taking your libation to go? Hard alcohol, beer, and wine are sold in package liquor ("packy") stores, except in "dry" towns (several of which are concentrated on Martha's Vineyard). Supermarkets can't sell liquor, and only a few are permitted to sell beer and wine, thanks to the outsize political clout of the state's beverage distributors, who don't want their profit margins squeezed by big chain retailers demanding volume discounts.

Take note that many areas have open-container laws, meaning you can't walk down the street with an open beer or bottle of whiskey in hand, although if you keep a low profile at your outdoor picnic, it shouldn't be an issue.

ACCOMMODATIONS

Familiar interstate hotel names are a distinct rarity in the region, with only a handful of chain affiliates on the Cape, a few on Martha's Vineyard, and none whatsoever on Nantucket. What you *will* find are hundreds of character-rich small hotels, inns, B&Bs, and B&B inns (that blurry category of establishments combining a motel's economies of scale with B&B frills and ruffles). Predictably, discounts of any kind (including those for AARP or AAA members, or for corporate travelers) are almost as rare as those chains, but, as always, it never hurts to ask.

Accommodations prices are generally on the high side, comparable to being in a big city (well north of $150 nightly for most of the year). But the region isn't completely devoid of cheap places to sleep. There are several Hostelling International-affiliated hostels, including one on each island, plus a variety of campgrounds, including some that offer cabins. Only Nantucket takes a dim view of sleeping under the stars; the fine for camping there is a hefty $200.

Whether romantic or rustic, a number of Martha's Vineyard and Nantucket bed-and-breakfasts still eschew air-conditioning, offering fans instead. First-time visitors—Southerners in particular—are skeptical about booking a room without air-conditioning, but island nights really are bearable—especially near the water—except during the muggy dog days of August. Just leave those flannel pajamas at home. And consider the upside of screen windows (the islands' most popular cooling system)—if you've slept in air-conditioned houses all your life, you've probably never had the pleasure of being awakened by songbirds perched outside your open window singing a gentle morning reveille.

Lodging Options

Not all the superlatives applicable to Massachusetts are favorable. The state ranks among the nation's top 10 most expensive in terms of dining and lodging costs, according to AAA's annual survey of American vacation costs. Boston can take a good chunk of the blame for this ranking, but the abundance of deluxe prices on the Vineyard and Nantucket surely contribute to skewing the average too. Private baths, generous breakfasts, large rooms, fireplaces, and proximity to water are all extras. Any one of them, as a rule, will add about 25 percent to the rate for your basic four walls and a mattress—and a combination of several can quickly spike the price from $150 to $350. In this book, exceptions—mostly among B&Bs rather than motels—are noted where they exist. It should go without saying that places with reputations for good value have darned low vacancy rates, so you need to plan ahead if you want to try to save a little.

Wheelchair travelers and anyone unable to negotiate stairs should never assume that anything in Massachusetts called a motel or inn (even in major resort areas) is in compliance with Americans with Disabilities Act guidelines for accessibility. Major national chains all have fully accessible guest rooms, but the situation is very different in smaller places—especially historic homes converted to quaint inns. It's easy to find out who does comply, though: Order a copy of the *Massachusetts Getaway Guide* from the Massachusetts Office of Travel & Tourism (617/973-8500 or 800/227-6277, www.massvacation.com). Its accommodations listings identify accessibility.

Airbnb is a popular option for the Cape, as is VBRO, though prices still run more expensive for the Cape and the islands than elsewhere. Value is more about what you're able to get rather than the price—and you run the risk of cancellations and so on. If you search carefully and weigh options, you'll be able to find some deals.

CAMPING

When it comes to state-owned campgrounds, Massachusetts is hard to beat. For $15 or less, the state offers some of the cheapest moonlit sleeping spots in the nation. There are four state-owned campgrounds in this region, all on Cape Cod. Shawme-Crowell State Forest campground and Nickerson State Park campground are nicer and thus more popular than the others.

The campgrounds on Cape Cod tend to be open mid-April-early October, although self-contained vehicles (RVs with septic and gray-water holding tanks) may use a couple of the Cape's campgrounds on weekends (Thurs.-Sat.) any time of year.

With a credit card, you can make reservations for most sites in the state campgrounds up to six months in advance with ReserveAmerica (877/422-6762, www.reserveamerica.com) for an additional $8.65 service fee per campsite reservation. The website is highly recommended—you can pick out specific campsites from easy-to-use interactive campground maps, obtain site-specific descriptions (double-wide driveway, shaded site, access for the disabled), and see what amenities each campground features.

More family-oriented camping is also available at some 20 private campgrounds in the region, which are often equipped with recreation and game rooms, playgrounds, convenience stores, RV hookups, and laundry facilities. Download a free, annually-updated Cape and islands regional directory (a full statewide version is also available) from www.campmass.com, the website of the Massachusetts Association of Campground Owners.

HOSTELS

Hostels are just about the only budget accommodations on Cape Cod or the islands that don't require sleeping outdoors. They are not just for kids: Budget-conscious travelers of all ages and backgrounds may be found enjoying the stereotypical dorm-room bunk beds of the region's hostels. There are five in the region, four of which are branches of Hostelling International, which means they offer discounts to HI members from around the world. The fifth is an independent backpackers' hostel in Provincetown.

Membership in HI can be purchased at any affiliated hostel in the world. Currently the annual fee in the United States for anyone ages 18-54 is $18. For a complete guide to affiliates in eastern Massachusetts, visit www.hiusa.org.

BED-AND-BREAKFASTS

There's plenty of charm in local B&Bs, but there are also several factors to keep in mind. For example, expect to encounter minimum-stay requirements in high season, or single-night surcharges, especially at very small owner-run properties (these may also pass along the fee they get docked for accepting your credit card, if they take plastic at all). If using a booking service, expect a reservation fee. Deposits are usually required by both services and individual properties, and you should take those cancellation policies seriously—they aren't just for show. As a courtesy to the many small B&B owners who have already logged a 10-hour workday by the time five o'clock rolls around, pay close attention to their check-in policies. Owner-operated B&Bs should never be confused with 24-hour hotels, and the fastest way to totally stress out your host—or even forfeit your room and its deposit if you haven't shown up when you were supposed to—is to neglect arranging for a late check-in, if needed. Finally, when comparing prices, keep in mind that places with three or fewer rooms are not required to charge tax, so you save some of what you'd pay at larger establishments.

You won't find many places truly overlooking the waves on Massachusetts's coast, because those places get washed away in storms. If you're looking for a room with windows speckled by salt spray, look to places on the firm granite ledges of the coast north of Boston. Oodles of places on Cape Cod and the islands are, however, within view and earshot of water. A few places also have "private beaches"—but on the islands this usually means something about the size of a sandbox, and on the Cape they're usually attached to large Daytona Beach-style motels catering to large families.

Purists who want to be sure they're getting both bed *and* breakfast must be sure to ask—nothing in this niche of the hospitality industry can be taken for granted anymore. If it's important to you, inquire closely about what is really meant by such terms as "hearty" or "gourmet continental"; a continental breakfast can be skimpy even if you have the whole box of shredded wheat and basket of mix-and-bake muffins to myself. Not all the onus for skipping full breakfasts rests with innkeepers, however—some communities, particularly on Martha's Vineyard and Nantucket, erect steep regulatory obstacles to prevent B&Bs from competing with local restaurants (at least, that's the innkeepers' side of the story; local health inspectors have a differing view).

Travelers with diabetes or other special needs will find most traditional owner-operated B&Bs willing to handle special breakfast requests if you give them clear guidance.

The increasingly common self-styled "B&B inn," which pretends to represent the best of both worlds, may prove less tractable to menu modifications—especially those run by seasonal staff who don't quite have the hang of the concept of "customer satisfaction."

Nothing substitutes for planning ahead when it comes to landing a room where and when you want it, but don't give up on last-minute luck—there's always a cancellation someplace, and with patience and a bit of phone work, you may just find it.

MOTELS AND HOTELS

Although many of the major chains are represented on Cape Cod, you'll find independently owned accommodations far outnumber them throughout the region. Don't use appearance as a gauge of price. Some of those pocket-size New Deal-era bungalows and dreary-looking little motel courts straight out of *Key Largo* are anything but cheap. Some of these places have had the same owners and the same regular customers for over a generation. While same-sex couples and younger adults may detect a coolness upon check-in, don't take it personally—the ice will thaw and downright gracious hospitality will blossom forth if you judiciously refrain from trashing your room, playing music at top volume in the wee hours, or otherwise enacting the owners' worst nightmares.

Health and Safety

No part of Massachusetts is so remote that it isn't within range of emergency services, so when an ambulance, firefighters, or police are required, dial 911 to be instantly connected with an emergency dispatcher. In most communities around the state the dispatcher's computer will track your number and address, enabling authorities to locate you should the call be cut off.

PRESCRIPTIONS

If you use any sort of prescription medication, be sure to bring the medicine (not the prescription) when you come to the state. Massachusetts pharmacists are prohibited from refilling any prescription from out of state.

TICKS

Before you go striding off through marsh reeds or bushwhacking through the woods in spring, summer, or fall, remember that this region is home to both the bloodsucking wood or dog tick and the more notorious deer tick, *Ixodes dammini,* which, as its Latin name suggests, is a little damn thing—no bigger than the period at the end of this sentence. Though indigenous throughout the state, these ticks are most common on Cape Cod and the islands.

To avoid getting bitten by a tick, wear a hat and light-colored clothes with long sleeves and legs that may be tucked into socks. Commercial tick repellent is also advisable. Avoid favorite tick habitats such as tall grasses and the edges of woods and meadows. If you do find a tick on you, there's still no reason to panic, but early removal dramatically improves chances for avoiding illness (it usually takes a day or two for any infectious agents to be transmitted to the host). The deer tick's larval stage, which it reaches in July-August, is when it is believed to be most capable of passing on bacteria or parasites, but it is infectious throughout its life.

Above all, use the proper removal technique (described by Dirk Schroeder in *Staying Healthy in Asia, Africa, and Latin America*): If it isn't visibly walking and can't be lightly brushed away, use tweezers to grasp the tick's head parts as close to your skin as possible and apply slow steady traction. (Don't squeeze—you don't want its saliva in your skin.) Don't attempt to get ticks out of your skin by burning them or coating them with anything like nail polish or petroleum jelly. If you remove a tick before it has been attached for more than 24 hours, you greatly reduce your risk of infection. After you've removed the tick, wash the bite with soap and clean water, and watch for signs of infection over the following days.

Tick-Borne Diseases

Precautions against tick bites are advisable because of the diseases they can transmit to their hosts. Dog ticks carry Rocky Mountain

Coronavirus in New England

At the time of writing in September 2021, Cape Cod, Martha's Vineyard, and Nantucket were still impacted by the effects of the coronavirus, and the situation is constantly evolving. By the time the book reaches shelves the situation may have significantly changed. Currently, Massachusetts has a high overall vaccination rate and seems to be keeping infections under control. Facemasks are often required to attend crowded events and at many indoor establishments. Social distancing is also highly encouraged, if not required. Some places, such as many restaurants, are only open for take-out dining.

Now more than ever, Moon encourages its readers to be courteous and ethical in their travel. Be respectful to residents and mindful of the evolving situation when planning your trip. Your contracting the virus may spread it to many people beyond you, some of whom may get seriously ill or die.

BEFORE YOU GO

- Check local websites (listed below) for **local restrictions** and the **overall health status** of the destination and your point of origin. If you're traveling to or from an area that is currently a COVID-19 hotspot, you may want to reconsider your trip.
- Moon encourages travelers to get **vaccinated** if your health status allows, and to take a **coronavirus test** with enough time to receive your results before your departure if possible. Some destinations may require proof of vaccination or a negative COVID test result before arrival, along with other tests and potentially a self-quarantine period, once you've arrived. Check local requirements and factor these into your plans.
- If you plan to fly, check with your airline for updated **travel requirements.** Some airlines may be taking more steps than others to help you travel safely, such as limited occupancy; check their websites for more information before buying your ticket, and consider a very early or very late flight, to limit exposure. Flights may be more infrequent, with increased cancellations.
- Check the website of any museums and other venues you wish to patronize to confirm that they're open, if their hours have been adjusted, and to learn about any specific visitation requirements, such as **mandatory reservations** or **limited occupancy.** Most trails and outdoor activities are open, but masking may still be required by the establishment.
- Pack **hand sanitizer,** a **thermometer,** and plenty of **face masks.** Consider packing **snacks, bottled water,** a **cooler,** or anything else you might need to limit the number of stops along your route, and to be prepared for possible closures and reduced services over the course of your travels.
- **Assess the risk** of entering crowded spaces, joining tours, and taking public transit.
- Expect **general disruptions.** Events may be postponed or cancelled, and some tours and venues may require reservations, enforce limits on the number of guests, be operating during different hours than the ones listed, or be closed entirely.

RESOURCES

- Massachusetts Department of Health: (mass.gov/orgs/department-of-public-health)
- Center for Disease Control: (cdc.gov)
- National Park Service: Cape Cod National Seashore (nps.gov/caco)

spotted fever, while deer ticks have been identified as carriers of Lyme disease, human babesiosis, and human granulocytic ehrlichiosis, or HGE. None of these maladies is serious if treated early and properly, since all are caused by either bacteria or microscopic parasites susceptible to antibiotics.

Lyme disease may produce a distinctive concentric-ringed rash—like a bull's-eye, sometimes as large as your palm—around the point of infection and such flu-like symptoms as fever, chills, aches, fatigue, and headaches. These first-stage indicators may not appear for up to a couple of weeks after a bite. As the disease progresses, it affects muscles, joints, the heart, and the nervous system, ultimately attacking the brain and producing Alzheimer's-like conditions. Because many visitors are unfamiliar with the symptoms of Lyme disease and because it may take years for the eventual effects to appear, it's important to treat it early and be aware of any tick bites. Babesiosis is a parasite that attacks the red blood cells much like malaria, with similar symptoms and results: fever, chills, swollen liver and spleen, and dangerously depressed red blood cell count. HGE is the latest addition to the deer tick's arsenal, a potential immune system suppressant with flu-like symptoms.

POISON IVY

Poison ivy is native to the entire region. Growing as either a plant or vine, it's often found amid beach grass, where it exacts its itchy revenge on those who ignore dune-climbing restrictions. It's recognizable by its three shiny leaves on woody or hairy stems, sometimes accompanied by clusters of small off-white berries. In fall, the leaves turn a beautiful red.

PERSONAL SAFETY

Most casual travelers to Cape Cod and the islands will never have to worry about making headlines as victims of violent crime. It's unlikely you'll witness the alcohol and drug abuse and domestic violence for which the region is known in law enforcement circles, unless you settle down in the community. On the other hand, petty theft is certainly a fact of life during the high season, so don't let the casual resort atmosphere lull you into leaving valuables conspicuously unattended in unlocked vehicles, at the beach, or overnight on the porch of your summer rental.

Information and Services

SMOKING LAWS

Massachusetts has completely banned smoking in civic buildings, theaters and cinemas, malls, and aboard public transit (including all the island ferries), plus wherever food and drink are served. That's right: There's no smoking allowed in any restaurant or bar anywhere on Cape Cod, the Vineyard, and Nantucket. Though cannabis has been legalized for personal use, smoking it in public or while driving is still illegal.

MONEY AND BANKING

Foreign Exchange

If you're traveling from abroad, you'll find that while credit cards are almost universally accepted, there are still certain kinds of transactions for which only cash will do. Parking and snack concessions at public beaches, for example, don't take plastic, and most of the region's public buses also require payment in currency or coin.

If you choose to bring traveler's checks, make sure they are denominated in dollars. True to the vendors' claims, almost everyone but taxi drivers will treat them like cash.

If you're spending any time in Boston at the start of your visit to the region, you can take care of your exchange needs there. Keep in mind that despite competition among the city's banks and brokers, there's enough range in rates and fees to make shopping around worth a few local phone calls. If Boston isn't in your travel plans, learn to recognize the Citizens Bank logo—it's the state's only bank chain with branches outside Boston that can handle on-the-spot foreign exchange of major international currencies. You'll find that only the most luxurious resorts offer immediate foreign exchange—and, even with competition within walking distance, you will pay dearly for the privilege of trading pesos and pounds for portraits of dead American presidents.

Be aware that different brands of traveler's checks are not treated equally if they're in the denominations of your own national currency. Foreign-denominated checks are cashed for free only by local affiliates of the issuer—and only American Express has a large number of such offices outside greater Boston.

ATMs

Destination chapters note specific ATM locations where necessary (for example, if they're obscure), and any unusual absence of the machines. Otherwise, you may assume some sort of ATM will be self-evident in the vicinity of listed attractions and restaurants. Most belong to the Cirrus, Plus, and NYCE banking networks. Most also charge you up to a couple of bucks to use them. ATMs are required to carry notices about their fees, or to alert you before you complete your transaction, so at least you needn't worry about being charged unknowingly.

Sales Tax

The statewide sales tax on all goods, except groceries and clothing, is 6.25 percent, while lodging tax is 5.7 percent. Bed-and-breakfasts with three or fewer guest rooms are tax-free. 2.75% is added to all Cape & Islands rooms for the Water Protection fund. Additional town taxes may also apply.

MAPS

Massachusetts is like one of those suspicious foreign nations in which accurate cartographic information is kept under lock and key—the better to foil the treasonous plots of enemies of the state. For getting to and from major destinations via numbered state and federal highways, the free map available at MassPike information booths is sufficient. For more detailed coverage of local roads, most existing maps are flawed, although most of the inaccuracies won't impede the casual visitor.

If you're a stickler for accuracy, consider forearming yourself with the series of combination bicycle and road maps from **Rubel BikeMaps** (https://bikemaps.com). One map covers both Cape Cod and the islands, another focuses solely on Martha's Vineyard and Nantucket. Look for them in Massachusetts at well-stocked bookstores and most bike shops, have your local bookstore order them through MapLink, or order them online from the eMapStore link at https://bikemaps.com.

COMMUNICATIONS

Mail

The U.S. Postal Service is not hard to find or to use. Seasonal workers or transient boaters will find general-delivery mail-holding services available from post offices in most communities.

Internet Access

Internet cafés came and went on Cape Cod and the islands since free wireless internet access is available in nearly all the region's accommodations and many of its coffee shops. Towns throughout the Cape and islands are also installing community-wide public Wi-Fi networks; much of the region is now covered. Signal strength, however, is quite fickle, which is why gaggles of summer visitors may often be seen seated on the steps, sidewalks, and benches near public libraries and other unsecured Wi-Fi hotspots hunched over their laptops.

If you are not carrying a laptop or smart phone, your surest bet for public internet terminals is a public library. You may find yourself subject to user limits and possible preferential treatment for local cardholders, but it's a free means of logging on if you're in need of a technology fix.

Telecommunications

Because every community in Eastern Massachusetts shares two active area codes, all phone calls, whether local or not, must be dialed with 1 plus the area code first. Since 774, the second, overlay area code for Cape Cod, Martha's Vineyard, Nantucket, and Cuttyhunk has not yet frequently shown up in daily use, you may safely assume that 508 should be dialed in front of any seven-digit phone number given to you by a Cape or island native or observed on local signage.

Public pay phones are not all alike. Of the dwindling number still available to cell phone-free travelers, many belong to third-party service providers, and rates for making collect or direct-dial calling-card calls on these phones are far from competitive. If a pay phone doesn't carry a brand name you recognize, use an access code to reach your own trusted long-distance carrier or you'll likely be billed for the equivalent of a conference call to Mars. Alternatively, you can purchase prepaid phone cards in varying denominations at every post office and most convenience stores in the region.

For local and national directory information, dial 411. To report an emergency or to summon police, firefighters, or emergency medical assistance, dial 911.

Some convenience stores are often able to handle outgoing faxes, although if you want the most experienced and reliable fax capabilities, look for a copy shop or ask the staff of your inn or motel.

TRAVEL TIPS

Travelers of Color

Massachusetts in general is diverse and Cape Cod, Martha's Vineyard, and Nantucket are no exceptions. Fortunately, incidents of hate or discrimination are unlikely.

Consider visiting one of the following websites for more information about traveling throughout the region:

- **Travel Noire** (https://travelnoire.com/search?q=cape%20cod)
- **Soul of America** (https://www.soulofamerica.com/us-cities/)
- **Eat Okra** (https://www.eatokra.com)
- **Nomadness** (http://nomadnesstraveltribe.com)

LGBTQ+ Travelers

With Provincetown a stone's throw away, Cape Codders have grown up seeing, accepting, and celebrating difference in all its myriad forms. Provincetown hosts a year-round Pride events, including various themed weekends, parades, and celebrations.

Considering visiting one of the following websites for more information about traveling throughout the region:

- **Ptown Tourism** (https://ptowntourism.com/lgbtq/)
- **Travel Gay** (https://www.travelgay.com/destination/gay-usa/gay-massachusetts/gay-cape-cod/)
- **Out Traveler** (https://www.outtraveler.com)
- **Advocate** (https://www.advocate.com/travel)

Travelers with Children

The Cape, Martha's Vineyard, and Nantucket have so much to offer children that generations of tourists have kept coming back to enjoy the same fun activities they did as a child: Beach going, hikes and swims, mini-golf, eating special foods they can't get at home...it's a mecca. Admission fees generally offer a student or child discount.

Travelers with Disabilities

The Cape and Islands has come a long way in accessibility, but that's not to say there's not room for improvement. Some beaches have wheelchairs retrofitted with over-sand tires, and walkways or boardwalks make use of a cane or walker feasible for visiting some sites. But shifting sands, uncertain weather, and lack of resources may mean you find it tough or impossible to enjoy your destination. Many buildings do not have elevators or ramps due to historical preservation exemptions, including some restaurants. Modern construction has taken the need for ensuring access to all, but there's still work to be done.

Consider visiting one of the following websites for more information about traveling throughout the region:

- **Disabled Travelers** (www disabledtravelers.com)
- **Curb Free with Cory Lee, a wheelchair accessible Cape Cod, Massachusetts Travel Guide** (https://curbfreewithcorylee.com/2020/10/10/wheelchair-accessible-cape-cod-massachusetts/)
- **Cape Days** (https://www.capedays.com/accessible-beaches.html)
- **Everyone Outdoors** (https://everyoneoutdoors.blogspot.com/2011/06/wheelchair-accessible-cape-cod.html)

Business Hours

Hours vary depending on the type of business. Generally speaking, banks are open 9am-5pm Monday-Friday, although some major consumer banks also open select locations for a half day on Saturday. Other public and private businesses keep the general hours of 9am-5pm daily, although hours do vary. Many retail stores are open extended hours, especially throughout the high season. Many convenience stores, some "super" supermarkets, and a few gas stations stay open around the clock. When in doubt, call ahead and confirm hours of operation.

Holidays

Major public holidays in the United States shut down the whole country (Christmas Day, New Year's Day, Fourth of July, and Thanksgiving, which is the fourth Thursday in November). Other holidays only affect private businesses, banks, government offices, mail and package delivery services, and schools. Retail stores, on the other hand, typically stay open, often with special holiday sales and extended hours. These legal holidays, usually observed on a Monday or Friday to create a three-day weekend, include the following: New Year's Day (Jan. 1); Martin Luther King Jr. Day (3rd Mon. in Jan.); Presidents Day (3rd Mon. in Feb.); Memorial Day (last Mon. in May); Labor Day (1st Mon. in Sept.); Columbus Day (2nd Mon. in Oct.); and Veterans Day (Nov. 11).

Many Massachusetts government offices and many stores, libraries, and so on also celebrate Patriot's Day (3rd Mon. in Apr.), which is also always the date of the Boston Marathon.

Time Zones

In winter, Cape Cod and the islands function on eastern standard time, five hours earlier than Greenwich mean time. From the second Sunday in March to the first Sunday in November, daylight saving time advances the clock one hour.

Weather

For current Cape-wide weather conditions, call the **WQRC-FM forecast phone** (508/771-5522).

Resources

Suggested Reading

RECREATION

Evans, Lisa Gollin. *Sea-Kayaking Coastal Massachusetts: From Newburyport to Buzzards Bay.* Boston: Appalachian Mountain Club Books, 2000. Sea-kayaking, a favorite Bay State pastime, is made even more accessible with this detailed guide to over 45 trips among the state's tidal estuaries, offshore islands, and other attractive coastal waters; it provides necessary contact information for outfitters and guides in case you aren't already a kayak owner.

Mullen, Edwin, and Jane Griffith. *Short Bike Rides: Cape Cod, Nantucket, & the Vineyard.* 7th edition. Guilford, CT: Globe Pequot Press, 1999. With this book in hand, riding around the state's most popular region for recreational cycling couldn't be easier.

Trull, Peter. *An Illustrated Guide to the Common Birds of Cape Cod.* Atglen, PA: Schiffer Publishing, 2011. 140 color plates of common Cape Cod and Islands birds, plus lots of explanatory text about where, how, and when to find them. Peter Trull is one of the Cape's most respected birders.

Weintraub, David. *Walking the Cape and Islands.* Birmingham, AL: Menasha Ridge Press, 2006. This book features descriptions of over 70 walks and hikes, all accompanied by a trail map, directions, lists of flora and fauna, and a wealth of practical details, ranging from overall sun exposure to the estimated number of calories you'll burn completing each one.

HISTORY

Primary Documents

Bradford, William. *Of Plymouth Plantation: 1620-1647.* Edited by Samuel Eliot Morison. New York: Alfred A. Knopf, 1952. The leader and sometime governor of the Pilgrim settlement in Plymouth tells the story in his own inimitable style (helpfully edited, annotated, and indexed by one of the foremost scholars of colonial and maritime history). Unless you have a special interest in Bradford's orthography, no other edition can compare—which is why this one has never gone out of print.

Burrage, Henry S., ed. *Early English and French Voyages, Chiefly from Hakluyt: 1534-1608.* New York: Barnes & Noble, 1959. Originally published 1906. There were two 16th-century Richard Hakluyts—cousins some 20 years apart in age. Each supported English colonial ventures in the New World, the elder as a lawyer-investor, the younger as a geographer-publicist. Burrage draws on the younger Hakluyt's 1589 *Principall Navigations, Voiages, and Discoveries of the English Nation,* a multivolume work compiled from interviews and first-person accounts. Precolonial Massachusetts and its inhabitants are described by several of the explorers featured.

Champlain, Samuel de. *The Works of Samuel de Champlain*. Edited by H. P. Biggar. Toronto: Champlain Society, 1922-1936. Six-volume work includes the observant French captain's detailed log of his anchorages along the Massachusetts coast during his 1605-1608 voyage, with descriptions and the harbor chart for the Indian village at Patuxet, which became the site of the Pilgrims' Plimoth Plantation.

Smith, John. *Travels and Works of Captain John Smith*. Edited by Edward Arber. Birmingham, UK: English Scholar's Library, 1884. The writings of the man who named New England, and whose map, used by the *Mayflower* Pilgrims, already contained the name of their settlement—Plimoth—thanks to the arbitrary choice of 10-year-old heir-apparent Prince Charles, with whom Smith wished to gain favor.

St. John de Crèvecœur, J. Hector. *Letters from Nantucket and Martha's Vineyard*. Bedford, MA: Applewood Books, 1986. Selections from this 18th-century French immigrant's well-observed correspondence about his life as an American farmer in both New York and Massachusetts. This one is a classic.

Wroth, Lawrence C., ed. *The Voyages of Giovanni da Verrazzano: 1524-1528*. New Haven, CT: Yale University Press, 1970. Includes the Florentine navigator's descriptions of the Massachusetts coast, particularly Martha's Vineyard and Cape Cod before either island or the commonwealth had those names, written during his attempt to find a sea lane to the Far East.

Native Americans and Colonial Interaction

Cronon, William. *Changes in the Land: Indians, Colonists and the Ecology of New England*. New York: Hill and Wang, 1983. Articulate and meticulously researched. The curious reader will easily amass a vast additional reading list on its interdisciplinary content—colonial history, Native American history, ecology, anthropology—from the exceptional bibliographic essay that ends this highly recommended prize-winning book.

Jennings, Francis. *The Invasion of America: Indians, Colonialism, and the Cant of Conquest*. New York: W. W. Norton, 1975. One of the major so-called revisionist histories, scrutinizing the motives of the Pilgrim and Puritan migration to these shores. Was war a deliberate strategy to abet land-grabbing, itself a policy stemming from a strict interpretation of Scripture? Read the evidence in this impressive work.

Other Historical Works

Allport, Susan. *Sermons in Stone: The Stone Walls of New England and New York*. New York: W. W. Norton, 1990. An exceptional miscellany full of history, geology, and local lore, including an interesting chapter about Martha's Vineyard. Demonstrates how much about the historical landscape one can learn from careful observation of a few piled stones.

Barbo, Theresa Mitchell, John Galluzzo, and W. Russell Webster. *The Pendleton Disaster off Cape Cod: The Greatest Small Boat Rescue in Coast Guard History*. Charleston, SC: History Press, 2007. An account of the nearly suicidal, but ultimately successful, 1952 rescue of the crew of a large tanker that foundered off the Cape in a fierce winter nor'easter.

Brown, Dona. *Inventing New England: Regional Tourism in the Nineteenth Century*. Washington DC: Smithsonian Institute Press, 1995. An excellent treatise on the artifices of "colonial" townscapes and quaint fishing villages designed purely to appeal to urban dwellers who wanted to see "real, natural New England."

Karttunen, Frances Ruley. *The Other Islanders: People Who Pulled Nantucket's Oars.* New Bedford, MA: Spinner Publications, 2005. An eloquent exploration of Nantucket's diverse heritage, thoroughly researched and beautifully illustrated. A marvelous keepsake.

Morison, Samuel Eliot. *The Maritime History of Massachusetts: 1783-1860.* Boston: Northeastern University Press, 1979. Another Morison classic, written with a clear love of the sea and sailing.

Nickerson, Joseph A., Jr. and Geraldine D. Nickerson. *Chatham Sea Captains in the Age of Sail.* Charleston, SC: History Press, 2008. A chronicle of 25 seafaring men from the town at the Cape's elbow and their adventures from the 18th through the early 20th centuries.

O'Connell, James C. *Becoming Cape Cod: Creating a Seaside Resort.* Durham, NH: University of New Hampshire Press, 2002. This history of Cape tourism over 150 years is a blend of comprehensive social documentary and ecological wake-up call, generously illustrated with antique and vintage postcards from the author's private collection.

Philbrick, Nathaniel. *Away Off Shore: Nantucket Island and Its People, 1602-1890.* Nantucket, MA: Mill Hill Press, 1994. In this richly anecdotal and factually grounded work, episodes in the lives of several dozen islanders become the lens through which three centuries of island history is refracted.

Railton, Arthur R. *The History of Martha's Vineyard: How We Got to Where We Are.* Beverly, MA: Commonwealth Editions, 2006. A journalistic narrative, broad in scope yet fleshed out with plenty of local detail, written by the highly regarded former editor of the Martha's Vineyard Historical Society's quarterly journal.

Schneider, Paul. *The Enduring Shore: A History of Cape Cod, Martha's Vineyard, and Nantucket.* New York: Owl Books, 2001. Skillfully weaves a broad historical narrative from the author's experiences exploring the region by kayak and afoot. An absorbing contemporary heir to the intellectually wide-ranging, wryly discursive, and personally ruminative style of Thoreau. Highly recommended.

MISCELLANEOUS

Beston, Henry. *The Outermost House.* New York: Holt Paperbacks, 2003. Originally published in 1928, this is a classic account of a year spent on the dunes of Outer Cape Cod.

George, Diana Hume, and Malcolm A. Nelson. *Epitaph and Icon: A Field Guide to the Old Burying Grounds of Cape Cod, Martha's Vineyard, and Nantucket.* Marstons Mills, MA: Parnassus Imprints, 1983. The title says it all.

Kurlansky, Mark. *Cod: A Biography of the Fish That Changed the World.* New York: Walker & Co., 1997. A highly readable exploration of one of the former economic mainstays of the region.

Miller, John, Tim Smith, and Alice Hoffman, eds. *Cape Cod Stories: Tales from the Cape, Nantucket & Martha's Vineyard.* San Francisco: Chronicle Books, 2002. Essays and excerpts from longer works by a wide-ranging cast of authors who have set foot in the region and then written about it, including Edgar Allan Poe, Helen Keller, John Updike, Kurt Vonnegut, Herman Melville, and many more.

Ruhlman, Michael. *Wooden Boats: In Pursuit of the Perfect Craft at an American Boatyard.* New York: Penguin Books, 2001. An eloquent, detailed profile of the construction of two wooden boats and of the builders, Ross Gannon and Nat Benjamin of Martha's Vineyard.

Thoreau, Henry David. *Cape Cod.* New York: Penguin Books, 1987. First published 1865. Thoreau, the travel writer hiking the Outer Cape, is as engaging and piquantly observant as Thoreau the pondside philosopher.

Whynott, Douglas. *Giant Bluefin.* New York: Farrar Straus and Giroux, 1995. A look at the lives of Cape Cod bluefin anglers, in the tradition of Tracy Kidder and John McPhee.

Williams, Wendy, and Robert Whitcomb. *Cape Wind: Money, Celebrity, Class, Politics, and the Battle for Our Energy Future on Nantucket Sound.* New York: PublicAffairs, 2007. A trenchant dissection of the hard-fought battle over the proposal to build the nation's first offshore wind farm near the summer homes of some of the country's wealthiest and most politically powerful families.

PUBLISHERS

Special mention must be given to the following small firms for their dedication to producing titles on local subjects that are good enough to deserve a much wider audience:

Parnassus Imprints (220 Rte. 6A, Yarmouthport, MA 02675, 508/362-6420) specializes in books about Cape Cod and maritime subjects. They're also the exclusive distributor for **Mill Hill Press,** a good source for Nantucket-related titles.

Internet Resources

Cape Cod Bike Guide
www.capecodbikeguide.com
Detailed descriptions of all the region's paved bike paths and off-road mountain bike trails, with an accompanying database of bike shops and links to other cycling-related resources.

Cape Cod Online
www.capecodonline.com
Owned and run by *The Cape Cod Times,* this is the place to find the area's latest news, beach information, and community happenings, plus shopping, events, and real estate listings.

Cape Cod Pathways
www.capecodcommission.org
A project of the Cape Cod Commission, supporting the development of a Cape-wide network of walking trails from the Canal to P-town.

Cape Cod Regional Transit Authority
www.capecodrta.org
Features information and a route-finder for the CCRTA's own fixed-route transit services—the Breeze—as well as links to regional bus lines, ferries, and airlines that provide service to the Cape and islands. Also has real-time local traffic reports, weather, roadway construction updates, and webcam links for the two Cape Cod Canal highway bridges.

Commonwealth of Massachusetts
www.mass.gov
The state's official website, with links to town URLs and "community profiles," which contain a wealth of local statistical census, economic, and demographic data.

The Fish Database
www.fishbase.org
After eating, catching, seeing, reading about, or hearing of a particular fish on the Cape and islands that you'd like to know more about, this is where you will want to turn. Over 30,000 species (and counting), with over 45,000 identification photos, plus a multilingual search engine for common names in English, Arabic, Russian, Greek, Chinese, and other languages.

Maptech USGS Maps
www.mytopo.com

Online U.S. Geological Survey topographical maps available for sale, with all areas of Barnstable county.

Massachusetts Department of Environmental Management
www.mass.gov/orgs/department-of-conservation-recreation

The website of the guardian of all Massachusetts state parks, forests, and reservations: hours, fees, camping seasons, phone numbers, and more.

Massachusetts Maritime Academy
www.maritime.edu

The maritime academy is located at the western end of the Cape Cod Canal and is home to the control center for all canal shipping. The MMA's homepage features links to their two live canal webcams.

National Weather Service
www.weather.gov

One-stop weather site for the whole state: Click for current forecasts, marine reports, aviation reports, and up-to-the-minute conditions at any of the NWS data collection stations in Massachusetts.

Barnstable County Resources page
www.barnstablecounty.org/barnstable-county/links-copy

This particular page is a list of resources and links to the websites of participating Chambers of Commerce on Cape Cod and the islands, most of which feature event calendars, member directories with links where available, current weather, and photos.

Index

D

E

F

G

H

O

P

QR

S

T

UVWXYZ

List of Maps

Photo Credits

All photos © Ray Barrlett, except page 3 © Jiawangkun | Dreamstime.com; page 6 © (top left) Lunamarina | Dreamstime.com; (top right) Tanyabird777 | Dreamstime.com; (bottom) © Chee-onn Leong | Dreamstime.com; page 7 © (top) Radomir Rezny, Capture Light / 123rf.com; (bottom right) Lei Xu | Dreamstime.com; page 10 © Andrew Kazmierski | Dreamstime.com; page 12 © (bottom) Jerry Coli | Dreamstime.com; page 15 © Ethan Daniels / Shutterstock; page 87 © (top right) Rolf52 | Dreamstime.com; page 89 © Yevgenia Gorbulsky | Dreamstime.com; page 103 © (bottom) Ritu Jethani | Dreamstime.com; page 118 © William J. Taylor | Dreamstime.com; page 129 © (top) Kspangler | Dreamstime.com; page 147 © (top right) Suse Schulz |Dreamstime.com; (bottom) Joaquin Ossorio Castillo | Dreamstime; page 150 © (top) Matthew Omojola | Dreamstime; (bottom) Matthew Omojola | Dreamstime; page 161 © (right middle)Wangkun Jia | Dreamstime; (bottom) Cindy Goff |Dreamstime.com; page 181 © Steven Rivieccio | Dreamstime.com; page 182 © (top left) Lei Xu | Dreamstime.com; (top right) Robert Malo | Dreamstime.com; page 191 © (right middle) Claire White | Dreamstime.com; (bottom) Steven Rivieccio | Dreamstime.com; page 196 © Garth Grimmer | Dreamstime.com

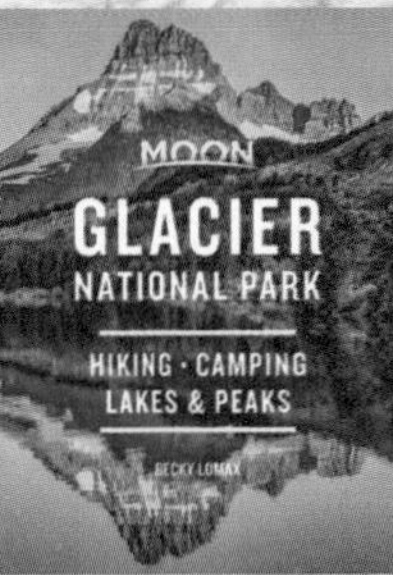

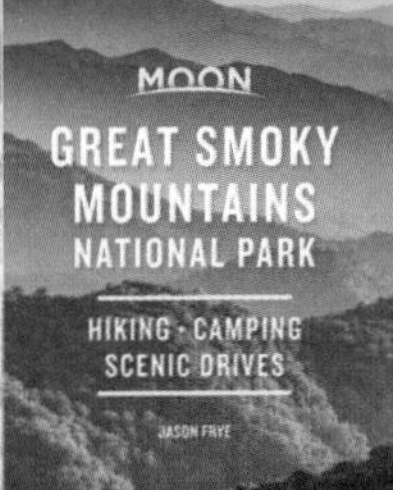

Spending only a few days in a park? Try Moon's Best of Parks guides.

Build your USA travel bucket list with Moon USA National Parks and the new Moon USA State by State.
MOON
USA
MOON
USA
STATE by STATE
The Best Things to Do in Every State for Your Travel Bucket List
MOON
BEST OF
GRAND CANYON
MAKE THE MOST OF ONE TO THREE DAYS IN THE PARK
TOP SIGHTS, TOP HIKES, TOP SCENIC DRIVES
TIM HULL
MOON
BEST OF
YELLOWSTONE & GRAND TETON
MAKE THE MOST OF ONE TO THREE DAYS IN THE PARKS
TOP SIGHTS, TOP HIKES, TOP SCENIC DRIVES
BECKY LOMAX
MOON
BEST OF
YOSEMITE
MAKE THE MOST OF ONE TO THREE DAYS IN THE PARK
TOP SIGHTS, TOP HIKES, TOP SCENIC DRIVES
MOON
BEST OF
ZION & BRYCE
MAKE THE MOST OF ONE TO THREE DAYS IN THE PARKS
TOP SIGHTS, TOP HIKES, TOP SCENIC DRIVES

MOON
SOUTH FLORIDA & THE KEYS
Road Trip
WITH MIAMI, WALT DISNEY WORLD, TAMPA & THE EVERGLADES
JASON FERGUSON

MOON
SOUTHERN CALIFORNIA
Road Trips
DRIVES ALONG THE BEACHES, MOUNTAINS, AND DESERTS WITH THE BEST STOPS ALONG THE WAY
IAN ANDERSON

MOON
SOUTHWEST
Road Trip
LAS VEGAS, ZION & BRYCE, MONUMENT VALLEY, SANTA FE & TAOS, AND THE GRAND CANYON
TIM HULL

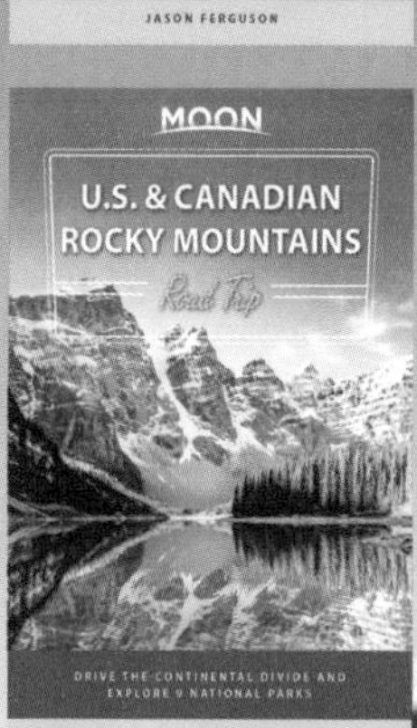
MOON
U.S. & CANADIAN ROCKY MOUNTAINS
Road Trip
DRIVE THE CONTINENTAL DIVIDE AND EXPLORE 9 NATIONAL PARKS
BECKY LOMAX
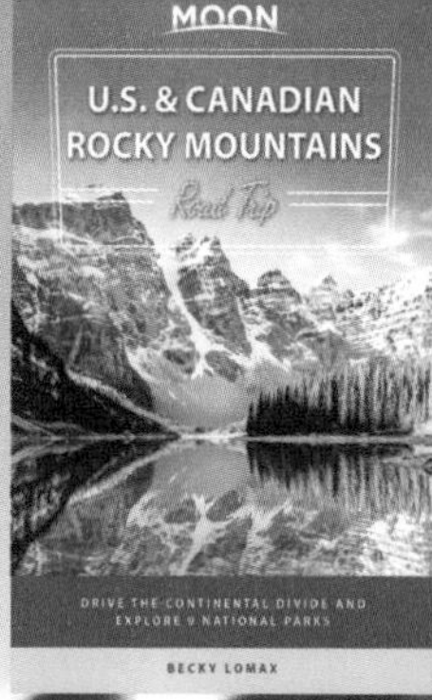

MOON
VANCOUVER & CANADIAN ROCKIES
Road Trip
VICTORIA, BANFF, JASPER, CALGARY, THE OKANAGAN, WHISTLER & THE SEA-TO-SKY HIGHWAY
CAROLYN B. HELLER

MOON
YELLOWSTONE TO GLACIER NATIONAL PARK
Road Trip
JACKSON HOLE, CODY, THE GRAND TETONS & THE ROCKY MOUNTAIN FRONT
CARTER G. WALKER

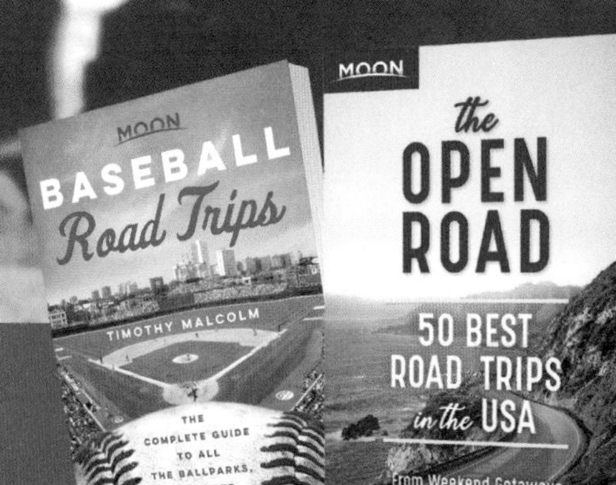
MOON
BASEBALL Road Trips
TIMOTHY MALCOLM
THE COMPLETE GUIDE TO ALL THE BALLPARKS, WITH BEER, BITES, AND SIGHTS NEARBY
MOON
the OPEN ROAD
50 BEST ROAD TRIPS in the USA
From Weekend Getaways to Cross-Country Adventures
JESSICA DUNHAM

MOON
Road Trip USA
25TH ANNIVERSARY EDITION
CROSS-COUNTRY ADVENTURES ON AMERICA'S TWO-LANE HIGHWAYS
Jamie Jensen

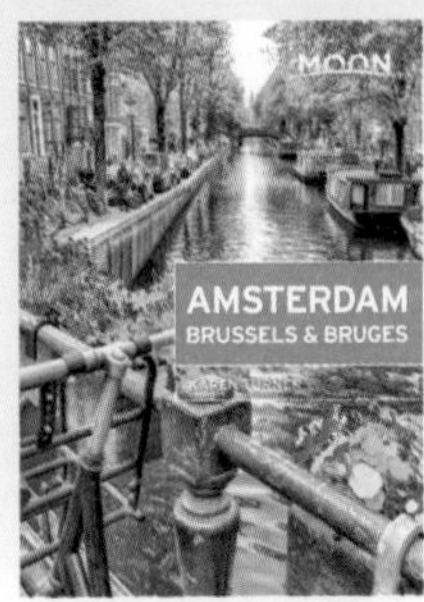

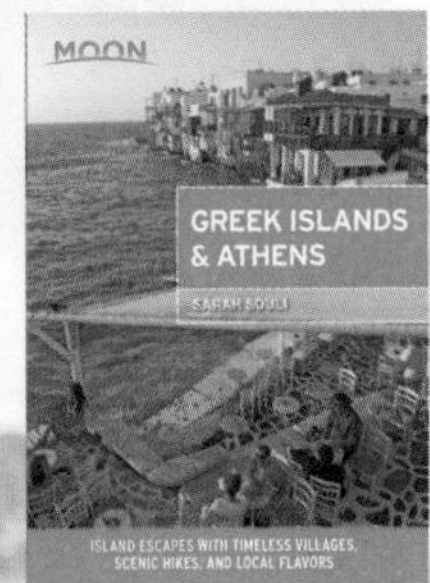

More Great Travel Guides from Moon

MAP SYMBOLS

- Expressway
- Primary Road
- Secondary Road
- Unpaved Road
- Trail
- Ferry
- Railroad
- Pedestrian Walkway
- Stairs
- City/Town
- State Capital
- National Capital
- Highlight
- Point of Interest
- Accommodation
- Restaurant/Bar
- Other Location
- Campground
- Airport
- Airfield
- Mountain
- Unique Natural Feature
- Waterfall
- Park
- Trailhead
- Skiing Area
- Golf Course
- Parking Area
- Archaeological Site
- Church
- Gas Station
- Glacier
- Mangrove
- Reef
- Swamp

CONVERSION TABLES

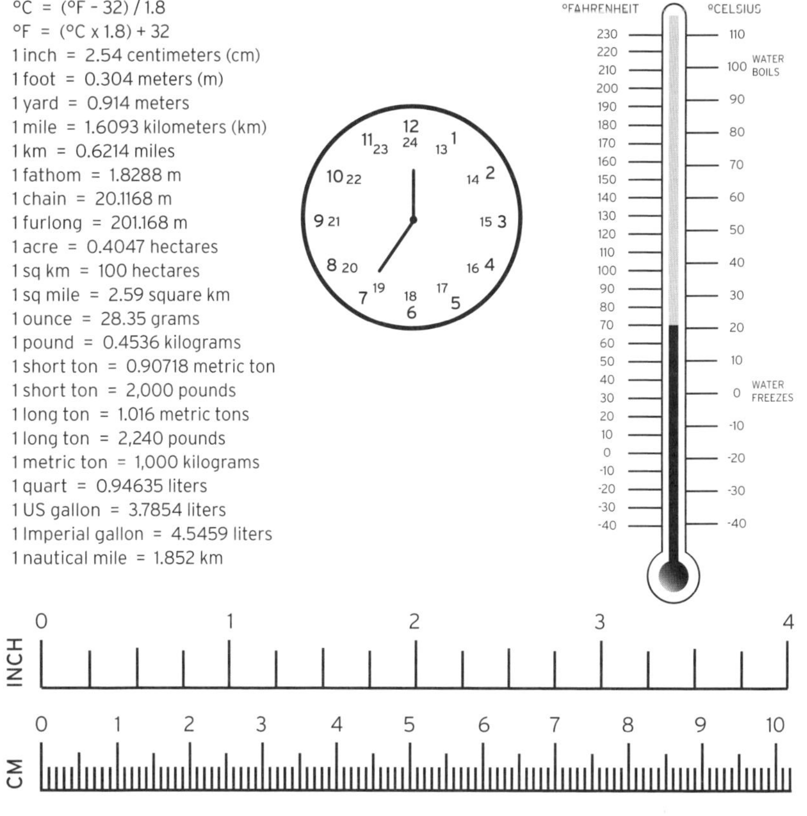

°C = (°F - 32) / 1.8
°F = (°C x 1.8) + 32
1 inch = 2.54 centimeters (cm)
1 foot = 0.304 meters (m)
1 yard = 0.914 meters
1 mile = 1.6093 kilometers (km)
1 km = 0.6214 miles
1 fathom = 1.8288 m
1 chain = 20.1168 m
1 furlong = 201.168 m
1 acre = 0.4047 hectares
1 sq km = 100 hectares
1 sq mile = 2.59 square km
1 ounce = 28.35 grams
1 pound = 0.4536 kilograms
1 short ton = 0.90718 metric ton
1 short ton = 2,000 pounds
1 long ton = 1.016 metric tons
1 long ton = 2,240 pounds
1 metric ton = 1,000 kilograms
1 quart = 0.94635 liters
1 US gallon = 3.7854 liters
1 Imperial gallon = 4.5459 liters
1 nautical mile = 1.852 km

MOON CAPE COD, MARTHA'S VINEYARD & NANTUCKET

Avalon Travel
Hachette Book Group
1700 Fourth Street
Berkeley, CA 94710, USA
www.moon.com

Editor: Kimberly Ehart
Acquiring Editor: Nikki Ioakimedes
Graphics and Production Coordinator: Suzanne Albertson
Cover Design: Faceout Studios, Charles Brock
Moon Logo: Tim McGrath
Map Editor: John Culp
Cartographers: Andrew Dolan, Albert Angulo, John Culp
Indexer: Greg Jewett

ISBN-13: 978-1-64049-605-7

Printing History
1st Edition — 2004
4th Edition — April 2022
5 4 3 2 1

Front cover photo: Woods Hole © Christian Delbert | Dreamstime.com
Back cover photo Provincetown Harbor © James Kirkikis | Dreamstime.com

Printed in Malaysia for Imago